A REPUBLIC, NOT AN EMPIRE
Reclaiming America's Destiny

A REPUBLIC, NOT AN EMPIRE
Reclaiming America's Destiny

PATRICK J. BUCHANAN

Since 1947
REGNERY
PUBLISHING, INC.
An Eagle Publishing Company • Washington, DC

Library of Congress Cataloging-in-Publication Data

Buchanan, Patrick J.
    A republic, not an empire : reclaiming America's destiny / Patrick J. Buchanan.
        p. cm.
    Includes index.
    ISBN 0-89526-272-X (alk. paper)
    1. United States—Foreign relations. 2. United States—Foreign relations—1989-
3. Intervention (International law)—History. I. Title.
E183.7.B83 1999
327.73'009—dc21   99-32102
                                             CIP

Published in the United States by
Regnery Publishing, Inc.
An Eagle Publishing Company
One Massachusetts Avenue, NW
Washington, DC 20001

Distributed to the trade by
National Book Network
4720-A Boston Way
Lanham, MD 20706

Printed on acid-free paper
Manufactured in the United States of America

BOOK DESIGN BY MARJA WALKER
SET IN BEMBO

10 9 8 7 6 5 4 3 2

Books are available in quantity for promotional or premium use. Write to Director of Special Sales, Regnery Publishing, Inc., One Massachusetts Avenue, NW, Washington, DC 20001, for information on discounts and terms or call (202) 216-0600.

To the loyal men and women of the
Buchanan Brigades of '92 and '96,

I will never forget you.

CONTENTS

The idea for *A Republic, Not an Empire* came out of my year-long campaign for the GOP nomination in 1996. From March 1995 through the California primary, I sought to persuade my party that the course on which America had embarked was replicating, with alarming exactitude, the course that brought the British Empire to ruin. The free-trade-*über-alles* policy of the administration, and its compulsive interventionism, I argued, violated America's greatest traditions and followed a course that had been repudiated and rejected by its greatest men.

What was most heartening about that campaign was the respectful and extensive coverage my ideas received in the mainstream media. What was most frustrating was to discover in my own party a reflexive hostility to any dissent on foreign policy, or any suggestion there might be a wiser trade policy than the unilateral industrial disarmament that travels under the passport of "global free trade."

Repeatedly, I found that my arguments were not being refuted, but airily dismissed as "isolationism" or "protectionism." This suggested to me that millions of Americans are oblivious to their own country's history and heritage. The propagandists in the educational establishment have done their work well. For not only was the party of Lincoln, McKinley, Theodore Roosevelt, Taft, and Coolidge born and bred in protectionism, it was defiantly and proudly protectionist. Moreover, the economic nationalism that carried Lincoln to the presidency was rooted in the ideas that Washington, Hamilton, and

Madison had taken to Philadelphia and written into the American Constitution, and that Henry Clay had refined to create "The American System" that was the marvel of mankind.

As for "isolationism," the term is a dismissive slur on a tradition of U.S. independence in foreign policy and nonintervention in foreign wars that is forever associated with Washington's Farewell Address, Jefferson's admonition against "entangling alliances," and John Quincy Adams's Independence Day Speech of 1821 declaring that it was neither America's duty nor its destiny to go "abroad in search of monsters to destroy." Not until our twenty-fifth president, McKinley, would that tradition be broken with our annexation of the Philippines. Following Wilson's failure at Versailles, nonintervention in foreign wars was again declared policy for both parties until after the election of 1940.

Why, I wondered, is this great tradition so reviled? After all, it was under the policies now derided as "isolationism" and "protectionism" that Americans, in a single century, expelled all French, British, Spanish, and Russian power from our continent to become the most powerful and secure republic the world had ever seen.

So it was that, after the momentum of our New Hampshire victory failed to carry us over the top in Arizona—against Mr. Forbes's millions and Mr. Dole's "push polls" and attack ads—I decided to write a book to explain and defend the ideas that animated the Buchanan Brigades.

After a year, I sent a 185,000-word manuscript to my editor, Fredi Friedman. She called to tell me I had written two books—one on trade policy and one on foreign policy—and that I should divide the manuscript into two books. So I did. After extracting the chapters and subchapters that dealt with the history, theory, and practice of economic nationalism versus free trade, and turning in the final draft of *The Great Betrayal*, I returned to the basement and the Mac. *A Republic, Not an Empire* is the product of that second year of nightly labor.

As with *The Great Betrayal*, many will disagree with my analysis and prescription. Yet I believe deeply that the foreign policy I advocate for the twenty-first century is not only right for America, but will also be seen to be right, and will one day be embraced by the entire nation, for a fundamental reason: Present U.S. foreign policy, which commits America to go to war for scores of nations in regions where we have never fought before, is unsustainable. As we pile commitment upon commitment in Eastern Europe, the Balkans, the Middle East, and the Persian Gulf, American power continues to contract—a sure formula for foreign policy disaster.

The day is coming when America's global hegemony is going to be challenged, and our leaders will discover they lack the resources to make good on all the war guarantees they have handed out so frivolously; and the American people, awakened to what it is their statesmen have committed them to do, will declare themselves unwilling to pay the price of empire.

A day of reckoning is approaching. It is my hope that the price in blood, treasure, and humiliation America will eventually be forced to pay for the hubris, arrogance, and folly of our reigning foreign policy elites is not, God forbid, war, defeat, and the diminution of this Republic—the fate of every other great nation or empire that set out on this same course.

PART ONE

AMERICA REACHES FOR GLOBAL HEGEMONY

CHAPTER 1

How Empires Perish

*I have but one lamp by which my feet are guided,
and that is the lamp of experience. I know of no other
way of judging the future but by the past.*[1]

—PATRICK HENRY, 1774

At the opening of the twentieth century there were five
great Western empires—the British, French, Russian, German, and
Austro-Hungarian—and two emerging great powers: Japan and the
United States. By century's end, all the empires had disappeared.
How did they perish? By war—all of them.

The Austro-Hungarian empire was crushed in World War I and
torn to pieces at Versailles, where Germany was also dismembered. A
vengeful Reich then began a second European war. Ruin was total.
Japan, believing its empire was being extorted, its place in the sun
denied, attacked America and was smashed like no other nation in history. The British and French empires, already bled in the trenches of
the Western Front from August 1914 to November 1918, did not long
survive Hitler's war.

Russia's empire, dismantled by the kaiser in 1918, was restored
by Lenin's Bolsheviks. Driven by traditional Russian imperialism and
a new fighting faith, communism, the Soviet empire expanded until
its reach was global. Overextended, bankrupt, exhausted by a fifty-
year struggle against a U.S.-led West that far surpassed the communist bloc in economic power and technological prowess, it collapsed

after a crisis of faith and a loss of will to maintain its rule over subject peoples who had grown to hate it.

America survives as the sole superpower because it stayed out of
the slaughter pens until the other great powers had fought themselves
near to death and avoided a cataclysmic clash with a nuclear-armed
Soviet Russia. In World War I Americans did not go into combat in
great numbers until 1918. In World War II America did not cross the
Channel until four years after France had fallen and three years after
the USSR had begun fighting for its life. We did not go to war
against Japan until the Japanese army had been bogged down for four
years fighting a no-win war against the most populous nation on
earth. U.S. casualties in the two world wars were thus the smallest of
the Great Powers, and America in the twentieth century has never
known the vast destruction that was visited on Russia, Germany, and
Japan—or even on France and England.

Yet, today, America's leaders are reenacting every folly that
brought these great powers to ruin—from arrogance and hubris, to
assertions of global hegemony, to imperial overstretch, to trumpeting
new "crusades," to handing out war guarantees to regions and countries where Americans have never fought before. We are piling up the
kind of commitments that produced the greatest disasters of the
twentieth century.

That is why I have written this book. Not for fifty years have
Americans had to think deeply about our foreign policy. It was made
for us—by Tojo, Hitler, Stalin, Castro, Ho, and Mao. For fifty years
America overcame enemies who either attacked us or declared our
destruction to be their highest ambition. "We will bury you!"
Khrushchev said. We took him at his word—and buried *them*. But in
the last days of the Cold War, something happened. Soviet propagan-
dist Georgi Arbatov said, "We are going to do the worst thing we can
do to you. We are going to take your enemy away from you." And so

they did, and so we have had to face the question asked in the war movies of our youth, "What are you going to do, Joe, when this is all over?"

Saddam Hussein's invasion of Kuwait briefly gave us a new Hitler and George Bush an opportunity to smash Iraq and to declare the building of a New World Order to be America's next crusade. But the nation did not buy in. After the Gulf War triumph, it turned its back on Bush, giving 37 percent of the vote to a president whose approval, eighteen months earlier, had stood at 91 percent.

As in the 1920s, Americans have tuned out foreign affairs and tuned in the stock market and the scandals. But as the good times of the 1920s ended in the Depression decade and World War II, the twenty-first century will not leave America serene in its preeminence. Already, enemies collude against what they consider an intolerable American hegemony.

There is a fundamental question any foreign policy must answer: What will we fight for? What are the vital interests for which America will sacrifice the blood of its young? With our great enemy gone, the answer is not a simple one. For we Americans disagree on what our vital interests are, what our role in the world should be, and whom we should defend. Without some new foreign peril, America is never going to know again the unity we knew in World War II and the early decades of the Cold War. It may be naive to believe we can ever again have a foreign policy that unites this divided and disputatious people. Nevertheless, we must try, for foreign policy is the shield of the Republic. Blunders here can be as fateful as they were for the other great empires and nations of the twentieth century.

The purpose of this book, then, is to revisit the history of American foreign policy, its successes, triumphs, and failures. From that history, we can expose the myths and identify the true traditions upon which we can build, and the lessons from which we can draw, to offer a foreign policy for the new century that might unite most of us and ensure that America endures as the greatest republic in history. As Patrick Henry said, only the "lamp of experience" can guide our way.

And the need for a course correction is urgent. For, with little discussion or dissent, America has undertaken the most open-ended and extravagant commitments in history. With the expansion of NATO, we have undertaken the defense of Eastern Europe, forever, as well as Central Europe from Norway to Turkey. American troops are, for the first time in history, policing the Balkans. We have undertaken the "dual containment" of Iran and Iraq and the ground and naval defense of the Persian Gulf. These new war guarantees have been added to old Cold War commitments to the security of Israel in a hostile Arab world, to the defense of Korea, Japan, Australia, and the SEATO pact nations of South Asia, not to mention every Latin American member-state of the Rio pact. Voices can even be heard in Washington asserting a "vital U.S. interest" in preventing Russia and Iran from dominating the south Caucasus.

U.S. war guarantees to Poland today, and Lithuania, Latvia, Estonia, and Rumania tomorrow, may seem costless, painless, and popular. But so did England's guarantee of Belgium's neutrality in 1839, which dragged Britain into the Great War, cost it hundreds of thousands of dead, and inflicted on the empire a wound from which it would never recover.

Our country is today traveling the same path that was trod by the British Empire—to the same fate. Do we want America to end that way?

CHAPTER 2

Courting Conflict with Russia

*He who wants to defend everything defends
nothing, and he who wants to be everyone's friend
has no friends in the end.*[1]

—FREDERICK THE GREAT

*The price of empire is America's soul and
that price is too high.*[2]

—J. WILLIAM FULBRIGHT

The Cold War was an exceptional time that called forth
exceptional commitments. A nation that had wanted to stay out of
World War II had declared by 1950 that an attack on Turkey would
be treated as an attack on Tennessee, that the 38th parallel of Korea
would be defended as though it were the 49th parallel of the United
States. But when the Cold War ended, the Cold War coalition collapsed and traditionalists declared the time had come to dissolve the
now-unnecessary alliances and bring the boys home.

Shocked at this outbreak of "isolationism," internationalists
quickly pressed America to seize the moment to begin an era of
"beneficent global hegemony."

THE WOLFOWITZ MEMORANDUM

The Republican establishment was first to advance this vision. Its
hand was tipped in early 1992 in a secret Pentagon memorandum
leaked to the *New York Times*. Prepared under the direction of
Undersecretary Paul Wolfowitz, the forty-six–page memo was

described by the *Washington Post* as a "classified blueprint intended to help 'set the nation's direction for the next century....'"[3] The document, wrote reporter Barton Gellman, "casts Russia as the gravest potential threat to U.S. vital interests and presumes the United States would spearhead a NATO counterattack if Russia launched an invasion of Lithuania." That Baltic republic had now become a "U.S. vital interest."[4] But how could the United States save Lithuania from Russia? Wrote Gellman:

> [The Pentagon] contemplates a major war by land, sea and air in which 24 NATO divisions, 70 fighter squadrons, and six aircraft carrier battle groups would keep the Russian Navy "bottled up in the eastern Baltic," bomb supply lines in Russia, and use armored formations to expel Russian forces from Lithuania. The authors state that Russia is unlikely to respond with nuclear weapons, but they provide no basis for that assessment.[5]

What made this scenario so astonishing was that only a year earlier George Bush barely protested when Mikhail Gorbachev ordered Spesnatz troops into Vilnius. Just three weeks before the leak, Bush and President Boris Yeltsin had issued a joint declaration that "Russia and the United States do not regard each other as potential adversaries."[6]

The Wolfowitz memo also envisioned U.S. war guarantees to Eastern Europe and permanent U.S. involvement on every continent. America's dominance was to remain so great as to deter "potential competitors from even aspiring to a larger regional or global role."[7] Preventing the emergence of rival superpowers was now declared a

> dominant consideration underlying the new regional defense *strategy* and requir[ing] that we endeavor to prevent any hostile power from dominating a region whose resources would, under

consolidated control, be sufficient to generate global power. These regions include Western Europe, East Asia, the territory of the former Soviet Union, and Southwest Asia.[8]

The Pentagon had decided the United States would never permit any nation—Russia, Germany, Japan, China—to rise ever again even to the status of regional superpower. To maintain global hegemony, the Pentagon anticipated U.S. military intervention for promoting ends far beyond the protection of vital interests. As the *Washington Post* noted:

> While the U.S. cannot become the world's "policeman," by
> assuming responsibility for righting every wrong, we will retain
> the preeminent responsibility for addressing selectively those
> wrongs which threaten not only our interests, but those of our
> allies or friends, or which could seriously unsettle international
> relations.[9]

Containment, a defensive strategy, had given way to a breathtakingly ambitious offensive strategy—to "establish and protect a new order."[10]

Reaction was sharp. Ex-Secretary of Defense Harold Brown warned that extending war guarantees to Eastern Europe would provoke Russian nationalism, risking the "same grave danger of nuclear war" that prevented intervention there for forty-five years.[11] Senator Joseph Biden ridiculed the memo as a formula for "a Pax Americana."[12] Senator Edward Kennedy said the Pentagon plans "appear to be aimed primarily at finding new ways to justify Cold War levels of military spending."[13]

The Wolfowitz plan seemed to have been laughed off the table. But by the end of the 1990s, crucial elements had been adopted by Congress and President Clinton, and passively accepted by the

American people. By 1998 the administration—with Biden and Kennedy's support—had indeed extended NATO to Poland, Hungary, and the Czech Republic and had offered membership to the Baltic states. Thus, NATO expansion is the first site at which to explore the new fault line in American foreign policy.

THE HEGEMONIST VISION

America's hegemonists argue the case for NATO expansion by citing justice, history, and the national interest. This, they say, is America's hour. The Eagle triumphant should spread its protective wings over liberated Eastern Europe to shield it from Russian revanchism and lock it onto a democratic path. To have left Poland, Hungary, and the Czech Republic outside of NATO, they argue, would have reenacted the betrayal of the Czechs at Munich, of the Poles at Yalta, of the Hungarians in 1956. In the phrase of Vaclav Havel, to deny the nations of Eastern Europe membership in NATO would have invited a return of "the Munich danger."[14] Indeed, we "owe" these people who suffered so under Hitler and Stalin.

The geostrategic argument is that the three new members of NATO are the eastern buffer states of Germany. To leave them outside the West's security zone is to invite the Russian Bear to go prowling again. "A larger NATO will make us safer," says Secretary of State Madeleine Albright, "by expanding the area in Europe where wars simply do not happen."[15] By putting Moscow on notice that Eastern Europe is now part of the West, we strengthen the alliance and ensure that the Bear keeps its claws off.

The argument from history runs thus: Conflicts in Europe often erupt into general wars, and the United States is inevitably dragged in to protect vital interests. Far better for America to put its weight in the balance before these wars begin. "If history teaches us anything," writes Senator Richard Lugar, "it is that the United States is always drawn into such European conflicts because our vital interests are ultimately... engaged."[16]

REBUTTALS FROM HISTORY

Yet history teaches no such thing. Between 1789 and 1914 there were seven major European wars: the wars of the French republic (1792–1802), Napoleon's wars (1803–1815), the Crimean War (1853–1855), the war of Piedmont and France against Austria (1859–1860), the Austro-Prussian War (1866), the Franco-Prussian War (1870–1871), and the Balkan wars (1912–1913). With the exceptions of an undeclared naval war with France under John Adams, and the War of 1812, the United States stayed out of them all. As for World Wars I and II, the United States kept clear of both conflicts for more than two years before going in.

For two consecutive decades between the beheading of Louis XVI and Napoleon's invasion of Russia, Europe fought. Yet America was neutral. Madison took us in in 1812 only because the opportunity to grab Canada, with the Iron Duke preoccupied, proved irresistible.

As for World War I, Wilson could have responded to U-boat attacks on U.S. merchant ships in 1917 with a naval war, without sending a single soldier to France. As late as December 1916 the president professed to see no difference in the war aims of the Allies and the Central Powers and no compelling U.S. interest to justify intervention.

In 1939 the United States anticipated that Britain and France would block any Nazi drive into Western Europe. When France was overrun, the United States rushed aid to Britain. By the fall of 1940 Hitler was contained at the Channel. By December 1941 he had been halted outside Leningrad and Moscow. U.S. policy was succeeding without one American ground soldier in combat. People forget: The United States did not declare war on Germany until after Hitler declared war on the United States on December 11, 1941. FDR's "date-which-will-live-in-infamy" speech did not even mention Germany.

After World War II America sent troops back to Europe to prevent it from being overrun by the Red Army. But Dwight Eisenhower pledged that the troops would remain only ten years.

True to his word, in 1961 Ike urged John F. Kennedy to begin bringing the troops home. Writes Kennedy biographer Richard Reeves:

> Eisenhower told his successor that it was time to start bringing
> the troops home from Europe. "America is carrying far more
> than her share of the free world defense," he said. It was time for
> the other nations of NATO... to take on more of the costs of
> their own defense. Their economies were more productive than
> ever in their histories and the costs of American deployment
> were creating a trade imbalance, draining gold from the United
> States Treasury.[17]

Kennedy nodded, but he ignored Eisenhower's advice. Had Ike's
counsel been heeded, America would have removed Europe's
crutches and forced the allies to walk on their own feet again. The
most successful alliance in history thus failed by the standards of its
founders. Half a century later, Europe remains a U.S. military
dependency.

Why did U.S. troops have to return to Europe? Because in
1943, at Casablanca, Franklin D. Roosevelt had foolishly declared
America's war aim to be the "unconditional surrender" of Germany.
That meant the Red Army would be in Berlin at war's end, and
Germany could not play its historical role of keeping Russia out of
Europe. That role would have to be assumed, as it was, by the United
States.

NATO, as a "temporary" alliance against a Soviet empire that
had declared the United States to be its main enemy, was consistent
with the tradition of George Washington. But expansion of NATO
into Eastern Europe, where no president had ever asserted a vital
interest and no U.S. army had ever fought, is an absolute break with
Washington's "great rule." Our foreign policy elite is making commitments previous generations could not have conceived of, ignor-

ing the warnings of wiser men, including columnist and liberal internationalist Walter Lippmann, who wrote, when America was at the
peak of its power:

> Our power is on the sea and in the air, not on the land, and our
> interest in the interior of the European continent is indirect....
> To encourage the nations of Central and Eastern Europe to
> organize themselves as a barrier against Russia would be to make
> a commitment that the United States could not carry out.[18]

NATO expansionists insist that America must defend Europe in
perpetuity because Europe's wars always put the U.S. economy at risk.
"History has taught us," writes Anthony Lake, Clinton's former
national security adviser, "that when Europe is in turmoil, America suf-
fers, and when Europe is peaceful and prosperous, America can thrive
as well."[19] But, again, history teaches no such thing. During the
Napoleonic Wars, America, cut off from trade by its own embargoes,
became a more self-sufficient nation. World War I pulled us out of the
recession of 1913–1914. World War II brought an end to the
Depression. In every great European war, a neutral America prospered.

Comes the counterargument: Perhaps that was true yesterday,
but, today, we are immersed in a Global Economy. When Russia, the
Pacific Rim, or Europe fails, we all fail. No nation is an island; no
nation can stand alone. Economic interdependence and military
interdependence are one and the same.

The answer to that argument: Rather than squander American
wealth propping up failed foreign economies, or spilling the blood of
America's young in foreign wars, let us restore the political, economic, and military independence that was the dream and purpose
of Washington, Hamilton, Madison, Clay, and the Republican Party
from Lincoln to World War II.

THE DEMOCRATIST TEMPTATION

Liberal internationalists contend that NATO's expansion into Eastern Europe will fix these nations forever in the democratic camp. But when did the kind of regime other nations adopt become a vital interest of the United States? NATO's founding fathers had no qualms about negotiating base agreements with Spain's General Franco. They also brought in Portugal, though ruled by a dictator, Dr. Salazar, whose successor would prove more reliable than Europe's democracies during the Yom Kippur War. Inclusion in NATO did not prevent Greece from succumbing to the dictatorship of the colonels from 1967 to 1974, or Turkey from passing repeatedly under military rule.

That democracy is putting down roots in Eastern Europe is welcome news. But democracy was not introduced to Warsaw, Prague, Budapest, or the Baltic republics by NATO; it sprang up before NATO membership was at issue. The nation America most needs to lock onto a democratic path is Russia. Yet, by making allies of countries once part of its empire, we treat Russia as the Allies treated Germany at Versailles, rubbing its nose in its defeat, pushing it outside the Western enclosure, virtually designating Russia a permanent enemy. To capture a pawn we are risking a queen.

The U.S. posture toward other nations should be based not on their internal arrangements but on their stance toward us. After June 22, 1941, Stalin's Soviet Union was no longer Hitler's partner, but our "ally." After victory in 1945, Stalin reverted to his natural hostility to America. China, an ally against Japan, was our enemy in Korea. Just as policies change and regimes pass, so, too, should alliances be temporary and transient.

Whether a nation is democratic should be of less concern to us than how it views America. In the Cold War, autocratic Pakistan was a better friend than democratic India, which sided with Moscow in the Afghan war. Chile's Pinochet was a better friend than the elected demagogue Salvador Allende. The authoritarians in Seoul and Manila supported America in Vietnam, while France and Britain traded with the enemy and Europe's socialists denounced what Reagan called a "noble cause" as a "dirty and immoral war." When we say a nation is democratic we say only that its leaders reflect the will of its people. Would America be better off with regimes in Morocco, Algeria, Egypt, Saudi Arabia, and Kuwait that better reflected the will of the Arab street? Is that a cause worth crusading for, fighting for, dying for? Of the Persian Gulf nations, perhaps the most "democratic"—if voter approval and popular support are our yardstick—is Iran.

The form of government nations adopt is their own business, and a foreign policy that declares global democracy as its goal is arrogant and utopian. Governments evolve out of a nation's history, culture, religious heritage, and traditions. Like alcoholics, democracies backslide. But the rise of autocrats does not threaten us if we decline to make the internal affairs of other nations our central concern.

While West Germany underwent years of "de-Nazification" before being brought into NATO, no nation in Eastern Europe has undertaken a purge of communist officials. NATO's newest members are democratic, but "[a]uthoritarian elements from the communist era still control… the military, the intelligence agencies, and the educational system."[20] War plans shared with these allies are likely to be weekend reading in Moscow.

BREAKING FAITH WITH RUSSIA

By pushing a U.S. alliance up to Russia's borders, we are violating solemn pledges given when Moscow agreed to German reunification. U.S. leaders say we never gave any *written* reassurances, but Gorbachev could never have brought the Red Army home had Russia's military believed its bases would be occupied by NATO troops. Regarding a high-level meeting in Moscow in which German Foreign Minister Hans Dietrich Genscher and Secretary of

State James Baker participated, Susan Eisenhower, a scholar on
Russia, writes:

> [Genscher] promoted a "no expansion of NATO" concept, an
> idea that Baker, too, had advanced. It was at the February meet-
> ing that the key words were spoken, words that are still a source
> of debate. If a unified Germany was anchored in NATO,
> Secretary Baker said to Gorbachev, "NATO's jurisdiction or
> forces would not move eastward."
>
> Apparently, Gorbachev was receptive to that assurance and
> emphasized that "any extension of the zone of NATO is
> unacceptable."
>
> "I agree," Baker said.
>
> Heartened by Baker's comments, several months later, in
> May, Gorbachev gave up his idea that Germany must remain
> neutral, or at least, a member of both blocs. He conceded (with-
> out consulting his advisers) that the German people should be
> able to choose the alliance they wished to join.[21]

"Against that background," writes Eisenhower, "it is not surpris-
ing that NATO expansion has been viewed with great hostility
across the entire Russian political spectrum."[22] Adds scholar Stanley
Kober, "Russians are now experiencing… [a] sense of betrayal
because they apparently were promised when Germany was reunited
that there would be no further expansion of NATO." In the words
of former Russian Prime Minister Yevgeny Primakov:

> In conversations with Mikhail Gorbachev, Eduard Shevardnadze
> and Dmitri Yazov, held in 1990–1991, i.e., when the West was
> vitally interested in the Soviet troop withdrawal from the German
> Democratic Republic and wanted us to "swallow the bitter
> pill"—the disintegration of the Warsaw Treaty Organization…

Francois Mitterrand, John Major, and [James] Baker, all of them said one and the same thing: NATO will not move to the east by a single inch and not a single Warsaw Pact country will be admitted to NATO. This was exactly what they said. These conversations were not codified in the form of official documents at that time.[23]

Former Soviet Ambassador to Britain Anatoli Adamishin contends that when Moscow let the Berlin Wall come down and began to withdraw its troops from Eastern Europe, "we were given repeatedly assurances that NATO would not expand an inch eastwards."[24] Jack Matlock, the U.S. ambassador to Russia in 1990, "confirms that Gorbachev had reason to believe that he had been given a 'blanket promise that NATO would not expand.'"[25]

In the early 1990s the romance of the age was between America and a Russia liberated from Leninism. Reagan was being toasted in Moscow for having been right about the evil empire. Boris Yeltsin was being toasted in America for having stood atop a tank and defied communists attempting to reestablish the *ancien regime*. How far away that all seems. An agitated Russia—believing America is taking advantage of Russia's present weakness to humiliate the nation—has sacked its pro-U.S. foreign minister, named an ex-KGB chief to be prime minister, refused to ratify the START II arms treaty, moved closer to Beijing, funneled weapons into the Caucasus to destabilize pro-U.S. regimes, sold weapons and nuclear technology to Iran, and sided with Saddam Hussein. "[T]he most fateful error of American policy in the entire post–cold war era," says George F. Kennan of the expansion of NATO.

Russia is today a bankrupt, demoralized nation whose presidency is lusted after by democrats, demagogues, ex-generals, and communists with a single conviction in common: All believe NATO expansion to be a provocation, an example of American bad faith in exploiting Russian weakness. Russian military analyst Pavel Felgenhauer warns that "public opinion is changing. NATO expansion will turn a whole generation of Russians anti-American."[26]

We soothingly reassure Moscow that NATO's expansion is benign. But if the Russians gave war guarantees to Mexico and began arming and training Mexican troops, would any Russian assurance diminish our determination to run them out of our hemisphere? If rising resentment in Russia leads to Yeltsin's replacement with an anti-American nationalist, full blame must rest squarely with a haughty U.S. elite that has done its best to humiliate Russia.

Why are we doing this? This is not 1948. Stalin is dead; the Soviet empire is dead; the Soviet Union is dead. European Russia is smaller than the Russia of Peter the Great. Between the vital interests of our two nations, there is no conflict. But these proud people retain thousands of nuclear weapons. A friendly Russia is far more critical to U.S. security than any alliance with Warsaw or Prague. If the United States has one overriding national security interest in the new century, it is to avoid collisions with great nuclear powers like Russia. By moving NATO onto Russia's front porch, we have scheduled a twenty-first–century confrontation. Europe's sick man of today is going to get well. When Russia does, it will proclaim its own Monroe Doctrine. And when that day comes, America will face a hellish dilemma: risk confrontation with a nuclear-armed Russia determined to recreate its old sphere of influence, or renege on solemn commitments and see NATO collapse.

Are we really willing to use nuclear weapons to defend Eastern Europe—for that is what NATO membership means. And if we make good on the commitment of Clinton and Madeleine Albright to bring in the Baltic republics, it is impossible to see how these tiny nations can be defended, short of an escalation to a nuclear crisis similar to Cuba, 1962.

FROM ALLIANCE TO PROTECTORATE

By expanding NATO to Eastern Europe, the United States has changed the character of the alliance from a defensive pact to an American protectorate. Europe knows this, and every ally has thus cut back on defense. After a NATO conference in Madrid in 1997, France declared it would contribute nothing to expansion. The Clinton administration claims NATO expansion will cost us only $1.5 billion over ten years. Whom are we deceiving? Does anyone believe a U.S. protectorate over Eastern Europe can be bought for less than the price of a B-2 bomber?

As Europeans slash budgets to maintain deficit targets demanded by the European Monetary Union, a crisis over who pays for NATO expansion looms. We claim this is being done for Europe's protection; Europe sees it as a scheme for permanent U.S. hegemony and has decided that if the Americans want to play Romans, let Americans pay the costs and take the risks.

What America has in Europe today are less allies than dependencies, and the brave Polish people would be well advised not to rely too heavily on guarantees that, in the event of any attack, NATO will declare war and send troops to its rescue. Surely the Poles remember 1939.

This generation has forgotten its own history. Five presidents were confronted with Soviet outrages in Germany, Hungary, Czechoslovakia, and Poland—Truman, Eisenhower, Kennedy, Johnson, and Reagan. Not one used force. Can anyone believe Clinton or Gore would go to Congress for a declaration of war if Polish and Russian soldiers clashed? Clinton has already said we will not move nuclear weapons or any significant number of troops into Poland, which should tell us all we need to know about this administration's resolve.

That Poland is independent and democratic is among the great peace dividends of our Cold War victory. But Poland has never been a vital U.S. interest. For the first 130 years of our existence, Poland

did not exist as an independent nation. Its partition by Nazis and
Stalinists did not even convince FDR to abandon neutrality. Its
incorporation into the Soviet empire was virtually acceded to by
FDR at Teheran. To assert that Poland's democracy and frontiers are
now matters over which we will fight a nuclear war is, in David
Lloyd George's phrase about British guarantees to Poland in 1939,
"demented... the most reckless commitment any country has ever
entered into."[27]

There is an element of fecklessness and immorality in a policy
that persuades nations to rely on guarantees we can no more honor
than Britain could honor its guarantees to Poland. General
Eisenhower commanded the greatest American army in history, but
even he halted before Berlin, Vienna, and Prague. Today's U.S. Army
is one-tenth the size of the American army of 1945. Yet the United
States has now declared it will not only defend and rescue Prague,
Warsaw, and Budapest, it is also ready to give the same solemn commitment to Vilnius, Riga, and Tallinn.

If America pushes to bring the Baltic states into NATO, Britain
and Germany will not go along. Thus Clinton and Albright have
scheduled a diplomatic collision in which NATO will face three
options: (1) The allies will buckle to U.S. demands and bring the
Baltic republics in, enraging Moscow; (2) the United States will use
Europe's opposition as grounds for backing away from its commitments to the Baltic states, which will be declared a "second Yalta"; or
(3) the United States will issue unilateral guarantees, creating a crisis
in U.S.-Russian relations.

With defense a smaller share of the budget and gross domestic
product (GDP) than at the time of Pearl Harbor, the only way the
United States could force Russia to disgorge Polish or Baltic territory would be with air strikes, a blockade, and the threat of nuclear
weapons. But, as the Russians have put the West on notice that the
diminished size of their army and navy means early reliance on the
use of nuclear weapons in any future war, is this wise?

Russia may be destitute and weak, but, should a nationalist regime take power, rebuild the army, impose Moscow's will on the Baltic states, and menace Poland, the United States will have to call up the reserves, reinstitute the draft, and be ready to impose a blockade and conduct air and missile strikes on Russian armed forces, risking atomic retribution. Let us pray Russia never tests the U.S.-NATO commitment to go to war for Poland.

A BRIDGE TOO FAR

Lost in the enthusiasm to include the liberated nations of Europe in NATO is the fact that NATO is not a social club. It is a *military* alliance. Under Article V, the heart of the treaty, "an armed attack against one [NATO nation] is to be considered an armed attack on all." Before 1949 America had never entered such an alliance. Whether we should have was hotly debated, but the guarantees were given. After Mao Tse-tung's armies overran China and South Korea was invaded, NATO was extended to Greece and Turkey. But the nation was assured that NATO's Red Line was at the Elbe. When Soviet tanks returned to Budapest in 1956, and to Prague in 1968, neither Eisenhower nor Johnson threatened military action. Yet, without a national debate, the United States has now moved its Red Line to Russia's border. Should Russian troops in the Kaliningrad enclave between Poland and Lithuania skirmish with Polish troops, America could be at war. Do we realize that? Should Belarus, ruled by an admirer of Hitler, clash with Poland, the 82nd Airborne could be on the way, F-16s could be making air strikes on Minsk, and Washington and Moscow could be careening toward confrontation. Are Americans aware of this? Is a nation that did not want to send peacekeeping troops to Bosnia willing to send combat troops to Bialystok?

Historically, nations enter alliances to strengthen themselves. How is America strengthened by an alliance with the Czech Republic? How do we respond if Moscow demands a corridor through Lithuania to Kaliningrad, where more Russian troops are stationed than there are U.S. troops in all of Europe? What do we do if Moscow decides to move its own defense line west by putting troops back in the Baltic republics? Where are those twenty-four NATO divisions of the Wolfowitz memo going to come from?

Since the Gulf War we have cut defense to 3 percent of GDP (from 6 percent in the Reagan years) and mustered 550,000 people out of our armed forces, a reduction in force equal to the army of Desert Storm. Yet triumphalism is pandemic. The *Washington Post* declares it is now our duty to set about "ensuring that no country, by virtue of size or history, can determine another's fate." This is hubris of the kind that got marines massacred in Beirut, where they had no more business than do U.S. Army troops on the Belarussian border.

Offering NATO memberships to Estonia, Latvia, Lithuania, and, as some urge, Ukraine is rashness bordering on madness. This would put the Russian base at Kaliningrad behind NATO lines and bring into a U.S.-led alliance three nations with huge Russian minorities. Latvia is almost half Russian; eastern Ukraine, almost entirely Russian. America could neither defend nor liberate these nations without the risk of nuclear war.

AMERICA'S LOST OPPORTUNITY

Consider again the opportunity America had in 1991. Moscow had let its empire collapse, pulled the Red Army back inside its borders, and allowed Germany to be reunited. The Baltic republics and Ukraine had been set free. And now, having overthrown communism, Russia stretched out its hand to America. Every goal of our Cold War policy had been achieved. Yet, instead of behaving toward Russia as we did toward Germany and Japan after World War II, we began treating Russia like a dangerous delinquent and probable recidivist, to be corralled and contained in the tight little box where history had put it. In 1997 U.S. Marines conducted exercises in the

Crimea, U.S. paratroops jumped into Kazakhstan, and U.S. strategists sought to cut Moscow out of the oil trade of the Caucasus. The imperious attitude seems to be: If the Russians don't like it, tough, what can they do about it?

Given the balance of power, Russia can only seethe. But the present balance will not endure forever. Like Weimar Germany, Russia is seeking friends where it can find them—in Teheran, Minsk, Belgrade, Baghdad, Beijing. In February 1998 Georgian leader Eduard Shevardnadze was the target of assassins. Suspected motive: to disrupt U.S.-backed plans to move Caspian Sea oil through an Azerbaijani-Georgian pipeline to the Black Sea, cutting Russia out. In Armenia a pro-Western president was ousted, and Russian arms began pouring in. The believed objective: to destabilize the region, block the pipeline. Even more ominous, Moscow has been berating Riga for maltreatment of its Russian minority. Latvia has 600,000 Russians, many of them retirees of the Red Army and Soviet navy. Yet America plans to bring Latvia into NATO.

WHAT THE FUTURE HOLDS

"Why the Rush to Expand NATO?" asked the *New York Times*. Answer: Handing out NATO memberships like White House souvenirs has produced popularity for U.S. politicians.

Warsaw, Prague, and Budapest are delighted, but Moscow seethes, and Belarus grows belligerent. Tension is greatest in the Baltic and Ukraine, where the U.S.-Russian crisis is likely to come. Never has so extravagant a commitment been made. We have put the world on notice that the Americans are never coming home, that our duty is, henceforth and forever, to defend virtually every border in Europe.

NATO expansionists have won the day, but they have scheduled a series of clashes that will mean a humiliating back-down by either Russia or the United States—or war. We have committed American

children yet unborn to fight Russians yet unborn over land no president ever considered vital. This hubristic attempt to impose a U.S.
protectorate over Europe will one day be challenged. That day we will
awaken to find that a new generation is not willing to send its sons to
fight in places they have never heard of, simply because this generation pledged they would go. NATO expansion is a rash and provocative act, unrelated to our true security interests and rooted in an
ignorance of American history and traditions.

Our hegemonists are confident that America's power is too great
for any to resist. History teaches otherwise. Every attempt to establish hegemony incites resentment and hostility. Weaker nations
instinctively seek security in each other, creating the very combina-
tions the hegemonists most fear. It is a law of history: The thesis calls
into being the antithesis; the weak collude to balance off the strong.

U.S. assurances that its hegemony is beneficent only confirm the
suspicions of those it is intended to constrict and circumscribe.
Fifteen years after Britain established hegemony over North
America, Americans were fighting alongside their old French enemies to overthrow it. Allied hegemony in Europe in 1919 persuaded
Germany to make common cause with Bolsheviks, whose agents
they had just liquidated—Lenin and Stalin were happy to accommodate at Rapallo. Hitler's conquest of France, our buffer state on
the Atlantic, aroused America to take Iceland, send aid to Britain, and
begin hunting German submarines. Stalin's hegemony over Central
Europe called into being the NATO alliance. When the Soviet
Union was in its ascendancy, Nixon, foremost anticommunist of his
generation, went to Beijing to embrace Mao. Even anticommunists
applauded, for they believed Nixon was trying to balance off the
power of the greater threat to the United States.

America's hegemonists have already begun to reap the pre-
dictable results. China and Russia, the two nations capable of doing
mortal damage to us, have formed a strategic partnership—to oppose
U.S. hegemony.

If we are to remain a republic, each generation should decide when and whether to risk the life of the nation and the lives of its young. We ought not to be foreclosing future generations' options or making their decisions. As Jefferson said, "The earth belongs to the living, not to the dead."[28]

CHAPTER 3

America's Future Wars

*The commonest error in politics is sticking to the
carcasses of dead policies.*[1]

—Lord Salisbury

*You don't need today's defense budget to defend
the United States; you need today's defense
budget to lead the world.*[2]

—Newt Gingrich

At the close of the twentieth century, U.S. foreign policy
seems frozen in time. Nostalgic for the clarity and certitudes of the
Cold War, our elites have resolutely refused to relinquish a single institution or commitment dating to that conflict. Yet the Soviet empire has
been dead for a decade. Indeed, commitments for America to fight, in
perpetuity, in defense of other nations are routinely added. Repeated
incantations to America as the "indispensable nation" are made to reassure ourselves our dominance is still desired. But the world has
changed since the Wall came down, and we must change with it.

BALANCE SHEET OF AN IMPERIAL REPUBLIC

Walter Lippmann once described the "preoccupation" of a statesman
as "bringing into balance, with a comfortable surplus of power in
reserve, the nation's commitments and the nation's power."[3] If a
nation's power fails to cover its commitments, its foreign policy is

bankrupt. While the insolvency might not be revealed until a run on the bank, as at Pearl Harbor, it will be exposed. Given U.S. military assets today, and the commitments they must cover, U.S. foreign policy is near bankruptcy.

Consider the asset side of our national security balance sheet. The Cold War Center-Right coalition has collapsed, our will to intervene has largely vanished, and U.S. power has undergone a historic contraction. Defense spending, 9 percent of GDP in Eisenhower's day, 6 percent in the Reagan era, is about 3 percent today. Under the "Proposed Active Force Levels" of the Pentagon, manpower is to be cut from 2,070,000 in 1990 to 1,453,000. Carrier battle groups, numbering fifteen during Desert Storm, are to fall to eleven; Air Force Wings are to drop from twenty-two in 1990 to thirteen.[4]

These, nevertheless, are impressive armed forces, and, were they needed only to protect U.S. vital interests, they would be adequate. But consider the astonishing and lengthening roster of global commitments that must be covered by these dwindling military assets:

✯ *North America and Europe.* Under Article V of the NATO treaty, an attack on any member state "shall be considered an attack against them all."[5] This means the United States, in perpetuity, must respond as though America were attacked in the event of any attack on any of eighteen NATO nations: Canada, Iceland, Britain, France, Holland, Luxembourg, Belgium, Denmark, Germany, Norway, Italy, Portugal, Spain, Turkey, Greece, Poland, Hungary, and the Czech Republic.

NATO expansionists are now demanding U.S. war guarantees for Austria, Slovenia, Macedonia, Bulgaria, Rumania, Slovakia, and the three Baltic states: Estonia, Lithuania, and Latvia. There is talk of Ukraine, which ten million Russians call home, joining NATO. This would commit America to fight Europe's wars in perpetuity all the way to the Urals. On November 4, 1996, was held the first meeting of the Security Committee of the U.S.-Ukraine Binational Commission to strengthen ties between the Pentagon and Kiev's Ministry of Defense, and to promote "Ukraine's integration into European and Transatlantic security structures."[6]

U.S. Marines have been involved in joint maneuvers with Ukrainian troops on the Crimean Peninsula; U.S. paratroopers have practiced jumps in Kazakhstan; and Washington has been providing military assistance to Tashkent and established a United States–Uzbekistan Joint Commission to study military and political cooperation.

✭ *The Balkan Peninsula.* Before President Clinton ordered air strikes on Yugoslavia in the early spring of 1999, U.S. soldiers had never fought in the Balkans. But today there are eight thousand U.S. troops in Bosnia and a U.S. presence in Macedonia. And the United States and NATO have battered Serbia to force Slobodan Milosevic to remove his army and security police from Kosovo. Yet Kosovo is part of Yugoslavia. Thus, for the first time, NATO, a defensive alliance, has taken offensive action against a country putting down an insurrection inside its own territory, and America has engaged in acts of war against a nation that did not perpetrate any act of violence against the United States or its allies. Secretary of State Madeleine Albright has been quoted as declaring that NATO must now extend its geographic reach even beyond the continent of Europe and evolve into a "force for peace from the Middle East to Central Africa."[7]

President Clinton's original ultimatum to Yugoslavia—to attack its troops and sovereign territory if it did not remove its forces from Kosovo—was made without the formal approval of Congress.

✭ *The Middle East.* While we have no treaty alliance with Israel, the United States, Britain, and France made a Tripartite Declaration in 1950, stating that they would take action if Arab nations or Israelis prepared to violate the armistice lines of 1948. "This declaration in effect supported Israel's right to exist within the frontiers established by force of arms pending a peace treaty,"[8] noted historians J. A. S. Grenville and Bernard Wasserstein. The United States signed a Mutual Defense Assistance Agreement with Israel in 1952. Under Presidents Johnson and Nixon, the United States made a moral commitment to Israeli security. That commitment led Nixon to put U.S. nuclear forces on alert when Moscow seemed about to intervene in the Yom Kippur War in October 1973.

After the Wye River meeting between Israel and the Palestinian Authority, a "memorandum of understanding" was signed committing the United States to enhance Israel's "defensive and deterrent capabilities" against chemical, biological, and nuclear weapons. Should Iran, Iraq, or Syria deploy missiles that can hit Israel, the United States will view that with "particular gravity" and consult promptly about the aid or support, "diplomatic or otherwise," it might provide. Clearly, the United States is moving toward further extension of its nuclear umbrella. As this was not a formal treaty, Senate approval was not required.[9]

Today, U.S. troops sit on Mount Sinai to monitor an Israeli-Egyptian peace. There is talk that, in return for recognition of a Palestinian state, Israel may be given security guarantees by the United States to come to its defense in any future Israeli-Arab war, of which there have been five. If Israel returns the Golan Heights to Syria, some Americans have suggested the United States might put its own forces there, to ensure Israel's security.

★ *The Persian Gulf.* After the Gulf War, America adopted a policy of "dual containment" of Iran and Iraq. Thousands of U.S. troops are stationed in the Gulf, and U.S. warships make routine visits to the United Arab Emirates, Oman, and Bahrain. It is understood that any attack on the pro-Western Arab nations of the Gulf would involve a U.S. response.

★ *South Korea.* After the armistice in 1953, the United States negotiated a Mutual Security Treaty with Korea. It reads, in part:

> Each party recognizes that an armed attack in the Pacific area on
> either of the parties in territories now under their respective
> administrative control... would be dangerous to its own peace
> and safety and declares that it would act to meet the common
> danger in accordance with its constitutional processes.[10]

Though Chinese forces left Korea forty years ago, 37,000 U.S. troops remain, and Defense Secretary William Cohen said in July 1998 that a U.S. military presence "should continue even if there is a unification of the two Koreas...."[11] The United States today spends more for the defense of South Korea than does Seoul, and if another war broke out, American soldiers would be in the thick of the fighting, and dying, from the first hours.

★ *Japan.* The U.S.-Japan Mutual Security Treaty of 1960 obligates the United States to treat any armed attack against any territories "under the administration of Japan" as "dangerous to [America's] own peace and safety...."[12] This would cover such islets as the Senkakus, also claimed by Beijing. Under the treaty, however, Japan is not obliged to treat an armed attack on the United States or its possessions as any threat to Japan. More than half a century after its defeat in World War II, Japan, which has a $4 trillion economy, spends 1 percent of its GDP on defense and relies on America to deal with any attack from Russia, China, or North Korea.

★ *Taiwan.* Though President Carter abrogated our mutual security treaty with Taiwan, signed in 1954, the United States, under Clinton, came close to a naval war with China over the island in 1996. There remains a U.S. moral commitment to Taiwan—much like that to

Israel—and the United States is obligated, by a Reagan communiqué of 1982, to permit Taiwan access to American defensive weapons. Since 1996 China has engaged in a steady buildup of missiles targeted on the island.

⋆ *The Philippines.* Under a mutual security treaty signed in August 1951, any attack on this island nation is declared dangerous to U.S. peace and security.[13] The treaty remains in force, though Manila years ago expelled U.S. forces from Clark Air Force Base and Subic Bay Naval Base. In late 1998, Manila, angry over China's building on disputed Mischief Reef in the Spratly island chain, suggested its U.S. pact might be invoked. "We don't think there will be a shooting war," said the Philippine defense minister, but, "[a]s far as we see it, the mutual defense treaty may still prove of value to us."[14]

⋆ *Thailand and Pakistan.* Under Article V of the Manila Pact of the Southeast Asia Collective Defense Treaty of 1954, SEATO was created by Secretary of State John Foster Dulles to oppose the communist aggression and subversion in the region. Signers included the United States, Britain, France, Australia, New Zealand, the Philippines, Thailand, and Pakistan. Under Article IV, in the event of an armed attack, each member would "act to meet the common danger in accordance with its constitutional processes."[15] De Gaulle's France withdrew from military cooperation in 1967, and Britain refused to assist the United States militarily in Vietnam. In 1972 Pakistan withdrew completely, and in 1977 SEATO was dissolved. But the Manila pact remains in force and, together with a 1962 U.S.-Thailand communiqué, constitutes the U.S. military commitment to Thailand, which remains a U.S. treaty ally.[16]

⋆ *Australia.* Under the ANZUS Pact of 1951, the United States is obligated to come to the defense of Australia and New Zealand if they are attacked, but they have no obligation to come to the defense of the United States if America, or one of its other allies, is attacked. In 1985 a Labour government refused to permit U.S. ships in Wellington Harbor unless Washington stipulated there were no nuclear weapons aboard. The United States declared that New Zealand had decided to "renege on an essential element of its ANZUS participation" and suspended its security obligations to New Zealand.[17] The ANZUS Pact between the United States and Australia, however, remains in force, and each year, under the Australia–United States Ministerial consultations, the two nations meet for high-level talks at the foreign and defense minister level.

★ *Latin America.* Under the Treaty of Rio (the Inter-American Treaty of Reciprocal Assistance) of 1947, which took effect in 1948, the United States is obliged to aid any country in the Western Hemisphere that comes under attack—with the exception of Cuba (Havana withdrew in 1960). Under Article III, signatories "agree that an armed attack by any States against an American State shall be considered as an attack against all the American States," and each signatory "undertakes to assist in meeting the attack."[18] Under this pact, the United States must come to the military rescue of Argentina, the Bahamas, Bolivia, Brazil, Chile, Colombia, Costa Rica, the Dominican Republic, Ecuador, El Salvador, Guatemala, Haiti, Honduras, Mexico, Nicaragua, Panama, Paraguay, Peru, Trinidad and Tobago, Uruguay, and Venezuela. Article IV adds: "This article defines the region to which the treaty refers, which extends from the North Pole to the South Pole, and includes Canada, Alaska, the Aleutians, Greenland, the Falklands, the South Orkneys, and Antarctica."[19]

Nothing can destroy this country except the overextension of our resources, Republican Senator Robert A. Taft once said. Indeed, it would be an understatement to describe the commitments above as an overextension of our resources. In their totality, they make the nineteenth-century British Empire look isolationist; truly, this is imperial overstretch.

America has taken on the historic roles of the German empire in keeping Russia out of Europe, of the Austrian empire in policing the Balkans, of the British Empire in patrolling the oceans and sea lanes and protecting the Persian Gulf, of the Ottoman Empire in keeping peace in the Holy Land, of the Japanese empire in defending Korea and containing China, and of the Spanish empire in Latin America. Thus, we have undertaken to come to the defense of half a hundred nations around the world on a defense budget that is less than 3 percent of GDP. As Paul Kennedy (*The Rise and Fall of the Great Powers*) wrote a decade ago:

> Decision-makers in Washington must face the awkward
> and enduring fact that the sum total of the United States'
> global interests and obligations is now far larger than the
> country's power to defend them all simultaneously.[20]

If not true a decade ago, it is surely true today. Our situation is unsustainable. The steady expansion of global commitments, as relative national power declines, is a prescription for endless wars and eventual disaster. Given these commitments, consider but a few scenarios, not at all remote, that could bring us into war, perhaps with nuclear powers, and with few allies, in but a few years, even where no vital interest is at stake.

SCENARIOS OF FUTURE AMERICAN WARS

The Second Balkan War. It is late 1999. Seething over a cut in Western aid, Nikola Poplasen, the deposed and rabidly nationalist president of Bosnia's Serb Republic, declares independence and asks to join Serbia. Poplasen orders NATO forces out. Within days,

Bosnia's Croats also break with Sarajevo, declare independence, and invite in the Croatian army. The landlocked remnant of a Muslim-dominated Bosnia calls on NATO to enforce the Dayton accords and bring the breakaway republics back.

The NATO high command in Brussels is in disarray; the allies are divided over what to do; the Russians are demanding that NATO stay out. Slobodan Milosevic's Belgrade regime has annexed the Bosnian Serb republic and is funneling in weapons and soldiers. Zagreb has agreed to unification with the Bosnian Croats. The Supreme Allied Commander estimates it will take 100,000 NATO troops to crush the Serbs and stop the fighting, more if the Croats fight. Meanwhile, Iran, Turkey, and Saudi Arabia pledge money, weapons, and volunteers to protect the Muslims.

Congress is split. One side says that the $12 billion already spent is enough trying to buy peace in Bosnia; our job is done; we should pack and go home; let the Bosnians settle their own quarrels. The other side says this means the end of NATO; if we cannot police the Balkans, NATO will become a "hollow shell," and Churchill's "soft underbelly of Europe" will be wide open to ethnic holocausts and penetration by Islamic fanatics.

Suddenly, a patrol of U.S. soldiers near Tuzla is ambushed, and the president orders air strikes and warns that Serbia is not off-limits to U.S. bombers. Russia, supporting its ancient Serb ally, vetoes a Security Council resolution authorizing air strikes. Berlin says it cannot pledge troops to any Balkan campaign, given its history there. France argues it may be time to pull out. The United States, backed only by Britain, determines to "stay the course." But with only 8,000 isolated American troops in Bosnia, and fewer than 100,000 in Europe, and many of these support troops, combat units must come from the United States. Marines are filmed hugging tearful wives and children and boarding ships at Norfolk. Poland offers troops, but Moscow warns that this would be an "unfriendly

act." Hungary offers its air bases and troops and begins to see, in a
NATO war on Serbia, a heaven-sent opportunity to take home its
Hungarian kinsmen who have been under Serb domination since
Versailles.

With Europe paralyzed, Milosevic decides now is an opportune
time to finish the Kosovo rebels. Serb forces pour in, depopulating
the villages of Kosovo adjacent to the Albanian border. Albania
begins funneling men and weapons back to their kinsmen, and the
Kosovars begin to match the Serbs, atrocity for atrocity. Greece says
Serbia is justified in crushing rebellion in its own country, but the
Turks begin air-lifting weapons to Sarajevo and Tirana.

The Balkan War spills over into the Albanian sector of
Macedonia; that tiny nation appears about to break up. All its neighbors, including Bulgaria, line up to take a bite. Greece and Turkey
begin maneuvers in the Aegean, and "Holy Warriors" arrive in
Sarajevo from Afghanistan, Iran, and Sudan. The United States is urging all sides to stand down, but no one is paying attention.

So, the question: Is America prepared to raise an army of 250,000
to invade the Balkans, crush Serbia, and occupy and police the peninsula for the next decade? That is what victory requires—and no one
wants another no-win war. Air, army, and navy reserves are called up;
there may be a need for a limited draft. The campuses are ablaze, and
talk-show populists of the Left and the Right are demanding the
United States stay out.

The Second Korean War. After the fiftieth anniversary of the North
Korean attack on the South—June 25, 2000—passes, nervous U.S.
and South Korean troops stand down. But in July, North Korean
infiltrators are captured. Under duress, one North Korean confesses
that they were sent to assassinate the South Korean president, his cabinet, and the military high command. Seoul abruptly breaks off all
contact, ending food shipments to the North. Congress votes to cancel further shipments of oil to the North and end all U.S. assistance

in building nuclear reactors to replace the plutonium-producing plants North Korea had agreed to shut down.

In late August, the attack comes. Thousands of North Korean soldiers slip through tunnels beneath U.S. and South Korean lines, and surface as suicide squads to create havoc, as thousands of artillery pieces lay down the greatest barrage in history along the Demilitarized Zone (DMZ), hitting targets all the way to the suburbs of Seoul. Scud missiles begin raining down on the South Korean capital. The North Korean army, taking heavy casualties, breaks the line between U.S. and South Korean troops and drives toward Seoul. Panic seizes the city.

After three weeks of savage fighting, Seoul is a ruin, but the North Korean army is stopped at the Han River, where all the bridges have been blown up. The invading North Koreans are now on the receiving end of round-the-clock air and cruise missile strikes from Okinawa, Guam, U.S. naval forces off the coast, and U.S. and South Korean air bases deep in the south of the country that have not been rendered inoperable by North Korean missiles.

North Korea now asks for a cease-fire in place, ominously warning that before it will accept being driven back across the DMZ, it will resort to its atomic weapons. The North Koreans have medium-range missiles and atomic bombs, but no one knows whether they have been able to marry the two or exactly where the missiles are. In the United States there is thunderous opposition to sending an army to fight another Asian war. But South Korea, invoking its treaty, demands that America pursue the war until the North Koreans are driven out and their criminal regime destroyed.

Meanwhile, Japan, fearing North Korea is not bluffing, indicates its interest in an armistice and tells the United States it cannot use bases in Japan or on Okinawa to support an invasion of North Korea. The United States replies that this could mean an end to the U.S.-Japan security treaty. Meanwhile, U.S. intelligence informs the president that Japan is now on its own crash program to build atomic weapons, and, given the advanced state of Japan's technology, this will take no more than eight weeks. In Washington the president is himself considering using low-yield atomic weapons on the nuclear storage and production sites of North Korea, but he is told by U.S. intelligence officers that they do not know where the North Koreans' atomic weapons are hidden, exactly how many they have, and what kind of fallout will result from hitting plutonium reactors.

The president warns Pyongyang that if any nuclear, chemical, or biological weapon falls on South Korea, retaliation will be "massive."

The Baltic War. It is 2001. Under a new president, the United States has kept its commitment to bring Lithuania into NATO, as recommended by Zbigniew Brzezinski. Latvia and Estonia are to be next. Russia angrily protests and ends its association with NATO. Germany and France warned that bringing in Lithuania would be a provocation, but the United States declared Vilnius had a commitment and America would not dishonor it.

In Moscow, the new president, who has won the election by playing the nationalist card—"All Russians back home under Mother Russia's roof"—is presiding over an economy still cut off from credit, due to the Yeltsin default of 1998. Russia's population has turned bitterly anti-American, believing the United States first humiliated, then robbed the country through International Monetary Fund (IMF) agents, currency speculators, and homegrown traitors the West calls "reformers." When Russian army and navy pensioners are roughed up in Riga and cry for help, Moscow orders the army into Latvia. Russia stands as one man and roars its approval.

The 100,000 sailors and soldiers at Kaliningrad, the Russian naval base wedged between Poland and Lithuania, go on alert, as Moscow tells both to keep their forces far away from the enclave. Belarus, still ruled by the neo-Stalinist Alexander Lukashenko, moves troops to the Lithuanian border. A surrounded Estonia protests, and the Russian army marches in and takes over in forty-eight hours. Moscow and Minsk are now eyeball-to-eyeball with NATO in the Baltic. Warsaw demands NATO ground troops, planes, and ships, and an allied ultimatum to Moscow not to invade Lithuania.

Moscow warns that any attack on Russian forces in the Baltic will invite retaliation on any nation permitting the attack from its soil, and U.S. intelligence picks up Russian tactical nuclear forces being moved onto higher alert. Germany, terrified of being dragged into a nuclear war over some Baltic ethnic dispute, announces it will not join any attack on Russian forces, nor will it permit air attacks from German soil. The American president declares there will be "no Munich in the Baltic" and, to show solidarity with Poland, dispatches the 82nd Airborne Division.

Russia and Belarus overrun Lithuania and ask for negotiations to make all three Baltic republics "a zone of peace, forever free of all military alliances." The U.S. president declares, "This will not stand." But no NATO nation offers to send troops to Poland or join the United States in a war on Russia.

The Joint Chiefs tell the president the United States lacks the manpower to force the reconstituted Russian army out of the Baltic states, without sending every combat division in the United States and Korea. The commander in chief is grimly told that any war will likely destroy the Baltic countries before they are liberated. As for air strikes from Poland on Belarus, or on Russian troops in Lithuania, that can be done, but it will risk air and missile counterstrikes on Polish cities.

The best option appears to be a naval blockade from Murmansk to the Black Sea. But this act of war entails risks from Russian submarines and potential resort to nuclear weapons by some rogue officer of a proud nation that is being strangled to death. The president goes on television to declare that a solemn commitment to an ally has been called, that the word of the United States is on the line, that the way to deal with aggressors is resolutely and early. If we do not overturn this outrage, he says, NATO is dead, and we have turned back the clock to 1939. The president announces a call-up of the reserves and asks Congress to reinstitute the draft on the basis of a lottery, with no student deferments. A U.S. blockade is imposed on every Russian port from Murmansk to the Black Sea to Vladivostok.

The Second Gulf War. By 2002 all the sanctions on Iraq have been lifted, and France and Russia have begun a brisk trade, including weapons sales. As three million barrels a day of Iraqi oil come into the world market, a global glut appears, and the price sinks to less than $10 a barrel. There is a spike in the price when the United States detects a nuclear test in the Iranian desert, and yet another when Israel warns that any Iranian attack will be met with "massive retaliation." Then the price collapses again.

With revenues falling, the Saudi monarchy has come to the end of its free-spending days. Resentment over belt-tightening is now added to the rising anger at the huge American presence on sacred Saudi soil. Yet another tragedy occurs at Mecca during Ramadan, when hundreds of pilgrims are trampled to death, causing the smoldering rage at the United States and the monarchy to explode. Army and police crush the riots, but the king declares that the U.S. presence in Saudi Arabia must be liquidated. We can both protect the holy places, the king says, and defend our soil ourselves.

At this point, U.S. intelligence picks up the movement of armored Iraqi Revolutionary Guard divisions toward Kuwait, where thousands of U.S. troops remain in defensive positions. The president warns Iraq that a new invasion will mean war and that this war will end with U.S. Marines in Baghdad. But when the president asks the Saudi king for permission to use U.S.-built bases for preemptive air strikes, the king balks, saying he will permit the strikes only if Kuwait is actually invaded. In trying to recreate the Gulf War coalition, the president finds that only Britain will agree to send warships and air-craft, and this time even the British say no troops. Egypt, France, and Germany refuse to participate.

In the situation room the Joint Chiefs lay out the options to the president's National Security Council.

First, the Iraqi forces, while inadequate to overrun U.S. forces in Kuwait, can inflict casualties. The American defensive positions have to be strengthened. And vital to limiting U.S. casualties is the need to strike at the guards *long before* they reach the border. This means round-the-clock bombing from bases in Saudi Arabia and transfer there of hundreds of U.S. strike aircraft. Israel's offer of bases cannot be taken up. U.S. strikes on Arab targets from Israeli territory will ignite anti-American riots from Morocco to Malaysia.

Second, there is no hope of recreating the Gulf War coalition. Not one Arab or European ally will send troops. If the United States intends a Gulf War II, it will have to be an all-American show, and there is now no certainty the Saudis will permit a huge Desert Storm–sized army back on their soil. And, given the Iranian atomic weapons, U.S. carriers must stay clear of Iran and the Persian Gulf. Turkey, too, is showing reluctance to allow the United States to use its air bases for another war on Iraq.

At this point, U.S. intelligence discovers that Iraqi armor is driving for Kuwait. Carrier-based strikes begin. The Pentagon gives the president a grim assessment: If Saudi bases can be used, an army of 100,000 can hold Kuwait and drive the Iraqis back to Basra, but 500,000 men, along with the two thousand planes General Norman Schwarzkopf had during Desert Storm, will be needed to take Baghdad. Not only does the United States not have the forces available, U.S. casualties this time will certainly be in the thousands, as the Iraqis have thousands of Stinger-like anti-aircraft weapons and anti-tank weapons, courtesy of France and Russia.

As U.S. troops are airlifted into Kuwait, a fierce debate begins in the United States. Half of Congress is arguing that if Europe and

Japan, who buy most of the Gulf oil, will not fight beside us in this war, we ought to get out of the Gulf and let the Arabs, Persians, Sunnis, and Shiites fight it out. But some members, contending that scuttling the Gulf means the end of the United States as a superpower, urge a warning to Iraq: Rather than see U.S. Marine positions overrun, or lose Kuwait, we will use atomic weapons.

At this point, Scuds strike Tel Aviv, and the Israeli air force heads to Baghdad to exact retribution. The "Arab street" explodes with calls for an Islamic jihad to drive Israelis and Americans out of the Middle East. Iran declares its solidarity with Iraq, against America and Israel. The nightmare scenario—with the United States and Israel on one side, and almost the entire Arab and Islamic world aligned against them—is at hand.

The China-Taiwan War. After backing down in the Taiwan Straits in 1996, the Chinese navy by 2004 is a more impressive instrument of war, while U.S. naval forces are down to less than half of Reagan's six hundred–ship navy. With lightning strikes, China settles all the disputed claims in the Spratly and Paracel island chains in the South China Sea.

After Chinese troops brutally put down riots in Hong Kong, now in its sixth year of depression, Taiwan declares independence in Jefferson's own language and asks the United States and the United Nations for recognition. Both refuse. Not one Western power recognizes Taipei. Nor does any Asian power. Taipei asks the United States at least to sell it weapons of self-defense and offers all its reserves— $100 billion—for antisubmarine aircraft, missile boats, F-16s, and antiship and air-to-surface missiles. Declaring Taiwan an outlaw regime, Beijing announces its intent to bring "the runaway home to the embrace of the Motherland." China demands that the United States confirm the Clinton commitment of 1998 not to recognize a breakaway Taiwan—and not to supply it with any new weapons.

The U.S. president warns China against settling the issue by force, but calls on Taiwan to reverse its declaration. Taiwan refuses, and startles the world by announcing that Beijing ought not assume that any response to a blockade or missile attack will be "solely with conventional weapons." U.S. experts concede Taiwan has the ability to build atomic weapons but doubt it has done so. No one is sure.

China warns that use of such weapons will mean total destruction of the Taiwanese regime and issues a warning to Asian nations to stay out of this Chinese internal affair. The warning is directed at Tokyo, which informs the United States it opposes Taiwan's independence and cannot support U.S. air or naval forces in a war with China—and that restriction applies to the giant U.S. base at Okinawa as well.

Conservative Republicans demanding that the president stand up to Beijing are reminded that China now has an estimated fifty intercontinental ballistic missiles, or ICBMs; that U.S. bases in Asia, Korea, and the Pacific will be easy targets for Chinese missiles; and that, on this issue of Taiwan, our intelligence is that the Chinese military is almost fanatical. What you must understand, the president tells his party, is that, for the Chinese, "this is *their* missile crisis, *their* Monroe Doctrine being challenged. Is Taiwan worth risking a nuclear war in which America, as well as Taiwan, could be a target of nuclear weapons?"

China declares a blockade and warns any merchant ship against entering Taiwanese waters. A day later, an air clash over the Straits brings a one-sided victory for the Taiwanese, whose U.S.-made planes and air-to-air missiles are still a generation ahead of China's Russian-made counterparts. The admiral in Hawaii commanding U.S. forces in the Pacific orders all his ships to sea and asks the president for instructions. Should the navy engage Chinese air and naval units in the waters around Taiwan—or stay out of the war?

The Terrorist War. It is in February of 2005 that the explosion occurs in the port of Seattle. It is a low-yield crude atomic device, but the devastation is incredible. Thousands are dead; thousands more are injured and wounded, many burned horribly. The device was smuggled in the cargo hold of a ship and detonated only hours after the ship had docked. No one knows for certain who put the device there. Iran condemns the act as an inhuman atrocity and an affront to Islam, but notes that America was the first to use such weapons. North Korea is also a suspect. But intense speculation focuses on a group associated with the financier of terror Osama Bin Laden, whom U.S. special forces ran down and killed years earlier. Bin Laden's agents reportedly acquired nuclear weapons from rogue army elements in Russia or Kazakhstan in the 1990s, or got one from a Pakistan now controlled by allies of the Afghan Taliban. But one thing is certain: The missile defense system America is completing has proven to be a Maginot Line. The enemy has gone around it.

The U.S. military now concedes there is no way to stop a Scud or cruise missile from being launched from a merchant ship a few miles off the United States coast. It will be a Herculean task to inspect thousands of such ships passing the American coast or entering U.S. ports each year.

At this point, a call comes to the U.S. Embassy in Bahrain warning that another device will be detonated within two months in another U.S. port, or in the locks of the Panama Canal, if America does not declare it is getting out of the Middle East and the Gulf. The CIA confirms that the caller demonstrated knowledge of how the Seattle bomb was delivered, knowledge that U.S. investigators have not yet given out to newspapers.

Meanwhile, there is panic in every American port. From Boston to Baltimore to New Orleans to San Diego to San Francisco, millions of people are refusing to go to work near port areas and are selling apartments in order to move inland. Manhattan and Brooklyn are in panic. Calls for retaliation are heard across the political spectrum, but no one knows against whom to retaliate. Pakistan, Iran, and North Korea are all nuclear powers, but no one can say for sure if their leaders had a hand in nuclear terrorism.

GOOD-BYE TO ALL THAT

In the scenarios above, none wholly implausible, the United States could find itself in a major war with few allies. Yet in none of the wars would any vital U.S. interest be at stake to justify sending a large American army to fight or to risk nuclear war. In each of the wars described above, America is drawn in because of commitments dating to a Cold War that has been over for a decade, a Gulf War that ended in 1991, or a commitment to a Balkan peninsula that should never have been made. Should simultaneous wars break out in the Gulf and Korea, and should the Middle East or the Balkans flare up, America will come face to face with what Lippmann called foreign policy bankruptcy.

In his 1996 book *The Next War*, former Defense Secretary Caspar Weinberger lays out other scenarios for major American wars. These include a U.S. invasion of Mexico to overthrow a radical leftist regime whose anti-American and Marxist policies bankrupted that country, sending millions of refugees pouring across the U.S. border; and Iranian terrorist strikes on Bahrain and Saudi Arabia, bringing down those pro-Western regimes.

If two or more of these scenarios played out, U.S. forces would be unable to fight these wars simultaneously, and America would confront disaster after disaster as its people refused to send their young to fight and die for an imperial policy they had never voted for and never understood.

Before any of these scenarios is played out, the United States desperately needs a "bottom-up" review of all its commitments to determine which remain vital to our security and which we must let go in order to stay out of future wars that are not our wars. For the United States has unthinkingly embarked on a neo-imperial policy that must involve us in virtually every great war of the coming century—and great wars are the death of republics. Finally, if we continue on this course of reflexive interventions, enemies will one day answer our power with the last weapon of the weak—terror, and eventually cataclysmic terrorism on U.S. soil with weapons of mass destruction. Then liberty, the cause of the Republic, will itself be in peril.

Yet any who raises a voice to demand that the United States reassess these insanely extravagant war guarantees, or at least stop adding to them, is shouted down as an "isolationist!" It is time to expose this malevolent myth of "isolationism," so our foreign policy debate can proceed on the grounds of what is best for America.

CHAPTER 4

The Myth of American Isolationism

Our first and fundamental maxim should be never to entangle ourselves in the broils of Europe; our second, never to suffer Europe to intermeddle in cisatlantic affairs.[1]

—THOMAS JEFFERSON, 1823

The occasion was the fiftieth anniversary of the Japanese attack on the Pacific fleet. A crowd gathered on the pier overlooking the hulk of the *Arizona*. The president that day was magnanimous toward the former enemy. "I have no rancor in my heart toward… Japan, none at all," said George Bush, who fought in the Pacific war. But the president did have rancor for those he held responsible for the "date which will live in infamy." In a savage remark Bush declared, "[I]solationism flew escort for the very bombers that attacked our men…. [I]solationists gathered together at what was known in those days as an 'America First' rally… at precisely the moment the first Americans met early, violent deaths right here at Pearl Harbor."[2]

The president urged his countrymen to repudiate the fatal delusion that had led to the disaster, and its disciples: "[W]e stand here today on the site of a tragedy spawned by isolationism. And we must learn and… avoid the dangers of today's isolationism and its economic accomplice, protectionism." At his party's convention in San Diego, five years later, the ex-president thundered: "Leadership means standing against the voices of isolation and protectionism."[3]

Yet, at Pearl Harbor, President Bush had stood history on its head. The United States found itself at war with Japan not because "isolationists" directed U.S. foreign policy but because Franklin Roosevelt, an interventionist, did. By December 1941 FDR was determined to block further Japanese expansion and was prepared to risk war to succeed. Japan attacked because it believed, correctly, that America meant to roll back its empire. The fleet was Roosevelt's weapon. As foreign policy scholar Christopher Layne wrote in response to Bush's 1991 address:

> Pearl Harbor… was the result of active U.S. engagement in Asian affairs, not of isolationism. America's commitment to maintaining its military presence in the Pacific and preserving its perceived political and economic interests in China put it on a collision course with a Japan determined to establish its strategic and economic predominance in East Asia. The Pacific Fleet had been deployed to Pearl Harbor for the specific purpose of dissuading Tokyo from its expansionist course….[4]

Bush's fear of a return to "isolationism" is echoed by the elites of both parties. Indeed, nothing can unite the U.S. establishment in greater solidarity than this dread specter. Which raises questions: Against what are they railing? Of whom are they afraid?

As "Munich" has become a synonym for craven and cowardly appeasement, "isolationist" is a term of abuse intended to silence an adversary, end an argument, and stifle debate. Brand an opponent an isolationist and you need not hear him out. But what is isolationism? Wayne Cole, the historian of the struggle between FDR and the America First Committee of 1940–1941, studied "isolationism" for fifty years and concludes:

[The very term] is an obstacle to clear thinking.... No president or national political party in the entire history of the United States... ever advocated isolating the United States from the rest of the world. In the eighteenth and nineteenth centuries the term isolationism was never used to describe the foreign policies of any presidential administration.[5]

The idea that America was ever an isolationist nation is a myth, a useful myth to be sure, but nonetheless a malevolent myth that approaches the status of a big lie. How did the term come into common usage? Cole explains:

"Isolationism" was a pejorative term invented and applied in the twentieth century to discredit policies that the United States had followed traditionally during the first one-hundred and forty years of its independent history. The term was never an accurate label for United States policies.[6]

The term is used today to disparage the foreign policy America pursued from the time of Washington until Wilson took us into war—and for the twenty years between the election of Harding and the third term of Franklin Roosevelt. What is today derided as isolationism was the foreign policy under which the Republic grew from thirteen states on the Atlantic into a continent-wide nation that dominated the hemisphere and whose power reached to Peking. Contrary to the impression left by the term, young America was no hermit republic. How can one characterize as a "century of isolationism" a period in American history in which:

⭑ John Adams fought an undeclared naval war with France.
⭑ Thomas Jefferson doubled the size of the country by relieving Napoleon of Louisiana, and sent ships to attack Barbary pirates.

⋆ James Madison seized West Florida from Spain, took us to war against the British Empire, and sent an army to invade Canada.

⋆ Andrew Jackson invaded Florida and packed the Spanish governor off to Havana, after which Secretary of State John Quincy Adams convinced Madrid to cede to the United States the "derelict province."

⋆ Colluding with Great Britain to prevent European powers from preying on the carcass of the Spanish empire, James Monroe declared the Western Hemisphere off limits to further colonization, an act Bismarck called an "insolent dogma" and "a species of arrogance peculiarly American and inexcusable."[7]

⋆ John Tyler annexed Texas and asserted a preeminent U.S. interest in Hawaii when a British naval officer tried to make a protectorate of the kingdom in 1841.

⋆ James Polk invaded Mexico and seized the northern half of the country, including California.

⋆ Millard Fillmore sent Commodore Matthew Perry to open up Japan to U.S. trade; that legendary sailor succeeded, and urged the annexation of Formosa and Okinawa.

⋆ Franklin Pierce purchased a swatch of Mexico larger than West Virginia, urged the Senate to annex Hawaii and grant statehood, and tried to annex Cuba, as U.S. clipper ships opened up China.

⋆ James Buchanan won the presidency on a platform that called for the annexation of Cuba.

⋆ Andrew Johnson sent a Union army to the border to drive the French out of Mexico and help overthrow Maximilian's regime.

⋆ William Seward bought Alaska, annexed Midway, and tried to acquire Hawaii, British Columbia, Greenland, and the Virgin Islands.

⋆ Ulysses S. Grant tried to annex the Dominican Republic, threatened Spain with war over the *Virginius* naval crisis, and gave the first presidential support to an isthmian canal controlled by the United States.

* Rutherford B. Hayes acquired a quasi-protectorate over the Samoan Islands, which later took us to the brink of war with Germany.
* Benjamin Harrison threatened Chile with war if it refused to apologize and indemnify America for a bloody fracas involving U.S. sailors in Valparaiso.
* Grover Cleveland threatened Great Britain with war over a border dispute between Venezuela and British Guiana.
* William McKinley declared war on Spain; invaded Cuba; annexed Puerto Rico, Hawaii, Guam, Pago Pago, and the Philippines; put down a Filipino insurgency; sent U.S. troops to Peking to crush the Boxer Rebellion; and declared an "Open Door" for the imperial powers in China.
* Teddy Roosevelt seized the Panama Canal Zone, sent the Great White Fleet to show Japan that the United States was a global power, mediated the Russo-Japanese War and the Moroccan crisis between France and Germany, and won America's first Nobel Peace Prize.

The nineteenth century witnessed a quadrupling of America's territory and its emergence as a world power. To call the foreign policy that produced this result "isolationist" is absurd. Americans were willing to go to war with the greatest powers in Europe, but only for American interests. They had no wish to take sides in European wars in which America had no stake. Our nation's ambitions always lay to the south, the west, and northwest—not to Europe. As early as the Congress of Vienna, the thrust of America's drive toward conquest was evident to the Spanish minister in Washington:

> If all Europe or its principal governments do not take steps in
> time against the scandalous ambition of this Republic... and [to
> obstruct] the well-established scheme of conquest which she has
> set for herself it may well be too late; and she may be master of

Cuba and of the New Kingdom of Mexico or whatever other region suits her.[8]

Henry Cabot Lodge would exult, even before America's "splendid little war" with Spain, "We have a record of conquest, colonization, and expansion unequaled by any people in the nineteenth century."[9] "For really three centuries," said Frederick Jackson Turner, "the dominant fact of American life has been expansion."[10] By 1898 America had, through diplomacy or war, eliminated all French, Spanish, Russian, and British power from the continent. As Talleyrand had predicted in the time of Napoleon: "The Americans mean to rule alone in America. Moreover, their conduct ever since the moment of their independence is enough to prove this truth; the Americans are devoured by pride, ambition, and cupidity."[11]

Those who describe U.S. foreign policy in its first 120 years as "isolationist" should take the matter up with Mexicans, Spaniards, American Indians, and Filipinos. Isolationism, writes historian Walter McDougall, is "but a dirty word that interventionists, especially since Pearl Harbor, hurl at anyone who questions their policies."[12] The word that best describes our earliest foreign policy tradition, he adds, is "unilateralism":

> [Unilaterism] never meant that the United States should, or for
> that matter could, sequester itself or pursue an ostrich-like policy
> toward all foreign countries. It simply meant, as Hamilton and
> Jefferson both underscored, that the self-evident course for the
> United States was to avoid permanent, entangling alliances and
> to remain neutral in Europe's wars except when our Liberty—
> the first hallowed tradition—was at risk.[13]

The message of Washington's Farewell Address was not to isolate America from Europe but to keep it independent of Europe. Stay out of foreign wars, Washington admonished; they are the great threat to liberty, and America is about nothing if not the preservation of liberty. Look west to the mountains, the great river beyond, the plains, the Pacific. That is where our destiny lies. Europe is the past. Avoid "permanent alliances"; devote your energies to our own country. Independence, not isolation, is the American tradition. Walter Lippmann in 1952 sought to explain to the British how the term isolationism "must be handled with the greatest care, or it can do nothing but confuse and mislead":

> The word isolationist conceals the dynamic and expansionist
> energy of the American nation. It suggests the United States did
> not have a foreign policy until recently. All that is quite untrue.
> The United States has never been neutral in the European sense.
> It has always had a very active foreign policy, of which the cen-
> tral purpose has been the determination to expand across the
> continent from the Atlantic seaboard to the Pacific Ocean.[14]

American foreign policy evolved even before independence, with colonial participation in British wars against the French and their Indian allies. Men like Washington fought in these wars for American reasons—to drive aliens and intruders out of land they themselves coveted. "Those whom we now call isolationists," wrote Lippmann, "are the true believers in the foreign policy of the men who conquered and settled the American continental domain."[15] The controlling principle was "to keep a free hand in order to expand westward to the continental limits." Twentieth-century "isolationists," said Lippmann,

> [wanted only] to isolate American decisions and actions, to have
> the final word wherever Americans are involved. They carry with
> them the thought and feeling which has come down from those

who in the eighteenth and nineteenth centuries managed in one
way or another, by war and by diplomacy, to expel all the foreign
powers who blocked the westward expansion of the American
people.[16]

Americans welcomed European immigrants to help build the
nation, but they drove relentlessly, sometimes ruthlessly, to expel
European power from the New World. We were to be masters of our
own house.

Why is this dynamic, triumphant foreign policy so reviled?
Because the hidden agenda of the globalists who now direct
America's destiny is to harness its wealth and power to causes having
little or nothing to do with the true national interests of the United
States. The savagery of today's attacks on "isolationism" is a measure
of the depth of establishment fear that the destiny of the Republic
will be torn away from it and restored to people who carry in their
hearts the great tradition of America First.

How did globalists capture the heights? As Wayne Cole writes,
the tradition derided as isolationism "was not simply downed by the
informed logic of a better ideology; it was quashed by every conceivable 'smear' and 'dirty trick' designed to make that once honorable approach seem to be ignorant, stupid, irresponsible, unpatriotic,
evil, and even fascist or Nazi."[17]

Victory achieved in such a fashion cannot be allowed to stand.
But to overturn the regime of the globalists, Americans must be rein-
troduced to the history made by the great men today mocked as isolationists, to the rules that guided them as they guided America, and
to the lessons they teach. For we are today on the threshold of a new
century, and it is in our power to reclaim our destiny. Will we be forever ensnared in entangling alliances that will involve us and bleed us
in every great new war on the Eurasian land mass until we are as
diminished as the other powers of the twentieth century? Or will we

recapture the freedom to decide ourselves when and where we go to war again?

America is today as overextended as any empire in history. We are committed to go to war to defend the borders of dozens of countries from Norway to Turkey, from Portugal to Poland, from Saudi Arabia to South Korea. U.S. soldiers patrol the lines between Bosnian Serbs and Bosnian Muslims, and between Macedonia and Kosovo. They sit on Mount Sinai to monitor a peace signed twenty years ago. Almost yearly, we issue new security guarantees to lock future generations into the wars of the coming century. But protest this mindless interventionism, and you are shouted down as an "isolationist!"

This transnational elite must not succeed in silencing the voices of American patriotism and enlightened nationalism. But if we are to answer insults designed to demonize us, to stifle dissent, to shut off debate, we need to rediscover the lost chapters of our history. We need to know the ideas and ideals of the Founding Fathers and America's great men, who would not believe where our leaders are taking us now.

"I think the nation-state is finished," an editor confided a few years ago.[18] That is what is at stake. Will America endure as a free independent republic, or become the North American province of a new world order as the globalists ardently desire? To prevent us from ever going "gentle into that good night," I wrote this book.

Now, back to the beginning.

PART TWO

1789–1823:
INDEPENDENCE AND EXPANSION

CHAPTER 5

Birth of an American Foreign Policy

The distinctions between Virginians, Pennsylvanians,
New Yorkers, New Englanders are no more.
I am not a Virginian, but an American![1]

—Patrick Henry, 1774

In the war preceding the Revolution, the colonials fought under British command, but for American causes—to drive the French and Indians back over the mountains in order to secure the land for themselves. But with French power broken and the French threat removed from North America, it had begun to dawn on the colonists that they no longer needed the British army. Before we even became a nation, a uniquely American foreign policy was taking shape in the minds of its most visionary leaders. Core doctrine: This land is our land; all European claimants must one day depart, so we may possess it whole and entire.

Few today defend the conduct of George III or his ministers. Yet there was an inevitability to what happened. The Americans were too far away, too many, and too independent-minded to be forever governed from abroad. When British policy in the French and Indian War coincided with American interests, Americans fought alongside the British. But when the Empire's interests began to collide with the core idea of America first, the break became unavoidable. Now the British also had to be expelled. Long before the phrase was ever coined, America's Manifest Destiny had been envisioned by the most farsighted of its sons.

There is a continuity to American foreign policy that dates back to Washington's march to Fort Duquesne in 1754 to clear the forks of the Ohio of the French who had entered the territory of the Mother Country. *Any power* in the path of America's westward expansion was to be removed by diplomacy or war. From the mid-eighteenth century to the twentieth, the new nation would be carved out of British, French, Spanish, Mexican, and Russian territory. Each European power in its turn would be expelled from our country, our continent, and our hemisphere.

"LET US ACT FOR OURSELVES"

When Washington returned to Mount Vernon after Yorktown, he was no longer simply a Virginian. The war had seared into his soul the first principle of the foreign policy he would shape for his country: sever all political and military ties to Europe. Four times in a century, Americans had gone to war because the Mother Country had. Never again. No cause on the blood-soaked continent was worth the life of a single American. In the first days of revolution, Tom Paine, in *Common Sense*, urged a total break with Europe:

> [A]ny submission to, or dependence on, Great Britain tends
> directly to involve this Continent in European wars and quarrels,
> and sets us at variance with nations who would otherwise seek
> our friendship, and against whom we have neither anger nor
> complaint.... It is the true interest of America to steer clear of
> European contentions.[2]

Washington had welcomed the 1778 Treaty of Alliance with France. It must, he said, "chalk out a plain and easy road to independence." That alliance had brought Rochambeau's army and

Admiral DeGrasse's fleet to Yorktown. But with victory Americans began to look for ways to sever the alliance. John Jay, the peace negotiator in Paris in 1782, though instructed to take no decision without the "knowledge and concurrence" of France, opened a back channel to the British in violation of the alliance's proscription against a separate peace. Jay confided to Benjamin Franklin, "Let us be grateful to the French for what they have done for us, but let us think for ourselves. And, if need be, let us act for ourselves!"[3] The French foreign minister felt betrayed by the United States' separate peace, and so told Dr. Franklin.

To George Washington, alliances were to be temporary, entered into when a crisis commanded, dissolved when the crisis passed. Just days before he took office as president, Washington wrote Lafayette:

> While you are quarreling among yourselves in Europe; while
> one King is running mad and others acting as if they were
> already so, by cutting the throats of the subjects of their neigh-
> bours, I think you need not doubt, my dear Marquis, we shall
> continue in tranquility here.[4]

Washington also differed from his great contemporaries in that he was a man of the West. "No other president," wrote James Thomas Flexner, "…before Andrew Jackson was so largely a product of the west and the frontier…. Washington had served in the wilderness as a surveyor, a messenger traversing unknown trails, an explorer, and an Indian fighter."[5] And he saw America's future there.

But as he looked west, Washington saw America's natural expansion blocked. Farmers and frontiersmen were unable to ship bulk goods over the mountains; they had to move them by water. But Spain controlled the Mississippi—outlet to the sea for the citizens of Kentucky, Tennessee, western Virginia, and western Pennsylvania— and had closed New Orleans to American commerce. West of

Georgia and south of the Tennessee, Creek, Choctaw, and Cherokee had been taken under Spanish protection and were being armed. Spain thus held the keys to peace, prosperity, and security in the Southwest.

In the Northwest the outlook was equally grim. Britain controlled the Great Lakes and St. Lawrence and had refused to honor that part of the peace treaty which dictated surrender of the forts that controlled access to the lakes. Britain was using what it held illegally to block America's trade.

Washington feared Britain or Spain would bribe the frontiersmen with access to the sea in exchange for allegiance. The crisis would be grave if either nation, "instead of throwing stumbling blocks in their [the western settlers'] way as they now do, should hold out lures for their trade and alliance."[6] The West might then become hostile territory. During one trip over the mountains in 1784, Washington noted, "The western settlers (I speak now from my own observation) stand as it were upon a pivot; the touch of a feather would turn them any way."[7]

With his country recovering from its Revolution, Washington did not want another war. Rather than confront Spain or Britain, he opted for the "arts of peace"—"clearing rivers, building bridges, and establishing conveniences for traveling" to link the West to the Atlantic through commerce, before the British or Spanish awoke to their opportunity.[8] If the seaboard could establish trade ties with the West, before Spain and Britain could lure them away, the West would be America's forever.

Foreign policy was thus inseparable from domestic policy and was high among the causes that brought Washington to Philadelphia. He feared a British-Spanish policy of encirclement, containment, and strangulation would abort a united America extending to the Mississippi, and he came to believe only a strong central government could deal with the crowding and bullying. Washington also wanted a new constitution to outlaw state tariffs and end the internal trade wars, so that the confederation could be tied together with bonds of commerce and America could gradually reduce its dependence upon Europe, especially Great Britain.

The Constitution created that executive. And in Washington, America had the indispensable man to steer it through the most perilous years of its existence. From 1789 to 1797 the policies of Washington effected the *de facto* annexation of the Northwest Territory that America had possessed only *de jure* before he became president. Equally critical, our first president kept his vulnerable country out of the wars exploding across Europe.

"STEER CLEAR OF PERMANENT ALLIANCES"

The great goal of the foreign policy advocated in Washington's Farewell Address was to buy still more time for America to grow and expand unmolested. In that address, published in September of 1796 but never delivered, Washington warned his countrymen to be forever vigilant against the "insidious wiles of foreign influence," the most "baneful foes of Republican Government." Behind the warning lay painful memories.

Washington was in his first year as president when the French Revolution erupted. By the end of Washington's first term, Louis XVI had gone to the guillotine. When France declared war on England in early 1793, Washington declared "impartial neutrality," a wildly unpopular decision. He now came face-to-face with a difficulty that has bedeviled many of his successors: a passionate attachment to foreign causes.

The neutrality decree sundered the cabinet. Jefferson's partisans, denounced as "Gallic jackals," mocked the Federalists as "British boot-lickers."[9] Alexander Hamilton, who accused Jefferson of a "womanish attachment to France and a womanish resentment

against Great Britain," was himself accused of leaking Jefferson's
strategies to the British.[10] In part because of Hamilton's interference
in his department, Jefferson resigned as secretary of state and was
replaced by Edmund Randolph, who was dismissed when the British
leaked letters to support a charge he had solicited bribes from the
French for acts of treason during the Whiskey Rebellion.

The memory of the savage cabinet battles was behind Washington's warning to Jeffersonians and Federalists in the campaign of
1796: "Let me now take a more comprehensive view and warn you
in the most solemn manner against the baneful effects of the spirit of
party generally." Wrote Washington:

> [That spirit] agitates the community with ill-founded jealousies
> and false alarms, kindles the animosity of one party against
> another.... It opens the door to foreign influence and corrup-
> tion, which find a facilitated access to the government itself
> through the channels of party passions. Thus the policy and will
> of one country are subjected to the policy and will of another.[11]

Clearly, the target here was Jefferson, whose pro-French sympathies in this era approached the fanatical.

Equally alarming to Washington was the conduct of "Citizen
Genet." In 1793 Edmond Genet arrived in America and began to
outfit privateers to raid British commerce, and to raise armies to
attack British interests. Many Americans enthusiastically supported
Genet's activities. Washington did not; he desperately wanted to
keep America out of the war. Hamilton penned his famous
"Pacificus" letters to support Washington's declaration of neutrality,
contending France had supported America's revolution for its own
motives, that we had given France the revenge it had sought against
England and owed it nothing more, that intervention in the
European war carried immense risks for virtually no reward.

Anticipating the Farewell Address he would help to write, Hamilton declared:

> Foreign influence is truly the Grecian horse to a republic. We
> cannot be too careful to exclude its entrance. Nor ought we to
> imagine that it can only make its approaches in the gross form
> of direct bribery. It is then most dangerous when it comes under
> the patronage of our passions, under the auspices of national
> prejudice and partiality.[12]

In their effort to maintain neutrality, Washington and Hamilton were vilified. Adams described these as times "when ten thousand people in the streets of Philadelphia, day after day, threatened to drag Washington out of his house and effect a revolution."[13] It was in his recalling these painful episodes that Washington warned against "inveterate antipathies" and "passionate attachments" to any nation other than our own. He wrote:

> The Nation, which indulges towards another an habitual hatred,
> or an habitual fondness, is in some degree a slave... to its ani-
> mosity or to its affection, either of which is sufficient to lead it
> astray from its duty and its interest....
>   [Such a] passionate attachment... produces a variety of evils.
> Sympathy for the favourite nation, facilitating the illusion of an
> imaginary common interest... where no real common interest
> exists, and infusing into one the enmities of the other, betrays
> the former into a participation in the quarrels and Wars of the
> latter, without adequate inducement or justification.[14]

Sage counsel for our coming century.

By the end of his term, Washington had persuaded his country-men of the wisdom of neutrality. When the French minister sought to interfere in the election of 1796 on behalf of Jefferson's Democratic-Republicans, his intrusion backfired. Indeed, it had been in part to help defeat Jefferson and assist Adams that Washington had released his Farewell Address two months before the election. Adams would cause that address to be read out in Congress every February, a tradition that continued until our own time.[15]

"The Great rule of conduct for us, in regard to foreign Nations, is in extending our commercial relations to have with them as little political connection as possible," said Washington, laying down a policy of nonintervention that would guide American presidents for a century. Pointing to our country's great and safe distance from Europe, he implored:

> Why forego the advantages of so peculiar a situation? Why quit
> our own to stand upon foreign ground? Why, by interweaving
> our destiny with that of any part of Europe, entangle our peace
> and prosperity in the toils of European Ambition, Rivalship,
> Interest, Humour, or Caprice?
>
> 'Tis our true policy to steer clear of permanent Alliances,
> with any portion of the foreign world. So far... as we are now at
> liberty to do it.[16]

The "great rule" was the wisest counsel left his countrymen by the greatest American. It was counsel bred of half a century as a soldier, a planter dependent on British trade, a commander of American forces, and a president who had seen his countrymen at each other's throats over a war in Europe. Washington knew his nation had the potential to be the greatest on earth, but he also knew America needed generations of peace to grow to its natural size and power before it could take its place in the world. It was crucial that young America stay out of old Europe's wars. As historian Charles Beard has written:

...Washington advocated strengthening the Union and creating suitable "defensive" forces, so that in a period "not far off" the United States could safely confront provocations and "choose peace or war, as our interest, guided by justice, shall counsel." In these cases of defensive action, if necessary "we may safely trust to temporary alliances."

This was not blind isolationism. It was not a rejection of all collaboration with foreign powers. It was a positive program for choosing peace or war... in the interest of our destiny and continental security, not in the interest of any European combination or balance of power.[17]

Precisely. For five generations America heeded Washington's counsel. After the Treaty of Alliance with France was dissolved by Adams in 1800, we would not enter another until World War I, and then only as an "associate power." In the century that followed Washington's Farewell Address, only once would America involve itself in war with a European power. That war, however, came only a dozen years after the great man had been laid to rest at Mount Vernon.

CHAPTER 6

"Mr. Madison's War"

A Nation, despicable by its weakness, forfeits
even the privilege of being neutral.[1]
—ALEXANDER HAMILTON, *THE FEDERALIST*, NO. 11

In the rating of presidents by historians, invariably the war leaders Lincoln, Wilson, and FDR are listed among the great or near-great, but few historians place John Adams there. Yet in his allegiance to Washington's "great rule" and successful effort to keep America out of Europe's wars, Adams merits a place of honor.

It was under our second president that America fought an undeclared naval war with France. The cause was the treaty John Jay brought home from England, which allowed the British to seize U.S. ships carrying goods bought by its enemy, France. Paris saw this as ingratitude, treachery, and a dishonoring of the Alliance of 1778, and retaliated by ordering warships to follow the British example and seize merchant ships flying the American flag. Between July 1796 and June 1797, French cruisers seized more than three hundred. To head off a war, Adams sent three delegates to Paris to negotiate. There they were met with an offer of women and demands for a large bribe and for a U.S. apology for Adams's allegedly anti-French statements to Congress. Only then might negotiations begin.

When word of the insult reached the United States, a national outcry went up—"Millions for defense, but not one cent for tribute!" Congress authorized the seizure of armed French ships, and the president recalled Washington to lead the defense of his country. Washington wanted to put Hamilton, a hero of Yorktown, in active command. Hamilton envisioned a campaign to seize Florida, New Orleans, and Texas from France's ally, Spain. With the Federalists elated to be aligned with Britain, the robust little U.S. Navy began attacking and seizing armed French cruisers.[2]

But Adams wanted no full-dress war. He sent a delegation to negotiate with the French first consul, who did not want America aligned with the British. After much haggling, the United States agreed to assume the cost of its shipping losses from French raiders, and America was allowed to terminate the alliance Washington had so rejoiced in after Saratoga. In the words of historian Thomas Bailey, "In effect, America consented to pay $20 million in alimony to secure a divorce from the twenty-two-year-old French marriage of [in]convenience, as represented by the Alliance of 1778."[3]

Adams's refusal to give the Federalists the war they wanted cost him the presidency. He would never again hold public office. Yet in his declining years he wrote:

> I will defend my missions to France, as long as I have an eye
> to direct my hand, or a finger to hold my pen. They were the
> most disinterested and meritorious actions of my life. I reflect
> upon them with so much satisfaction, that I deserve no other
> inscription over my gravestone than: "Here lies John Adams,
> who took upon himself the responsibility of the peace with
> France in the year 1800."[4]

Obedient to Washington's admonition, Adams had ended his career on an act of statesmanship. He had redeemed America's honor and exacted proportionate retribution on France's navy, but refused to engage his country in a war in which the costs would never have been justified by any conceivable gain. And by severing the Alliance of 1778, Adams kept the United States out of a decade of Europe's bloodiest wars.

JEFFERSON'S DUEL WITH NAPOLEON

When Jefferson assumed the presidency, he was unaware Spain was negotiating to cede back to Paris the Louisiana territory France had given up in the 1763 treaty that ended the French and Indian War. When word reached America, there was panic. Rumors circulated that Spain was ceding not only Louisiana, but the Floridas as well—all the land south of the 31st parallel from St. Augustine to Baton Rouge. If true, a weak Spain was about to be replaced on America's southern and western frontier by the greatest power on the European continent. With British Canada to the north, and British fleets to the east, the Republic would be encircled.

What was France up to? Napoleon envisioned a new empire in the Western Hemisphere centered on Santo Domingo and the "sugar islands" of the Caribbean, sustained by the "Granary of America." Talleyrand saw in Louisiana "a wall of brass forever impenetrable to the combined efforts of England and America."[5] That "wall of brass" was what America feared.

Jefferson had been an impassioned champion of revolutionary France, penning intemperate statements for which history would excoriate him. After the September 1792 massacres in Paris—in which hundreds of French aristocrats, including women, were horribly butchered—he had written to William Short: "My own affections have been deeply wounded by some of the martyrs to this cause, but rather than it should have failed, I would have seen half the earth desolated. Were there but an Adam and an Eve left in every country, and left free, it would be better than as it now is."[6]

But as the French republic evolved into the Napoleonic empire, the ardor he had felt for France cooled, and it was an alarmed Jefferson who heard reports of France's taking over Louisiana and Florida. Vital U.S. interests were now at risk, and Napoleon had put them there. Jefferson discussed colluding with the British to drive the French out. As the final transfer of Louisiana was taking place in 1802, the United States received another shock. Spain had withdrawn the "right of deposit" in New Orleans, outlet to the sea for the West. Jefferson feared that Napoleon was behind Spain's action and that, on taking Louisiana and the Floridas, he would close the Mississippi and Gulf Coast to U.S. commerce. Jefferson ordered military preparations in the West, and, in an open letter to Robert Livingston, U.S. minister in France, issued a pointed warning to the emperor:

> There is on the globe one single spot, the possessor of which
> is our natural and habitual enemy. It is New Orleans, through
> which the produce of three-eighths of our territory must pass
> to market.... France, placing herself in that door, assumes...
> the attitude of defiance.... The day that France takes posses-
> sion of New Orleans... [f]rom that moment, we must marry
> ourselves to the British fleet and nation.[7]

Not wanting war, but facing a clamor from his western allies, the president instructed Livingston to offer to buy New Orleans and the Floridas, and ordered James Monroe to Paris to press the negotiations. Before Monroe's departure, congressional Republicans gave him a public dinner. The most remarked-upon toast: "Peace, if peace is honorable, war if war is necessary."[8] French diplomats were led to believe that if Monroe did not succeed in Paris, his next stop would be London, where the United States would seek a formal alliance.

But when Monroe arrived, he found a sensational develop-ment. Talleyrand had offered to sell not only New Orleans but all Louisiana for $25 million. What had changed? Napoleon's dream of a New World empire had been drenched in blood when a French army of 50,000, sent to subdue Santo Domingo, had succumbed to yellow fever and massacre by the rebels of Toussaint L'Ouverture. Louisiana no longer appeared to Paris as a granary to sustain an American empire; rather, it seemed an issue that might force the United States into alliance with Britain, and an unprotected province likely to be ripped away in the event of a war, which was exactly what Napoleon was planning.

Setting aside personal jealousies, Monroe and Livingston negotiated the purchase for $15 million. "We have lived long," said Livingston, "but this is the noblest work of our whole lives."[9] The pair had acted just in time. The formal agreements were dated April 30, 1803. Two weeks later, Britain and France were at war, and America learned that British war plans had included the immediate capture of New Orleans.

Jefferson embraced the purchase. While Bonaparte had no right to transfer Louisiana, which he had pledged "not to sell or alienate," and Jefferson had no authority to buy it, that seemed not to matter to either of them. America was taking possession of stolen goods being fenced by the greatest thief in Europe, but there was no denying the bargain. "This accession of territory affirms forever the power of the United States," said Napoleon. "I have just given England a maritime rival that sooner or later will lay low her pride."[10]

If Jefferson's presidency has a claim to greatness, it rests on the diplomatic triumph in which, confronted by the two greatest powers in Europe, he played one off against the other and effected the transfer to the United States of 800,000 square miles of terri-tory at three cents an acre. As for Spain's protests that Louisiana had been illegally sold by Napoleon, the Americans ignored them. Spain did not have the power to enforce its claim, and power, not legalisms, was all that concerned the Americans reveling in their new empire. As for the unconstitutionality of it all, our strict constructionist president coolly observed that he could not let "metaphysical subtleties" impede the Republic's westward expansion.

UNILATERAL DISARMAMENT

During the Napoleonic Wars, America endured repeated humiliations traceable to a fundamental failing. Jefferson had declared neutrality, but with his visceral dislike of industry and suspicion of a strong navy intact, he failed to maintain the power to guarantee the nation's rights as a neutral.

Despite the splendid showing of America's navy in the undeclared war with France in 1797–1798, "pure Republicans" of Jefferson's party, like John Randolph, believed a navy was a natural enemy of liberty. Jefferson himself believed in a policy not far distant from unilateral disarmament. On his taking office, the army was reduced by a "chaste reformation," as Jefferson called it, from 3,500 to 2,500 men, while his navy was being scuttled. "I believe that gunboats are the only *water* defense which can be useful to us, and protect us from the ruinous folly of a navy," Jefferson had written.[12] Federalists hooted at Jefferson's naiveté and his Lilliputian fleet. In a world at war, the brilliant intellectual who was president had chosen to defend America's peace and honor by leaving it naked to attack by land and sea, while trading vigorously with both sides.

With much of the navy rotting in dry dock, American merchants began shipping with abandon to both England and Napoleon's Europe. British merchants whose markets we were pirating were incensed; even more so were British patriots. In England, Americans were looked upon as avaricious collaborators of a criminal regime. Desperate for seamen to replace crews lost in battle or to desertion, the Royal Navy began boarding U.S. ships and removing "British subjects" for impressment into service. Eight thousand to ten thousand Americans were eventually taken, many kidnapped.

In 1807 the British went too far. On June 22 the warship *Leopard* pulled alongside the American frigate *Chesapeake* off Hampton Roads; its captain demanded to send a party aboard to search for British nationals. Captain James Barron refused. *Leopard* opened fire, pouring broadside after broadside into *Chesapeake*, killing three and wounding twenty. The British boarded; four sailors were taken off. When the crippled frigate limped back into port, there was a clamor for war.[13] "I had only to open my hand and let havoc loose," said Jefferson. He told friends that "the British had 'their foot on the threshold of war' and the United States 'has never been in such a state of excitement since the battle of Lexington.'"[14]

Reluctant to go to war against the world's greatest sea power, Jefferson resorted to economic sanctions and persuaded Congress to pass the Embargo Act of 1807. No U.S. ship could carry cargo to Europe. To punish Britain, and France, which had also harassed American shipping, the United States had imposed a blockade on itself. This was the policy of "peaceable coercion," as explained by Jefferson in a letter to George Mason:

> Our commerce is so valuable to them that they will be glad to
> purchase it when the only price we ask is to do us justice. I
> believe we have in our own hands the means of peaceable coer-
> cion; and that the moment they see our government so united as
> that they can make use of it, they will for their own interest be
> disposed to do us justice.[15]

"Peaceable coercion" was a colossal bust. Jefferson was the first president to learn that economic sanctions are an overrated tool of

foreign policy. The British and French continued kidnapping American seamen, and the Embargo Act ravaged U.S. exports. Tariff revenue fell by more than half.[16] Infuriated New England merchants
faced bankruptcy, and a huge market was created for smuggling from
U.S. ports and through Canada. So rampant was the defiance of
Jefferson's embargo that when Napoleon invaded Spain in 1808 and
put his brother on the throne, the French discovered 250 American
ships in Spanish ports and seized their cargoes. When the U.S. minister to Paris protested, Napoleon calmly informed the envoy he was
only helping to enforce the Embargo Act.[17]

Before leaving office, Jefferson saw the act repealed and
replaced by a Nonintercourse Act which prohibited U.S. ships
from trade only with Britain and France. Jefferson retired to
Monticello believing himself to have been a failed president. He
wrote to a friend: "Within a few days I retire to my family, my
books, and my farms [at Monticello].... Never did a prisoner,
released from his chains, feel such relief as I shall on shaking off the
shackles of power."[18]

A FLORIDA LAND GRAB

From the birth of the nation, the Virginia fathers had their eyes on
Florida. When the Spanish governor, weary of feeding his garrisons by depending on Mexico, opened the territory to immigration in 1790, Secretary of State Jefferson wrote Washington
with conspiratorial glee:

> Governor Quesada, by order of his court, is inviting foreigners
> to go and settle Florida. This is meant for our people.... It will
> be the means of delivering to us peaceably, what may other-
> wise cost us a war. In the meantime, we may complain of this
> seduction of our inhabitants just enough to make [the
> Spaniards] believe we think it very wise policy for them, and
> confirm them in it. This is my idea of it.[19]

Having seen how his neighbor and patron had written a glorious page in history with Louisiana, Madison was determined to write one of his own. "The acquisition of the Floridas," the insightful French minister in Washington noted, "is the object of all of Mr. Madison's prayers."[20]

While Louisiana had given America control of the west bank of the Mississippi, on the east bank there extended a sliver of coastal land which ran like the barrel of a pistol along the Gulf of Mexico from Baton Rouge to Pensacola. This was West Florida, and it belonged to Spain. Some Americans insisted it had been part of Louisiana, but the U.S. claim was weak. Others had an idea how the claim might be strengthened. With Spain occupied with the Napoleonic Wars, American settlers in West Florida were encouraged to revolt. Seizing the Spanish fort at Baton Rouge, a mob tore down the Bourbon banner, dragged it through the dirt, and replaced it with a new flag—the flag of the Republic of West Florida. The "republic" immediately petitioned to join the Union. On October 27, 1810, Madison acceded. West Florida from the Mississippi to the Perdido River was declared U.S. territory, though Americans had cautiously occupied only the land from Baton Rouge to the Pearl River. John Quincy Adams, minister to Russia, undertook to explain it all to the tsar. Acquainted with Bonaparte, Alexander I replied pleasantly, "Everyone always grows a little in this world."[21]

Spain was helpless, as was its British ally. Jefferson's prediction of 1790 had come true. By allowing Americans to emigrate, the Spanish had almost guaranteed they would have West Florida wrested from them by the very settlers they had invited in. Europe's powers seethed at the exhibition of American avarice. Four years later, the *Times* of London would remind Parliament, "Mr. Madison's dirty swindling manoeuvres in respect to Louisiana and the Floridas remain to be punished."[22]

"KNIFING THE MOTHER COUNTRY"

The British despised "Little Jemmy," as they called Madison, who was five feet two inches tall, and they held in equal contempt his coastal fleet of little boats. But soon Americans had reasons of their own to be enraged. From over the mountains came reports that British Canada had begun arming the Indians, who were scalping Americans in the Northwest.

On November 7, 1811, in a bloody battle on Tippecanoe Creek, a tributary of the Wabash, warriors of Tecumseh killed two hundred Americans out of a force of one thousand under the command of William Henry Harrison, the governor of the Indiana Territory. Among the weapons left behind by the retreating Indians, Harrison found that some had been made in Britain. America's patience with John Bull had run out. "[T]he period has now arrived," declared the Virginia House of Delegates, "when *peace, as we now have it*, is disgraceful, and war is honorable."[23]

When Congress reconvened in November, half its members were new, and they chose as speaker the thirty-four-year-old firebrand Henry Clay of Kentucky, who dispensed all the positions of House power to "coonskin congressmen" from the South and West who began agitating for war.

"War Hawks," John Randolph christened them, "buckskin statesmen." The brilliant, acidulous Virginian mocked the idea of going to war with Great Britain: "What!... [S]hall this great mammoth of the American forest leave his native element and plunge into the water in a mad contest with the shark?"[24] But the War Hawks did not have in mind engaging the British navy. They envisioned a land battle—for Canada. Americans had begun looking to war to end our British problem once and for all, and Canada with its vast territory and tiny population appeared easy pickings. Clay boasted to colleagues: "The conquest of Canada is in your power. I trust that I shall not be deemed presumptuous when I state that

I verily believe that the militia of Kentucky are alone competent to place Montreal and Upper Canada at your feet."[25] Even the Sage of Monticello was caught up in the war enthusiasm, trumpeting to his White House successor:

> The acquisition of Canada this year [1812] as far as the neighborhood of Quebec, will be a mere matter of marching, and will give us experience for the attack on Halifax the next, and the final expulsion of England from the American continent. Halifax, once taken, every cockboat of hers must return to England for repairs.[26]

With a spirit of covetousness added to the passions of patriotism, Madison bowed to congressional demands and sent up a war message on June 1, 1812. Three days later, it passed the House, 79–49. In the Senate the margin was 19–12. Neither Congress nor the nation was united on war; nevertheless, on June 18, America declared war. Had the Senate known that, two days earlier, Parliament had suspended its rules regarding America's commerce, a longtime U.S. goal, four Senate votes might have been changed and the War of 1812 averted. Though Napoleon's outrages against U.S. shipping and sailors seemed as offensive as Britain's, a declaration of war against France was narrowly defeated in the Senate, 18–14. Four days after the United States declared war, Napoleon ordered the Grand Army into Russia. Hitler would choose the same day, June 22, to invade the Soviet Union. British fury now knew no bounds, and historian Thomas Bailey finds it fully justified:

> As the leading champion of constitutional government in the New World, [America] should have been waging war on the greatest despot of the age, Napoleon, at the side of England, the surviving champion of constitutional government in the

Old World. The British, in a sense, were fighting America's
battle. This explains why New England Federalists could
prayerfully drink Pickering's famous toast: "The world's last
hope—Britain's fast-anchored isle." Yet at the very moment
when the fate of constitutionalism was trembling in the balance, when Napoleon was launching his mighty invasion of
Russia with 500,000 men, when England was nerving herself
for the last desperate struggle, the United States knifed the
Mother Country in the back and threw what strength it had
on the side of despotism. Britain's extremity seemed to be
America's opportunity.[27]

But Britain's peril aside, historian Bailey is dead wrong.
Madison's war was a just and righteous cause. For years the young
republic had been absorbing insults to the national honor. The
British had kidnapped its sailors, treated its protests with contempt, even turned the Indians loose on American settler families
along the frontier. The young republic had endured a decade of
humiliations and had had enough of John Bull. War was the only
way left to salvage the national honor, and America bravely took
it. Provocation aside, a declaration of war on the greatest naval
power on earth was an act of astonishing audacity. The British had
the capacity to raid and ravage our coasts. And though we had
gone to war with great bluster and cockiness, we had no plan of
how to win it.

Disaster followed disaster. General William Hull, dispatched to
seize Canada, surrendered Detroit, hardly firing a shot. New
England, which looked on Napoleon as the anti-Christ, and war
with Britain as immoral, refused to call its militia into service. In
Maine, oaths of loyalty were taken to George III. American warships won dramatic victories, but the British would emerge in
1815 with eight hundred vessels in the Royal Navy, while the

United States ended the war with its first-line warships reduced to three.

NADIR OF INDEPENDENCE

"Despicable in the cabinet, ridiculous in the field!" one London newspaper wrote of America. Asked another: "Is Great Britain to be driven from the proud eminence… by a piece of striped bunting at the mastheads of a few *fir-built frigates,* manned by *a handful of bastards and outlaws?*"[28] The *Times* of London exploded:

> [The Americans] are struck to the heart with terror for their impending punishment,—and oh! may no false liberality, no mistaken lenity, no weak and cowardly policy interpose to save them from the blow! Strike, Chastise the savages; for such they are…. With Madison and his perjured set, no treaty can be made; for no oath can bind them.[29]

With Napoleon defeated in Russia and in exile on Elba, the Duke of Wellington turned his attention to the treacherous cousins. To the cheers of the British, veterans of the peninsula campaign in Spain boarded ships to "give Jonathan a good drubbing." In August 1814 a squadron sailed up the Chesapeake Bay with four thousand British regulars. They disembarked to march down the road to pay Little Jemmy a visit. At Bladensburg, the British encountered a U.S. force of seven thousand. At the shock of battle, the Americans fled. Many did not stop running until they reached the safety of Arlington Heights across the Potomac. The British camped in Washington, ate the dinner prepared for the president and Mrs. Madison, stacked the furniture inside the Executive Mansion, and burned it down. Only the walls remained. James and Dolley Madison had fled on horseback to Tenleytown to watch the flames and smoke pour out of their home. Then they galloped out the Brookville road to the security of Maryland. British marines burned the Capitol, the War and Treasury buildings, a federal arsenal, and the offices of the *National Intelligencer.*[30]

Four days later, Admiral Sir George Cockburn moved to demolish the town Washington had called home. Alexandria capitulated and turned over all the requested provisions as ransom. Where the War Hawks were at this moment is not known. On August 30 the British lifted anchor and sailed away. Cockburn was chastised by his superior officer Admiral Cochrane: "I am sorry you left a house standing in Washington—depend upon it, it is mistaken mercy."[31] Informed of the burning of America's capital, Britain's prime minister muttered: "Let them feast on Washington."[32]

America was at the nadir of independence. A British force of ten thousand was headed for New Orleans from the West Indies under Major General Sir Edward Pakenham, brother-in-law of the Iron Duke. Word was expected of another crushing defeat for the motley American forces. Many feared imminent detachment of the Southwest and breakup of the nation. Such was not far from the British plan. After the British captured New Orleans, which they assumed would be easy work, America's inland trade was to be cut off. The army would then sail to Baltimore and, if Madison rejected terms, negotiate a separate peace with New England.

At a Hartford Convention called by the Massachusetts legislature and attended only by New England Federalists, secession and renewal of ties to the England of George III were openly discussed. The convention's leading lights crowed with delight at their country's humiliations. "From the moment the British possess New Orleans, the Union is severed," predicted the smug, hawk-faced Puritan Pickering, who had served in Washington's cabinet and despised republican France.[33] Anticipating a disaster in New Orleans, the convention sent a delegation to Madison to present him an ultimatum. But American honor, glory, and hope were to be restored by one of the great men of American history who now moved on stage.

"VALOR DIRECTED BY STUPIDITY"

Andrew Jackson hated the British. Of Scotch-Irish heritage, he had been a fourteen-year-old fighter in the Revolution who had been captured and ordered by one of Banastre Tarleton's officers to clean his boots. The lad refused. When the officer raised his sword, Andrew raised a hand to ward off the blow. The sword slashed his hand to the bone and left him with a head scar he would carry the rest of his life.

The bleeding boy was forced to march with his brother Robert, also slashed, to Camden, South Carolina. There, they were jailed as prisoners of war. A tiny Irish woman came to beg their release. Elizabeth Jackson had come too late for Robert, who died within days of smallpox and an infection of his wounds. Andrew was delirious with smallpox, and his mother stayed with him for weeks. When Andrew was restored to health, she left to help the sons of friends. Elizabeth Jackson never returned. She succumbed to the plague, and her body was buried in an unmarked grave. The fourteen-year-old was desolate, an orphan of the Revolution: "I felt utterly alone and tried to recall her last words to me."[34] A third of a century later, Andrew Jackson was waiting below New Orleans to take his revenge.

A veteran Indian fighter and head of the Tennessee militia, Jackson had crushed an uprising of Creeks at Horseshoe Bend, Alabama, on March 27, 1814. His reward: a generalship in the regular army and command of the defense of New Orleans. Jackson's forces consisted of "Kentuckians and Tennesseans… legendary riflemen… a couple of regiments of regulars, two volunteer battalions of Free Negroes of New Orleans, a battalion of wellborn New Orleans white folk, and a band known as the New Orleans sharpshooters," plus a contingent of Choctaw Indians and hundreds of Jean Lafitte's bayou pirates.[35] The pirate-patriot had written to plead with the governor of Louisiana to be allowed to fight beside his countrymen: "I am the Lost Sheep who desires to return to the flock."[36]

Jackson was leading an all-American army.

When the British army disembarked below the city and began to advance, it did not know it was facing Americans different from the boys on the Bladensburg Road. On the foggy morning of January 8, 1815, the Redcoats, led by Pakenham, who was contemptuous of militia, moved up in a massed frontal assault. A wind rose to blow away the fog. Entrenched behind ramparts, Jackson's men saw a solid red line marching toward them. It was a massacre: Jackson's militiamen, Creoles, Negroes, pirates, and sharpshooters firing volley after volley cut the British lines to pieces, killing two thousand. The Americans suffered seven dead and six wounded.

"I begin to be of opinion with you that there is nothing as stupid as a gallant officer," Wellington had written a friend in the Spanish campaign.[37] "[V]alor directed by stupidity," wrote one historian of Pakenham's army.[38]

When the British invaders sailed away, they carried in a casket of rum the corpse of General Pakenham; the ship also carried his grieving widow, who had expected to be governess of Louisiana. British humiliation was total. As Franklin D. Roosevelt told the story, when the British aboard ship discovered Pakenham's body, they put pipes into the barrel and drank the rum. Poor Pakenham arrived home in awful condition.[39]

Though Jackson's victory had come after peace had been agreed to at Ghent—the news had not crossed the Atlantic—that does not diminish its significance. Jackson's victory meant that Britain, which had refused to recognize the seizure of West Florida or the purchase of Louisiana, would accept both. Had Jackson lost at New Orleans, and the city been occupied, Great Britain, according to the terms of Ghent, would have been within its rights to restore the Gulf Coast and all of Louisiana to Spain. As Monroe reported to Madison, that is exactly what the British would have done.[40] Jackson's victory thus gave America uncontested title to half of the land claimed by the United States.

AS EUROPE BLED, AMERICA PROSPERED

Not for eight decades would America become embroiled in another war with a European power. But there were lessons to be learned from the War of 1812 and the sixteen years of rule by the neighbors from the Tidewater.

There is no security in disarmament. In war even a neutral must maintain the power to defend its rights. To protests that the British had no right to board our ships and remove U.S. citizens, Foreign Secretary Lord Harrowby had replied, "The pretension advanced by Mr. Madison that the American Flag should protect every Individual sailing under it on board of a Merchant Ship is too extravagant to require any serious Refutation."[41] As Thucydides observed, the strong do what they will, the weak suffer what they must.

American ships had been boarded and seamen kidnapped within sight of our coast because we were weak. Having beached his navy to rely on single-shot gunboats that could be turned into kindling by British ships of the line, Jefferson had to resort to sanctions to defend his nation's honor. But sanctions did not work. The Embargo Act failed to stop the press-gangs and damaged America more than Britain. Jefferson and Madison, neither a soldier, had believed a disarmed America would be a respected America. If we threatened no one, no one would threaten us. Both had been proven disastrously wrong. America was bullied and insulted until the affronts forced us to fight to defend our honor. "Our commerce on the ocean… must be paid for by frequent war," Jefferson wrote in 1785.[42] Yet neither he nor Madison prepared us, and the nation almost paid a terrible price for their failure.

Had Jefferson and Madison used the decade of British humiliations to build an army, and invaded and held Canada as hostage to end the outrages at sea, U.S. goals—peace, security, and respect for our rights as a neutral—could have been achieved. But neither Jefferson nor Madison, though given a decade to prepare, acted to build an army that could defeat the British on our own continent. Providence alone spared us the customary consequences of such failures. But, then, fortune favors the brave.

Anglophiles argued, then and now, that as we and the British shared a heritage of liberty, we should have fought at England's side against the despot of the age. But the British had violated our sovereignty, kidnapped our seamen, incited Indians to massacre pioneers, attacked a U.S. warship in peacetime, and exploited a momentary advantage to try to tear the young republic apart. Unlike Jefferson, his old rival, Hamilton put no trust in the supposed beneficence of the more democratic regimes:

> Sparta, Athens, Rome, and Carthage were all republics; two of them, Athens and Carthage, of the commercial kind. Yet were they as often engaged in wars, offensive and defensive, as the neighboring monarchies of the same times…. In the government of Britain the representatives of the people compose one branch of the national legislature. Commerce has been for ages the predominant pursuit of that country. Few nations, nevertheless, have been more frequently engaged in war….[43]

Most important, Britain alone threatened U.S. vital interests; Britain alone had the power to tear America apart; Britain alone could arm Indians along our frontier to kill Americans. With Louisiana in America's control, Napoleon, lacking a fleet to overwhelm the British, presented no immediate or mortal threat.

When Washington warned against a "passionate attachment" to any country other than our own, his warning included the Mother Country. But France had behaved no better. "His Majesty loves the Americans," France's foreign minister, the Duc de Cadore, wrote in a fawning letter to a U.S. envoy.[44] Many believed it, even as American ships were being seized by Napoleon with the same contempt for their nationality as the British had shown. Anglophiles, and Francophiles who once held a romantic view of the Revolution and the Republic, now had a more realistic view of the world.

According to balance-of-power theorists, should any single power control Europe, America must be in mortal peril. But America saw no threat in Napoleon's domination of Europe from the Atlantic to Moscow, for between the French army and the United States stood the British fleet. Napoleon was held in check by the nation that could still do America the greatest harm: Great Britain.

And far from being imperiled by Europe's war, America prospered mightily from the conflict. Napoleon had sold us Louisiana to prevent a U.S.-British alliance and to strengthen America as a rival to British power. Madison had seized on Europe's distraction to pirate West Florida. Napoleon's return from Elba and the renewal of war had caused Britain to back down on its demand that the United States accept an Indian buffer state in what is today's Midwest, as a condition of peace. The British agreed to settle for the *status quo ante*, so Wellington could get back to Napoleon.

It is a myth that America has been imperiled by Europe's wars; more often, the opposite has proven true. During the Napoleonic Wars, the United States doubled its size for just $15 million, the loss of Madison's reputation for honest dealing, and a minimal cost in life.

MADE IN ENGLAND: THE MONROE DOCTRINE

Jefferson and Madison were not isolationists. They had, like Adams, internalized Washington's "great rule." Both were prepared to risk war, but only for America's vital interests. Jefferson did not want to go to war over the impressment of our seamen or national honor in the *Chesapeake* affair, but he was prepared to form an alliance with Britain and go to war to keep France from taking New Orleans, Louisiana, and the Floridas, and thereby acquire the ability to choke America's commerce and block her expansion. Madison was willing to risk war with Spain and Britain if the prize was something tangible, like West Florida. Neither Jefferson nor Madison had any interest in going to war to help rid Europe of the despot of the age. Napoleon was Europe's problem, not ours. As long as he did not threaten us, it was not our responsibility to rein him in.

Finally, America's economy was not imperiled by Europe's war. Far from it. As a result of the Embargo Act, the Nonintercourse Act, the war, and British-French depredations at sea, the United States, forced to fall back on its own resources, had become a manufacturing power and self-sufficient nation. Indeed, to kill the infant American industries that had sprouted up, the British in 1815 began dumping manufactures on us, but the assault on U.S. industry was defeated by Madison's Tariff of 1816, which was powerfully supported by Henry Clay and John C. Calhoun.

In 1817 Madison went home to Montpelier and was succeeded by James Monroe, who, with John Quincy Adams as secretary of state, would expand on the noninterventionist policy of Washington. To Washington's dictum that we stay out of Europe's affairs, Monroe would add a corollary that would carry his name into history: Europe must henceforth stay out of the Western Hemisphere.

> In the wars of the European powers in matters relating to themselves we have never taken any part, nor does it comport with our policy so to do....
>
> [But] the American continents, by the free and independent condition which they have assumed and maintain, are henceforth not to be considered as subjects for future colonization by any European powers....
>
> We owe it, therefore, to candor and to the amicable relations between the United States and those powers [of Europe] to declare that we should consider any attempt on their part to extend their system to any portion of this hemisphere as dangerous to our peace and safety.[45]

This was the Monroe Doctrine of 1823. The idea had originally come from British Foreign Minister George Canning, who had invited the United States to enter a strategic partnership. On the advice of Adams, Monroe decided on a unilateral declaration. It would be "more dignified," Adams had said, "to avow our principles explicitly... than to come in as a cock-boat in the wake of a British man-of-war." Made aware by Monroe of British instigation of the initiative, Jefferson agreed: "Great Britain is the nation which can do us the most harm of any one, or all on earth; and with her on our side we need not fear the whole world."[46]

For decades the Royal Navy would be the enforcer of the Monroe Doctrine, and the Americans would be "free riders" on the naval power of the British Empire. We should do well to emulate our forefathers, and let the nations of Europe and Asia become our first line of defense again, while keeping U.S. power intact and America's powder dry.

CHAPTER 7

How We Took Florida

*Diplomacy without power is feeble, and power without
diplomacy is destructive and blind.*[1]

—Hans J. Morgenthau

We must have the Floridas and Cuba.[2]

—Thomas Jefferson, 1809

At the end of the eighteenth century, Spain's empire in
North America was breathtaking. At the close of the Seven Years War
in 1763, Spain had received the Louisiana territory from a defeated
France; at the end of the American Revolution, Britain had restored
Florida to Spain. As Jackson biographer Robert Remini writes:

> Thus, in 1790, Spain controlled a vast empire that stretched from
> Florida to Louisiana and Texas, up the west bank of the
> Mississippi to some indefinite point close to Canada, and west-
> ward to the Pacific Ocean north of California—an empire that
> reached from ocean to ocean across a continent.[3]

Again and again in the nineteenth century, Americans would
tear off a piece of this empire and digest it. First Louisiana, then the
Floridas, then Texas, then all of northern Mexico and California. At
century's end, America expelled Spain from a hemisphere it had been
first to explore, robbing His Most Catholic Majesty of possessions
Spain had held for four centuries. If any nation had reason to hate
America, it was Spain.

JACKSON STORMS FLORIDA

The first decades of the nineteenth century were a "time of troubles" for the Spanish. Louisiana had been sold to America by the French, although Napoleon had agreed never to "alienate" the territory. And most of West Florida had been torn away by Madison. Madrid still held East Florida and part of West Florida, but both had been stripped of troops to put down rebellions across Latin America. The unpoliced Floridas thus became a haven for fugitive slaves, pirates, renegades, and marauding Indians who regularly crossed into U.S. territory to pillage, burn, and murder. Monroe gave the assignment to clean out the nests of villainy to the hero of New Orleans. Jackson looked forward to going back to fighting Indians.

Earlier, General Edmund P. Gaines had been authorized to chase the Indians out of Georgia, back into Florida, but to respect the Spanish forts and flag. Jackson was more ambitious. He wrote the president, "The whole of East Florida [should be] seized and... this can be done without implicating the Government."[4] And how might that be done? "Let it be signified to me through any channel... that the possession of the Floridas would be desirable... and in sixty days it will be accomplished."[5] Jackson's letter to the president going north crossed one from Monroe coming south, which stated with fine diplomatic ambiguity: "The mov'ment... against the Seminoles... will bring you on a theatre where you may possibly have other services to perform.... Great interests are at issue.... This is not a time for repose... untill our cause is carried triumphantly thro'."[6]

In April 1818 Jackson stormed into Florida, seized St. Marks, tore down the Spanish flag, and hoisted the Stars and Stripes. Two British subjects had the misfortune to fall into his custody: Alexander Arbuthnot, a seventy-year-old Scot who sympathized with the Indians, and Robert Ambrister, twenty-one, a former lieutenant in the Royal Colonial Marines. Jackson ordered them court-martialed.

Arbuthnot was convicted of alerting the Indians to Jackson's coming and of providing them with ten barrels of powder, and was sentenced to be hanged. Ambrister was charged with "assuming command of the Indians in... a war with the United States." Pleading "guilty with justification," he threw himself on the mercy of the court. Ambrister was sentenced to be shot, but one of Jackson's officers who had sentenced Ambrister, who was popular with his guards, reversed himself and resentenced the soldier of fortune to fifty lashes and a year's confinement. The next morning, Jackson reviewed the sentences and reversed the act of clemency. Arbuthnot and Ambrister were executed. Jackson reported back to the secretary of war, the thirty-five-year-old, back-country, Scotch-Irish South Carolinian, John Caldwell Calhoun:

> I hope the execution of these two unprincipled villains will
> prove an awful example to the world, and convince the
> Government of Great Britain, as well as her subjects, that certain,
> though slow retribution awaits those unchristian wretches who,
> by false promises, delude and excite an Indian tribe to all the
> deeds of savage war.[7]

Jackson was not finished. Claiming he had reports of hostile Indians near Pensacola, he marched there, seized that capital of West Florida, and packed the Spanish governor and his garrison off to Havana. Historian Thomas Bailey sums up Jackson's visit to Florida:

> Thus in a few weeks he chastised the Indians, seized every
> important post in Florida except St. Augustine, confiscated the
> royal archives, deposed the Spanish governor and named an
> American in his place, executed two British subjects, and
> declared in force "the revenue laws of the United States." He
> later expressed regret that he did not hang the Spanish
> governor.[8]

PANIC IN THE CABINET

When word of Jackson's rampage reached Washington, a shaken president fled to his farm in Loudoun County, leaving Secretary of State John Quincy Adams to deal with the towering rage of a Spanish envoy who had just delivered a virtual ultimatum: "In the name of the King, my master, I demand a prompt restitution of St. Marks, Pensacola, Barrancas, and all other places wrested by General Jackson from the Crown of Spain. I demand... indemnity for all injuries and losses, and the punishment of the general."[9]

Monroe wanted to be rid of Jackson, but did not wish to incite the wrath of the general's growing host of idolaters. He wrote Jefferson to get the great man's opinion about making Jackson minister to the tsar's court. In the words of historians David and Jeanne Heidler: "Jefferson thought the idea absurd; Jackson's temper would provoke a Russian-American crisis within weeks of his arrival. Monroe agreed and dropped it."[10]

When Monroe returned, his cabinet began daily meetings on the crisis. To seize Spanish forts and the Spanish capital and expel the governor were acts of war; but to hang or shoot British subjects and crow about it was to insult the greatest power on earth. In exceeding his orders, Jackson had dragged the United States to the brink of war. Calhoun urged a court-martial.[11] But Jackson had one resolute defender in the cabinet. For days Secretary of State John Quincy Adams defended the general.

An unrepentant Jackson returned home the toast of the Republic. He had chastised Indians, humiliated Spaniards, and hurled defiance at the British Empire. A rousing resolution was passed in his honor at Tammany Hall:

> Resolved... That the conduct of General Jackson... was
> justified by the law of nations, and the laws of war, and the
> immutable principles of retaliation and self-defence; and we

highly approve of the manly spirit of the American general, who
promptly punished the offenders and culprits against humanity
and the rights of his country, and taught foreign emissaries that
the United States was not to be outraged by spies, traitors, and
lawless adventurers.[12]

CASTLEREAGH CALMS AN INCENSED ENGLAND

When the report reached London of the executions of Ambrister
and Arbuthnot, and Jackson's exultation, official and public opinion
moved swiftly toward a demand for apologies and reparations—or
war. As Heidler and Heidler noted:

> The public, churned by sensational accounts in the press, per-
> ceived the executions as an affront of the first rank, and
> Castlereagh glumly noted in the fall of 1818 that if the govern-
> ment wanted a brawl with the United States, a large number of
> Britons would eagerly hold the government's coat.[13]

But Foreign Secretary Castlereagh had other fish to fry. He was
engaged in negotiations with the Americans over the encouragement
of trade, use of the North American fisheries, and fixing the U.S.-
Canadian border. War would abort the talks. After a drawn-out investigation, Castlereagh concluded that Ambrister and Arbuthnot had
been engaged in "practices of such a description as to have deprived
them of any claim on their own government for interference."[14]
England neither demanded redress nor supported Spain's protests.
The poet Shelley might revile him ("I met Murder on the way/He
had a mask like Castlereagh"), but America had a convenient friend
in the foreign secretary.[15]

Surely in the back of Castlereagh's mind was the futility of
another war with the Americans. While Great Britain might thrash
the cousins, the empire had no vital interest in Florida, and no inter-

est at all in reengaging General Jackson. Then, there was Britain's enduring vulnerability to an invasion of Canada. Best for all concerned if old Arbuthnot and young Ambrister were left to rest in peace.

America's first warrior had made many friends, but also enemies envious of his popularity and fearful of his ambition. Foremost among them was Henry Clay. For twenty-seven days, Congress debated Clay's call for Jackson's condemnation, with members carrying pistols after the general, wild with rage, threatened to cut off the ears of his enemies. At the debate's close, Congress rejected Clay's motion by huge margins. The hero of New Orleans and Florida was now America's hero. Jackson was feted in Philadelphia and New York in day-long celebrations. Not since Washington returned from Yorktown had America had such a celebrity. But Jackson, believing his honor had been impugned, was incensed by the conduct of his fellow westerner, who had darkly reminded the Senate that "it was in the provinces that were laid the seeds of ambitious projects that overturned the liberties of Rome."[16] When Congress adjourned, Jackson confided to friends, he intended to challenge Clay to a duel and kill the Speaker of the House.[17]

"THE FRUITS OF EXPEDIENCY OVER PRINCIPLE"

In defending Jackson, John Quincy Adams had shown a statesman's grasp of the larger issue. While Jackson had exceeded his authority, and perhaps disobeyed orders and committed acts of war against a nation with which America was at peace, splendid indeed were the fruits of his insubordination. In the words of Heidler and Heidler:

> Jackson's exploits had... roused in Adams the instincts of the
> shrewd Yankee trader. Far more important than Jackson's

deliberate disregard of his orders was the practical benefit the
United States might enjoy because he had done so. Fifteen years
earlier, a younger John Quincy Adams had fretted over the constitutional irregularities of Jefferson's purchasing Louisiana until
Secretary of State James Madison had told him to be still and
reap the occasional fruits of expediency over principle. Now in
1818, Adams was older, wiser, and ready to do some harvesting
of his own.[18]

Jackson's unauthorized act of war against Spain, Adams felt,
might be overlooked if America could but keep the fruits of his
transgression. Calhoun, however, "remained adamant. How was he
ever to control… his department if Jackson were allowed to behave
with such impunity?"[19]

Fearful of Jackson's soaring popularity, Monroe backed away
from a confrontation with his general. While he returned the Spanish
posts, he refused to apologize to Madrid. Dissatisfied, Spain again
demanded full apologies, reparations, and the punishment of Jackson.
Now came Adams's moment. On shaky legal ground but full of
righteousness, the secretary sent a long letter to Madrid. The crisis
had arisen, wrote Adams, because Spain had proven incapable of controlling the Indians. Adams luridly described the Indian atrocities, laid
out the offenses of Arbuthnot and Ambrister, and asserted that
Jackson had had a right to execute both, even without a trial.
America, Adams thundered, had a God-given right to protect its citizens, and if Spain could not control the Indians on its own territory,
it should cede that territory to a nation that would. And if ever again
attacks on American citizens came out of Florida, Jackson's remedy
would be applied again. The next time, moreover, America might not
return Florida. An inherent right of self-defense, declared Adams, "is
engraved in adamant on the common sense of mankind."[20]

No precedent in diplomacy or international law could be found

for Adams's "derelict province" principle, but it was brazen and brilliant. Adams had turned a brief in defense of Jackson into an indictment and a virtual ultimatum to Spain: Control Florida or cede
Florida! Since Spain had all but admitted it could not control Florida,
it had an obligation to cede. Adams then turned face up the card
Spain feared most. If this offer were rejected, the United States would
have to consider recognizing the Latin American revolutionaries in
rebellion against the Spanish empire.[21]

At the Spanish court nationalistic rage gave way to sober reflection.
With Britain refusing to stand by it and revolution spreading across
Latin America, Spain could not long hold Florida if the rapacious
Americans were determined to seize it. Better to relinquish with
honor than have Florida ripped away. Spain's apprehension was justified, for Calhoun was in receipt of a new message from his general.
Asserting that the return of Pensacola was being taken by the Indians
as a sign of American weakness, Jackson was urging another expedi-
tion to seize St. Augustine.[22]

Adams sat down with Spanish envoy Don Luis de Onis and
came away with Spain's ceding East Florida, validating America's
claim to all of West Florida, and relinquishing all claims to Oregon.
In return, the United States agreed to settle the claims of Americans
against Spain for losses to the Indians and to concede that Texas had
not been part of the Louisiana Purchase. The diplomacy of Adams
backed by the threat of Jackson had left the Spanish no choice but to
yield and retrieve what honor they could. Historian Samuel Flagg
Bemis would say of Adams's acquisition of clear title to the two
Floridas, and of all of Spain's rights in the Oregon territory that
reached to the Pacific, "It was the greatest diplomatic victory won by
a single individual in the history of the United States."[23]

But Clay, who believed he should have been Monroe's choice as
secretary of state—stepping-stone to the presidency—protested that

the West had been betrayed by acceptance of Spain's claim that Texas was not part of Louisiana. Clay was echoed by the *Louisiana Advertiser*, which bellowed that Texas was "worth ten Floridas."[24]

The Spanish court balked at the Adams-Onis treaty, and the Senate was forced to give its consent twice. On February 19, 1821, with but four dissenting votes, clear title to all of Florida passed to the United States. A year later, Monroe took the step Madrid dreaded. The United States recognized the independence of the Latin American republics that had broken from Spain.

ADAMS EXPANDS ON WASHINGTON'S GOSPEL

How the great aspirants to national power had conducted themselves in the Florida crisis would have a profound effect on their ambitions and America's future. The two men who had behaved with the greatest audacity, Adams and Jackson, would occupy the White House from 1825 to 1837. Other careers suffered permanent damage. Clay had made a lifelong enemy of Andrew Jackson. In the cabinet Calhoun had argued for Jackson's censure; but after Monroe backed away in the face of public acclaim, Calhoun sent word to the general through aides that he had been Jackson's staunch defender. Not for a dozen years, until the battle over nullification and the "Tariff of Abominations," would Jackson discover the truth. When he did, Calhoun was his vice president.

Jackson and Adams were men of vision, unapologetic about the means they employed to realize the destiny they foresaw for America. Adams once declared, "North America appears to be destined by Divine Providence to be peopled by one nation, speaking one language, professing one general system of religious and political principles, and accustomed to one general tenor of social usages and customs."[25] Jackson, who would be Adams's rival in the 1824 presidential election and would win a plurality of the popular and electoral votes but lose the presidency in the House because of Clay, was at one with the New Englander on this matter:

> What good man would prefer a country covered with forests
> and ranged by a few thousand savages to our extensive
> Republic, studded with cities, towns, and prosperous farms,
> embellished with all the improvements which art can devise or
> industry execute, occupied by more than 12,000,000 happy
> people, and filled with all the blessings of liberty, civilization,
> and religion?[26]

As his biographer Robert Remini wrote, "More than any other man, [Jackson] kept the British from returning to the Gulf Coast. More than any other man, he expelled the Spanish from their southern stronghold and made possible the transformation of the United States into a continental power."[27] Jackson and Adams believed they belonged to a people with a glorious destiny, and to a superior civilization with the right to conquer and rule—and they acted on this belief. But while Adams was aggressive in defending America's rights on its own continent, he was a passionate and articulate foe of enlistment in alien causes or foreign crusades. When the Greeks rose in rebellion against centuries of rule by Ottoman Turks, many wanted America to intervene on the side of liberty in Europe, as France had intervened on the side of liberty in America. But Adams blocked intervention, rendering the most succinct and famous expression of Washington's "great rule" ever penned. In his Fourth of July speech in 1821, Adams declared:

> Wherever the standard of freedom and independence has been
> or shall be unfurled, there will [America's] heart, her benedic-
> tions, and her prayers be. But she goes not abroad in search of
> monsters to destroy. She is the well-wisher to the freedom and

independence of all. She is the champion and vindicator only of her own....[28]

Intervention in Europe, even if carried out under "the banners of foreign independence," Adams continued, would involve America in

all the wars of interest and intrigue, of individual avarice, envy, and ambition, which assume the colors and usurp the standard of freedom. The fundamental maxims of her policy would insensibly change from liberty to force....

    She might become the dictatress of the world. She would no longer be the ruler of her own spirit.[29]

America's ideals of "freedom and independence" would be set aside for an "imperial diadem, flashing in false and tarnished luster, the murky radiance of dominance and power." To be true to herself, America must restrict intervention to "recommend the general cause with the countenance of her voice and the benignant sympathy of her example."[30]

Not since the Farewell Address had U.S. foreign policy been stated with such clarity, force, and eloquence.

If you like laws and sausages, it is said, you ought not watch them being made. The same may be said of great nations and empires. The often duplicitous and ruthless way in which Madison, Jackson, Monroe, and Adams took the Floridas would prove a model for how we would take Texas, California, Hawaii, the Philippines, and the Canal Zone. That is the way the world worked in that age of empires; and that appears to be the way the world will work in the twenty-first century, now that the West has given up its empires to lecture other nations on how to behave. But aspiring great powers are more likely to emulate the example of Jackson than the exhortations of Clinton.

Jackson had seen in Florida the land of a dying empire, there for the taking, as Iraqis saw in Kuwait oil-rich and undefended land left behind by a defunct British Empire. In 1991 America had the power and will to force Iraq to disgorge Kuwait. In 1818 Spain lacked the power or will to take back Florida. But the day is coming when Americans will tire of imperial burdens. Then the Gulf, too, will come to be dominated by the most powerful of its littoral states. Just as Castlereagh sagely decided that no vital British interest was at risk in who controlled Florida, so must America one day soon decide what is vital and what we can let go.

PART THREE

1845–1869:
MANIFEST DESTINY

CHAPTER 8

"Jimmy Polk's War"

[It is] the right of our manifest destiny to overspread and to possess the whole of the continent which Providence has given us for the development of the great experiment in liberty and federative self-government entrusted to us.[1]

—JOHN L. O'SULLIVAN,
NEW YORK EDITOR, 1845

Every great fortune, it is said, is the fruit of some great crime. Was America's tearing away of the Southwest and California from Mexico an act of imperial aggression? Was our war with Mexico the "most unjust war in history," as Ulysses S. Grant described it?[2] Among guilt-ridden Americans, and south of the Rio Grande, this belief is widespread. But the charge is but another big lie in the Blame America First series. To see the critical distinction between naked aggression and Manifest Destiny, we must review the history of 1835–1848, when the United States almost doubled in size to reach the Pacific.

TEXAS'S WAR OF INDEPENDENCE

As far back as the early 1820s, Americans setting out for the West began to take up an offer from a newly independent Mexico to settle in Texas. By 1825 President Adams, who regretted having signed away U.S. claims on Texas in the 1819 treaty with Spain that gave us Florida, sought to purchase the territory. He was rebuffed, as was his successor, Jackson. The "Yanquis" were despised in Mexico City. Any Mexican who sold territory to them would have risked his life.

But by 1835 more than thirty thousand Americans lived in
Texas, where they outnumbered the Mexican population ten-to-
one. Among them were adventurers like Jim Bowie, inventor of
the eighteen-inch knife they called the "genuine Arkansas tooth-
pick"; Davy Crockett, frontiersman and former congressman from
Tennessee; and Sam Houston. On March 27, 1814, Ensign Houston
had been first to leap the Creek barricades at Horseshoe Bend on
the Tallapoosa, where eight hundred braves had fought to the
death. His commander at Horseshoe Bend had been Andrew
Jackson.

Allowed to enter Texas on condition they become Mexican citizens and Catholic converts, the settlers still thought of themselves as
Americans and began to chafe at the demand that they give up their
citizenship and convert to another faith. After a series of revolutions
in Mexico City thrust into power the brutal and corrupt General
Antonio Lopez de Santa Anna, who set aside Mexico's liberal constitution and began to repress the Texans, even moderates like
Stephen Austin, the son of Moses Austin, who had been invited in by
Mexico to settle Texas, now thought it time to declare independence.
In 1835 the Texans rose in rebellion and chased the weak Mexican
army garrisons over the Rio Grande.

But the Mexican dictator was determined not to lose his
province. Leading seven thousand troops, Santa Anna crossed the Rio
Grande and encountered 180 defiant Texans holed up at Alamo mission. Crockett and Bowie were among the defenders. For twelve days
the Texans held off the warlord's army. When the frustrated and
enraged Mexicans overran the mission, they put every last man and
boy to the sword. Moving east, Santa Anna encountered another
band of Texans at Goliad. Outnumbered ten-to-one, these Texans
surrendered. As historian Alexander DeConde recounted:

> In violation of the surrender terms, the Mexicans roused the
> prisoners from their sleep, marched them a short distance from

the town, and shot them in cold blood on Sunday morning,
March 27. Like the slaughter at the Alamo, the massacre at
Goliad sent aroused volunteers flocking to join Houston's army.[3]

"Exterminate the Sabine!" was the war cry of Santa Anna's army
as it continued east. For thirty-eight days, Sam Houston retreated. At
the juncture of Buffalo Bayou and San Jacinto River, his small force
halted, wheeled, and surprised the Mexicans at their siesta. With cries
of "Remember the Alamo!" "Remember Goliad!" and "Death to
Santa Anna!" the Texans stormed the Mexican camp, slaughtered six
hundred soldiers, and captured seven hundred others. The dictator
was discovered cowering in the grass, disguised as a common soldier.

The Texans wanted vengeance, but Houston knew the prize he
had. On May 14, 1836, a quaking Santa Anna was coerced into signing two treaties. The first declared an end to the fighting and called
for a Mexican withdrawal; the second, which was secret, recognized
the Texas republic, with its border on the Rio Grande.[4] But no
sooner had Santa Anna been turned loose and sent home than he
repudiated what he had signed.

DO WE REALLY WANT TEXAS?

Texas was now free, but its situation was precarious. Unrecognized by
a brooding Mexico with a population two hundred times as great,
the Lone Star Republic sought the protection of the Eagle; Houston
wanted immediate U.S. annexation and statehood.

Jackson, however, was hesitant, for the dreaded slavery issue had
reared its head. In the clamor for statehood, northern abolitionists
saw a plot by slave states to increase their power in Congress. William
Lloyd Garrison, editor of *The Liberator*, dipped his quill pen in abolitionist acid:

Texas is the rendezvous of absconding villainy, desperate adventure, and lawless ruffianism—the ark of safety to swindlers, gam-

blers, robbers, and rogues of every size and degree. Its distinguishing characteristic is unmitigated depravity. Nothing homogeneous is found among its population, except a disposition to extend and perpetuate the most frightful form of servitude the world has ever known, and to add crime to crime.[5]

Fearful that annexation would divide his party and defeat his heir, Vice President Martin Van Buren, and perhaps even ignite a war with Mexico, Jackson acted with caution. Not until his last day in office, a year after San Jacinto, and only after both houses of Congress had voted to recognize Texas, did he recognize the independence of Texas.

Now Texas was Van Buren's problem. Yet no sooner had he taken office than the Panic of 1837 struck, the result of the economic turmoil following Jackson's war with Nicholas Biddle's Bank of the United States (BUS). The Philadelphia banker had foolishly challenged Jackson in terms certain to arouse the old warrior: "This worthy President," Biddle had boasted, "thinks that because he has scalped Indians and imprisoned judges, he is to have his own way with the Bank. He is mistaken."[6] Biddle misread his man. "It is trying to kill me, but I will kill it," Jackson told friends of Biddle's bank. Inaugurated for a second term, the president yanked all government deposits out of the BUS, persuaded Congress not to renew its charter, and effectively starved it to death. He then put the government deposits into state-chartered banks, derided by foes as "pet banks." Less responsible than the BUS, these banks began multiplying the number of bank notes in circulation. Money expanded by 50 percent, creating a speculative boom in land and stocks. The boom of 1835–1836 begat the Panic of 1837, inherited by the luckless Van Buren.[7]

His plate full, Van Buren put Texas on the back burner. When the Texans petitioned again for statehood, "the Little Magician" brushed aside the offer. Spurned again, Houston withdrew it and, fearful of Mexico's dictator, began to court Great Britain, where Parliament was receptive. An independent Texas would block America's westward expansion. British merchants were enthusiastic. If the Texans could be persuaded to embrace free trade, British goods could enter duty-free and be easily transported to the southern and western states, undercutting Yankee manufactures. Texas could also become a source of Britain's cotton and a magnet to lure the free-trade South away from the high-tariff North. The American South could be converted into a virtual colony of the empire.

In Texas's independence, Britain and France saw a way to divide the upstart Americans and establish a bulwark against Yankee expansionism. Both recognized the Lone Star Republic. And the situation simmered.

TYLER'S DREAM AND ADAMS'S THREAT

Eight years after San Jacinto, a worried John Tyler sat brooding in the Executive Mansion, a president without a party. A Calhoun Democrat, Tyler had broken with Jackson in 1832, when Calhoun had resigned the vice presidency in the nullification battle, and been put on the Whig ticket in 1840 to win over southern Democrats to William Henry Harrison. "Tippecanoe and Tyler, too" had carried the nation, and Tyler took office when the sixty-nine-year-old ex-soldier, a month after being sworn in, succumbed to pneumonia contracted during a two-hour inaugural speech he made in the cold without wearing an overcoat.

"His Accidency" needed an issue to win the presidency in his own right in 1844, and thought he had found it in the annexation of Texas with its appeal to a South that saw in the Lone Star Republic a new slave state, and the possibility Texas might be broken up into as many as five new slave states with ten senators. John Quincy Adams, now in the House, saw the same possibility; only he viewed it as a threat to the Union. The former president issued a warning:

We hesitate not to say that annexation… WOULD BE IDEN-
TICAL WITH DISSOLUTION. It would be a violation of our
national compact… so deep and fundamental… as, in our opinion, not only inevitably to result in a dissolution of the Union,
but fully to justify it.[8]

Adams was threatening secession, and, again, Americans began to
talk of disunion. In 1814 New England Federalists had threatened to
secede over "Mr. Madison's War." In 1820 there had been rumbles of
secession if Missouri were allowed into the Union, giving the slave states
a two-vote margin in the Senate; even the aging Jefferson had heard a
"firebell in the night." In 1832 Calhoun's South Carolinians had been
ready to secede over the "tariff of abominations." Now, Tyler's proposed
annexation of Texas was threatening to break apart the nation.

But Tyler was determined to go ahead. His agents assured Texans
that if they would request annexation again, two-thirds of the Senate
would vote to take Texas in. Relying on his assurances, Texas swal-
lowed its pride and for the third time requested admission. Texas
President Sam Houston, however, wrote to his old chief at the
Hermitage with a warning:

Now, my venerated friend, you will perceive that Texas is presented to the United States as a bride adorned for her espousals;
but if, in the confident hope of the Union, she should be
rejected, her mortification would be indescribable. She has been
sought by the United States, and this is the third time she has
consented. Were she now to be spurned… she would seek some
other friend.[9]

Andrew Jackson had no doubt who that "other friend" might
be.

CALHOUN RETURNS TO THE CABINET

Fate intervened to kill Tyler's dream. Captain Robert F. Stockton had persuaded Congress to build the *Princeton*, a revolutionary frigate designed by Swedish engineer John Ericsson, inventor of the screw propeller. *Princeton* carried two revolutionary, smooth-bore, twelve-inch, wrought-iron guns. One, brought from England by Ericsson, was called "Oregon"; the other, designed by Stockton, cast in an American foundry, was "Peacemaker." Both had been tested, but on a gala cruise down the Potomac, "Peacemaker" exploded, killing Secretary of State Abel Upshur. Upshur had been handling the Texas negotiations.[10]

For Tyler the tragedy was not unmitigated. The blast that killed Upshur, the secretary of the navy, and a state senator hurled into Tyler's arms the senator's daughter, Julia Gardiner, whom the president proceeded to make the second Mrs. Tyler and mistress of the Executive Mansion.[11]

Upshur's post was now offered to Calhoun. Seeing himself as Tyler's successor, Calhoun quickly accepted. Believing that statehood for Texas was a foregone conclusion, the Senate unanimously approved his nomination, and assumed Calhoun's primary role was to negotiate a favorable settlement with the British over Oregon.[12]

But success required a subtlety of which Calhoun proved incapable. While to Northerners and Westerners the annexation of Texas was an appealing way to frustrate Britain's anti-U.S. policy, to Calhoun, annexation meant added political weight for the South. Unfortunately, on taking office, Calhoun immediately conflated the Texas issue with slavery.

While the British had been working to abolish slavery in Texas, to Old Hickory, England's motives were the darkest—to destabilize his beloved Union: "Would not... our slaves in the great valley of the Mississippi [be] worth nothing, because they would all run over to Texas, and under British influence, liberated, and lost to their owners!"[13]

Calhoun's sentiments exactly. Thus, when the new secretary of state received a note from British Minister Richard Pakenham, he used his reply to instruct the envoy. Slavery, wrote Calhoun, was being misrepresented. It was not an institution of brutality and force, but of piety and love which benefited master and slave alike. Moreover, the U.S. government was obliged to defend the institution, would do so, and intended to annex Texas to keep Britain from undertaking, via diplomacy, to free its slaves.[14]

Calhoun's letter found its way into the press, and North and West were suddenly arrayed against the South—over Texas. In a thundering oration to the young men of Boston, Adams came close to calling for a civil war of emancipation:

> Your trial is approaching. The spirit of freedom and the spirit of slavery are drawing together for the deadly conflict of arms. The annexation of Texas to this union is the blast of the trumpet for a foreign, civil, servile, and Indian war, of which the government of your country, fallen into faithless hands, have already twice given the signal—first by a shameless treaty, rejected by a virtuous senate; and again by the glove of defiance, hurled by the apostle of nullification, at the avowed policy of the British empire peacefully to promote the extinction of slavery throughout the world. Young men of Boston: burnish your armor, prepare for the conflict, and I say to you, in the language of Calgacus to the ancient Britons, think of your forefathers! Think of your posterity![15]

Tyler's treaty went down to crushing defeat. With a two-thirds Senate vote needed for approval, the annexation of Texas was rejected, 35–16—more than two-to-one against.

THE DARK HORSE

Jackson was sick: "I fear Texas is gone from us and in the embrace of England. Houston has been most cruelly treated." He poured out his contempt on "those craven hearted Senators, Traitors to the best interests of our country, and to our Glorious Union.... [Must we now] go to war with England and France, to gain Texas, offered to us in peace and honorable terms, [and] rejected for political effect...?"[16] Old Hickory saw in Britain's maneuvers a violation of the Monroe Doctrine. The Empire was seeking a protectorate in Texas, Jackson believed, a satellite nation set down in the path of his Union.

As the election of 1844 approached, the divisions grew bitter and deep. Texas was "the all absorbing question, stronger even than the presidential," said Calhoun. "If lost now, it will be forever lost; and, if that, the South will be lost."[17] Dixie "fire-eaters" were talking "Texas or disunion!"

Jackson had written off Clay, the probable Whig candidate, as "a dead political Duck!" when he learned that Clay was opposed to annexation.[18] Then, Jackson was handed a letter written by his successor, Van Buren. Angling to return to the White House, Van Buren, now the front-runner for his party's nomination, had joined Clay in opposition to annexation, to remove the divisive issue from the election. Certain his old friend and protégé would ride the Texas issue back into the White House, Jackson could not believe what he was reading. "It's a forgery," he raged. "Mr. Van Buren never wrote such a letter."[19] Unfortunately, Mr. Van Buren had.

In Jackson's eyes, Van Buren had to change his position. But the man from Kinderhook refused. Jackson wrote to Francis P. Blair, editor of the *Globe*, which had published the Van Buren letter:

> I am quite sick really, and have been ever since I read V.B. letter.... Texas [is]... the... key to our future safety.... We cannot bear that Great Britain should have a Canedy on our west as

she has on the north…. Some good democrat must be selected
with Polk [as Vice President]…. [C]an Wright be brought out
and will he pledge himself, will Woodbury, or Buchannan.[20]

James K. Polk's supporters were calling regularly at the Hermitage, and the Tennessean had pledged to conduct a campaign on the
issues dearest to Jackson's heart: annexation of Texas and the settlement of the Oregon boundary dispute in favor of the United States.

As the Baltimore convention opened, Van Buren had a majority,
but Senator Robert J. Walker of Mississippi pushed through a rule
requiring support of two-thirds of the delegates for nomination. The
hurdle was too high for the Little Magician. The convention dead-
locked, and history's first "dark horse" emerged. Backroom king-
makers stitched together a ticket of Polk and George Dallas of
Pennsylvania. The convention chant began: "Polk and Dallas! Texas
and Oregon!"

Polk carried the convention and, narrowly, the election. But
from November to March, Tyler was still president and determined
to annex Texas to secure his place in history. The British, meanwhile,
worked feverishly to create the satellite state of Jackson's fears.
Foreign Secretary Lord Aberdeen hatched a plan to have Britain,
France, and Mexico sign a treaty guaranteeing the independence of
Texas; but France was fearful of offending the United States, and
Mexico dithered. "You always do everything too late," an exasperated
Aberdeen told the Mexican minister.[21] In years past, Texans would
have welcomed a guarantee of independence, but were no longer
interested. They had lived for a decade under a Mexican threat, and
preferred to nest under the Eagle's wings than rely on the word of a
Mexican government or the distant power of a British fleet.

Unable to win a two-thirds vote for a treaty, Tyler settled for a
joint resolution of Congress by simple majorities in each house.
Annexation passed in Tyler's final hours as president.

Jackson had been right. An independent and free-trade Texas, supported by Britain and France, would have blocked America's expansion to the Pacific, lured the southern states away from the North,
and been in endless conflict with the Union over smuggled goods,
fugitive slaves, and imports that circumvented Union tariffs. "Let us
take [Texas] now," the old general thundered, "and lock the door
against future danger."[22] America did.

Jackson's life's work was now over. As he wrote a friend, "I have
the pleasure to inform you that Polk and Dallas are elected and the
Republic is safe.... I am now like Simeon of old; having seen my
country safe, I am prepared to depart in peace.... I await with resig-
nation the call of my God."[23] On June 8, 1845, the call came:

> At dusk a coach drawn by galloping horses careened into the
> Hermitage drive. A travel-stained arresting figure dismounted,
> leading a very small boy by the hand. The newcomer towered
> half a head above the next tallest man present. Not everyone at
> first recognized Sam Houston.
>
> The greatest of Old Hickory's expeditionary captains stood
> motionless before the candle-lit couch of death. Then he
> dropped to his knees, and sobbing, buried his face on his chief-
> tain's breast.
>
> The proprietor of the Texas Republic drew the boy to his
> side.
>
> "My son, try to remember that you have looked on the face
> of Andrew Jackson."[24]

POLK'S PATIENCE RUNS OUT

Texas now belonged to the United States. But Polk's ambitions did
not end at the Rio Grande. His eyes were on California. To negotiate its purchase and resolve a dispute over the Texas border, the
president authorized John Slidell to go to Mexico City. Mexico

insisted that Texas's border was the Nueces River; the Texans held it to be 120 miles further south, at the Rio Grande. The disputed territory amounted to scores of thousands of square miles. When Slidell's mission became public, he was rudely treated by the Mexican government and denounced by a fiercely nationalist Mexican press. "Be assured," Slidell wrote Polk, "nothing is to be done with these people until they shall have been chastised."[25] Polk had reached the same conclusion.

When a revolution erupted in Mexico, vaulting to power a faction led by General Mariano Paredes that was spoiling for a fight with the United States, Polk decided to settle the boundary dispute—by force if necessary. He ordered Brigadier General Zachary Taylor to the Rio Grande. "Old Rough and Ready" marched to the river and built a fort overlooking Matamoros. On April 11, 1846, Mexican General Pedro Ampudia arrived on the opposite bank with three thousand troops and demanded Taylor's withdrawal. Old Rough and Ready responded by blockading the river. Hotheads in Mexico City were clamoring for an invasion to recapture Texas, and the minister of war had predicted his army would have an easy time of it, as it would face only "some miserable colonists, a few hundred adventurers, and a handful of speculators from New Orleans and New York."[26]

At a May 9 cabinet meeting Polk discussed a declaration of war on Mexico for defaulting on its debts and for its treatment of the Slidell mission. Secretary of State James Buchanan, an ardent expansionist along with the rest of the cabinet, was not averse to war, but wanted to maneuver Mexico into firing the first shot. That night, word came from Taylor that on April 25 Mexican troops had crossed the Rio Grande and fired on his men, killing sixteen. Two days before, Mexico's president had declared a "defensive war" on the United States.[27] His cabinet now united, Polk drafted a war message and sent it to Congress on May 11. What he wrote was not a wholly objective rendering of recent events:

> The cup of forbearance had been exhausted even before the recent information from the frontier.... But now, after reiterated menaces, Mexico has passed the boundary of the United States, has invaded our territory and shed American blood upon the American soil. She has proclaimed that hostilities have commenced, and that the two nations are now at war.
>
> As war exists, and, notwithstanding all our efforts to avoid it, exists by the act of Mexico herself, we are called upon by every consideration of duty and patriotism to vindicate with decision the honor, the rights, and the interests of our country.[28]

News of U.S. casualties inflamed Congress, and President Polk's declaration was cheered through the House, 174–14. The Senate vote was 40–2. "Destiny beckons us to hold and civilize Mexico," said Buchanan.

Begun with patriotic passion, the Mexican War would come to be denounced as "Jimmy Polk's War" by Whigs and abolitionists who saw in it a plot to expand the slave states. One congressman called it "unholy, unrighteous, and damnable." Were he a Mexican, said Ohio Senator Thomas Corwin, he would say to Americans: "Have you not room in your own country to bury your dead men? If you come into mine, we will greet you with bloody hands; and welcome you to hospitable graves."[29]

In 1847 a newly elected congressman from Illinois introduced what came to be known as the "spot" resolution, demanding to know the exact spot on which Americans had been fired upon. Representative Abraham Lincoln's "spot" was not for certain on "American soil," as Polk had asserted; it was on the U.S.-claimed territory that was in dispute. But if the U.S. Army was on disputed land, so was the Mexican army—and the Mexicans had fired first and drawn first blood. The truth: Polk was determined to hold Texas to the Rio Grande and keep California out of the clutches of the British, who had eyes on the prize, even at the price of war. "The vision of golden California as part of the United States," wrote one historian, "was the real cause of the Mexican war."[30] But as the Slidell mission demonstrated, Polk always wanted a peaceful annexation of Texas and purchase of California.

HUBRIS IN MEXICO CITY

Mexico, with an army five times the size of the U.S. Army, and a press even more bellicose, had gravely miscalculated. It assumed that Polk's desire for negotiations meant the Americans were afraid to fight. The British press encouraged Mexico in its hubris. As "an aggressive power," sniffed the weekly *Britannia*, America "is one of the weakest in the world… fit for nothing but to fight Indians." The *Times* of London echoed the contempt: "The invasion and conquest of a vast region by a State which is without an army and without credit, is a novelty in the history of nations."[31]

That Polk desired a peaceful resolution of the conflict is evident from his acceptance of a plea from President Santa Anna, who had been impeached and banished to Cuba. The Butcher of the Alamo asked to be allowed to return to Mexico to negotiate a settlement. Polk ordered the scoundrel passed through the U.S. blockade. Once home, Santa Anna rallied to the Mexican cause and called for the expulsion of the Americans.

Polk concluded that, to end the conflict, the United States had to seize all disputed territory and dictate terms. Zachary Taylor's army pushed deep into northern Mexico, where it routed Santa Anna's at Buena Vista in "a splendid picture-book battle on a sun-soaked plain" where Taylor's son-in-law, Colonel Jefferson Davis, distinguished himself by breaking up a Mexican cavalry charge.[32] Colonel Stephen Kearny moved out of Fort Leavenworth, captured Santa Fe, and drove west to San Diego and Los Angeles. Commodore J. D. Sloat had already occupied Monterey and declared California part of the United States. Sloat acted on secret orders from the secretary of the navy to strike instantly if he heard "with certainty" war had broken out.[33] Fifty years later, Commodore George Dewey would receive identical orders from Assistant Secretary of the Navy Theodore Roosevelt.

Polk now held all the land he wanted, but the Mexicans were still full of fight. The president determined that to end the war he had to occupy the enemy capital. An army under Major General Winfield Scott was sent by ship to Veracruz. It seized the city in three days and set out on the road trod three centuries before by Cortés.

Polk was by now feeling the scorching heat of a Whig press and a House of Representatives that in January 1848 voted to denounce the war as "unnecessarily and unconstitutionally begun by the President of the United States."[34] Henry David Thoreau protested in Massachusetts by refusing to pay his state poll tax. After he spent one night in the lockup, Thoreau's aunt came and paid the tax. He retreated to his cabin on Walden Pond to write *Civil Disobedience*.

In Mexico, things were going much better. In a brilliant feat of generalship, Scott fought his way, six battles in five months, to the Mexican capital. Among his officers were Captains Robert E. Lee and George B. McClellan, and Lieutenant Ulysses S. Grant. Lee had made possible Scott's movement to flank the Mexicans at Cerro Gordo. Now, for the first time in history, the Stars and Stripes flew over a foreign capital.

Traveling with Scott was Nicholas P. Trist, chief clerk of the State Department, whom Polk had authorized to negotiate. Trist was now busy writing himself a page in history. Though orders had been sent to Scott recalling him, Trist ignored them and returned with the Treaty of Guadalupe Hidalgo, which transferred to the United States all of Texas and the northern half of Mexico, 1.2 million square miles, including California. Mexico's debts up to $3.25 million were to be taken over by the United States, and the Mexican government was to be paid an additional $15 million.

Polk accepted. On February 21, 1848, the day that Trist's treaty arrived at the Senate, John Quincy Adams, who had served his nation for five decades, suffered a paralytic stroke in the House chamber. The voice of the "Old Roman" would never be heard again.[35]

Suspicious, jealous of rivals, not given to sharing credit, Polk fired poor Trist and replaced Scott with a Democratic major general.[36] But the Senate approved what was now Polk's treaty 38–14, and the Mexican War was history. Though he had enlarged U.S. territory by an area as great as Louisiana, some Americans expressed disappointment that Polk had not annexed Mexico. They were wrong. Manifest Destiny was never about imposing American rule on alien peoples; it was about extending the frontiers of American liberty and freedom.

Even as he was going to war, Polk was negotiating a settlement with Britain over the Oregon territory, which extended from the northern boundary of today's California to the southern tip of Alaska, from the Rockies to the Pacific, an immense tract equal in size to Great Britain, Ireland, France, Germany, Austria, Holland, and Belgium combined.[37] The British agreed to split the land at the 49th parallel.

Thus did James K. Polk give his country clear title to Texas, virtually all of New Mexico and Arizona, Nevada, California, Oregon, Idaho, and Washington, and vast tracts of Kansas, Oklahoma, Colorado, Utah, and Wyoming. He had pledged to serve one term and kept his word. In four years he had done all he had promised Old Hickory.

"My... great labor has exceedingly exhausted me," the small and sad-faced man wrote in his diary.[38] Pledges fulfilled, his nation almost doubled in size, the "last man of yesterday" went home to Tennessee in March 1849, and, within a hundred days, Young Hickory was dead—the most underrated president in American history.

IMPERIALISM OR MANIFEST DESTINY?

Again, then, the questions: Were Texas, the Southwest, and California the fruits of some great crime? Was the Mexican War a war of aggression against a weak and vulnerable neighbor? Was it "the most unjust war in history"? The answer to all three is no.

Texas had won its independence honorably in 1836 in a struggle for freedom from a brutal dictatorship. Texas's rebellion was as legitimate as the Mexican revolution of 1821. Americans in Texas outnumbered the Mexicans ten-to-one in 1835, and had a right to declare independence of a distant tyranny and create a government of their own choosing. While the United States had hardly been neutral in Texas's war of independence, these were, after all, Americans fighting Mexicans.

Moreover, the United States waited nine years before acceding to Houston's entreaties for annexation. Not once in those years had Mexico made a serious attempt to recapture its lost province. By 1845 Texas's independence had been recognized by the United States, Britain, and France, and Mexico's rights there were no greater than British rights in Virginia in 1789. As an independent republic, Texas had the right to determine its own destiny and America a right to accept its plea to enter a union of free and independent states.

The Mexican War was not begun by U.S. soldiers on Mexican soil, but by Mexican soldiers on disputed land that Santa Anna had signed away to the Texans. Mexicans had fired the first shots and inflicted the first casualties. Assuming that Polk's desire for negotiations meant he would shrink from war, Mexico underestimated him and the fighting spirit of the U.S. Army. As has often proven true, it is not the size of the dog in the fight, it is the size of the fight in the dog. The Mexicans belatedly came to appreciate Tocqueville's insight: "The truth is well understood in the United States as anywhere else: the Americans are already able to make their flag respected; in a few years they will make it feared."[39]

As for the hoary claim, widely believed at the time, that Texas's war of independence and its annexation were part of some "slaveholders' plot," historians have found nothing to substantiate it.

Adams, who raged that annexation was grounds for secession, had himself sought to purchase Texas in 1825. Most Americans wanted Texas for the same reason they had wanted Florida, Louisiana, the Southwest, California, and Oregon—to expand to the continental limits. America's appetite for contiguous land was insatiable.

Mexicans who believe the United States robbed their nation when it was weak must reconcile that charge with Mexico City's snapping up of a cash offer in 1853 for a huge swath of its territory. In the Gadsden Purchase of Franklin Pierce and his agent James Gadsden, Mexico sold to the United States, for $10 million, the Gila River Valley of New Mexico and Arizona. Pierce wanted the 29,640 square miles (an area twice the size of Massachusetts, Rhode Island, and Connecticut combined) for a southern railroad to California. A greedy Mexican regime offered to sell Pierce even more land. Only congressional niggling prevented us from acquiring Baja California for another $10 million.[40] Congress did not want it at that price, and, as always, there was the Yankee fear that this would mean still more slave states.

Annexation of Texas, the Southwest, and California was Manifest Destiny, not imperialism. These lands were contiguous, largely empty, easily defensible with a small army, and involved no entanglement with the great powers of Europe. Imperialism is the rule of other peoples against their will, and most Americans recoiled at the idea of colonizing Mexico or making Mexicans a subject people. Warned Calhoun, "Mexico is to us the forbidden fruit; the penalty of eating it would be to subject our institutions to political death."[41]

Out of the vast open territory taken from Mexico would be created half a dozen states. Each would enter the Union with the same rights as the original thirteen. Every citizen of those states, including those of Spanish heritage and Mexican descent, would become full citizens of the United States. Spanish loyalists in California, who had rebelled against Mexican governors sent north, preferred Americans as overlords. Indian tribes like the Pueblos rejoiced that they now had Americans, rather than indifferent Mexicans, to defend them from roving Apaches. The Mexican War was a historic inevitability. Two emerging countries collided along a disputed frontier, and the stronger prevailed.

Was Washington's admonition against foreign wars violated by the Mexican War? The opposite is true. Texas was on our continent, its annexation as natural an acquisition as the taking of the North-west Territory, Louisiana, and Florida.

British intrigue had played a role in the Texas affair and been much on the minds of Jackson and Polk. Just as the British, after the burning of Washington in 1814, had sought to impose on the defeated Americans an Indian buffer state in the Ohio Valley, so, in backing an independent Texas, the British had sought to block America's expansion. Jackson sensed that British enthusiasm for an independent Texas was born of traditional British policy—to "contain" America, to keep it divided and weak, to get around the U.S. tariff, and to use trade to draw the South into the imperial orbit and pull the Republic apart. Another clever scheme by our endlessly scheming cousins, but it blew up in the face of the Foreign Office when Polk accepted war to accomplish everything the British were trying to prevent.

So it was that Jackson died at peace with himself and his God, six decades after a British officer had slashed a fourteen-year-old boy's hand and head for refusing to shine his boots.

"MASTERLY INACTIVITY"—ABROAD

In the last year of the Mexican War, revolutions shook every throne in Europe. Caught up in the events, captivated by the spirit of the times, America yet remained true to Washington's legacy. When the leader of Hungary's struggle for independence, Louis Kossuth, came seeking United States recognition for Hungary's independence and the dispatch of U.S. warships to the Mediterranean to keep the tsar at bay, he was wildly feted in every city he visited. But he departed only with America's cheers, not with any commitment to act. Calhoun and Clay stood together in opposition to aiding Kossuth— and to any break with Vienna. Both opposed intervention in Europe. Said Clay:

> Far better is it for ourselves, for Hungary, and for the cause
> of liberty, that, adhering to our wise, pacific system, and avoiding
> the distant wars of Europe, we should keep our lamp burning
> brightly on this western shore as a light to all nations, than
> to hazard its utter extinction amid the ruins of fallen or falling
> republics in Europe.[42]

Calhoun called for a "masterly inactivity" toward Europe: "If we remain quiet… and let our destinies work out their own results, we shall do more for liberty, not only for ourselves but for the example of mankind, than can be done by a thousand victories."[43] For the first time, the term "isolationist" was thrown into the faces of those opposed to breaking ties with Vienna.

Secretary of State Daniel Webster, however, sensed the political sentiment and, with an eye on the presidential prize that had eluded him, played the nationalist card. When the Austrian chargé in Washington, Chevalier J. G. Huelsemann, protested U.S. support for Kossuth, he was made the recipient of a towering insult, forever known as the Huelsemann Note. Seeking to arouse the national pride, Webster declared in a bombastic boast that the events in Hungary "appeared to have their origin in those great ideas of responsible and popular government on which the American consti-tutions themselves are founded." Webster went on to instruct the ancient House of Hapsburg:

> The power of this republic at the present moment is spread over
> a region one of the richest and most fertile on the globe, and of

> an extent in comparison with which the possessions of the
> house of Hapsburg are but as a patch on the earth's surface.[44]

Austria demanded Webster's ouster, but President Millard Fillmore refused. Webster's push for intervention failed, however, just as he had failed three decades before when he had sought U.S. intervention on the side of Greece in its struggle for independence from the Turks. John Randolph had then risen in Congress to excoriate Webster for his notion that the United States should intervene on behalf of liberty all over the world as breaching "every bulwark and barrier of the Constitution."[45] Stop looking for our assistance, Randolph admonished the Greeks, and look rather to America's example: "Let us say to those seven millions of Greeks, 'We defended ourselves, when we were but three millions, against a Power, in comparison to which the Turk is but as a lamb. Go and do thou likewise.'"[46]

The most passionate champions of intervention against monarchy in Europe were German and Irish immigrants who flocked into the "Young America" movement and Democratic Party that nominated Franklin Pierce in 1852. British Minister John Crampton described Young America as made up of those

> who possess extreme democratic doctrines in the usual sense of
> the word...; and also those who urge it to be a duty, as well as
> the true policy of the United States to intervene in the affairs of
> Foreign Nations in support of Democratic and Republican
> Principles.[47]

Crusaders for "global democracy" may trace their lineage to Young America. But such doctrines depart from the teachings of Washington. It was Clay and Calhoun, not the ambitious secretary of state, who remained true to the "great rule."

CHAPTER 9

"One War at a Time"

Who does not see, then, that…
the Pacific Ocean, its shores, its islands, and the
vast regions beyond, will become the chief theatre of
events in the world's great hereafter?[1]
—WILLIAM H. SEWARD, 1852

Not even 1814, with the burning of Washington, was as ominous a year as 1861. When Lincoln took the oath, South Carolina, Georgia, and all five Gulf states had seceded. On April 11, in response to Lincoln's resupply of Fort Sumter (against the advice of Winfield Scott and most of his cabinet), the South Carolinians opened fire.

President Lincoln issued a call for 75,000 volunteers to bring the "erring sisters" home, in chains if necessary. Four southern states that had remained loyal—Virginia, North Carolina, Tennessee, and Arkansas—refused to join a war against their kinsmen and seceded to join the rebellion.

On April 19 Lincoln declared a blockade of the South; Britain instantly recognized a state of belligerency, declared neutrality, and claimed its rights as a neutral. The Union was stunned. As one English writer put it, Lincoln forced London's hand: "The Northern party in fact demanded that we should recognize a state of war by admitting their blockade, and at the same time deny a state of war by treating Southern vessels as pirates."[2] Napoleon III seized the opportunity to turn Mexico into a vassal state.

Americans are familiar with the story of how this iron-willed president persevered through four years of bloodletting. Less well
known is the story of Lincoln's diplomacy, which was indispensable to Union victory.

During four years of war, there was one overriding foreign
policy objective of the Confederacy: win Europe's recognition and
British aid in breaking the blockade. The goal of Union diplomacy
was thus to prevent European recognition of the South. Jefferson
Davis's failure would be Abraham Lincoln's triumph, and the triumph of the rival he had chosen as secretary of state—William H.
Seward. Indispensable to their success was Charles Francis Adams,
son and grandson of presidents and the third Adams to serve as
minister to the Court of St. James.

As remembered by Charles's brother, Henry Adams, Seward was a
"slouching, slender figure" with a "head like a wise Macaw; a
beaked nose; shaggy eyebrows; unorderly hair and clothes; hoarse
voice; offhand manner; free talk, and perpetual cigar."[3] A militant
abolitionist, and governor and senator from New York who had
lost the nomination to Lincoln, Seward believed he was Lincoln's
superior in accomplishments and leadership and looked to a
tenure as prime minister to a figurehead president. But his stew-
ardship of foreign policy did not begin on an auspicious note.

On April 1 Seward presented Lincoln with his plan to restore
the Union titled "Some Thoughts for the President's Consider-
ation." Wrote Seward, "We are at the end of a month's administration and yet without a policy either domestic or foreign."[4] His
proposal: The Union should adopt a policy of hostility, even war,
against France, Britain, Spain, or Russia to stoke the fires of patriotism, bring America together, and arrest the plunge toward civil war.
Lincoln pocketed Seward's "Thoughts," which would come to be
known as the April Fools' Day proposition.

THE *TRENT* AFFAIR

To convince Europe to recognize the South, Davis dispatched as special commissioners to London and Paris James M. Mason of Virginia and John Slidell of Louisiana. Slidell had headed Polk's mission to Mexico before the war of 1846. Slipping the blockade at Charleston, the agents sailed to Havana, where they boarded the British steamer *Trent* for the neutral Danish West Indies port of St. Thomas. From there, they expected to sail to England.

On hearing that Mason and Slidell were aboard the *Trent*, Captain Charles Wilkes of the Union sloop *San Jacinto* intercepted it in the Bahama strait, fired two shots across its bow, boarded the ship, collared Slidell as he tried to escape through a porthole, and sailed for Boston, where the pair was incarcerated at Fort Warren. Wilkes was a national hero, and the nation, desperate for good news after the defeat at the battle of Bull Run, roared its approval. As Charles Francis Adams, Jr., would write, long after the affair:

> I do not remember in the whole course of the half-century's
> retrospect... any occurrence in which the American people
> were so completely swept off their feet, for the moment losing
> possession of their senses, as during the weeks which immedi-
> ately followed the seizure of Mason and Slidell.[5]

But Great Britain—forgetting how, a half century before, it had seized American sailors off merchant ships and impressed them into His Majesty's service—was enraged. To the British government, Mason and Slidell had been kidnapped from aboard a British ship, and Wilkes had committed an act of piracy. The Royal Navy cleared its decks for action, and eight thousand British troops boarded transports for Canada.

Queen Victoria warned a war would result in "utter destruction to the North Americans," and Lord Palmerston, Britian's prime minister, drew up an ultimatum.[6] Only intervention by a dying Prince Albert, the queen's consort, succeeded in toning it down. The situation was grave. Charles Francis Adams wrote that the British were "now all lashed up into hostility," and that the "leading newspapers roll out as much fiery lava as Vesuvius is doing, daily. The Clubs and the army and the navy and the people in the streets generally are raving for war."[7] An American resident in London wrote Seward:

> There never was within memory such a burst of feeling as has been created by the news of the boarding of [the *Trent*]. The people are frantic with rage, and were the country polled, I fear 999 men out of a thousand would declare for immediate war. Lord Palmerston cannot resist the impulse if he would.[8]

Henry Adams wrote his brother back home, "This nation means to make war. Do not doubt it."[9]

Lincoln had reveled in the seizure of Mason and Slidell, but was instantly aware of the awful implications if he did not find some way to back down. The Union was isolated, almost friendless. Official Europe detested America for its trumpeting of republicanism against monarchy, and for its rude seizures of the remnants of Europe's American empires. In the *Trent* affair, the continent sided with Great Britain. In seizing Mason and Slidell—and not bringing the *Trent* into port to remove its contraband and ask for judgment by a prize court—Wilkes had violated international law. It smacked of impressment, though Mason and Slidell had enjoyed the hospitality of Wilkes's table on the voyage to Boston.

President Lincoln knew that any clash with a European power could mean loss of the objective that consumed his every waking hour: restoration of the Union. "One war at a time," he cautioned Seward.[10]

On Christmas day, 1861, the cabinet met and voted unanimously to release Slidell and Mason. Had Lincoln and his men not done so, it would have meant war, the Royal Navy's shattering of the blockade, destruction of the Union navy, and victory for the South. Seward covered America's retreat with a December 26 letter claiming victory in that England had, after fifty years, accepted the American principle on impressment.

Only because Lincoln backed down did the Union avoid war. For the British were as anxious to drive a knife into the back of the Union in the fight of its life as Americans had been to drive a knife into the back of Britain in 1812. As Charles Beard wrote, in 1861 Great Britain was dominated by a "Tory class that profoundly hoped for the destruction of the American Republic."[11] The bristling hostility between the two great nations with more in common than any others on earth was proof of the wisdom of Washington, who had warned in his Farewell Address, "there can be no greater error than to expect, or calculate upon real favours from Nations."[12]

Throughout 1861 and 1862, with battle after battle ending in Union defeat, Britain toyed with recognizing the South. But Seward, almost surely bluffing, warned that recognition meant war. Should Europeans even attempt mediation, he wrote in July 1862, "this civil war will, without our fault, become a war of continents—a war of the world."[13] Implied threat: If Britain recognized the Confederacy, the United States would invade Canada.

Anxious to recognize the South and to effect a permanent breakup of the Union, Palmerston was looking for a Southern victory that would point to the rebellion's ultimate triumph. It was in part to win recognition by the British that Lee's Army of Northern Virginia crossed the Potomac and met McClellan's at Antietam Creek in the bloodiest battle in American history. When Lee retreated back across the Potomac, the Confederacy's best chance of European recognition had passed.

THE LAIRD RAMS

Lincoln's appeasement in the *Trent* affair paid off. By the time the second crisis with Great Britain occurred, the Union army was a mighty instrument of war and Lincoln was on his way to a thousand-ship navy.

The initial blockade of the South had been feeble, but it began to tighten as new Union warships came on line. The South's counterstrategy was to build privateers in foreign shipyards to roam the oceans and drive Union shipping from the seas. Under their own neutrality laws, the British were forbidden from equipping and arming privateers, but ships could be built in British yards, ostensibly for nations at peace, then sail off to where they could take on their cannons and Confederate identity.

When the *Oreto*, supposedly built for a firm in Italy, slipped out of England and took aboard its guns in Nassau, rechristened as the *Florida*, Adams protested to Foreign Secretary Earl Russell and provided evidence that another sloop being built in British yards was a Confederate raider. Russell agreed to block the vessel from sailing. But the British official responsible for signing the papers to halt the departure suffered a stroke. The ship slipped out to the Azores, where she took aboard British cannons and a British crew to become the most successful raider in history—the *Alabama*. Davis's raiders would sink or burn more than 250 Union ships.

Now something even more ominous to the Union than the raiders appeared. The Confederacy had ordered from William Laird & Sons two ships of 1,500 tons, covered by four-and-a-half inches of iron plate, with a seven-foot "piercer" extending from the prow, three feet below the water line. Purpose: ram, pierce, and sink wooden warships. If the Laird rams reached the Confederacy, many feared the Union blockade was history and the South would prevail. "We have no defense against them," warned the secretary of the navy. "It is a matter of life and death."[14]

With the **Alabama** *incident in mind,* Adams did not mince words. On September 5, 1863, he wrote Russell a note with the compelling line, "It would be superfluous in me to point out to your Lordship that this [the escape of the rams] is war."[15] Within days, the British had blocked their departure and bought both rams for the Royal Navy.

How close did the Union come to war with Great Britain in 1863? Historians have found that Russell, on September 3, informed Palmerston he was seizing the rams, and did so on September 8, three days after Adams's note. And read in its entirety, the Adams note did not exactly threaten war. But had the rams reached the Confederacy, there would have been a crisis in U.S.-British relations as grave as the *Trent* affair, and by this time the Union was not inclined to back down. Since the seizure of Mason and Slidell and the escapes of the *Florida* and *Alabama*, much had changed to cause Palmerston's government to show greater respect for the United States. Lincoln's army was no longer the rabble of Manassas, but the huge and blooded army of Gettysburg. In the event of war, the U.S. Navy would now give the Royal Navy a hellish fight, and Canada would have been an easy march for the Army of the Potomac.

Union victories and Union power had fortified Lincoln's diplomacy.

"GET YOUR LEGS UNDER NAPOLEON'S MAHOGANY"

With the United States preoccupied, Europe felt free to exploit the U.S.'s inability to enforce its Monroe Doctrine. The target: Mexico.

Benito Juarez, a full-blooded Indian, had taken power in January 1861 and defaulted on Mexico's debts. France, owed 40 million francs, supported by Britain and Spain, sent an army to collect. Behind the cover of debt collection lay a strategic French goal.

Napoleon III wanted to alter the balance of power in the New World by creating a Catholic monarchy and ally on the border of Texas to block further expansion by the Americans.

Britain had sent only a token force, and, with Spain, dropped out of the game in 1862, leaving Napoleon to play out the hand. Conquering Mexico proved more difficult than anticipated; at Puebla, French troops suffered a major defeat. But on June 7, 1863, Napoleon's army entered Mexico City. The French general called together a Council of Notables, who dutifully voted to invite to Mexico to become their new emperor the Austrian Archduke Maximilian, the brother of Franz Joseph, who had been pre-selected by Napoleon before the French troops had set sail.

Napoleon's scheme to take advantage of the sundering of the United States is understandable, but by mid-1863 the emperor should have seen that a victorious Union would command a million-man army to enforce the Monroe Doctrine. Yet he plunged ahead with his Mexican adventure, and on May 28, 1864, the archduke and his wife, Carlotta, arrived in Vera Cruz.

Seward had repeatedly made known to Paris the U.S. attitude toward what was happening in Mexico. Not once, however, did he mention the Monroe Doctrine. The author of the April Fools' Day proposition was now a seasoned diplomat following Lincoln's counsel, "One war at a time." When a U.S. diplomat in Paris, John Bigelow, urged Seward to use tougher rhetoric with the emperor, the secretary shot back:

> With our land and naval forces in Louisiana retreating before
> the rebels instead of marching to Mexico, this is not the most
> suitable time for offering idle menaces to the Emperor of
> France. We have compromised nothing, surrendered nothing
> and I do not propose to surrender anything. But why should

we gasconade about Mexico when we are in a struggle for
our own life?[16]

After Appomattox, Seward became direct, and Andrew Johnson,
at the urging of Generals Grant and Sherman, sent forty thousand
American troops to the border. Juarez's agents were urging intervention. Instead, Seward called in General John Schofield, who had
wanted to lead an army of volunteers into Mexico, made him a special emissary to France, and gave him his marching orders: "I want
you to get your legs under Napoleon's mahogany and tell him he
must get out of Mexico."[17]

In January 1866 Napoleon agreed to evacuate the first contingent of troops in November. He then reversed himself, saying
the troops would leave in the spring of 1867. Seward sent a long
cable to Paris: Not soon enough. Napoleon got the message.
French forces began to pull out. Maximilian should have departed
with them, but the proud, stubborn, young monarch now believed
Mexico was his country. In 1867 he was captured. Spain urged the
secretary of state to intercede with the Mexicans to spare him.
Replied Seward, while crunching a radish, "His life is quite as safe
as yours and mine."[18] Juarez put Maximilian before a firing squad
as a lesson to Europe to leave his country alone.

THE PARAGON OF MANIFEST DESTINY

[G]ive me fifty, forty, thirty more years of life, and I will
engage to give you the possession of the American continent
and the control of the world.[19]

—William H. Seward, 1867

With the war over and the French out of Mexico, Seward was free
to pursue his vision of Manifest Destiny; his achievements, in the
years left to him, rank him among our greatest secretaries of state.

During the war the Union navy had had a hellish time chasing down Confederate raiders in the Caribbean. So in January 1866, under the guise of a vacation, Seward took a month-long cruise of the islands with an eye to acquiring a naval base. He settled on the first port he visited, St. Thomas. Negotiating with the Danes, Seward cut their price in half to $7.5 million for two of the three islands. Referenda held on both islands showed overwhelming support for transfer to a United States that had just abolished slavery. Seward sent the Danish Treaty up to the Senate, but it became ensnared in the politics of the impeachment of President Johnson and was ultimately rejected.

The Dominican Republic offered itself for sale to the United States, and Seward took up that offer as well. But it, too, was rejected by the Senate. Failing in a bid to buy the Hawaiian Islands, Seward acquired the Midway Islands, a thousand miles to the northwest. But, disliked by the hugely popular 1868 Republican nominee, Ulysses S. Grant, who had called the Danish Treaty a "scheme of Seward's," the secretary was unable to realize his ambitions to annex Cuba, Puerto Rico, St. Bart's, Canada, Greenland, Iceland, and, according to enemies, part of China.

Seward had looked to a revival of Manifest Destiny to give America new land to explore to unite the broken country on some great purpose. There are many reasons for his failures. Some were sound. Believers in the old Republic were willing to annex empty land, but not peoples; they wanted no part of empire. Among other reasons Seward was thwarted are: senatorial hatred of Johnson for resisting a harsher reconstruction of the South, congressional unwillingness to give the president a triumph, the sense the nation was already surfeited with land, and the House's refusal to appropriate money after the enormous expenditures of the war. Also, America was chopping up and selling off its navy, and had no further need of Caribbean bases. But for all his frustrations, Seward wrote his place in history with the acquisition of Alaska—in a night's work.

SEWARD PUTS THE ROOF ON

During the war, most of Europe's powers reveled in the early Union defeats, and the nation felt itself alone. But in 1863 Russian naval squadrons sailed into New York and San Francisco. Spirits soared. The largest nation on earth had come to give moral support to the Union cause. Night after night, the Russian captains and crews were feted and toasted.

The Russian ships, however, had not sailed out of any solidarity with America, but in apprehension of England. The tsar feared his crushing of a Polish rebellion would lead to war with Great Britain and destruction of his fleet. He had ordered the squadrons to seek safe haven in the neutral ports of the United States. Not until the Romanov archives were opened, half a century later, did Americans discover what was behind the gesture. But in 1867 relations between the world's greatest republic and its largest autocracy were warm, for it was believed that Russia, in the line of Oliver Wendell Holmes, "was our friend when the world was our foe."[20]

The two nations also had more in common than their enormous size. Alexander II was the "Tsar Liberator" who had freed the serfs as Lincoln was emancipating the slaves. Both nations also shared a dislike of Great Britain and a fear of its navy.

The tsar knew that in the next war with its archenemy, Russia was powerless to prevent the Royal Navy from seizing Russian America. In the Crimean War, Britain and Russia had agreed to neutralize Alaska; in the next war, the territory would be fair game. An early transfer to the Union, however, would frustrate British ambitions in the Pacific and strengthen its American rival. Moreover, sale to the Yankees would preclude a repeat of what had happened in West Florida and Texas. The Russians, too, were familiar with the "Texas game."

Seward had long had his eye on Alaska. During the war, the raider *Shenandoah* had wrought havoc on the whaling fleets in the far north; Seward also wanted naval outposts there as well as in the Caribbean. When the tsar's minister in Washington, Edouard de Stoeckl, dropped word to a friend of Seward's that the tsar might sell, Seward leaped at the bait. In March 1867 he began to haggle with the Russian minister on a price. The two settled on $7.2 million, $2 million above the tsar's rock-bottom figure; the $200,000 was thrown in as bribe money to grease the sale through a balky Congress.

Stoeckl sent the offer to St. Petersburg. Approval came by cable, and the minister arrived at Seward's house on the evening of March 29 to give him the news and suggest they meet to settle the matter the next day.

Rising from a game of whist, a smiling Seward replied, "Why wait till tomorrow, Mr. Stoeckl? Let us make the treaty tonight."[21] Seward told Stoeckl to be at the State Department by midnight. By 4:00 AM the two had drafted and signed the treaty, transferring 586,000 square miles to the United States. That afternoon it was on its way to the Senate.

Seward had taken the precaution of inviting Charles Sumner, chairman of the Senate committee on foreign relations, to his house—and to the department for the drafting, if he wished. Seward's deference to the prickly Sumner, who disliked him, would ensure the success of his great coup.

Initial reaction to the purchase was shock and rage—"a dark deed done in the night." Americans knew nothing of Alaska, and, believing it to be covered by ice, most mocked the purchase as "Seward's Icebox," "Walrussia," and "Johnson's Polar Bear Garden." Seward was also hated for his loyalty to the president. Some senators told the Russian minister they would vote against the treaty simply to spite the secretary. So hostile was the reaction, Sumner urged Seward at one point to withdraw it, lest a treaty rejection be seen as an affront to a friendly Russia. But Seward was relentless. He provided information on Russian America to the press and invited senators, one by one, to his office to describe the enormous prize and its benefits to the United States.

Public opinion began to turn. On April 7, in a three-hour speech his contemporaries called the capstone of his career, Sumner gave Alaska its name and persuaded the Senate to approve the treaty, 37–2. A motion was made to make the vote unanimous as a gesture to Russia—"the old and faithful friend of the United States."[22]

Seward's problem was now the House, which had to appropriate the $7.2 million. Again the matter of not affronting a friendly Russia, and Seward's depiction of the land's strategic potential, proved decisive. There was another potent argument: If America did not take Alaska, Britain would. But if America snatched it from the British lion's jaws, then British Columbia, caught in a vise between Alaska and the United States, might fall into America's lap like ripened fruit.

When these arguments fell short, Stoeckl went to work. He paid the press for favorable articles on Alaska, hired lobbyists, and finally resorted to bribery. But the decisive argument was that America simply could not throw Alaska back into the face of a friendly tsar. On July 14, 1868, the appropriation passed the House, 113–43. Alaska belonged to America, and William Seward had put the roof on the Republic.

Decisive in the transfer of this majestic land were two events—the arrival of Alexander II's naval squadrons in 1863 and the immense goodwill that generated toward Russia, and the failure of John Wilkes Booth's accomplice to assassinate Seward the night Booth shot Lincoln.

By the time Seward left office, America was a completed nation. From Trist's Treaty of Guadalupe Hidalgo in 1848 to Seward's purchase of Alaska in 1867, Manifest Destiny had given the United

States a vast Pacific frontage and its continental borders. Between Washington's first oath as president and Seward's departure as secretary of state, eighty years elapsed. In that time the country tripled in size, from a nation with Georgia as its southernmost state and the Mississippi River as its western frontier to a continent-wide nation that touched Russia and that, save Russia and China, was the largest on earth. Foremost among the soldiers and statesmen who created that American miracle were Washington, Jefferson, Madison, Jackson, John Quincy Adams, James K. Polk, and William Seward. This was not the fruit of "isolationism."

AMERICA AT THE GREAT DIVIDE

By 1869 four of America's foreign policy traditions had been established, and historian Walter McDougall names them: Exceptionalism, Unilateralism, the Monroe Doctrine, and Manifest Destiny. He writes:

> To qualify as a genuine tradition, a principle or strategy must have commanded solid bipartisan support, outlived the era that gave it birth, entered the permanent lexicon of our national discourse, and continued to resonate with a portion of the American public even during eras when it did not directly inspire policy.[23]

Exceptionalism was the belief that America is a providential nation set apart, "a shining city on a hill," God's country.

Unilateralism was the "great rule" laid down by Washington: America must remain free of permanent alliances, at liberty to determine its own destiny, and stay out of wars where the vital interests of the Republic are not at risk. Only then could liberty, the cause for which America came into being, be assured. Another name for Unilateralism might be taken from John Adams's deathbed toast,

"Independence, Forever!" After Washington's Farewell Address, this idea found its most eloquent exponent in Adams's son, John Quincy Adams.

The Monroe Doctrine held that no alien power shall be permitted to establish a new colony in the hemisphere. To this dogma had been added "Polk's Corollary." When Yucatan cast about to be annexed by some great power, perhaps the British Empire, Polk declared in 1848 that no American land would be permitted to transfer its sovereignty to a foreign power, even by popular referendum.

Manifest Destiny was the idea that America's westward expansion to the Pacific had been ordained by Providence.

By 1869 America was a completed nation. But a coming generation would contend that Manifest Destiny required not just American rule from Panama to the Pole, but also expansion west to Hawaii, the Philippines, even China—as the United States assumed its rightful place among the great imperial powers, acquired distant colonies, and undertook the instruction of alien peoples in the superior American way of life. Thus was Seward, that paragon of Manifest Destiny, a transitional figure. Near manic in his acquisition of territory, Seward, like the turn-of-the-century American imperialists, would accept the burden of ruling alien peoples.

It was under William McKinley, Theodore Roosevelt, and Woodrow Wilson that we would eat of the forbidden fruit of imperialism and go out into the world in search of monsters to destroy— leading to America's involvement in all the great wars of the twentieth century.

PART FOUR

1898–1919:
THE TURNING POINT

CHAPTER 10

"Splendid Little War"

*The great nations are rapidly absorbing for their
future expansion and their present defense all the
waste places of the earth.... As one of the
great nations of the world the United States must not
fall out of the line of march.*[1]

—SENATOR HENRY CABOT LODGE, 1895

*We are face to face with a strange destiny.
The taste of empire is in the mouth of the people even
as the taste of blood in the jungle. It means an
imperial policy, the Republic renascent, taking her
place with the armed nations.*[2]

—*WASHINGTON POST*, 1898

With the hammer blows of Sherman and Grant did Lincoln reforge a Union of free states into a centralized nation. Under William McKinley the nation became an empire. The years from McKinley's annexation of the Philippines in 1898 to Wilson's return from Versailles in 1919 mark the great turning point in U.S. history, when America turned its back on George Washington to join the imperial powers in a mad scramble for global preeminence. Why did it happen? Was it inevitable?

"UNPROTECTED AS A JELLYFISH"

One of the first signs that America was looking outward can be found by looking at its navy. Nine months after Appomattox, the axe and the auctioneer had reduced the Union fleet from 971 ships to 29 ships. Lincoln's mighty navy had been junked. In 1874, during a skirmish with Spain off Cuba, fleet maneuvers in the Gulf of Mexico exposed the U.S. Navy as a "heterogeneous collection of naval trash" and "antiquated and rotting ships."[3] One warship from the modern navy of Chile, which had bested Peru and Bolivia in the Pacific War (1879–1884), could have sunk the entire U.S. Navy. "China's fleet today, if properly manned," quipped Rudyard Kipling, "could waft the entire American navy out of the water and into the blue. The big, fat Republic that is afraid of nothing... is as unprotected as a jellyfish."[4]

In 1882, the year that Egyptian fortifications at Alexandria were pounded to pieces by eighty-ton British naval guns, the USS *Tallapoosa* was run down by a coal barge on the Hudson River. In the rueful observation of Captain Alfred Thayer Mahan, America's prophet of sea power, the U.S. Navy had neither the strength to fight nor the speed to run away.[5]

Yet, by this time, a revolution had begun in naval technology. Steam was replacing sail, and the screw propeller replacing wind. Breech-loading rifled guns were being brought on line as old muzzle-loading smooth-bore cannons were removed from decks. Iron and armored plate were replacing wood.

It was Benjamin Harrison and Grover Cleveland who began to rescue the navy, building first the 7,000-ton battleships of the *Maine* class, then the 10,000-ton *Oregon*-class battleships that boasted speeds up to seventeen knots and carried four thirteen-inch and eight eight-inch guns. In 1898 *Oregon* would sail from Puget Sound around Cape Horn to join the U.S. Atlantic squadron in blockading Santiago.[6]

TWISTING THE LION'S TAIL

In 1895, toward the close of his second term, Cleveland, who had endured the terrible Panic of '93, got caught up in the jingoistic spirit. The British were in a dispute over the border between British Guiana and Venezuela, over a few hundred square miles of jungle. When gold was discovered in the 1880s, the land suddenly acquired value. With the bellicose American press demanding that the United States enforce the Monroe Doctrine, Cleveland's friends told him he had an issue on which he could not lose. "Turn this Venezuela question up or down, North, South, East or West," said one, "and it is a winner."[7]

Tom Paschal of Texas urged Secretary of State Richard Olney to consider how a clash with the British might steal the thunder of the radicals and populists who were clamoring for government action to rein in the robber barons of the Gilded Age: "Why, Mr. Secretary, just think how angry the Anarchistic, socialistic, populistic boil appears on our political surface, and who knows how deep its roots extend or ramify. One cannon shot across the bows of a British boat… will knock more *pus* out of it than would suffice to inoculate and corrupt our people for the next two centuries."[8] Paschal was suggesting, inelegantly, what Henry IV had proposed on his deathbed to his son Prince Hal:

> Therefore, my Harry,
> Be it thy course to busy giddy minds
> With foreign quarrels….[9]

Cleveland decided to intervene on the side of Venezuela. The assignment to draft the message to Britain went to the new secretary of state, Olney, an unbending descendant of Puritans who had made his reputation as an aggressive railroad attorney. Olney's note of July 20, 1895, was arrogant, swaggering, and belligerent. Grossly misrepresenting British conduct in the dispute (Olney probably relied on Venezuelan sources), the note invoked the Monroe Doctrine and declared:

> To-day the United States is practically sovereign on this conti-
> nent, and its fiat is law upon the subjects to which it confines its
> interposition. Why? It is not because of the pure friendship or
> good will felt for it. It is not... because wisdom and justice and
> equity are the invariable characteristics of the dealings of the
> United States. It is because, in addition to all other grounds, its
> infinite resources combined with its isolated position render it
> master of the situation and practically invulnerable as against any
> or all other powers.[10]

"[T]he best thing of the kind I have ever read," chortled Cleveland, who described Olney's note as a "twenty-inch gun" blast.[11] The British were stunned. But their new prime minister, Lord Salisbury, was not a man easily intimidated. He treated Olney's ulti-matum as he might have a challenge to a duel from his tailor. Salisbury took four months to reply. In his return note of November 26, he picked apart Olney's rendition of events like a tenured professor tak-ing apart a freshman term paper, and informed Olney the border dis-pute was none of his business:

> The disputed frontier of Venezuela has nothing to do with any
> of the questions dealt with by President Monroe. It is not a
> question of the colonization by a European Power of any por-
> tion of America. It is not a question of the imposition upon the
> communities of South America of any system of government
> devised in Europe. It is simply the determination of the frontier
> of a British possession which belonged to the Throne of England
> long before the Republic of Venezuela came into existence.[12]

Now it was Cleveland's turn to be stunned. A secretary of state had demanded that Britain accept U.S. arbitration, and the British had told the American the quarrel was none of his concern, and to keep out. The dispute was no longer about a patch of jungle; it was about national honor, and Cleveland was not a man to back down. He sent a strong message to Congress asking for the appointment of a commission to determine the correct boundary. If, after this commission had ruled, Britain attempted to alter the boundary by force, said the president, the United States would consider it "willful aggression" and resist "by every means in its power."

Jingoism swept the country. "WAR IF NECESSARY" roared the *New York Sun*.[13] "I rather hope that the fight will come soon," said Teddy Roosevelt. "The clamor of the peace faction has convinced me that this country needs war."[14] British jingoes were not to be outdone by their bellicose cousins. In a letter to the *Times* of London, novelist and journalist Morley Roberts wrote:

> No Englishman with imperial instincts can look with anything
> but contempt on the Monroe Doctrine. The English and not the
> inhabitants of the United States are the greatest power in the
> two Americas; and no dog of a Republic can open its mouth to
> bark without our good leave.[15]

Fortunately, history intervened with a distraction. In December 1895 there took place in South Africa what has come to be known as the Jameson Raid. At the instigation of Cecil Rhodes, six hundred settlers from the Cape Colony under Dr. Leander Starr Jameson invaded the Boer Republic of the Transvaal to bring all South Africa under British rule. Jameson's raiders were routed and captured, to the great delight and public applause of the kaiser. "Instantly," writes the historian Barbara Tuchman, "every British gaze, like spectators' heads at a tennis match, turned from America to Germany, and British wrath was diverted from President Cleveland, always unlikely in the role of menace, to the Kaiser, who played it so much more suitably."[16]

Voices of reason on both sides of the Atlantic now arose with calls for compromise on Venezuela, and the border question was settled by arbitration. Looking back, a war between the two great English-speaking peoples would have been disastrous. A superior British navy might have ravaged U.S. fleets and shut down U.S. ports, but Britain's defense of vast, vulnerable, and empty Canada from jingoistic and expansionist Americans would have proven no easy task.

As the Venezuela crisis dissolved, a relieved Arthur Balfour declared that a time must come when a statesman even greater than Monroe "will lay down the doctrine that between English-speaking peoples war is impossible."[17] Balfour was right, and the now-forgotten Venezuela incident marked a sea change in British policy that profoundly affected the history of the twentieth century.

THE GREAT RAPPROCHEMENT

From the Boston Tea Party to the Venezuelan imbroglio, American-British relations had undergone repeated crises, often bringing the two nations to the brink of war, and, in 1812, over it. No nation could make America's blood boil more rapidly than Great Britain. Baiting John Bull, twisting the Lion's tail, was a campaign tactic of American politicians as reliable as waving the bloody shirt. Irish-Americans made up a voting bloc that could be depended upon to cheer any politician who offended Great Britain and punish any perceived as too cozy with the Empire.

After the Civil War, Irish-American Fenians had attempted several invasions of Canada to provoke a U.S.-British war they believed would bring independence to Ireland; and throughout the latter half of the nineteenth century, Irish-Americans stood in the path of any rapprochement. In 1896 Republicans would seek to enhance their candidate's appeal with a tract entitled "How McKinley is hated in England."

Toward the century's end, however, the British Empire was being challenged not only by traditional rivals Russia and France, but also by rising powers like Japan, Germany, and the United States. Britain could no longer go it alone in the world, antagonizing whom it pleased. Like other nations, Britain now needed powerful friends, and to the most farsighted of its statesmen, America was a natural ally. For two decades following the Venezuela crisis, Britain courted the Americans. At international conferences, British and U.S. diplomats collaborated; in the Spanish-American War, Britain alone sided with the United States, and America's elite, proud of its blood ties to the great empire, warmly reciprocated.

This wise and patient policy would pay off a thousandfold when the United States would tolerate British interference with trade in World War I, tolerance it would have afforded no other nation. Had there been a U.S.-British clash over Venezuela, with U.S. ships sent to the bottom and U.S. sailors burned and drowned, there might have been no doughboys beside British Tommies in the trenches of France. If Lord North had handled it all rather badly back in the days of the Revolution, the British diplomats who conducted American policy from 1895 to 1914 handled it brilliantly. They had not forgotten the admonition of Palmerston to the House of Commons in 1848:

> It is a narrow policy to suppose that this country or that is to be marked out as the eternal ally or the perpetual enemy.... We have no eternal allies, and we have no eternal enemies. Our interests are eternal and perpetual, and those interests it is our duty to follow.[18]

"BUTCHER WEYLER" COMES TO CUBA

Cleveland's successor was a reluctant imperialist. There will be "no jingo nonsense in my administration," McKinley had written Carl Schurz, the anti-imperialist German-American leader, in 1897.[19] In his inaugural address the new president placed himself in the tradition of Washington:

> We have cherished the policy of non-interference with the
> affairs of foreign governments wisely inaugurated by Washington,
> keeping ourselves free from entanglement, either as allies or foes,
> content to leave undisturbed with them the settlement of their
> own domestic concerns.... We want no wars of conquest; we
> must avoid the temptation of territorial aggression.[20]

Yet McKinley, too, would yield to the tides of history—to become America's first imperialist president. How did it happen?

Cuba had been a Spanish colony for four hundred years. The "Ever-Faithful Isle" had remained loyal when Spain's other American colonies had broken away. But Cuban revolutionaries were now determined to drive Spain out and had adopted a "scorched earth" strategy, devastating the island to force a Spanish withdrawal, because Madrid could not afford to hold on. Hoping that chaos would bring intervention, the rebels burned American property, shook down U.S. planters, and dynamited passenger trains.

Madrid's answer was General Valeriano Weyler, who arrived in 1896. Weyler believed the key to victory was to deny the rebels access to the peasants aiding their cause. He decided to concentrate much of the Cuban rural population in camps where, without proper sanitation, the women and children began to die in the thousands. Pathetic stories from the camps, embellished by the American press, incited a congressional clamor for a war with Spain—to liberate Cuba.

But Cleveland did not have a high regard for the "rascally Cubans" and was determined to stay out. He warned Congress that if it declared war, he would not send the army to fight. When

Congress recognized Cuban belligerency, however, some Spaniards went wild. In Barcelona a mob of 15,000 shouting, "Down with the American pig killers," stoned the U.S. consulate and tore up the Stars and Stripes.[21]

Though vilified in the jingo press as a toady of Spain, Cleveland showed courage and resolve in resisting the war clamor. When he left office in 1897, the nation was still at peace, and McKinley entered determined to avoid war. But the "yellow press"—as it was known from the name of one of its comic strips, "The Yellow Kid"—was in a frenzy. Led by William Randolph ("You-furnish-the-pictures-and-I'll-furnish-the-war!") Hearst's *New York Journal* and Joseph Pulitzer's *New York World*, the papers competed daily in the vitriol they poured on the Spanish. For the first but not the last time in U.S. history, the media beat the war drums of intervention until the nation rose and followed.

Playing a supporting role was the "black legend," the "stereotype of Spaniards as blood-thirsty despots that Americans had inherited from their English forebears."[22] The Protestant press was up in arms over Spanish barbarities and wanted Catholic Spain driven out of the hemisphere in humiliation. "And if it be the will of Almighty God that by war the last trace of this inhumanity of man to man shall be swept away from the Western Hemisphere," thundered the Presbyterian journal *Evangelist*, "let it come."[23]

Like most antiguerrilla wars, the campaign waged by Weyler was brutal, though probably no more so than the subsequent U.S. war to crush the insurrection of Emilio Aguinaldo in the Philippines. But to the American press Weyler was a monster, a beast. "Butcher Weyler" he was called, "Wolf" Weyler, a "human hyena," a "mad dog" who "massacred prisoners or threw them to the sharks; dragged the sick from their cots, shot them, and fed their bodies to the dogs."[24] The *Journal* solemnly asserted:

It is not only Weyler the soldier... but Weyler the brute, the devas-
tator of haciendas, the destroyer of families, and the outrager of
women.... Pitiless, cold, an exterminator of men....There is nothing to prevent his carnal, animal brain from running riot with
itself in inventing tortures and infamies of bloody debauchery.[25]

Circulation at the *Journal* soared to 800,000 daily.

Pulitzer's *World* rose to Hearst's challenge by lowering itself to
Hearst's depth. "Blood on the roadsides, blood in the fields, blood on
the doorsteps, blood, blood, blood!" its correspondent in Havana
telegraphed. "Is there no nation wise enough, brave enough, and
strong enough to restore peace in this bloodsmitten land?"[26]

"REMEMBER THE *MAINE*"

Still, McKinley refused to yield. "I have been through one war," he
told a friend. "I have seen the dead piled up, and I do not want to see
another."[27] Unlike most of the hawks of 1898, McKinley knew war.
Within months of Fort Sumter, seventeen-year-old Bill McKinley
had enlisted in the 23rd Ohio and was on his way to the Shenandoah
to face the army of Stonewall Jackson. On a Maryland field near
Antietam Creek, where more men died than had been killed in battle in all of America's previous wars, the teenager rode into the thick
of battle carrying hot food and coffee for the Union troops. The
memory of the dead and wounded on that field would never leave
McKinley.

In 1897 his patience seemed to be rewarded. A liberal government came to power in Madrid, anxious to resolve the crisis. It
recalled Weyler, modified the camps policy, released all Americans
from prison, and gave Cubans a measure of autonomy. In his annual
message on December 6, 1897, McKinley urged the country to give
the new government time: "I shall not impugn its sincerity, nor

should impatience be suffered to embarrass it in the task it has under-taken."[28] But Spain's luck had run out. As George F. Kennan writes:

> Unfortunately, two things happened during the winter which
> changed the situation quite drastically. First, the Spanish minister
> in Washington wrote an indiscreet letter in which he spoke
> slightingly of President McKinley, calling him a "bidder for the
> admiration of the crowd," and a "would-be politician... who
> tries to leave open a door behind himself while keeping on
> good terms with the jingoes of his party." The letter leaked; it
> was published in the New York papers, causing much indigna-
> tion and resentment. And a few days later the American public
> was profoundly shocked and outraged to hear that the battleship
> "Maine" had been sunk in Havana harbor with the loss of
> 266 American lives.[29]

The letter was a blunder, but hardly unusual for an envoy to put in private correspondence; and the insult was surely less egregious than the cutting remark of Assistant Secretary of the Navy Theodore Roosevelt, who had called the president "as spineless as a chocolate eclair."[30] Nor was evidence ever discovered that a Spanish mine had sabotaged the *Maine*. Nonetheless, Hearst's headlines screamed:

THE WARSHIP MAINE WAS SPLIT IN TWO BY AN
ENEMY'S SECRET INFERNAL MACHINE!

THE WHOLE COUNTRY THRILLS
WITH WAR FEVER

THE MAINE WAS DESTROYED
BY TREACHERY[31]

Hearst was echoed by Theodore Roosevelt: "The *Maine* was sunk by an act of dirty treachery on the part of the Spaniards."[32]

McKinley's friend and patron Senator Mark Hanna had warned against sending the *Maine* to Havana, comparing it to "waving a match in an oil well for fun."[33] The Spanish in Cuba and the U.S. consul general had pleaded with the president not to send the ship. After the disaster, Spain offered to cooperate in any investigation. Since Spain was desperate to avoid war, the least logical explanation of the *Maine* disaster is that Madrid ordered it. But an American court of inquiry conducted by naval officers concluded on March 28, 1898, that the *Maine* had been sunk by a submarine mine. Slogan of the hour:

Remember the *Maine*!
To hell with Spain!

In its hour of desperation Spain appealed to Europe. No nation offered aid. The German secretary for foreign relations was blunt: "You are isolated, because everybody wants to be pleasant to the United States, or, [at] any rate, nobody wants to arouse America's anger; the United States is a rich country, against which you simply cannot sustain a war."[34]

Many Americans were by now wild for war—but still McKinley resisted. Discussing the crisis with a friend, he reportedly broke down and cried "like a boy of thirteen."[35] Roosevelt was disgusted. Coming out of a White House meeting, he told one friend, "Do you know what that white-livered cur up there has done? He has prepared *two* messages, one for war and one for peace, and doesn't know which one to send in!"[36]

Facing congressional elections in six months and a 1900 rematch with William Jennings Bryan—a hawk where Spain was concerned, already running on "Free Cuba!" and "Free Silver!"—the president, on April 11, 1898, joined the crowd. "Better a foreign war than an internal upheaval; better that Spain should be ejected from Cuba than the Republicans be ejected from Washington," wrote one historian.[37] A *Times* of London correspondent captured the thoughtful and reflective mood in Congress:

> Men fought; "Liar," "Scoundrel," and other epithets were bandied
> to and fro; there were half-a-dozen personal collisions; books
> were thrown; members rushed up and down the aisles like mad-
> men, exchanging hot words, with clenched fists and set teeth;
> excitement was at fever heat. Not for years has such a scene
> occurred.[38]

Had Congress delayed but a few days, the United States might have won a diplomatic triumph. In the final hours before war was declared, it became clear Spain was casting about for an honorable way to capitulate, even if it meant ceding Cuba to the United States. Four days before the McKinley war message, the American minister in Madrid wired home:

> I hope that nothing will now be done to humiliate Spain, as I
> am satisfied that the present government is going, and is loyally
> ready to go, as fast and as far as it can. With your power of action
> sufficiently free you will win the fight on your own lines.[39]

Too late. Eleven days after the declaration of war, Commodore George Dewey attacked and sank a Spanish squadron in Manila Bay. He lost one man, an engineer, who died of heat stroke. Only days later, McKinley ordered preparations for the dispatch of troops to complete "the reduction of Spanish power in that quarter" and give "order and security to the islands while in the possession of the United States."[40] Since the war declaration mentioned only a

demand for Spain's withdrawal from Cuba, what was going on
10,000 miles from Washington? Kennan speculates:

> We know that Theodore Roosevelt, who was then the young
> Assistant Secretary of the Navy, had long felt that we ought to
> take the Philippines; that he wangled Dewey's appointment to the
> command of the Asiatic fleet; that both he and Dewey wanted
> war; and that he had some sort of a prior understanding with
> Dewey to the effect that Dewey would attack Manila, regardless
> of the circumstances of the origin or purpose of the war.[41]

Quick to grasp the meaning of Manila was the *Washington Post*:
"The guns of Dewey at Manila have changed the destiny of the
United States. We are face to face with a strange destiny and must
accept its responsibilities. An imperial policy!"[42]

HAPPY DAYS ARE HERE AGAIN

The Spanish–American War brought Americans together as they had
not been since Monroe's Era of Good Feelings. During a presidential trip to Atlanta, the veteran of Antietam affirmed that the care of
Confederate graves was a national duty and named two ex-
Confederate soldiers as major generals to command U.S. troops.
"Fighting Joe" Wheeler, who had "laid away a suit of gray to wear
the Union blue," took part in the surrender of Spanish forces.[43] In the
campaign before Santiago, the old cavalryman was heard shouting,
"We've got the Yankees on the run!"[44]

On May 28, 1898, the Sixth Massachusetts marched through
Baltimore on its way to camp. In 1861 the regiment had been stoned
by a mob while changing trains in Baltimore en route to defend the
capital. Now the Sixth was wildly cheered as it tramped through, its
regimental band playing "Dixie." Senator Lodge journeyed up from
Washington to see the parade. He wept unashamedly. "It was," he

said, "'roses, roses all the way'—flags, cheers, excited crowds. Tears
were in my eyes. I never felt so moved in my life. The war of 1861
was over at last and the great country for which so many men died
was one again."[45] So great was the patriotic fervor after the *Maine* was
sunk that when McKinley put out a call for 25,000 men to fight, a
million men answered.[46]

The war lasted from late April to early August, a few weeks longer
than the three months Captain Mahan had predicted. At its end
America made a decision it had never made before. The United
States annexed Spain's colonies of Puerto Rico, Guam, and the
Philippines, acquiring control of lands we had no intention of con-
verting into states, and of peoples we had no intention of allowing to
become U.S. citizens. We also annexed Hawaii. The Republic had
become an empire.

"THE VOICE OF THE SERPENT"

Even in the flush of victory some warned against the course on which
America was embarking. From Grover Cleveland to Speaker Thomas
B. Reed, from labor statesman Sam Gompers to industrialist Andrew
Carnegie, they implored the Republic to resist the temptation. "The
fruits of imperialism, be they bitter or sweet," declared Bryan, "must
be left to the subjects of monarchy. This is one tree of which citizens
of a republic may not partake. It is the voice of the serpent, not the
voice of God, that bids us eat."[47] To annex foreign peoples without
their consent, said Massachusetts Senator George Hoar, contradicted
the Constitution and Declaration of Independence. The Founding
Fathers would not believe, said Hoar, that their heirs

> would be beguiled from these sacred and awful verities that
> they might strut about in the cast-off clothing of pinchbeck
> emperors and pewter kings; that their descendants would be

excited by the smell of gunpowder and the sound of the guns
of a single victory as a small boy by a firecracker on some
Fourth of July morning.[48]

An Anti-Imperialist League was founded in September of 1898.
"The serious question for the people of this country to consider,"
said Frederick Gookin, "is what effect the imperial policy will have
upon ourselves if we permit it to be established."[49] In his poem—
"On a Soldier Fallen in the Philippines"—about an American who
died suppressing the Filipino uprising, William Vaughn Moody
"urged us never to let the deceased know of the rotten cause for
which he died":

Let him never dream that
his bullet's scream went wide of its island mark,
Home to the heart of his darling land
where she stumbled and sinned in the dark.[50]

"We cannot maintain an empire in the Orient and maintain a
republic in America," said Mark Twain.[51] "What do the people get
out of this war?" asked Senator Tom Watson of Georgia. "The fighting and the taxes.... What are we going to get out of this war as a
nation? Endless trouble, complications, expense. Republics cannot go
into the conquering business and remain republics."[52] William
Graham Sumner gave a speech he titled "The Conquest of the
United States by Spain." In it he said:

...[W]e are submitting to be conquered by her on the field of
ideas and policies.... If we believe in liberty, as an American
principle, why do we not stand by it? Why are we going to
throw it away and enter upon a Spanish policy of dominion and
regulation?[53]

To the charge he was lacking in patriotism, Sumner responded, "My patriotism is of the kind which is outraged by the notion that the United States never was a great nation until in a petty three months campaign it knocked to pieces a poor, decrepit, bankrupt old state like Spain."[54]

Ironically, Bryan was as responsible as any man for annexation of the Philippines. When the peace treaty came up for a Senate vote, with two-thirds needed for approval, the prairie populist urged his party's senators to vote yes. Bryan told followers that this would give the nation a formal peace and that when Democrats took back the presidency in 1900, they would liberate the Philippines. The treaty passed 57–27, one vote more than needed. "One word from Mr. Bryan," said a bitter Andrew Carnegie, "would have saved the country from disaster. I could not be cordial to him for years afterwards. He had seemed to me a man who was willing to sacrifice his country and his personal convictions for party advantage."[55] It is difficult to defend Bryan from a charge of rankest cynicism. After the treaty had been adopted, Bryan exulted, "We are now in a better position to wage a successful contest against imperialism [in the 1900 election] than we would have been had the treaty been rejected."[56]

In Mahan's dismissive term, the anti-imperialists were "isolationists." And in 1901 the *Oxford English Dictionary* gave us the word to describe "one who favors or advocates isolation. In U.S. politics one who thinks the Republic ought to pursue a policy of political isolation."[57] Thus did the term of derision, invented by interventionists for those who adhere to the wisdom of Washington, formally enter the political lexicon.

The anti-imperialists were principled, but history does not validate their direst warnings. The character of the Republic was not altered by the annexations, and U.S. imperialism proved far more enlightened than that of most European states, and surely more benign than

that of Japan. Still, what was a republic, born of revolution against
British colonialism, doing crushing rebellions and collecting
colonies? "In what respect does the position of the Republican Party
differ from the position taken by the English government in 1776?"
Bryan had asked.[58]

But across the sea Britain's poet of empire was egging us on:

> Take up the White Man's burden,
> Send forth the best ye breed—
> Go, bind your sons to exile
> To serve your captives' need.[59]

Kipling mailed a copy of his poem to Roosevelt, who wrote
Lodge that he found it "rather poor poetry, but good sense from the
expansionist standpoint."[60] Yet within a few years even Roosevelt
would come to see the islands as a strategic liability, a "heel of
Achilles." But before annexation was complete, a brutal war had to
be fought against Filipino guerrillas in which many more American
lives would be lost than in the war with Spain. Thousands of Filipinos
perished in that war and the famine it produced. But the harsh realities of putting down the insurrection and ruling a subject people had
one sobering, beneficial effect: It killed the spirit of imperialism in
the American people and was among the reasons the United States
never annexed Cuba. By late 1899, a year after victory, the *Boston
Transcript* was writing:

> O Dewey at Manila
> That fateful first of May,
> When you sank the Spanish squadron
> In almost bloodless fray,
> And gave your name to deathless fame;
> O glorious Dewey, say,

Why didn't you weigh anchor
And softly sail away?[61]

The *New York World* had its own reply to Britain's poet of empire:

We've taken up the white man's burden
Of ebony and brown;
Now will you kindly tell us, Rudyard,
How we may put it down?[62]

The "ruling of distant peoples is not our dish," said George
Kennan in his 1951 lectures gathered together in *American Diplomacy*.
"[T]here are many things we Americans should beware of, and
among them is the acceptance of any sort of paternalistic responsibility to anyone, be it even in the form of military occupation, if we
can possibly avoid it."[63]

As for the Spanish, they had fought bravely. On Sunday morning,
July 3, 1898, a squadron led by the *Infanta Maria Teresa*, bottled up
in Santiago harbor and facing capture by American troops besieg-
ing the city, sallied forth for the honor of Spain. "The Spanish ships
came out as gaily as brides to the altar," said Captain John Philip
of the *Texas*.[64] The U.S. ships stoked up and gave chase, sinking or
beaching every Spanish vessel with the loss of but a single man. As
American sailors exulted and gloated over the burning Spanish
ships, the pious Captain Philip admonished his men: "Don't cheer,
boys, the poor fellows are dying."[65]

With the battle ended, American bluejackets braved shark-
infested waters to rescue drowning Spanish sailors. They fed and
clothed the survivors, while consigning the dead to the deep with
prayer. "So long as the enemy showed his flag, they fought like
American seamen," Captain Robley Evans wrote of his *Iowa* crew,

"but when the flag came down they were as gentle and tender as American women."[66]

The Civil War veteran Dewey became a legend. His order to the commander of the *Olympia*, "You may fire when ready, Gridley," became the stuff of legend.[67] And Roosevelt proved himself no armchair warrior. While a jingo to the core who clamored for war and plotted its victory, he had always planned to fight. He became a lieutenant colonel of the Rough Riders, sailed to Cuba, fought gallantly at Kettle Hill, and emerged a national hero, the personification of the young America that had strutted onto the world stage. "It has been a splendid little war," wrote Secretary of State John Hay, "begun with the highest motives, carried on with magnificent intelligence and spirit, favored by the fortune which loves the brave."[68]

Most Americans exulted in our new empire. Albert Beveridge, Indiana's newly elected thirty-five-year-old senator, an unabashed imperialist, declared that Americans were among God's chosen people, and that it was the destiny of the Anglo-Saxon and Germanic peoples to rule over the earth:

> It is elemental. It is racial. God has not been preparing the English-speaking and Teutonic peoples for a thousand years for nothing but vain and idle self-admiration.... He has made us the master organizers of the world to establish system where chaos reigns.... He has made us adepts in government that we may administer government among savage and senile peoples.[69]

Beveridge believed in a foreign policy of "America first, and not only America *first*, but America *only*."[70] William Allen White's *Emporia Gazette* saw a tribal destiny beckoning: "It is the Anglo-Saxon's destiny to go forth as a world conqueror. He will take possession of all the islands of the sea. He will exterminate the peoples he cannot subjugate. This is what fate holds for the chosen people. It is so written."[71] Such sentiments were far removed from what the Founding Fathers had intended the young Republic to become, but that was the spirit of the confident years.

WHY WE TOOK THE PHILIPPINES

"When we received the cable from Admiral Dewey telling of the taking of the Philippines I looked up their location on the globe. I could not have told where those darned islands were within 2,000 miles!" said McKinley.[72] Nevertheless we had taken them. Turning our backs on eleven decades of American history, we had begun to behave like Europeans. We had become imperialists. Attacking the Spanish squadron at Manila was a bold, brilliant, and legitimate act of war. But why did we annex the Philippines? Why did we annex Puerto Rico rather than extend a protectorate over the island, as we did with Cuba?

McKinley reportedly came down after a night of prayer to tell a startled press: God told me to take the Philippines. In an interview with the General Missionary Committee of the Methodist Episcopal Church, which supported annexation, as did most of the Protestant press, he reportedly offered this explanation of how his apparition had come:

> I walked the floor of the White House night after night until
> midnight, and I am not ashamed to tell you, gentlemen, that I
> went down on my knees and prayed [to] Almighty God for light
> and guidance more than one night. And one night late it came
> to me this way—I don't know how it was but it came... that
> there was nothing left for us to do but to take them all, and to
> educate the Filipinos, and uplift them and civilize and
> Christianize them, and by God's grace do the very best we could
> by them, as our fellow-men for whom Christ also died. And
> then I went to bed, and went to sleep, and slept soundly, and the
> next morning I sent for the chief engineer of the War

Department (our map-maker), and I told him to put the
Philippines on the map of the United States, and there they are,
and there they will stay while I am President![73]

Among Catholics, aware that baptisms had begun in the islands
fifty years before the English landed at Jamestown, and that two million Filipinos had already been received into the Church, the idea
that Americans had been sent by God to "Christianize" the islands
caused some puzzlement.[74]

"Contingent necessity" was a second argument. Had we not
taken the islands, the Germans or British—who had squadrons larger
than Dewey's in Manila Bay in that spring of 1898—would have
gladly taken them off our hands. But so what? While annexation of
Hawaii, Midway, and Guam strengthened the U.S. defense line and
extended it to mid-Pacific, the same could not be said of the
Philippines. From the beginning, the islands were "a military and
diplomatic liability... the Achilles heel of American defense, a
hostage to Japan for American foreign policy in the Far East." [75] They
were impossible to defend without investments of men and money
their economic and strategic benefit could not justify. In October
1898 British Admiral P. H. Colomb wrote in *North American Review*
of what might befall the United States from having taken the islands.
For the first time, he said:

[America was giving] hostages to fortune, and [was] taking a
place in the world that will entail on her sacrifices and difficul-
ties of which she has not yet dreamed…. [W]ith outlying territories, especially islands, a comparatively weak power, has
facilities for wounding her without being wounded in return.[76]

Another reason given for annexation was historic inevitability.
By the century's end, America had become the greatest economic
and industrial power on earth, with the potential to become the

world's first military power. The nation had begun to sense that power. It was inevitable that, having subdued the continent, Americans would go out into the world, that when we did we would collide with other nations, that if we prevailed we would take what was theirs. Brooks Adams, of the great American Adams family, gave voice to the idea of the predestination of nations:

> It is in vain that men talk of keeping free of entanglements.
> Nature is omnipotent; and nations must float with the tide.
> Whither the exchanges flow, they must follow; and they will follow as long as their vitality endures.... These great catastrophes escape human control.[77]

But Adams's fatalism and determinism are belied by the history of his own family. His father's diplomacy helped avert a war with Britain at the time of the *Trent* affair. His grandfather kept America from enmeshing itself in the Greek struggle for independence. His great-grandfather put his presidency on the line to keep the United States out of an open war with France, and to sever the 1778 Treaty of Alliance with Paris, which could have involved America in a decade of Napoleonic Wars. No, our destiny is not preordained; we determine it.

Some scholars contend that imperialism was the inevitable next step of Manifest Destiny, as Marx argued that imperialism was the last, highest form of capitalism. But this also denies the possibility of statesmanship, of the leader who knows his country's limits. Annexation of the Philippines was no more inevitable than annexation of Cuba or Mexico, both of which had been advocated, neither of which was ever consummated. Where we resisted the imperial temptation in 1848, we embraced it in 1898.

Yet another reason for annexation was the desire of American merchants and manufacturers to acquire bases of operation off the Asian coast to give America a foot in the door to the lucrative China trade. But in that day as well as this, the "China trade" would prove a mirage. Historian Charles Beard exonerates the captains of industry and indicts the policies and propaganda of America's navalists and imperialists, particularly Captain Mahan:

> Loyalty to the facts of historical record must ascribe the idea of imperialist expansion mainly to naval officers and politicians rather than to businessmen.... By universal consent, Captain Alfred Thayer Mahan was the principal formulator of imperialism for the United States.[78]

Annexation of the Philippines, writes Beard, "was a flat, violent, and revolutionary breach with old American policy" and a fateful error.[79] Reinhold Niebuhr, the pastor turned international ethicist, would decry the war as an unconscionable act of aggression by the United States, bred of the "will to power of an adolescent nation and the frustrated impulses of pugnacity and martial ardor of the pitiful little 'men in the street.'"[80]

For years, Americans fought a war against Filipino *insurrectos* who felt betrayed by the nation that had made the world's first revolution. Although the governor appointed by McKinley, William Howard Taft, would urge his countrymen to regard the Filipinos as our "little brown brothers," U.S. troops crushing their rebellion had another view:

> He may be a brother of Big Bill Taft,
> But he ain't no friend of mine.[81]

Half a decade after the United States became the first non-European nation to enter the imperialists' club, the first Asian applicant appeared in a fashion even more dramatic. Believing itself swindled by Russia out of the fruits of its victory over China during a war in 1894–1895, Japan, on February 6, 1904, launched a surprise attack on the Russian naval squadron at Port Arthur. Humiliated before Europe, the tsar sent his Baltic squadron on a six-month voyage of vengeance. Waiting at Tsushima Straits, between Korea and Japan, was Admiral Togo. When the Russian fleet was sighted, he attacked for two days. Thirty-five Russian ships went to the bottom, reducing the Russian navy from the world's third greatest to sixth in thirty-six hours. "Neither Trafalgar nor the defeat of the Spanish Armada," said TR, "was as complete—as overwhelming."[82]

The Japanese had launched their surprise attack on Port Arthur before any declaration of war. Yet the U.S. press thought it a splendid piece of work. Our Asian protégés had caught the Russian Slav with his guard down. "Was not the way the Japs began the fight bully?" wrote an admiring Elihu Root, the former secretary of state.[83] Interesting observation in light of what the Japanese would manage in December of 1941.

America in 1898 had humiliated a fading European power with a population one-fourth its own. Japan had sent to the ocean floor the navy of the largest nation on earth. The Philippines suddenly seemed less a forward base of U.S. power than the vulnerable island possessions of which Admiral Colomb had lately written. But the great turn had been taken. The Americans had become imperialists, and the nation endorsed the new course in the McKinley landslide of 1900. Even before that election, U.S. troops were marching beside British imperial troops to Peking.

CHAPTER 11

The New Imperialists

Nothing in all history had ever succeeded like America, and every American knew it.[1]
—Henry Steele Commager

Even before America became a world power, other great powers had begun carving out spheres of interest in a disintegrating Chinese empire—Britain in the Yangtze Valley, Germany in Shantung, Russia in Manchuria. To prevent partition and keep the United States from being shut out of the China trade, John Hay advanced an idea said to have sprung from the fertile mind of an old British China hand, Alfred E. Hippisley: declare an "open door" for all imperial powers in China. The original source of the idea was—the British Foreign Office. Alarmed at encroachments on its China preserve, London wanted the United States to jointly support a policy by which all imperial players would be entitled to equal treatment in all spheres of interests. Thus, the imperial latecomers would be prevented from excluding the British.

When London first broached the idea, America was preoccupied with Spain. But after the annexation of the Philippines, Hay in 1899 unilaterally proposed an "open door" under which each imperial power would retain its sphere of interest, but all would be subject to the same port fees and customs duties. China would keep control of its trade. Hay sent a note outlining the new U.S.

policy to the imperial capitals. When all, save Russia, nodded some form of assent, Hay declared the Open Door in force.

A revolution in China in 1900 caused Hay to broaden the concept. Zealots of the Order of Liberty Patriotic Harmonious Fists—"Boxers" in Western slang—began to attack "foreign devils" and Chinese converts to Christianity. After several massacres, the imperial powers demanded that the dowager empress suppress the Boxers. She refused. The Boxers then demanded that all foreign envoys get out. They refused.

When a German ambassador and a Japanese diplomat were murdered in Peking, foreign officials and businessmen fled to the Legation Quarter, which was defended by 377 soldiers from eight countries, including fifty-six U.S. Marines with the lone machine gun. Another fifty men had hunting rifles to which they attached butcher knives as bayonets. They took their place on the wall as "Thornhill's Roughs." The 149 women served as nurses. Seventy-nine children were in the compound, and 2,700 Chinese converts had taken refuge there. In an epic story, this *ad hoc* force held off a horde of Boxers and dynastic troops for fifty-five days.

To relieve the siege, 2,500 U.S. soldiers joined an international force of 18,000 that marched from the port of Tientsin to Peking in a dramatic rescue. Tientsin had been attacked by 10,000 Boxers and dynastic troops, but they failed to dislodge the 2,400 allied defenders due to the barricades built under the guidance of a U.S. engineer named Herbert Hoover.

U.S. troops spearheaded the drive into the Forbidden City, and China was forced to pay a large indemnity and erect monuments honoring the Westerners and Chinese Christians killed. Only U.S. pressure kept the indemnity within reason, and America used the few millions it had been awarded to finance scholarships for Chinese students in the United States.

Hay now feared that the presence of a multinational army in

Peking, coupled with rampant anti-Chinese sentiment among the imperial powers, would mean partition of China. Russia was already using the attacks on its citizens in Manchuria as a pretext for annexation. In 1900 Hay boldly and unilaterally declared it to be U.S. policy to "preserve Chinese territorial and administrative entity."[2]

The Open Door was seen as "a triumph of idealism over power politics, an American policy that saved China."[3] Henry Adams declared that "nothing so meteoric had ever been done in American diplomacy."[4] This was gross hyperbole. Yet out of an effort to preserve a commercial *status quo* in China would come a cardinal dogma of U.S. foreign policy to rival the Monroe Doctrine. America had signed no treaty, but the Open Door would come to be regarded as a unilateral U.S. guarantee of China's territorial integrity.

Despite Hay's declaration, the imperial powers continued their encroachments. And there was a measure of insincerity in the Open Door. In the Philippines, the United States had slammed the door shut to all rivals, and in 1900 Hay secretly instructed the U.S. minister in Peking to obtain a naval coaling station on China's coast at Samsah Bay.[5] Japan, which looked on Samsah as within its own sphere, blocked the move, politely reminding Hay of his commitment to China's territorial integrity.

As the Russians pressed China virtually to cede Manchuria, Tokyo asked Hay if the United States would stand by Japan and resist any further Russian seizures. Hay's reply: The United States "was not prepared... singly, or in concert with other Powers, to enforce these views in the east by any demonstration which could present a character of hostility to any other Power."[6] Japan concluded the Open Door was merely American bluster and bluff.

The American Century had begun in 1898 at Manila Bay. By 1900 McKinley had abandoned the tradition of nonintervention outside the hemisphere and entangled the nation in world politics through the back door of Asia. His motivation had been that familiar Yankee cocktail of high-minded idealism and commercial interest, of morality and money; the purpose of U.S. foreign policy was to make the world safe for American capitalism. As for the "China trade," the lure of which had persuaded U.S. businesses to back annexation of the Philippines and an open door to 400 million Chinese customers, it proved a mirage. In 1900 China had taken 1 percent of U.S. exports. For thirty years after the Open Door was declared, China never took much more than 2 percent—with up to 70 percent of that accounted for by sales of tobacco and cigarettes.[7]

IMPERIAL OVERSTRETCH IN ASIA

Since Russia had been most aggressive in preying on the carcass of the Manchu Dynasty, America began to look to Japan as Asia's buffer against tsarist expansion. Theodore Roosevelt, now president, said openly that in the event of war, he hoped Japan would defeat Russia. When war did come, the United States tilted toward Tokyo. But the stunning Japanese victory at Tsushima Straits in 1905 dramatically altered the American perspective. Russia was suddenly a defeated empire, rife with revolution, and Japan an emerging threat to the Philippines.

Asked by a victorious but near-bankrupt Japan to mediate the war, Roosevelt invited the belligerents to New Hampshire. In the Treaty of Portsmouth, Japan was awarded the South Manchuria Railroad, Liaotung peninsula, and the southern half of Sakhalin Island, and Russia recognized Japan's paramount interest in Korea. Tokyo wanted all of Sakhalin and a large monetary indemnity, but Russia balked and threatened to walk out. Having failed to break Russia's armies, Japan grudgingly accepted the deal. But Japan blamed TR for its having been shortchanged and looked aside as anti-American riots broke out in Tokyo. Four American churches were burned, and the U.S. Embassy had to be put under guard. For his diplomatic coup, Roosevelt won worldwide popularity and America's first Nobel Prize for Peace—but United States–Japan relations had now begun their long downhill slide.

Roosevelt did not want conflict with Japan and sought to recreate the old warmth with the Taft-Katsura Agreement of 1905. Signed in Tokyo by Secretary of War William Howard Taft, it contained Japan's disavowal of "any aggressive designs whatever" on the Philippines and America's recognition of Japan's dominant interest in Korea. In November 1905 the United States became the first great power to close its legation in Seoul. Korea's independence came to an end. Roosevelt and Taft-Katsura are not fondly remembered by Koreans, but the United States was only acceding to what it was powerless to prevent. When Japan occupied the peninsula, TR conceded:

> Korea is absolutely Japan's. To be sure, by treaty it was solemnly
> covenanted that Korea should remain independent. But Korea
> was itself helpless to enforce the treaty, and it was out of the ques-
> tion to suppose that any other nation… would attempt to do for
> the Koreans what they were utterly unable to do for themselves.[8]

Brutally frank, and utterly true. "Who would be free themselves must strike the blow." So the poet Byron wrote.

But while he spoke softly, TR brandished his big stick. In 1907 he sent the U.S. battleship fleet to circle the globe and impress on Japan the full extent of U.S. naval power. When the fleet reached the Pacific, the emperor invited it to pay a visit. As the warships steamed into Tokyo Bay, the Japanese were impressed. The reception was tumultuous; talk of war dissipated. "Every particle of trouble with the Japanese Government and the Japanese press stopped like magic," said Roosevelt, "as soon as they found that our fleet had actually sailed, and was obviously in good trim."[9]

By the time TR left office, the Open Door was "more a phrase than a fact."[10] Russia had ignored it in Manchuria. Japan had slammed it shut in Manchuria and Korea. Other imperial powers did not feel bound by U.S. declarations, and America was unwilling to back it up with force. As revisionist historian William Appleman Williams wrote, the Open Door "was conceived and designed to win the victories without the wars."[11] Roosevelt summed it up succinctly:

> The Open Door policy in China was an excellent thing, and I hope it will be a good thing in the future, so far as it can be maintained by general diplomatic agreement; but, as has been proved by the whole history of Manchuria, alike under Russia and under Japan, the 'Open Door' policy, as a matter of fact, completely disappears as soon as a powerful nation determines to disregard it, and is willing to run the risk of war rather than forego its intention.[12]

"That was the heart of the matter," writes Alexander DeConde. "It was not to the interest of the United States to risk war over principles not vital to its foreign policy."[13] By its inaction as Russia and Japan trampled on the principle of the Open Door, America was saying that preserving China's territorial integrity was not a cause worth fighting for.

The Open Door was a classic example of the American penchant for "declaratory overstretch"—noble and sweeping statements of policy and purpose the United States lacks the will or power to back up. Such declarations mislead friends into trusting our words, and cause enemies to hold us in contempt, and to miscalculate. Seeing that the Open Door contained elements of fakery and fraud, Tokyo set out on a course that would bring it into direct collision with the United States in 1941.

Annexation of the Philippines had produced a three-year guerrilla war, embroilment in imperial rivalries in China, an Open Door we were unprepared to keep open with force, deteriorating relations with Japan, and acquiescence in Tokyo's seizure of Korea—in return for Japan's promise to respect our position in the Philippines, which even TR was now calling our "heel of Achilles."[14] The Republic's maiden voyage into the realm of *realpolitik* had been a limited success.

A NOBEL FOR THEODORE

McKinley had ended the U.S. tradition of nonintervention in Asia, and Roosevelt led America into the power politics of Europe. The issue was the Moroccan crisis of 1905, and it was serious. Britain and France had formed their Entente Cordiale in 1904, aimed at Germany. France had recognized Britain's paramount interest in Egypt in return for British recognition of France's interest in Morocco, where the French were busily taking over and closing the door to foreign merchants. Egged on by his foreign minister, the kaiser one morning in March 1905 showed up in Tangier, riding a charger, to visit the sultan and show Berlin's support for Moroccan independence. There, Wilhelm delivered a saber-rattling speech. A full-blown crisis was at hand. France's foreign minister wanted to threaten Germany with war over the insult but was overruled by the cabinet and resigned. Emotions ran high. There was talk that the long-anticipated European war was at hand.

A nervous kaiser urged Roosevelt to convene a conference to mediate, and to maintain an open door for Germany in Morocco. He gave TR a pledge: If a deadlock developed, he would accept the president's arbitration. A mistake—for TR was more alarmed at the prospect of a German presence on the Atlantic than about closing the open door and a possible partition of Morocco. Roosevelt agreed to mediate.

The conference was called in Algeciras, a Spanish seacoast town near Gibraltar. The resulting General Act of Algeciras proved a defeat

for a Germany that was unprepared to face down the entente. The
principle of the open door was upheld for German merchants, but
France was left in a privileged position with the Moroccan police.
Roosevelt's popularity soared, but many were alarmed that, for the
first time, the United States had intruded in the power politics of
Europe when no vital interest was at risk.

INTERNATIONALISTS VS. GLOBALISTS

Wilson is said to have been the first president to lead America out of
"isolation," but this, as we have seen, is myth. The United States was
never isolationist. Only if one looks at the world from a Eurocentric
vantage point—as some foreign policy scholars do—can one make
such a case. For twelve decades before Wilson, America was the most
expansionist nation on earth, and, by 1900, had become an empire.
McKinley and Hay had sent troops to Peking and enmeshed us in
the politics of China. They had been first to accept Tsar Nicholas II's
invitation to the 1899 Hague conference on disarmament. Teddy
Roosevelt was the most famous and popular leader on earth for
mediating the Russo-Japanese War and Moroccan crisis. He had
declared a "Roosevelt Corollary" to the Monroe Doctrine whereby
the United States asserted a right to intervene in Latin America to
prevent defaults and chaos that might otherwise invite European
intervention. Closer to the mark about this era is the dictum credited to Captain Mahan about the guiding principles of U.S. foreign
policy: In the Far East, cooperation; in Europe, abstention; in Latin
America, dominance.[15]

Progressive Imperialism was America's fifth great foreign policy
tradition. Forever associated with McKinley, Roosevelt, and Henry
Cabot Lodge, it broke with the vision of the Farewell Address and
raised Manifest Destiny to a new level. America's destiny now
entailed overseas annexations and domination of other peoples. The
British Empire was no longer our great antagonist, but an exemplar

in advancing the hegemony of the Anglo-Saxon race and civilization. Rooted in a belief that American ideals and institutions were superior, Progressive Imperialism incorporated the conviction that any who got in our way were blocking the path of progress and must be removed without apology. Talk that God Himself had instructed McKinley to take the Philippines and "Christianize" our "little brown brothers" nicely encapsules the basic idea.

The leading Republicans of this era were unmoved by some gauzy vision of a world without war or altruistic idea of what was best for mankind. They made decisions based on what would enhance U.S. power and glory. McKinley and TR were imperialists, not globalists; unilateralists, not multilateralists. Throughout the years prior to and during the Great War, Theodore Roosevelt would strive to make clear how different was his internationalism from that of Wilson and Bryan:

> I regard the Wilson-Bryan attitude of trusting to fantastic peace treaties, to impossible promises, to all kinds of scraps of paper without any backing in efficient force as abhorrent. It is infinitely better for a nation and for the world to have the Frederick the Great and Bismarck tradition as regards foreign policy than to have the... Bryan-Wilson attitude.... A milk-and-water righteousness unbacked by force is to the full as wicked as and even more mischievous than force divorced from righteousness.[16]

TR was a better and greater man than Wilson, and he and Lodge were instinctively right about the nature of the Hobbesian world of the twentieth century we had entered. But Wilson and Bryan, the men of "milk-and-water righteousness," would prove, in their desire to keep America out of the horrifying and futile wasteland of blood and lives on the Western Front, wiser than Roosevelt, whose idea of warfare was that glorious charge up Kettle Hill.

CHAPTER 12

"He Kept Us Out of War"

*We are participants, whether we would or not,
in the life of the world. The interests of all nations
are our own also.*[1]

—WOODROW WILSON, MAY 27, 1916

By November 1916 Europe had been at war for more than
two years. Millions of Europe's best and bravest had already fallen at
the Marne and Gallipoli, at Verdun and in the Somme offensive. The
Great War was producing sickening and endless casualty lists of
British, French, Germans, Russians, and Austrians. And America
wanted to stay out. That is why it reelected the peace president who
alone stood between America and the war hawks like Theodore
Roosevelt.

Had Taft lost the nomination to Roosevelt in 1912, the Rough
Rider would have led a united party into that election and won.
America would have gone to war far sooner than 1917. Roosevelt
loved war. In 1897 he had told students at the Naval War College,
"No triumph of peace is quite so great as the supreme triumphs of
war."[2] Taft said of him that Roosevelt was "obsessed with his love of
war and the glory of it. That is the secret of his present attitude....
He would think it a real injury to mankind if we would not have a
war."[3]

When the guns of August began firing in 1914, Roosevelt initially took neither side in the charge that Germany had violated the

neutrality of Belgium. By October, however, he was writing the British minister in Washington, "If I had been President, I should have acted [against Germany] on the thirtieth or thirty-first of July."[4] Given his belief in the purifying and ennobling powers of war, his support of the British Empire, his dislike of "Bill the Kaiser," and his wish to have America play a dominant role in the world arena, Roosevelt would have converted an event like the sinking of the *Lusitania* in 1915 into a *casus belli*. In a 1916 essay titled "America First—a Phrase or a Fact?" Roosevelt excoriated the policies of Taft and virtually charged Wilson with cowardice:

> [T]his course of national infamy on our part began when the last
> Administration surrendered to the peace-at-any-price people,
> and started the negotiation of its foolish and wicked all-inclusive
> arbitration treaties. Individuals and nations who preach the doc-
> trine of milk-and-water invariably have in them a softness of
> fibre which means that they fear to antagonize those who preach
> and practise the doctrine of blood-and-iron. It is true of our
> people, as once it was true of the fellow countrymen of Ruskin
> when he said: "We have been passive when we should have not
> have been passive, for fear. The principle of non-intervention, as
> now practised among us, is as selfish and cruel as the worst
> frenzy of conquest, and differs from it only by being not only
> malignant, but dastardly."[5]

By his failure to act when neutral Belgium was overrun, said TR, Wilson had "played the part which nineteen hundred years ago was played by the Levite toward the wayfarer who fell among thieves near Jericho."[6] But when the war he so wanted finally came, TR would find it a different kind from the "splendid little war" in which he had charged up Kettle Hill. All four of his sons would fight; Quentin would be killed, and Theodore, Jr., wounded on the Western Front.

Roosevelt's lifelong friend Lodge shared his fear that America was being left on the sidelines of the great struggle for global pre-eminence. As described by historian Eric Nordlinger:

> The chief hawk, Senator Henry Cabot Lodge, laid out the secu-rity argument for intervention as early as 1915. He feared that "unarmed, unready, undefended, we offer a standing invitation to aggression and attack." Hearkening back to his position of twenty years earlier, Lodge maintained that the "ocean barrier which defended us in 1776 and 1812 no longer exists. Steam and electricity have destroyed it."[7]

Lodge was wrong. In the quarter century before 1915, the United States had built a navy second only to Britain's and was invul-nerable to German naval and military power. During the entire war, the German High Seas Fleet dared venture out of port but once, for the inconclusive battle of Jutland. But the bellicosity of Roosevelt and Lodge shows that it was not Wilson who, from 1914 to 1917, was most anxious to involve the United States in the bloodletting of the Western Front.

Wilson's image as Christ-like opponent of violence aside, the man was no pacifist, but a proud idealist: "Sometimes people call me an idealist. Well that is the way I know I am an American."[8] Like Roosevelt and Lodge, he believed in the superiority of Anglo-Saxon peoples. Pressed by a British diplomat to explain his Mexican policy, Wilson retorted, "I am going to teach the South American republics to elect good men."[9] More than any other president, Wilson used military force in Latin America. Twice he invaded Mexico—order-ing the U.S. Navy to occupy Veracruz in 1914, after U.S. Marines were assaulted in Tampico, and sending General John Pershing to pursue Pancho Villa in 1916, after Villa's renegades invaded New Mexico and murdered Americans.

Wilson would add a sixth tradition to U.S. foreign policy: Liberal Internationalism. In his Fourteen Points we see his vision. Wilson believed that through the global expansion of free trade, democracy, and disarmament, the way would open up to global governance and universal peace. His ideas are traceable to the classical liberals of the nineteenth century. Wilson parted with Roosevelt and Lodge in his globalist, rather than nationalist, perspective; his willingness to subordinate U.S. sovereignty to multilateral institutions; and his distaste for balance-of-power politics. History would afford Wilson an opportunity to impose his vision on mankind, but not until his second term would the great chance come.

AN OUT-OF-CONTROL PEACE RALLY

Woodrow Wilson set the scenario for his own renomination convention in St. Louis. It was to be a roaring celebration of "Americanism," the nation's patriotic unity under the stresses imposed by war. "Demonstrations were to hinge upon nationalism and the flag," wrote Wilson biographer Ray Stannard Baker. "The music of 'Dixie,' the classic rouser of Democratic conventions, was to be subordinated to the 'Star Spangled Banner.'"[10]

The feature was to be a relentless assault on the "hyphenate groups," as Wilson liked to call them, in echo of TR's denunciations of "hyphenated-Americanism." Like Roosevelt, Wilson was deeply suspicious that some of America's foreign-born harbored a dual loyalty. In one address near the Washington Monument, he charged some immigrants with virtual treason:

> There is disloyalty active in the United States, and it must be
> absolutely crushed. It proceeds from a minority, a very small
> minority, but a very active and subtle minority. It works under-
> ground, but it also shows its ugly head where we can see it; and
> there are those at this moment who are trying to levy a species of

political blackmail, saying, "Do what we wish in the interest of
foreign sentiment or we will wreak our vengeance at the polls."[11]

Wilson himself drafted the "Americanism plank" for inclusion
in the party platform. But when Newton D. Baker brought it to
St. Louis, he found the convention had turned into an out-of-control
peace rally. Within minutes of rising to speak, keynoter Martin
Glynn, former governor of New York, had the crowd on its feet.

The sinking of the *Lusitania* by a German submarine with the
loss of 128 Americans was fresh in mind, as was Roosevelt's mock-
ery of Wilson's response—"There is such a thing as a nation being
too proud to fight." Glynn cited example after example of presidents
turning the other cheek rather than leading America to war.

"When Grant was President, during the war between Spain and
the Spanish West Indies, a Spanish gunboat seized the vessel
'Virginius,' flying the American flag, and a Spanish commandant
in cold blood shot the captain of the 'Virginius,' thirty-six of the
crew and sixteen of the passengers.

"But we didn't go to war. Grant settled our troubles by
negotiation just as the President of the United States is trying to
do today."

The convention burst into wild applause.

The orator cited cases of violations under Harrison and
Lincoln:

"But we didn't go to war."

He paused for the roar of approval.

"And so goes our history. I don't want to take too much
time to enumerate—"

But the great throng, thrilled and excited, was not to be
denied.

"Go on, go on—give it to them."

It was such a moment as comes rarely in any orator's life.

"All right, I'll hit them again—"

He cited precedents under Pierce, Van Buren, Jefferson, Adams, Washington:

"But we didn't go to war."

The crowd was delirious with joy.[12]

Bryan, who had resigned as secretary of state because he feared the Wilson administration was taking the first steps that would lead to war, was seen weeping in the gallery. Glynn roared on:

"In the face of this record, do Republicans realize that when they arraign the policy of the President of the United States today, they arraign the policy of Harrison, of Blaine, of Lincoln and of Grant? For the pleasure of criticizing a Democratic President, are they willing to read out of the Republican Party the greatest men the Republican Party has ever had?...

"This policy may not satisfy those who revel in destruction and find pleasure in despair. It may not satisfy the fire-eater and the swashbuckler. [Laughter and applause]... this policy does satisfy the mothers of the land, at whose hearth and fireside no jingoistic war has placed an empty chair.... It does satisfy the fathers of this land and the sons of this land, who will fight for our flag, and die for our flag—"

The crowd was completely intoxicated.[13]

On the second day of the convention, Senator Ollie James of Kentucky, who had the "face of a prizefighter, the body of an oak, and the voice of a pipe organ," mounted the podium knowing what the crowd wanted.[14] James gave it to them:

Without orphaning a single American child, without widowing a single American mother, without firing a single gun, without

the shedding of a single drop of blood, he [Wilson] wrung from
the most militant spirit that ever brooded above a battlefield an
acknowledgement of American rights and an agreement to
American demands.[15]

Next came the Boy Orator of the West, Bryan himself, now deep
into middle age:

My friends, I have differed with our President on some of the
methods employed, but I join with the American people in
thanking God that we have a President who does not want this
nation plunged into this war.[16]

Yet, still, Wilson wanted his Americanism plank to take primacy
in the platform—for two reasons: to denounce the widespread
propaganda of groups supporting both sides in Europe's war, and to
serve notice on the Republicans that if they pandered to these "disloyal groups," Wilson would make patriotism the issue. Americanism
was to be Wilson's plank and the heart of his campaign, but the near-
runaway convention had inserted a plank of its own:

In particular, we commend to the American people the splendid
diplomatic victories of our great President, who has preserved
the vital interests of our Government and its citizens, and kept us
out of war.[17]

He kept us out of war! Democrats had their slogan.

But Wilson was nervous. As he told Secretary of the Navy
Josephus Daniels, "I can't keep the country out of war. They talk of
me as though I were a god. Any little German lieutenant can put us
into the war at any time by some calculated outrage."[18]

HAMMERING THE "HYPHENATES"

As the fall campaign began, Wilson began his assaults on the dual loyalty and treasonous behavior of the "hyphenate" groups:

> The passions and intrigues of certain active groups and combi-
> nations of men amongst us who were born under foreign flags
> injected the poison of disloyalty into our most critical affairs.... I
> am the candidate of a party, but I am above all things else an
> American citizen. I neither seek the favour nor fear the displea-
> sure of that small alien element amongst us which puts loyalty to
> any foreign power before loyalty to the United States.[19]

Republican rival Charles Evans Hughes was boxed. The president had already attracted the pro-British vote by allowing armed
British merchant ships to enter U.S. ports and take home what they
could carry. He was now winning the peace vote and bringing over
German-Americans who felt Wilson would keep the country out of
a war with their kinsmen. The National German-American Alliance
boasted two million members; German-Americans desperately
wanted the United States to stay out. They recoiled from a party
whose loudest voice was that of the bellicose Roosevelt, who had
charged German immigrants with "moral treason to the republic."[20]

A heaven-sent opportunity came for the president with receipt
of a telegram from one Jeremiah A. O'Leary of the America Truth
Society, a stridently anti-British, pro-German, propaganda organization. O'Leary baited the president in almost insulting language: "Your
foreign policies, your failure to secure compliance with all American
rights, your leniency with the British Empire, your approval of war
loans, the ammunition traffic are issues in this campaign."[21]

"Your telegram received," Wilson fired back. "I would feel
deeply mortified to have you or anybody like you vote for me. Since
you have access to many disloyal Americans and I have not I will ask

you to convey this message to them."[22] Wilson scored a direct hit. Closer and closer he moved toward a charge that the Republican Party was hell-bent on taking America into a European war in which it had no business. Addressing the Young Democrats League on September 30, 1916, he declared:

> All our present foreign policy is wrong, they say, and if it is
> wrong and they are men of conscience, they must change it; and
> if they are going to change it, in what direction are they going
> to change it?
>   There is only one choice as against peace, and that is war.
> Some of the supporters of that party, a very great body of the
> supporters of that party, outspokenly declare that they want war;
> so that the certain prospect of the success of the Republican
> Party is that we shall be drawn in one form or other into the
> embroilments of the European war.... Some young men ought
> to be interested in that.[23]

Wilson's speech rang "like a firebell in the night, and response was so encouraging" he returned to the theme again and again.[24] Edward Mandell House, the *éminence grise* of the White House, was elated with the success of his man's "peace" campaign. "The Republicans," House wrote Wilson, "are much concerned over that part of your last Saturday's speech [on September 30] in which you declared that Hughes' election would mean war. I would suggest that you emphasize this again."[25]

WILSON AND PEACE WITH HONOR!

As progressives in both parties were antiwar, and their strength was in the West, it was here that Wilson hoped to win. Henry Morgenthau, Sr., chairman of the Democratic Party's Finance Committee, had reported back to Wilson on the potency of the peace issue:"During my western trip I met and talked with... a great many people, and found that they are not as 'heroic' as T.R. wants them to be. They want [you] to keep us out of the war at almost any price."[26]

Up and down the Great Plains, Bryan and other Democrat orators echoed the slogan "He kept us out of war!"[27] Party pamphlets and newspaper ads took up the themes: progressivism and peace. Paid ads in major newspapers spelled out the difference between the parties:

> You are Working;
> —*Not Fighting!*
> Alive and Happy;
> —*Not Cannon Fodder!*
> Wilson and Peace with Honor?
> or
> *Hughes with Roosevelt and War?*[28]

As Wilson had kept their children out of sweatshops, mines, and mills, so the peace president had "saved their sons and their husbands from unrighteous battlefields!"[29] Democrats seized on a note from Hughes congratulating TR on a belligerent speech given in Maine. "Complete Accord with Roosevelt," the pamphlet was titled. In it Democrats accused Hughes of being pro-British and anti-German.

> If Mr. Hughes is elected President on this issue, it is notice to all
> the world that America repudiates her policy of peace for the
> Roosevelt-Hughes policy of war. Let the issue not be misunder-
> stood.... A vote for Hughes is a potential vote for war.[30]

In 1916 the United States was still a Republican country. Only through party splits had Cleveland and Wilson, the only Democrats elected president since 1856, been able to win. With the GOP

reunited, party hopes ran high. In the early returns, Hughes was leading. Confident of victory, he went to bed. As the story is told in journalistic circles, when the late returns came in from California giving
the nation to Wilson, a reporter called at Hughes's door.

"The president is sleeping," the butler replied.

Snapping his notebook shut, the reporter replied:

"Well, when he wakes up, tell him he isn't president any more."

On election eve Wilson partisans stood in front of Democratic
Party headquarters in Washington, chanting, "We want peace, we
don't want war/We want Wilson four years more."[31]

Within weeks of taking his oath of office for a second term, the
president who had won reelection on the slogan "He Kept Us Out
of War!" went to Congress to ask for a declaration of war.

CHAPTER 13

"Wilson's War"

[T]he day has come when America is privileged to spend her blood and her might for the principles that gave her birth and happiness and the peace which she has treasured.[1]

—WOODROW WILSON, APRIL 2, 1917

*If any question why we died,
Tell them, because our fathers lied.*[2]

—RUDYARD KIPLING

Why did Woodrow Wilson break with all tradition and lead America into a slaughterhouse that had consumed millions of the best and bravest of Europe's young, when no vital U.S. interest was at risk? Anglophilia is one reason. The most important fact of the twentieth century, it has been said, is that Americans spoke English. A cultural affinity and common Anglo-Saxon heritage helped us identify with the English; among America's elite, pro-British sympathies were almost universal. Wilson and most of his cabinet were viscerally pro-British. Writes historian Ralph Raico:

> The President and most of his chief subordinates were dyed-in-the-wool Anglophiles. Love of England and all things English was an intrinsic part of their sense of identity. With England threatened, even the Chief Justice of the United States Supreme Court, Edward D. White, voiced the impulse to leave for Canada to volunteer for the British armed forces.[3]

"England is fighting our fight," the president once confided. "I
shall not... place obstacles in her way when she is fighting for her
life—and the life of the world."[4] From boyhood Wilson had been
enamored of things British. As Walter McDougall wrote:

> As a Princeton undergraduate, "Tommy" Wilson drafted class-
> mates into games and clubs so that he could play the leader and
> indulge his love of things British. In war games he fancied him-
> self a British squadron commander, in political clubs a British
> minister swaying Parliament with his rhetoric. He kept a portrait
> of the crusading Christian prime minister William Ewart
> Gladstone on his desk.[5]

Theodore Roosevelt, the most popular Republican of the day,
was also an Anglophile. Though of Dutch descent like the Boers, TR
backed the British in the Boer War: "[The] downfall of the British
Empire, I should regard as a calamity to the race, and especially to this
country."[6]

Also, since the Venezuela crisis in 1895, British policy had turned
pro-American. In the Spanish-American War, Britain sided with the
United States. When American troops took Manila on August 13,
1898, the British squadron, to get a better view of U.S. naval gunfire,
maneuvered between the American and German squadrons, leading
Americans to believe the Royal Navy had covered Dewey's flank.
Some Americans had begun to see an intertwined destiny. As the war
against Spain began, Albert V. Beveridge, the young Indiana firebrand,
called on America to emulate "our mother" and with her take over
the markets of the world:

> If it means Anglo-Saxon solidarity; if it means an English-
> American understanding upon the basis of a division of the
> world's markets, and English-speaking people's league of God for

the permanent peace of this war-worn world, the stars will fight for us, and countless centuries will applaud.[7]

In 1900 American and British troops marched and fought side-by-side to rescue the besieged foreign legation in Peking. At the Hague disarmament conferences of 1899 and 1907, Americans collaborated with the British to block any arms limitations that might weaken either nation. Britain had settled the Alaska border dispute in America's favor, enraging Canadians, and signed the Hay-Pauncefote Treaty of 1900 guaranteeing that any interoceanic canal in Central America would be an exclusively American project. Britain then granted the United States the right to fortify such a canal, reduced its garrisons in the West Indies, and removed its naval squadron from the Caribbean.

London had concluded that U.S. hegemony in the Western Hemisphere was inevitable, and had decided to accommodate reality and convert the world's greatest industrial power from an antagonist into an ally. Call it appeasement, but it was among the wisest policies the British ever took. The blunders of Lord North and George III were somewhat compensated for by the brilliance of the British statesmen who for twenty years pursued what historians now call "The Great Rapprochement."[8]

America thus never fully stood up for its rights when the British interfered with U.S. trade with Germany and neutrals such as Denmark and the Netherlands. When the State Department issued one sharp protest, U.S. Ambassador Walter Hines Page read the message to Foreign Secretary Sir Edward Grey, then added, "I have now read the dispatch, but do not agree with it. Let us consider how it should be answered!"[9] Grey thought this the "highest type of patriotism." A U.S. historian describes Page as a "good English spaniel."[10]

THE SWORD OF LAFAYETTE

Second, though there was deep anti-British sentiment among Irish-
and German-Americans, most Americans had a dislike for militaristic
Germany and "Kaiser Bill." Anti-German feeling was strengthened by
British propaganda alleging atrocities by the "Hun." Stories of Belgian
babies being tossed about on German bayonets and of raped Catholic
nuns were believed. Years later, there would come an emotional back-
lash against "lying British propaganda" and "false atrocity stories." But
the British hidden persuaders succeeded for a reason:

> …Britons, in this war as on other occasions, were the most
> effective spokesmen for their country's cause because of their
> national gift of restraint and understatement. This made it easy
> for them to identify more or less convincingly British interests
> with the requirements of reason, logic, and morality.
>
> By contrast German publicity efforts, heavily handicapped
> by the severance of direct cable communication between
> Germany and the outside world, seemed clumsy, bumbling, and
> heavy-footed, and generally fell on skeptical ears.[11]

The British had cut the cable.

Third, Americans are romantics. We saw France bleeding and
believed we owed it a debt. Wrote Robert Underwood Johnson:

> Forget us, God, if we forget
> The sacred sword of Lafayette![12]

When, on July 4, 1917, Colonel E. S. Stanton stood at the Paris
grave of the hero of the American Revolution and declared, "Lafayette,
we are here!" a thrill of pride swept over every American heart.

Americans also sympathized with "brave little Belgium" as the
Germans marched over it, dismissing as a "scrap of paper" the 1839

treaty that had guaranteed Belgian neutrality. In that time an invasion in wanton violation of a nation's neutrality was a shocking event. With great emotion, the editor of the periodical *Life* declared:

> For us the great, clear issue of this war is Belgium. If we see any-
> thing right at all in all this matter, Belgium is a martyr to civi-
> lization, sister to all who love liberty or law; assailed, polluted,
> trampled in the mire, heelmarked in her breast, tattered, home-
> less....The great unconquerable fact of the great war is
> Belgium.[13]

U-BOATS AND BLUNDERS

Fourth, there were the U-boats. As soon as the war began, Britain determined to use its navy to choke off all trade of the Central Powers, and mined the North Sea in November 1914. Britain's goal, First Sea Lord Winston Churchill candidly admitted, was to "starve the whole population—men, women, and children, old and young, wounded and sound—into submission."[14]

Britain also applied the doctrine of "continuous voyage" to cargoes headed for neutral ports, if the goods could be transported by land to Germany. Previously, the doctrine had applied only to the second leg of a sea voyage.[15] America took no action to force Britain to stop the violations of its neutral rights. Robert Lansing, who succeeded Bryan as secretary of state, gave the reason in his memoirs:

> [I]n dealing with the British Government there was always in
> my mind the conviction that we would ultimately become an
> ally of Great Britain and that it would not do, therefore, to let
> our controversies reach a point where diplomatic correspon-
> dence gave place to action.[16]

In contrast to his flexibility in coping with Britain's abuses, Wilson warned Germany it would be held "strictly accountable" for any loss of life or property from submarine attacks, which began in February 1915 in response to Britain's mining of the North Sea. U.S. neutrality was thus seen by many as a sham, benevolent toward the Allies, bristling toward the Germans. The newly born *New Republic* found Britain's policy more offensive: "The German threat to innocent neutral commerce with England was wanton, but it was incidental. The English threat to innocent neutral commerce with Germany is polite and benevolent in form, but in substance it is deadly."[17] Historian H. W. Brands agrees:

> The British couldn't hide behind the rationalization that their
> policy spared the innocent, as they said the German policy did
> not, for while German submarines did indeed take a toll of the
> crews of merchant vessels, the Allied blockade had the objective
> of starving an entire nation, of which women and children
> would be the first to succumb.[18]

Since the U-boats were under orders not to attack U.S. ships, there was no major peril to American citizens from submarines, if they traveled on American ships. Prior to the break in relations with Berlin, February 3, 1917, only three Americans had perished aboard U.S. ships, lost on the *Gulflight,* torpedoed while sailing in a British convoy that was not entitled to American protection.[19] The danger to Americans came from their insistence on traveling on British and French ships. Wilson stubbornly asserted Americans' right to travel on belligerent merchant ships and demanded that German U-boats follow the rules of cruiser warfare. These rules required a submarine to surface and fire a warning shot before a ship was searched. Such rules were utterly unworkable for submarines, which were small and flimsy. A surfaced U-boat could be attacked, rammed, and sunk.

Indeed, the British Admiralty had given orders to ram surfaced submarines and developed decoy merchant ships called "Q ships" with hidden guns to lure U-boats to the surface, where they could be blasted out of the water.[20]

To avoid a clash with the United States, Germany made an offer. Its submarines would follow the rules of cruiser warfare, if the British would disarm their merchant ships. Britain refused, and Wilson put no pressure on London to agree. Weaker at sea, the Germans were willing to abide by the rules of sea warfare as demanded by the president. This got them nowhere with Woodrow Wilson.

Bryan, a principled man, had grasped the contradiction in Wilson's policy: The president wanted to stay out of the war, but his unyielding stand on neutral rights—especially the dubious right of Americans to travel safely aboard belligerents' ships—must lead to incidents that would lead to war. Bryan believed Wilson had to choose between his stand on neutral rights and his desire to stay out of the war; he pressed on the president the course he believed would achieve the higher goal. He urged Wilson to deny armed merchant ships entry to U.S. ports and forbid U.S. citizens from traveling on the vessels of belligerents. Historian Charles Callan Tansill believed that had Wilson taken Bryan's advice, there might have been no World War I for America. He wrote:

> America finally entered the war because of serious difficulties
> with Germany arising out of the submarine warfare.... If the
> President had taken any decisive action against the admission of
> armed British merchantmen into American harbors, and if he
> had warned American citizens of the dangers that attended passage on belligerent vessels, America might well have been spared
> the great sacrifice of 1917–1918.[21]

"America's entry into the World War," Tansill argued, "may be traced in part to this failure of the President to follow a course dictated by American rather than Allied interests."[22] *The New Republic* agreed: "No American lives would have been lost had we acquiesced in Germany's policy as we have in Britain's."[23]

Although Wilson's administration had accepted Britain's blockade of German ports, Germany's retaliatory blockade of Britain produced repeated collisions. The first and greatest was over the sinking of the *Lusitania* on May 7, 1915, with a loss of 1,198 passengers, among them 128 Americans. Germany protested that it had given fair warning in newspaper ads that the ship was carrying contraband and Americans ought not to sail on her, but the reaction in America was fury and disgust.

"Why be shocked by the drowning of a few people, if there is to be no objection to starving a nation?" Bryan asked.[24] When the president refused, once again, to take his counsel to avoid war with Germany, Bryan resigned. The last great antiwar Democrat in the cabinet was gone.

ALL THE PRESIDENT'S MEN

This leads to a fifth reason Wilson went to war. After Bryan left, all of the president's key foreign policy advisers, House, Page, and Lansing, were more pro–Ally and prointervention than Wilson, who wanted to stay out even it meant a German victory. Page was so pro-British that Wilson grew weary of reading his cables. House wanted to stay out, but would accept war to prevent a German victory. By the summer of 1915, writes historian Robert Tucker, "House believed America's participation in the war on the Allied side to be all but inevitable. With the passage of time this belief was to harden."[25] This was the confidant of whom Wilson said, "Mr. House is my second personality... my independent self. His thoughts and mine are one."[26]

By the time he took over from Bryan, Lansing had decided the war was between autocracy and democracy and that Germany must

not be allowed to escape even with a draw. In a private memorandum, Lansing wrote, "Germany must not be permitted to win this
war and [*sic*] to break even, though to prevent it this country is forced
to take an active part."[27] On the eve of war, Lansing was exultant and
resolute:

> Things have turned out right and the days of anxiety and uncer-
> tainty are over.... It may take two or three years. It may even
> take five years. It may cost a million Americans; it may cost five
> million. However long it may take, however many men it costs
> we must go through with it.[28]

Adds Tucker:

> A case can be made that Wilson's advisers were never really can-
> did in their dealings with him, that their counsel often obscured
> their real convictions, and that if the result was not to deceive
> the president it was at least to mislead him. Even Page, the most
> open of Wilson's assistants, was occasionally guilty of voicing
> apparent convictions that in all likelihood he did not hold. But
> Lansing and House made a regular practice of doing so. Never
> once did Lansing reveal his true position to the president.[29]

These men knew the president wanted to stay out of the
European war even if it meant a German victory. Not one shared his
view, but none was forthright. They feared banishment if they openly
disagreed; so, they dissembled and served the president badly. Wilson
deserved better. But he had refused to heed the counsel of the one
honest, open adviser, Bryan, who, like the president himself, put
peace above any sweeping construction of neutral rights in a world
at war.

MEXICO GETS AN OFFER

A sixth cause of war was Teutonic blundering. Repeatedly, diplomats
of the Central Powers were caught in anti-American activity. Documents fell into U.S. hands proving that the German Embassy's army
attaché, Captain Franz von Papen, and naval attaché, Captain Karl
Boy-Ed, had been plotting against the United States. Papen confided
to his wife in a letter, "I always say to these idiotic Yankees that they
should shut their mouths...."[30] Austria-Hungary's ambassador, Dr.
Constantin Dumba, was caught fomenting strikes at U.S. munitions
plants. The *Boston Post* memorialized his expulsion:

> O Constantin Theodor Dumba,
> You've roused Uncle Sam from his slumba:
> That letter you wrote,
> Got the old fellow's goat—
> Now his path you'll no longer encumba.[31]

Spectacularly, on March 1, 1917, headlines brought news of a
secret cable from German Foreign Minister Arthur Zimmermann to
his minister in Mexico City, instructing him to offer, as a reward if
Mexico joined the Central Powers in the event of war, return of "lost
territory in Texas, New Mexico, and Arizona." British naval intelligence had intercepted and deciphered the telegram and delightedly
made it public. The Zimmermann telegram brought Americans to the
boiling point, though the idea that Mexico could recapture the
Southwest, or that Germany could assist an invasion, made it obvious,
writes Tansill, that "Secretary Zimmermann had certain attributes of
the celebrated Baron Munchausen."[32] The absurdity of the plan aside,
the Zimmermann note was perfectly crafted to enrage Americans and
humiliate and silence Germany's remaining friends—not a brilliant
moment in the diplomatic history of the Second Reich.

"UNDER THE COMMAND OF GOLD"

Finally, there was the money power. In early 1914 the United States was sliding toward depression. Bankruptcies were at an all-time high; the U.S. industrial plant was operating at only 60 percent of capacity. Allied purchases helped pull the country out of recession. Americans began to get rich on the war trade, and the Allies began to depend on it for survival. The Central Powers came to believe that only American food, money, and munitions kept the Allies fighting. An embittered German-American cried: "We prattle about humanity, while we manufacture poisoned shrapnel and picric acid for profit. Ten thousand German widows, ten thousand orphans, ten thousand graves bear the legend, 'Made in America.'"[33]

As early as October 1914, Wilson, who had implored Americans to be "impartial in thought as well as action," had secretly allowed credits for the Allies. By the time America went to war in April 1917, $2.3 billion in cash and credits had been extended by U.S. banks. Ninety percent of these loans went for arms, munitions, and supplies from the United States. During these years of neutrality, America moved from a debtor nation to become the world's greatest creditor. But it was doubtful these loans would ever be repaid without an Allied victory and the imposition of heavy reparations on Germany. The U.S. financial community thus had a huge stake in an Allied victory. But, by 1917, victory was not in the cards—unless the U.S. Army was thrown into the fight. The vital interests of U.S. financial houses thus argued aloud for doughboys in the trenches of the Western Front. As Thomas W. Lamont of the House of Morgan later declared:

> Those were the days when American citizens were being urged to remain neutral in action, in word, and even in thought. But our firm had never for one moment been neutral: we didn't know how to be. From the very start we did everything that we could to contribute to the cause of the Allies.[34]

As the flower of Europe's youth was being mowed down, Yankee dollars kept the war going and American farms, factories, and financiers profited from the slaughter. "[T]he munitions trade was about as essential to the economic life of America as it was to the military life of the Allies," notes one historian.[35] Years later, the progressive senator George W. Norris wrote that when Americans ought to have remembered the advice of the Father of their Country and kept out of European wars, they were pushed and pulled "into war under the command of gold."[36] Norris placed full blame for U.S. intervention on the doorstep of plutocrats "concealed in their palatial offices on Wall Street, sitting behind mahogany desks, covered up with clipped coupons... coupons tainted with mothers' tears, coupons dyed in the lifeblood of their fellow men."[37]

By January 1917 the Allies had overdrawn their credit by nearly $500 million. Only the U.S. government could now bail out the bankrupt Allies and save the bankers' investments. But the government could not help unless America was at war, for a neutral could not legally lend to a belligerent. Thus, by 1917, not only were America's sympathies with the Allies, America's corporate and financial elite also had an enormous monetary stake in an Allied victory, which was nowhere in sight.

Wilson, however, was contemptuous of corporate power. In 1913 he had declared it a "very perilous thing to determine the foreign policy of a nation in terms of material interest. It is not only unfair to those with whom you are dealing, but it is degrading as regards your own actions."[38] Thus war would not reach America's shore unless Germany insulted U.S. honor; and in one of the greatest blunders in history, the Germans did just that.

THE KAISER'S FATAL GAMBLE

Even on the very eve of war, Wilson did not believe it was coming. On January 4, 1917, he told Colonel House: "[T]here will be no war.

This country does not intend to become involved in this war. We are the only one of the great white nations that is free from war today, and it would be a crime against civilization for us to go in."[39] The colonel confided this to his diary, but was not so sure:

> The President may change this view for, as I said before, he changes his views often.... I told him, as I have many times before, how unprepared we were and that [French Ambassador Jean] Jusserand had called my attention to it, expressing the hope that we would take some steps particularly if there was any chance of a break with Germany. Jusserand thought there would be from 20,000 to 40,000 Germans in the Eastern States who would for the moment have things their own way; blowing up bridges, powder magazines, munitions, etc. He did not consider it improbable that they might capture Washington and the President himself. Neither the President nor I was disturbed at this thought, but I took the occasion to express the feeling that we should not be so totally unprepared in the event of war.[40]

Whose loyalty Wilson had been questioning with his ferocious attacks on the "hyphenates... born under foreign flags [who] had injected the poison of disloyalty in our political affairs" is clear—the immigrants who had come to America from Germany.

But as the president was confiding to House his sense that the war threat had passed by, Germany's high command was nearing desperation. Unfortunately for the kaiser's men, they did not know fortune was about to smile upon them. The abdication of the tsar and the overthrow of the Romanov dynasty were only two months away. But in January, Germany was still fighting a two-front war, the end of which it could not see. Thus the Reich was about to gamble all on a last desperate throw of the dice. As historian Foster Rhea Dulles noted:

Germany's only means of cutting off the flow of American
munitions which enabled her enemies to go on fighting was
submarine warfare directed against all cargo ships, regardless of
nationality. Sooner or later she was certain to accept the risk of
being held to account by the United States [for] turning her
U-boats loose. To allow the constant re-enforcement of the Allies
was to accept defeat.[41]

On January 9, 1917, Field Marshal Paul von Hindenburg, General
Erich Ludendorff, Admiral Henning von Holtzendorf, and Chan-
cellor Theobald von Bethmann Hollweg arrived at Pless Castle on the
German-Polish border, Supreme Headquarters of the German army.
They were joined the next day by a "pale, irritable, and excited" kaiser.
Hindenburg had warned, "Things cannot be worse than they are now.
The war must be brought to an end by whatever means as soon as
possible."[42] Questions on the table: Should Germany declare unre-
stricted submarine warfare around the British Isles and risk sinking
U.S. ships, bringing America into the war? Could Britain be starved
out before the Americans crossed the Atlantic in sufficient force to
turn the tide of battle?

Holtzendorf said if his submarines were allowed to prowl free, he
would guarantee victory before harvest time. Hindenburg and
Ludendorff seconded the admiral, warning the kaiser he must do
something to weaken a near-certain Allied spring offensive. For an
hour Bethmann argued that the Americans might prove stronger
than imagined. But in 1917 the U.S. Army was ranked seventeenth
in the world in effectiveness, behind Portugal's, and since the question of how much power the United States might bring to bear in
France was a military one, the chancellor deferred to the warlords.
They placed before the kaiser a secret order calling for unrestricted
submarine warfare to commence on February 1, 1917. The kaiser
signed. He and his admiral and generals marched out, leaving the

diplomat slumped in his chair. An aide entered and asked what was wrong.

"Finis Germaniae," said the chancellor of the Second Reich.[43]

THE WAR BECOMES A CRUSADE

Germany had wagered its survival on a military assessment that the Americans could not raise a great army, and train and transport it across a submarine-infested Atlantic, before the Allies had been forced to sue for peace. It was a desperate gamble to end the war, and it failed. Had Berlin not declared unrestricted submarine warfare, the Americans would likely have stayed out. But when Germany began sinking U.S. ships and killing American seamen, war became certain. In Wilson's words, the war had been "thrust" upon us. In the next collisions between German submarines and U.S. merchantmen, four U.S. ships went to the bottom. Wilson went to Congress for a declaration of war.

Yet even in his war message there is a vagueness about America's aims, suggestive of what was true: No vital U.S. interest was at risk to justify sending two million American soldiers to France.

> It is a fearful thing to lead this great peaceful people into war,
> into the most terrible and disastrous of all wars, civilization itself
> seeming to be in the balance. But the right is more precious
> than peace, and we shall fight for the things which we have
> always carried nearest to our hearts,—for democracy, for the
> right of those who submit to authority to have a voice in their
> own governments, for the rights and liberties of small nations,
> for a universal dominion of right by such a concert of free peo-
> ples as shall bring peace and safety to all nations and make the
> world itself at last free.[44]

To Filipino rebels, whose cause had lately been crushed by U.S.

troops, this must have appeared a remarkable statement. And if this messianic vision was Wilson's war aim, there was trouble ahead. For whatever motivated the idealist in the White House, the men entrusted with the destinies of the British, French, Russian, and Japanese empires were not waging any war for democracy. Not only did the universal nature of Wilson's war aims contradict his call only weeks earlier, on January 22, 1917, for a "peace without victory," there could now be no compromise peace, if the future of mankind was at stake.

A year before the war became, in Wilson's eyes, a crusade in which the fate of civilization was at issue, the president could not even fathom what it was all about. With the objects and causes of Europe's war, he had said in 1916, "we are not concerned. The obscure fountains from which its stupendous flood has burst forth we are not interested to search for or explore."[45] In December 1916, as Wilson sought to mediate between the belligerents, he suggested that the goals for which the Allies and the Central Powers both claimed to be fighting were "virtually the same."[46]

In Wilson's call for war can be found not a trace of national interest. "We have no selfish ends to serve. We desire no conquest, no dominion. We seek no indemnities for ourselves, no material compensation for the sacrifices we shall freely make."[47] We want nothing, said Wilson.

Polk had gone to war for Texas, Lincoln to save the Union, McKinley to avenge the *Maine* and drive the Spanish out of Cuba. Each achieved his aim. Wilson went to war to build a better world and would come home with a peace that spat upon his ideals and guaranteed a second world war. His words in 1917 had masked the truth: The greatest war in history was not begun to "make the world safe for democracy." It had been ignited, as Bismarck had predicted it would be, by "some damn fool thing in the Balkans."

Why, ultimately, did America come in? Some contend the United States entered the war for no higher motive than to defend a right to ship and sell, unmolested, to one of the belligerents; but with the blood of a generation of Europe's young spilled, the statesmen needed to endow the war with a higher, nobler purpose. Wrote Reinhold Niebuhr, "Every nation is caught in the moral paradox of refusing to go to war unless it can be proved that the national interest is imperiled, and of continuing the war only by proving that something much more than the national interest is at stake."[48]

Historian Robert Ferrell believes such explanations are cynical and ahistorical, and that this generation cannot comprehend the magnanimity and belief in principles of the idealistic Americans of 1917. He writes:

> The American people, having enjoyed throughout their history
> an abundant life in a material sense, having from their own suc-
> cesses come to believe that their principles were correct princi-
> ples, lacking bitterness and cynicism about the motives and
> behavior of foreign peoples, were willing to take a stand against
> what most students even today would grant was a ruthless
> Germany military ambition. The American people, to the entire
> disbelief of contemporary foreign observers and to the disbelief
> of their own children of the next generation, were willing to
> take that stand in the world for principle.[49]

With doughboys pouring into France in the hundreds of thousands by mid-1918, the tide began to go out on Germany. Its armies breaking, Berlin, in October, asked Wilson for an armistice on the basis of his Fourteen Points. On the eleventh hour of the eleventh day of the eleventh month, the Great War ended. Wilson sailed for Europe. Ten months before, he had gone before Congress and put forth with great eloquence America's war aims: the Fourteen Points.

The purpose of his speech had been to keep Russia fighting after Lenin had come to power, by announcing more idealistic war aims. Wilson listed eight points as crucial to peace: open diplomacy, freedom of the seas, disarmament, lifting of trade barriers, an impartial settlement of colonial claims, restoration of Belgium, evacuation of Russian territory, and the establishment of a League of Nations.[50]

Rooted in liberal idealism rather than the brutal realities of a world of imperial powers in a death struggle, Wilson's vision entailed certain disillusionment. He may have come to believe this vision, but to British Prime Minister David Lloyd George and French Premier Georges Clemenceau, the Fourteen Points had been useful war propaganda, of no relevance to the business at hand: settling accounts with the *Boche*. In December 1918 Lloyd George had won reelection on a pledge to "hang the kaiser" and "squeeze the German lemon until the pips squeak."[51] Said Clemenceau, "Wilson bores me with his Fourteen Points; why, God Almighty has only ten."[52]

A CARTHAGINIAN PEACE

During the war, not one Allied soldier had set foot on German soil. As late as April 1918 the Allies were on the defensive and a German army was on the Marne within forty miles of Paris. But after agreeing to an armistice on Wilson's terms, Germany was treated as a war criminal whose atrocities justified stripping it of all property and rights.

At the Paris peace conference, Alsace-Lorraine was separated from Germany and ceded to France. Recalling how close the German army had come to Paris, Clemenceau wanted to occupy all of Germany to the Rhine, or create a buffer state there. Wilson fought this violation of his principle of self-determination. Clemenceau compromised. France would occupy the Rhineland, and the coal-rich Saar would be put under the League of Nations for fifteen years, after which a plebiscite would be held. In return, Paris demanded a security treaty that pledged America to come to France's defense if it were ever again attacked by Germany. Wilson agreed.

The patches of Eupen and Malmedy were taken from Germany and given to Belgium. Croatia and Slovenia were stripped from Austria and force-marched into a new kingdom of the Serbs, Croats, and Slovenes, to be called Yugoslavia. South Tyrol, north to the Brenner Pass, was given to Italy to fulfill a secret deal whereby Rome had switched sides. This put a quarter of a million Austrians under Italian control. The Middle East, taken from the Ottoman Empire, was divided between the British and French. Germany's African colonies were awarded to Britain and its island colonies in the Pacific divided between Britain and Japan, thus ratifying a secret London-Tokyo deal of 1917 whereby Britain had agreed to support Japan's claims in Shantung peninsula, home of Confucius, and to the German islands north of the equator, if Tokyo would support Britain's claims to Germany's islands south of the equator. Thus did Japan take control of the Marshalls, Marianas, and Carolines, chains of islands the names of which would become familiar to a generation of U.S. Marines.

"Open covenants, openly arrived at."

Observing Wilson's cave-ins to reality, Clemenceau mocked that the president "talked like Jesus Christ but acted like Lloyd George."[53]

But this was only the beginning of the stripping of Germany and Austria-Hungary. Lithuania was given the East Prussian city of Memel, and the Sudetenland—and 3.25 million German subjects of the Hapsburg empire—was given to a new nation: Czechoslovakia. Learning later of the Sudeten Germans, Wilson blurted, "Why Masaryk never told me that."[54] A million Hungarians and half a million Poles passed under Prague's rule. German Danzig was declared a "free city" under the League of Nations, and a 130-kilometer–wide strip was torn out of West Prussia and given to Poland as its promised

"corridor" to the sea, which cut East Prussia off from the rest of
Germany. In his "Four Principles" speech, a month after the Fourteen Points address, Wilson had declared:

> There shall be... no punitive damages. People are not to be
> handed about from one sovereignty to another by an inter-
> national conference.... National aspirations must be respected;
> peoples may now be dominated and governed only by their
> own consent. "Self-determination" is not a mere phrase.... Every
> territorial settlement involved in this war must be made in the
> interest and for the benefit of the populations concerned, and
> not as a part of any mere adjustment or compromise of claims
> amongst rival states.[55]

Not one of Wilson's principles was left unviolated at Versailles.
    Self-determination was granted former subjects of Germany and
Austria-Hungary, but denied millions of Germans and Austrians who
were marched under French, Italian, Czech, and Polish rule. Divided
and dismembered, Germany was put on the rack and ordered to pay
the entire cost of the war, including pensions of Allied soldiers, and
to accept moral responsibility for having started the war. A "war
guilt" clause was inserted in the treaty:

> The Allied and Associated Governments affirm and Germany
> accepts the responsibility of Germany and her allies for causing
> all the loss and damage to which the Allied and Associated
> Governments and their nationals have been subjected as a conse-
> quence of the war imposed upon them by the aggression of
> Germany and her allies.[56]

The "war guilt" clause was the intolerable humiliation. In 1914
the kaiser had not wanted war, had not plotted war, and, after blundering in giving Austria the "blank check" to punish Serbia for the

murder of the Austrian archduke, had begged the tsar to stop mobilizing for war. But truth did not matter. Germany must confess to its immorality. As historian Erik von Kuehnelt-Leddihn wrote:

> There is no better way to generate hatred than by forcing a person to sign a confession of guilt which he is sacredly convinced is untrue. This wanton humiliation, unprecedented up to that time in the annals of Christendom, created the thirst for revenge which the National Socialists so cleverly exploited.[57]

On the fourth anniversary of the sinking of the *Lusitania*, Berlin's diplomats were summoned by Clemenceau to Versailles's Trianon Palace, where the French premier staged his humiliation of the hated Germans:

> Delegates of the German state! It is neither the time nor place for superfluous words. You have before you the accredited plenipotentiaries of all the small and great Powers united to fight together in the war that has been so cruelly imposed upon them. The time has come when we must settle our accounts. This is the hour of heavy reckoning! You have asked for peace. We are ready to give you peace.[58]

The Germans were given six weeks to review the treaty and sign. To convince them, Marshal Foch made ready to march at the head of the Allied armies, and the Royal Navy and U.S. warships maintained a "hunger blockade" that had never been lifted at war's end. Within six months of the armistice, that blockade had, in the words of Otto Friedrich, "achieved a casualty list of 700,000 children, old people and women.... The German people, starved and dying by the hundred thousand, were reeling deliriously between blank despair, frenzied revelry, and revolution."[59] A visitor to Germany wrote:

"The starvation is done quietly and decently at home. And when
death comes, it comes in the form of influenza, tuberculosis,
heart failure or one of the new and mysterious diseases caused
by the war and carries off its exhausted victims." In Frankfurt,
even as late as March 1920, the funerals never ceased all day.[60]

One half of Europe has knocked the other half down and is
kicking it to death, wrote an observer. When the treaty was brought
to him, German Chancellor Philip Scheidemann rejected it and
resigned, saying, "What hand would not wither that binds itself and
us in these fetters?"[61]

Given an ultimatum that the Allies would march in a week, on
June 28, 1919, five years to the day after Gavrilo Princip shot the
archduke in Sarajevo, the Germans signed—as crews aboard the
German warships in captivity scuttled battleships, cruisers, and
destroyers, rather than turn them over to the Allies. The High Seas
Fleet, which by 1914 had begun to challenge England's historic naval
supremacy, committed suicide at Scapa Flow.

The Versailles Treaty had detached from the Reich an eighth of
its territory and a tenth of its population. Their noble work done, the
peacemakers went home and were astonished, fourteen years later,
that so many Germans could vote for a man like Hitler. In
"September 1, 1939," the poet W. H. Auden would later write,
"Those to whom evil is done/Do evil in return."[62]

WILSON'S FAILURE

The "collapse of the president has been one of the decisive moral
events of history," wrote a bitterly disillusioned John Maynard
Keynes, a Paris observer. More than any other man, Wilson had
failed at Versailles.[63] The Germans had agreed to an armistice based
on the president's word that the Fourteen Points would be the basis
of peace. While Wilson could not dictate terms to the Allies, he had
a moral duty to oppose the dishonoring of his commitments. But

he failed to halt the amputations of the German nation. What Wilson brought home was Clemenceau's treaty of vengeance imposed in violation of everything he had pledged. All he had to show for it was allied agreement to join his League of Nations, a Western-dominated parliament of man that Wilson believed could forever enforce peace, but that his critics said was nothing more than a scheme for the preservation of the British Empire. Perhaps there was truth in the savage verdict of his own secretary of war, Lindley Garrison, that Wilson was a man of high ideals and no principles.[64]

France's position is understandable. Crushed in the Franco-Prussian War of 1870–1871, invaded in 1914, with 1,350,000 dead, 3 million wounded, and lands ravaged by four years of trench warfare, France was determined to punish Germany and eliminate it as a threat. "There are twenty million Germans too many," Clemenceau once blurted.[65] France's goals: strip Germany of its fleet, deny it the right to maintain an army, reduce its population by tearing off provinces, destroy its capacity to recover by seizing or crippling its industrial heartland, and crush it with debt.

France's desire for revenge may be understood in terms of European power politics, Franco-German history, and the horrific losses France had just suffered. But Clemenceau's demands only underscored the point: These old world hatreds and quarrels were none of America's business.

Versailles was worse than an unjust, dishonorable peace; it was a historic crime, justifying Senate rejection and repudiation of Wilson's League of Nations, which would have required American soldiers to enforce it. Wilson had forgotten the wisdom of his own words that January day in 1917 when he warned against a victory that would mean a

peace forced upon the loser, a victor's terms imposed upon the vanquished. It would be accepted in humiliation, under duress, at an intolerable sacrifice, and would leave a sting, a resentment, a bitter memory upon which terms of peace would rest… as upon quicksand.[66]

So it did. Defenders of Versailles retort that what the Allies did to Germany was nothing less than what the Germans had done to a defeated Russia at Brest-Litovsk—where in March 1918 Berlin had stripped away Poland, the Baltic republics, and Ukraine—or what a victorious Reich would have done to France. Had not Wilhelm I and Bismarck demanded a huge indemnity of a defeated France in 1871? All of which may be true, none of which was relevant. Versailles was an act of colossal stupidity. Instead of tying a defeated Germany to the West, it drove outcast Germans to collude with that other pariah state, Bolshevik Russia, in the Rapallo Pact of 1922. Decrying the injustice of Versailles would become a universally popular plank in the platform of the Nazi Party. As Kennan wrote:

> Truly, this was a peace which had the tragedies of the future
> written into it as by the devil's own hand. It was a peace, as the
> French historian Bainville said, which was too mild for the hard-
> ships it contained. And this was the sort of peace you got when
> you allowed war hysteria and impractical idealism to lie down
> together in your mind, like the lion and the lamb; when you
> indulged yourself in the colossal conceit of thinking that you
> could suddenly make international life over into what you
> believed to be your own image.[67]

The war's carnage, the hatreds engendered, and the lust for vengeance blinded the Allied statesmen. They could not see that with Lenin, Trotsky, and Stalin coming to power in Russia, a unified, democratic Germany was Europe's bulwark against the rise of totalitarian barbarism to the east. Rather than create conditions from which such a Germany might emerge, the Allies stripped it naked and tore it apart, discrediting German democracy at birth by forcing its diplomats to sign a peace no patriot could defend. Wrote Keynes, "Never in the lifetime of men now living has the universal element in the soul of man burnt so dimly."[68]

Moreover, it was not a workable peace. By dismembering the most powerful nation in Europe and surrounding it with weak neighbors against whom Germany had huge grievances, the treaty-makers had scheduled a war of revenge and reunification, once Germany got to its feet. Toward the end of negotiations, Lloyd George sensed the calamity the Big Three had wrought. On March 23 he withdrew to draft a memorandum that he circulated. The Fontainebleau Memorandum proved prophetic:

> [I]njustice, arrogance, displayed in the hour of triumph will never be forgotten or forgiven.
>   …I am, therefore, strongly averse to transferring more Germans from German rule to the rule of some other nation than can possibly be helped. I cannot conceive any greater cause of future war than that the German people, who have certainly proved themselves one of the most vigorous and powerful races in the world should be surrounded by a number of small states, many of them consisting of people who have never previously set up a stable government for themselves, but each of them containing large masses of Germans clamouring for reunion with their native land.[69]

"We must regain our power," said General Hans von Seeckt, who would take command of the German army, "and as soon as we do, we will naturally take back everything we lost."[70]

THE COSTS OF INTERVENTION

No one can say for certain how history would have unfolded had America stayed out of the Great War. Russia, whose tsar abdicated only weeks before U.S. entry, would still have collapsed. The same German divisions would have been released to the west, where the French army was in mutiny. Without the U.S. government becoming the lender of last resort to finance the war effort, with no prospect of millions of American troops pouring into the trenches, the Allies would probably have been forced to negotiate an armistice or sue for peace. The kaiser's army, bloodied but undefeated, would have gone home. Germany would have become a fire wall against any drive into Central Europe by a Soviet Russia diminished by Brest-Litovsk. As the character of the Bolshevik regime revealed itself, Germany would surely have considered going back to correct the blunder of having transported Lenin through German lines in the infamous sealed train. Lenin, Trotsky, Stalin, and the whole grisly gang might have been hung from the lampposts of Petrograd. A strong, united, and prosperous Germany would not have spawned a Hitler. There might have been no Holocaust, no quarter-century reign of Stalin, no Cold War. Had America stayed out, there would have been no Versailles, no occupation and dismemberment of the German nation, no American war dead, no debt, no era of disillusionment. Had America not financed the war, it would surely have ended earlier than it did, with far fewer dead. "For of all sad words of tongue or pen,/The saddest are these: 'It might have been!'"[71]

What had intervention wrought? As the doughboys went off to France, wives and sweethearts had sung the old rebel song "When Johnny Comes Marching Home Again." Some 116,000 Johnnys never came home again. Dead of shot, shell, and gas on the battlefields of Belleau Wood, Chateau Thierry, and the Argonne, and of the diseases that swept the Western Front, they lay in places like the hill country around the river Meuse. War had seemingly produced only "debt, inflation, prohibition, influenza, and ingratitude from Allies whom [America] had strained herself to help...."[72] That first modern income tax of 1913, which had 6 percent as its highest rate, by war's end had soared to 77 percent. U.S. national debt, $1.2 billion in 1916, passed $25 billion in 1919.[73] It would never be repaid.

World War I was an unrelieved disaster for Western civilization. Three ancient European houses and empires had collapsed in ruins: the Hapsburgs, Hohenzollerns, and Romanovs. The Ottoman Empire had also collapsed. Britain and France had suffered wounds from which they would never recover. The war to make the world safe for democracy made the world safe for Bolshevism, fascism, and Nazism. Such were the fruits of U.S. intervention, victory, and Versailles. Perhaps the most eloquent epitaph of the Great War was written a decade after the guns fell silent, in the somber reflection of that most bellicose of leaders in the British war cabinet, First Lord of the Admiralty Winston Churchill:

> Governments and individuals conformed to the rhythm of the
> tragedy, and swayed and staggered forward in helpless violence,
> slaughtering and squandering on ever-increasing scales, till
> injuries were wrought to the structure of human society which a
> century will not efface, and which may conceivably prove fatal
> to the present civilisation....Victory was to be bought so dear as
> to be almost indistinguishable from defeat. It was not to give
> even security to the victors....The most complete victory ever
> gained in arms has failed to solve the European problem or to
> remove the dangers which produced the war.[74]

WILSON VS. THE "IRRECONCILABLES"

On March 3, 1919, near midnight, Senator Henry Cabot Lodge, who had vowed to kill Wilson's League of Nations—"this evil thing with a holy name"—showed his hand.[75] It was a strong one. Lodge introduced the "Republican Round Robin" signed by thirty-nine colleagues, well over one-third of the Senate, enough votes to kill the league and the entire treaty:

> Resolved... That it is the sense of the Senate that while it is
> their sincere desire that the nations of the world should unite to
> promote peace and general disarmament, the constitution of the
> league of nations *in the form now proposed* to the peace conference
> should not be accepted by the United States [emphasis added].[76]

Message to President Wilson: Unless there are changes in the league to protect America's rights, we have the votes to keep the United States out. But Lodge knew that if Wilson made concessions, the president would win. Arrogant, proud, and stubborn, Wilson defiantly announced he was going to ram the treaty and league through the Senate, as written. How? By tying the treaty and league together, and forcing the Senate to vote up or down:

> [W]hen that treaty comes back gentlemen on this side will find
> the Covenant not only in it, but so many threads of the treaty
> tied to the Covenant that you cannot dissect the Covenant from
> the treaty without destroying the whole vital structure. The
> structure of the peace will not be vital without the League of
> Nations, and no man is going to bring back a cadaver with
> him.[77]

Would Wilson entertain reservations to his league? "I shall consent to nothing," the president said. "The Senate must take its medicine."[78] As historian Walter McDougall writes, the Senate "refused the spoon."

In many histories Wilson is portrayed as a martyr to peace whose

League of Nations was a bold and idealistic institution that would have enabled America to play its rightful role in the world and prevented World War II. To the contrary, American membership would have produced a debacle. Not only did the league contradict the counsel of Washington and Jefferson to stay aloof from European politics and avoid "permanent" and "entangling" alliances, but had America joined, U.S. troops would have been called upon to enforce a dishonorable peace. Were Americans to spill the blood of their sons to enforce a peace from which all the victors had grabbed territory and booty but the United States? To have joined the league as founding father and most powerful member would have put America into the middle of every ethnic quarrel and nationalist conflict in Europe, including the clash between Great Britain and the Irish.

Irish-Americans were outraged; they believed that Ireland's right to independence had been compromised. German-Americans saw Versailles as a peace of vengeance. Italian-Americans were enraged that Wilson had supported Yugoslavia's control of Fiume. This treaty, said the *Springfield Republican*, "was dictated in a paroxysm of hate."[79] It is a myth that reactionary Republicans killed the treaty; opposition came from every quarter. The Battalion of Death was led by the great progressive "Lion of Idaho," William E. Borah. Had he his way, the senator roared, Wilson's league would be put "twenty thousand leagues under the sea," and this "treacherous and treasonable scheme... buried in hell." Borah vowed he "would not change his mind [even] if Jesus Christ himself came to earth and pleaded for the Covenant."[80]

Declared *The New Republic* in a cover editorial entitled "This Is Not Peace":

> Americans would be fools if they permitted themselves now to
> be embroiled in a system of European alliances. America promised to underwrite a stable peace. Mr. Wilson has failed. The

peace cannot last. America should withdraw from all commitments which would impair her freedom of action.[81]

While holding no brief for Germany, *The New Republic* warned
that a "Punic peace of annihilation" carried within it "the specifica-
tions for future revolution and war."[82] "In so far as its terms are actually carried out, it is bound to provoke the ultimate explosion of
irreconcilable warfare."[83] *The New Republic* began to serialize Keynes's
The Economic Consequences of the Peace, which portrayed Wilson as a
"blind and deaf Don Quixote" who had been outmaneuvered by
Clemenceau and the "Welsh witch."[84] Progressives piled on. Robert
La Follette denounced the league as a "super-legislature" created to
exploit the "lusty manpower and rich resources of the United States."
Versailles, said Clarence Darrow, is the "machinery for fastening an
unjust and war-breeding peace on the world."[85] Walter Lippmann
called the treaty "illiberal and in bad faith... [and] in the highest
degree imprudent."[86]

With revolts erupting in Ireland, Egypt, and India, five senators
from Wilson's party wrote him on March 28, 1919: "It is quite generally believed here that Great Britain is most desirous of launching the
league."[87] There was a widespread view that "the league was a British
scheme designed for the perpetuation of the British Empire."[88]
Moreover, Lloyd George had made sure the British Empire got six
votes in the league—to one vote for the United States. Even Lansing
was shocked by the implications of Versailles. Wilson, he wrote, had
"abandoned international democracy and become the advocate of
international autocracy."[89]

Then there were the Republican internationalists led by Lodge, who
detested Wilson. "I never expected to hate anyone in politics with the
hatred I feel towards Wilson," Lodge had said.[90] First ever to take a
Ph.D. in political science at Harvard, Lodge sniffed at Wilson's treaty,

"It might get by at Princeton but not at Harvard."[91] But Lodge was no isolationist; he had been an early war hawk who believed in a commanding role for his country in the world, a defense second to none, and a U.S.-British guarantee of France's security. What enraged Lodge was Wilson's surrender of sovereignty and America's freedom of action to an alien institution. Lodge believed Wilson had committed the unpardonable sin—delivering to the League of Nations authority to conscript American blood for ends unrelated to America's vital interests.

Wilson was a believer in multilateralism and collective security. He was willing to put U.S. soldiers at the service of universal ideals and under global institutions not controlled by the United States. Advancing democracy was a driving passion with Wilson. He was certain that global free trade and the spread of democracy would one day usher in the millennium.

Between December 1916, when Wilson was still casting about for a way to end the war before America was dragged in, and December 1918, a change had taken place in the man. Wilson informed Felix Frankfurter that the League of Nations (originally another British idea) was divinely inspired, and that he, Wilson, was "the personal instrument of God."[92] It had come about, said Wilson, "by no plan of our conceiving but by the hand of God who had led us into this way. We can only go forward, with lifted eyes and freshened spirit, to follow the vision."[93] Scholar Marvin Olasky writes of an astonishing scene at the peace conference:

> Wilson's "most extraordinary outburst," according to Lloyd
> George, came when he explained the failure of Christianity to
> achieve its highest ideals. "Jesus Christ so far [has] not succeeded
> in inducing the world to follow His teaching," Wilson stated,
> "because He taught the ideal without devising any practical
> scheme to carry out his aims." In Lloyd George's account,

"Clemenceau slowly opened his dark eyes to their widest
dimension and swept them round the Assembly to see how the
Christians gathered around the table enjoyed this exposure of the
futility of their Master."[94]

To Lodge, Wilsonism was un-American and unconstitutional.
He believed American soldiers should fight only when the national
interest commanded and ought never to be conscripted for foreign
crusades. To his eternal credit, Lodge led the Senate to reject Versailles
and the League of Nations.

THE LAST CRUSADE

Lodge's strategy was to delay a Senate vote until public opinion had
begun to turn against the treaty. To save his league, Wilson, against the
advice of his friends and doctor, undertook a strenuous national
speaking campaign. As he traveled west by train, through Montana
and Idaho, the demonstrations were enormous and heartfelt. But by
the time he began his return trip, Wilson's strength was gone. At
Pueblo, Colorado, where the crowd cheered for ten minutes before
he began to speak, Wilson finished exhausted and near collapse. He
was taken back to the White House. A few days later, a stroke paralyzed one side of his body.

Wilson was never the same man. He cut all ties to Colonel
House, never speaking to him again, dismissed Lansing, and stubbornly resisted any suggestion of compromise on his league. Reading
a fragment from one of his speeches on that final journey, one gets a
sense of the tragedy of the man as he rode that train from state to
state knowing the work of his life was in the balance. In St. Louis,
where the convention had been held to nominate him for a second
term, Wilson declared:

If it [the Covenant of the League of Nations] should ever in any
important respect be impaired, I would feel like asking the

Secretary of War to get the boys who went across the water to
fight together on some field where I could go and see them. And
I would stand up before them and say,

"Boys, I told you before you went across the seas that this
was a war against wars, and I did my best to fulfill the promise;
but I am obliged to come to you in mortification and shame and
say I have not been able to fulfill the promise. You are betrayed.
You fought for something that you did not get."

And the glory of the Armies and Navies of the United States
is gone like a dream in the night, and there ensues upon it, in the
suitable darkness of the night, the nightmare of dread which lay
upon the nations before this war came; and there will come
sometime, in the vengeful Providence of God, another struggle in
which not a few hundred thousand fine men from America will
have to die, but as many millions as are necessary to accomplish
the final freedom of the peoples of the world.[95]

The words are Lincolnian. But like Wilson's Fourteen Points, this
is utopianism, the substitution of liberal sentimentality for hard
thought. No League of Nations, enforcing the vengeful peace of
Versailles, could lift from mankind the scourge of war. When the test
came for the league's concept of collective security, with Japan's invasion of Manchuria in 1931 and Mussolini's invasion of Ethiopia in
1935, the league failed. Britain and France refused to cut off oil to
Italy. Can anyone believe that America in the 1930s would have conscripted and sent soldiers to Manchuria or Ethiopia?

Lodge and his allies appended fourteen "reservations" to the league.
As McDougall writes, "Clearly, these reservations were designed not
to gut the peace that Wilson had fashioned, but to ensure that his
new order did not gut the sovereignty and Constitution of the
United States and the Monroe Doctrine."[96] Adds historian Paul
Johnson, "[T]he Europeans would have accepted Lodge's reservations

and in some cases welcomed them."[97] Even House and Bryan favored the reservations. But the president who had given the rapacious Allies all they wanted at Paris, at the expense of his own principles, refused to compromise with a Republican Senate.

Nor would Wilson accept any weakening of Article X, which bound the United States to "preserve as against external aggression the territorial integrity and existing political independence" of all league members. To Wilson this was the heart of the covenant. To California Senator Hiram Johnson, Article X meant the "British Empire can demand American blood to subdue Ireland."[98] A delegation from the Foreign Relations Committee confronted Wilson in the White House on Article X. Wilson failed the test. The senator who called him out was Warren Harding. It was on Article X that Wilson lost the support of Herbert Hoover, Calvin Coolidge, Charles Evans Hughes, and Henry L. Stimson. While these men did not wish to be associated with the imperialism of old-time expansionists like Elihu Root and William Howard Taft, they were even more averse to the "moral imperialism" of Wilson.[99]

By refusing to take Republicans to Paris to give Congress's majority a hand in and a stake in the treaty, by insisting any alteration was a breach of faith with Britain and France, Wilson painted himself into a corner. There was no escape, once the Senate determined to exercise its constitutional right. Thus when the vote came on the treaty with the Lodge reservations attached, Wilson instructed Democratic senators to vote no. They joined Johnson, Borah, and the "Irreconcilables," and, together, killed the treaty. Several Senate Democrats proposed milder reservations which would have enabled the treaty to pass, but Wilson, who saw them as concessions to the hated Lodge, recoiled: "Never, never! I'll never consent to adopt any policy with which that impossible man is so prominently identified."[100] Democratic Senator Harry F. Ashurst of Arizona said bitterly:

As a friend of the President, as one who has loyally followed
him, I solemnly declare to him this morning: If you want to kill
your own child because the Senate straightens out its crooked
limbs, you must take the responsibility and accept the verdict of
history.[101]

Wilson did.

Subsequent efforts to revive the treaty, with the reservations,
failed. The Irreconcilables would vote the treaty down, and Democrats, loyal to Wilson, would help them kill it. Said William Howard
Taft: "Wilson's greatness is oozing out, as it ought to. He will live in
history as a man with great opportunities which were not improved
but which were wrecked by his personal egotism, selfishness, vanity,
and mulishness."[102]

Taft was right. Far from being "isolationists" who wanted to turn
their backs on Europe, Lodge Republicans and many progressives
wanted America to play the lead role in the rebirth of Western civilization. What they would not do was surrender America's sovereignty, its freedom of action, or the hallowed tradition that Americans
alone decide when, where, and whether the Republic goes to war.
Irreconcilables and Roosevelt-Lodge Republicans agreed that only
Americans could be relied upon to defend the national interest,
which must come first. Wilson was defeated because he placed his
vision above his country; he had failed to put America first.

PART FIVE

1921–1941:
TRIUMPH OF THE INTERVENTIONISTS

CHAPTER 14

Disarmament Decade

A closer examination of the so-called isolationists of the Nineteen-Twenties reveals that many of them were in fact busily engaged in extending American power.[1]
—WILLIAM APPLEMAN WILLIAMS, 1956

Not once had Americans voted for Wilsonian internationalism. In 1916 Wilson had run as the president who had "kept us out of war." On November 5, 1918, on the eve of armistice, he was repudiated, when the country turned both Houses of Congress over to Republicans. In 1920 Warren Harding and Calvin Coolidge, rejecting Wilsonism and the League of Nations, won the greatest popular landslide in American history: 16.1 million votes to 9.1 million for James Cox of Ohio and Franklin Roosevelt.

Yet the Harding-Coolidge triumph was no victory for isolationism. As the historian A. J. P. Taylor wrote, "American policy was never more active and never more effective in regard to Europe than in the nineteen-twenties. Reparations were settled; stable finances were restored; Europe was pacified: all mainly due to the United States."[2]

A HARDING-HUGHES INITIATIVE

In December of 1920, four months before Wilson left office, the same Senate that had rejected his League of Nations passed, 74–0, a resolution calling on the new president to convene a world conference to limit arms. The House endorsed it 332–4. Chief sponsor of

the resolution: William Borah.[3] America had turned its back on
Wilsonism, not the world. And the new president was an activist
in foreign policy. Harding began his administration with an international thunderclap, summoning the Allies to a Washington Conference on the Limitation of Armaments, the greatest such conference
in modern history. Historian Thomas Bailey describes the curtain-
raising address of Secretary of State Charles Evans Hughes:

> When the delegates first assembled in beautiful Memorial
> Continental Hall, on November 12, 1921, the dynamic Secretary
> Hughes bowled them over. In an astonishingly candid speech he
> declared that the way to disarm was to disarm, and that the time
> to begin was at once—not in the distant future. He thereupon
> proposed a ten-year holiday in the construction of capital
> ships—that is, battleships and battle cruisers. In addition, he
> would scrap other warships built and building, so that the navies
> of the three great naval powers—America, Britain, and Japan—
> would ultimately be left in the ratio of 5–5–3 in all categories.
> "Thus," he declared, "the number of capital ships to be scrapped
> by the United States, if this plan is accepted, is 30, with an aggre-
> gate tonnage (including that of ships in construction, if com-
> pleted) of 845,740 tons."
>
> Hardly pausing for breath, Hughes proceeded to tell the
> British and Japanese delegates in a tomblike silence just what
> they should scrap—19 and 17 capital ships respectively. In less
> than fifteen minutes, he destroyed 66 ships with a total tonnage
> of 1,878,043—more, as one British reporter put it, "than all the
> admirals of the world have sunk in a cycle of centuries."[4]

Hughes sat down to a thunderous ovation. Congressmen, senators, and Supreme Court justices rose cheering in what appeared a
political rally. William Jennings Bryan was seen with tears streaming
down his face.

But not all rejoiced. As Hughes was listing the British ships to be sunk, wrote British journalist Mark Sullivan, Admiral Sir David Beatty "came forward in his chair with the manner of a bulldog sleeping on a sunny doorstep who has been poked in the stomach by the impudent foot of an itinerant soap-canvasser seriously lacking in any sense of the most ordinary proprieties or considerations of personal safety."[5]

Even more distraught were the Japanese, who had drawn the low number in the 5–5–3 ratio. When news of the U.S. proposal reached the home islands, anti-U.S. demonstrations erupted. The U.S. ratios were an affront to the national honor. Japan demanded a ratio of at least 10–10–7. Tough negotiations followed, and Japan offered to compromise. Tokyo would accept 5–5–3, if the United States would agree to build no new fortifications on Guam, Wake, Samoa, the Aleutians, or in the Philippines. The United States agreed, as did Britain, which pledged to cease fortifying its Pacific possessions or Hong Kong. Japan seemed satisfied. But the negotiators were unable to extend the ratios for battleships and aircraft carriers to cruisers, destroyers, and submarines. These were left outside the treaty.

In carrying out the Five Power Treaty of the naval conference— France and Italy had also signed, with both given a ratio that allowed them one-third the amount of the United States and Britain—the United States scuttled more ships than any other nation. We tore up battleships while they tore up blueprints, said unhappy American admirals. "Anybody can spit on the Philippines and you can't stop them," muttered Admiral William S. Sims.[6] Sims had a point. At Paris, Wilson had agreed to Japanese control of the Carolines, Marshalls, and Marianas, the natural invasion route to the Philippines. At Washington, we had agreed to cease fortifying the Philippines. How did we propose to defend them? As the men of the Bataan Death March would discover, America could not.

This, then, is the strategic failure of Wilson and the Republicans: If the United States intended to hold the Philippines, it should have built a Pacific fleet equal to the task, continued to fortify the islands, and, at Paris, demanded Germany's islands as our legitimate spoils of victory, and as essential to defend our Pacific possessions. After all, America had been decisive in winning the war; Japan had been peripheral. Only if America were ready to let the Philippines go did it make sense to reduce our navy. Wilson and the Republicans had wanted both disarmament and the Philippines. So, we disarmed; and in 1942 we lost the islands.

America, however, made a strategic breakthrough at Washington. With adoption of the Four Power Treaty on December 13, 1921, the United States, Britain, France, and Japan agreed to respect each other's possessions in the Asia-Pacific region and to confer in a crisis. Through this vehicle, a twenty-year-old Anglo-Japanese Alliance was severed. Bemoaning the loss, one Japanese diplomat muttered, "We have discarded whiskey and accepted water."[7] Japan was thus the big loser in Washington. It had accepted inferiority in capital ships, given up a security treaty with Britain, and agreed to surrender China's Shantung peninsula, taken in World War I.

The Washington naval treaty passed the Senate with one dissenting vote, and Harding and Hughes were the toast of the internationalists. They had negotiated history's greatest agreement to control strategic arms—in that era, battleships and the emerging aircraft carriers. The 1924 GOP platform modestly claimed credit for the "greatest peace document ever drawn."[8] Another Republican landslide ensued.

This, then, was the Republican alternative to Wilson. If Democrats believed in collective security and a League of Nations to preserve the peace, Republicans believed in peace through disarmament by solemn treaty. Both had forgotten the wisdom of Washington: *Si vis pacem, pare bellum* (If you want peace, prepare for war). Twenty years after the Washington treaty was signed, Walter Lippmann would look back in deep remorse:

> ...I was too weak-minded to take a stand against the exorbitant folly of the Washington Disarmament Conference. In fact, I followed the fashion, and in editorials for the old *New York World* celebrated the disaster as a triumph and denounced the admirals who dared to protest. Of that episode in my life I am ashamed, all the more so because I had no excuse for not knowing better.[9]

Lippmann, here, overdoes the contrition. The problem, as we shall see, was not in the terms of the Washington treaty, but in the failure of statesmen to adapt to political, military, and strategic changes that took place in the following decade, the 1930s.

BATTLESHIPS—OR TAX CUTS?

A prime motive behind Harding's drive to halt the growth of the navy was a desire to balance the budget and cut taxes. The Republican business community strongly supported deep cuts in federal spending, which still consumed 6 percent of the gross national product (GNP) when Harding took over.

In March 1921 *The Saturday Evening Post* declared, "Let those who do not love taxes reach an agreement concerning disarmament, for here is a present evil, a grievous burden gratuitously borne, a punishment inflicted by stupidity."[10] On August 6 the governor of the Federal Reserve Bank of Philadelphia wrote, "There can be no relief from present tax burdens until expenditures for excessive armies and navies are revised downward sharply."[11] Primary target of the budget-balancers: the new battleships being built for the navy, the first with sixteen-inch guns. The *Dallas News* was appalled at this extravagance:

"At best a waste, at worst a menace, and always a burden and a drain on the resources of America, the *Maryland* isn't good for anything except for use as an argument—against further waste in armament—$42,000,000 worth of argument."[12]

Due to the "battleship holiday" declared by the Washington naval treaty, *Maryland* and her sister ships *Colorado* and *West Virginia* would be the last constructed before World War II. But these warships would prove not quite so useless as the *Dallas News* had insisted.

On December 7, 1941, *Maryland* was riding at anchor at Pearl Harbor and took two direct hits. She limped back to Bremerton, Washington, and was repaired in time to cover Hawaii during the Battle of Midway. *Maryland* shielded the resupply convoys for the U.S. Marines on Guadalcanal. With *Colorado* and *Tennessee*, she provided naval gunfire at Tarawa. And during the Battle of Leyte Gulf, *Maryland* and five other survivors of battleship row, including *Colorado* and *West Virginia*, exacted retribution for Pearl Harbor, ambushing a Japanese task force of battleships and cruisers in Surigao Straits in a night battle, sinking every enemy ship but a lone destroyer that escaped. In November 1944 and April 1945, *Maryland* took kamikaze hits, the last one sending her back to Bremerton for the duration. In a thirty-year career in defense of the United States, *Maryland* would show there are sometimes even more important priorities than balanced budgets and tax cuts.

Looking back, one sees that it was not the terms themselves of the Washington treaty that proved disastrous. After all, the United States had severed the British-Japanese alliance and negotiated an arms regime that left the United States and Britain with better than a three-to-one superiority over Japan in capital ships, and Japan in 1922 was an ex-Ally and cooperative power. The mistake America and Britain made was believing their security resided in those treaties rather than in their warships.

Like most arms control agreements, the Washington naval treaty had unanticipated consequences. By setting a limit on capital ships, it triggered an arms race in the uncovered categories: cruisers, destroyers, submarines. From 1922 to 1930, the numbers of keels laid for these exempted warships among the treaty powers were as follows[13]:

Japan	125
France	119
Italy	82
Britain	74
United States	1

Americans, by the late 1920s, should have begun to ask themselves: For what purpose, as it was threatened by no sea power, was Japan conducting this remarkable naval buildup?

AMERICA AND FRANCE "OUTLAW" WAR

With Harding's death in 1923, Coolidge began naval maneuvers geared to the defense of Pearl Harbor, but found himself under attack by Wilson's assistant secretary of the navy for an anti-Japanese provocation. "[I]t is hardly tactful," Franklin D. Roosevelt wrote in the *Macon Daily Telegraph*, "for the American Government to give… the impression… that we are trying to find out how easy or how difficult it would be for the Japanese navy to occupy Hawaii."[14]

Columnist Roosevelt was more supportive of the 1924 legislation that cut immigration to 2 percent of each foreign-born resident group in the United States as of 1890, and excluded Asians, enraging Japan. FDR heartily approved: "Californians have properly objected [to Japanese immigration] on the sound basic ground… that the mingling of Asiatic blood with European or American blood produces, in nine cases out of ten, the most unfortunate results."[15] The mindset that would produce the internment of 110,000 Japanese-Americans is here on early display.

To emulate his predecessor's triumph, Coolidge, in 1927, called a second naval conference in Geneva to extend the 5–5–3 ratios to all warships. But now Britain balked, rejecting parity in cruisers with the United States. The British, with a worldwide empire, preferred more cruisers with more guns, while Americans preferred heavier cruisers with large guns. In six weeks the conference collapsed, U.S.-British relations chilled, and an upset Congress responded by voting to construct fifteen new 10,000-ton cruisers.

The famous Kellogg-Briand Pact traces its paternity to the fertile mind of the French foreign minister, Aristide Briand. Terrified that Germany might rise again, Briand wanted to tie the United States into a European security system. He offered a pact whereby America and France would pledge never to go to war with each other. At first glance, this seemed innocuous. However, as historian Robert Ferrell writes:

> The proposal of perpetual peace between the United States and
> France was in truth a negative military alliance. If America were
> to sign such a promise it meant that regardless of how hard the
> French pushed the United States in violation of neutral rights (as
> the British had done in 1914–1917), in any future war when
> France was, say, fighting Germany, the Americans could not side
> in reprisal against France, for the antiwar treaty would prevent it.[16]

Secretary of State Frank B. Kellogg countered by offering a treaty which all nations might sign, outlawing war as "an instrument of national policy." Briand was trapped in the snare of his own devising. On August 27, 1928, the Kellogg-Briand Pact was signed by fifteen nations. Within months, sixty-two had signed on. "Observance of this Covenant," said Coolidge modestly, "...promises more for the peace of the world than any other agreement ever negotiated among the nations."[17]

The pact, however, contained no provision to punish nations that chose the more traditional way of settling disputes. Of the fifteen High Contracting Parties—the United States, Britain, Germany, Italy, Japan, France, Poland, Belgium, Czechoslovakia, Canada, South Africa, Australia, New Zealand, Ireland, and India—all save Ireland would be at war in little more than a decade.

Wilson had declared America to be "the only national idealistic force in the world, and idealism is going to save the world." Lodge had mocked him, calling Versailles "the beautiful scheme of making mankind virtuous by statute or a written constitution." Now Lodge's party had embraced Wilson's folly, with Hiram Johnson solemnly declaring, "War may be banished from the earth more nearly by disarmament than by any other agency or in any other manner."[18]

So revolted were Americans by the horrors of the Great War, so desperate were they to avoid another, they had begun to invest their hopes for peace in parchment. Theodore Roosevelt and Lodge were dead, their realism sorely missed from the leadership of their party.

A companion failing of the 1920s Republicans was their unwarranted faith in a rising prosperity as the solution to mankind's ills. They were the first generation of Republicans to buy into the Myth of Economic Man. Rational and decent, many had a utopian belief in man's perfectibility and the idea of progress that ran as deep as Wilson's. With the soldier-statesmen of America's past like Washington, Hamilton, and Jackson—men who knew war and had a healthy regard for mankind's propensity for evil—they had little in common, and not a great deal in common with the generation of TR, Lodge, and Mahan.

Kellogg became the fourth American to win the Nobel Peace Prize; and with Kellogg-Briand as his foreign policy legacy, Coolidge went home and left the nation in the capable hands of his world-renowned secretary of commerce, whom Coolidge privately referred to as "Wonder Boy."

THE CRUISERS PROBLEM IS SOLVED

Herbert Hoover was an internationalist and a hero of peace. After World War I, he had delivered millions of tons of U.S. grain to a starving Europe, and to Russia after its terrible civil war. Even Lenin had praised Hoover's assistance to the Russian people. His reputation as a statesman gave hope of a great presidency. A progressive, Hoover spoke at the 1929 Memorial Day ceremonies at Arlington Cemetery of his vision that arms control and disarmament would bring peace to the world:

> Limitation upward [of naval ships] is not now our goal, but actual reduction of existing commitments to lowered levels.
>
> Such a program, if it is achieved, is fraught with endless blessings. The smaller the armed forces of the world, the less will armed force be left in the minds of men as an instrument of national policy. The smaller the armed forces of the world, the less will be the number of men withdrawn from the creative and productive labors. Thus we shall relieve the toilers of the nations of the deadening burden of unproductive expenditures, and above all, we shall deliver them from the greatest of human calamities—fear. We shall breathe an air cleared of poison, of destructive thought, and of potential war.[19]

Motivated by such ideals, dismayed by the arms race in cruisers, Hoover determined to end it, and sought out Ramsay MacDonald, the new British prime minister. Their common hope: repair the old relationship that had been torn at Geneva.

France, Italy, Japan, the United States, and Great Britain were the five powers invited to the London Naval Conference of 1930. Another Republican triumph followed with Britain's acceptance of parity with the United States in all categories of warships. But Japan

emerged as the big winner. Locked into the old 5–5–3 ratio in battleships, Tokyo was awarded a better ratio in cruisers, a 10–10–7 ratio
in destroyers, and equality in submarines. As America needed a two-
ocean navy, and Britain had to keep sea lanes open to the
Mediterranean and the Middle East, to South Africa and the Persian
Gulf—as well as to India, Burma, Singapore, and Hong Kong—
Japan, with a small slice of ocean to defend and a large and burgeoning navy, had just taken a long step toward naval supremacy in
the western Pacific.

Hoover nevertheless had an abiding faith in naval arms control as
the path to peace and warned in his treaty message to the Senate of
those foolish men who would dissipate America's wealth on warships:

> We must naturally expect opposition from those groups who
> believe in unrestricted military strength as an objective of the
> American Nation.... Nevertheless, I am convinced that the over
> whelming majority of the American people are opposed to the
> conception of these groups....
>
> The only alternative to this treaty is the competitive build
> ing of navies with all its flow of suspicion, hate, ill-will, and ulti
> mate disaster. History supports those who hold to agreement as
> the path to peace. Every naval limitations treaty with which we
> are familiar, from the Rush-Bagot agreement of 1817, limiting
> vessels of war on the Great Lakes, to the Washington Arms Treaty
> of 1921, has resulted in a marked growth of good will and confi
> dence between the nations which were parties to it.[20]

Thus did men believe. In July 1930 Hoover's treaty carried the
Senate. And later FDR sought vainly to replicate the arms control
triumphs of his Republican predecessors. His administration called
for a second London naval conference in 1935. But in the run-up,
Japan, which had by now occupied all of Manchuria, declared that

the old ratios would no longer do. This talk of 5–5–3, said a Japanese diplomat, sounds to us like "Rolls-Royce—Rolls-Royce—Ford."[21]

Japan demanded naval parity with the United States. As Japan had a tenth of the ocean to patrol as the U.S. Navy, America balked. Tokyo gave notice it would no longer abide by the Washington ratios.

At this point, early in FDR's first term, America should have begun to see the handwriting on the wall in the Pacific. It did not. But, for that failure, the departed Republicans cannot be held accountable.

From 1922 to 1932, Harding, Coolidge, and Hoover had authorized construction of only forty-two warships—three carriers, sixteen cruisers, eleven destroyers, six subs, six miscellaneous ships.[22] President Roosevelt, as a Depression-era stimulus, allotted $238 million from the 1933 National Recovery Act to warship construction, approved the Vinson-Trammel Act of 1934 calling for an additional 102 ships, and declared it to be "the policy of the United States to build up to the London Naval Treaty limits."[23]

Unfortunately, not until war broke out in 1939 did FDR begin the urgent implementation of his own policy.

LE BOCHE PAYERA TOUT!

By 1921 the Allies had decided that Germany's reparations came to $33 billion. Handed the astronomical bill, the Germans threw up their hands. "*Le Boche payera tout!*" was the unrelenting French reply. Furious, Paris ordered its army into the Ruhr in 1923 to take out the reparations in kind. German workers sat down; the French learned you cannot dig coal with bayonets. Graver consequences ensued. France's action so disgusted America that all U.S. troops were pulled out of the Rhineland. French intervention had brought an end to the U.S. occupation. "Not even the most liberal internationalists," wrote

Henry Kissinger, "any longer discerned an American interest in sustaining a flawed postwar settlement."[24]

With the Ruhr occupied, Germany lost its source of iron, coal, and steel. Inflation ran rampant, destroying the mark and demoralizing and impoverishing the middle class. "The result of the inflation," wrote Otto Friedrich, "was to undermine the foundations of German society in a way which neither the war, nor the revolution of November 1918, nor the Treaty of Versailles had ever done. The real revolution in Germany was the inflation."[25]

Democratic France had humiliated a democratic Germany. With that nation in chaos, a new party, the National Socialist Party, attempted a coup d'état in Munich. The "beer hall putsch" was crushed, its leader prosecuted and sent to prison, where he wrote a manifesto he titled *Mein Kampf.* The harsh peace was creating a hardened German people.

With the Dawes Plan of 1924 and Young Plan of 1929, Republicans tried to ease the reparations burden and bring the Weimar Republic back to life. America lent money, negotiated reductions in reparations, lengthened Germany's payments schedule. But every effort to lighten the crushing weight of Versailles, or insist on Allied repayment of war debts, earned the enmity of France. "L'Oncle Shylock," the French called Uncle Sam. To which Coolidge replied, "Well, they hired the money, didn't they?"[26]

By decade's end, anti-Americanism was rife in France.

THE "GOOD NEIGHBOR POLICY"—OF HOOVER

To generations of schoolchildren, the Good Neighbor policy has always been associated with FDR. Yet that policy and its famous name were lifts, expropriations, plagiarisms. The phrase had been a staple in international diplomacy for a century. Four years before Roosevelt rode to his inauguration with Hoover, President-elect Hoover had gone on a ten-week tour of ten Latin American nations, where he repeatedly declared that the United States would pursue the policy of the "good neighbor."

In Honduras, Hoover said, "We have a desire to maintain not only the cordial relations of governments with each other but also the relations of good neighbors."[27] A Quaker, Hoover had an aversion to military interventions of the kind associated with TR and Wilson. In his inaugural address, he declared, "It never has been and ought not to be the policy of the United States to intervene by force to secure or maintain contracts between our citizens and foreign States or their citizens."[28]

Under the Republicans of the 1920s, the United States had begun to lay down TR's Big Stick. In 1921 America paid Colombia $25 million, the exact price the United States had offered for the right to dig and control a canal in the isthmus of Panama, before Panama, at U.S. instigation, broke away from Bogota. In 1924 the U.S. Marines were withdrawn from the Dominican Republic and temporarily from Nicaragua. Hoover also repudiated the Roosevelt corollary to the Monroe Doctrine, under which the United States had asserted a right to intervene in Latin America to prevent chaos or defaults that might invite European intervention.

Hoover also reversed Wilson's moralistic policy of not recognizing regimes that had come to power by other than constitutional processes. He adopted a policy of *de facto* recognition of Latin American governments that accepted their international obligations. In 1930 a pro-U.S. Brazilian regime was ousted by Getulio Vargas. Hoover promptly recognized the Vargas regime. He removed the last of the marines from Nicaragua, and would have taken them out of Haiti had Haiti accepted U.S. terms for withdrawal. Most Latin nations preferred Hoover in 1932 to TR's cousin, who had been the assistant secretary of the navy and had helped Wilson carry out interventions in Haiti, the Dominican Republic, and Mexico. As historian Alexander DeConde concludes, "[T]he Good Neighbor idea took

root in the Hoover years."[29] Yet it is FDR to whom credit is customarily given, which tells us more about historians than about history.

WHO WAS TO BLAME FOR UNPREPAREDNESS?

From 1921 to 1933 America did not cut herself off from the world.
The nation led the world into the greatest strategic arms agreements
in history, and in helping to resurrect a Germany that was sick unto
death. The Republican failure was in embracing the naive notion that
disarmament treaties build trust, and upon that trust peace can rest
secure. U.S. leaders failed to look beyond the treaties—to the changing character of the men signing them. Yet after the war, disarmament
had become a fetish, and the Republican presidents who pursued
it reflected public opinion and were rewarded with landslide after
landslide.

History condemns these presidents for making disarmament an
idol. They succeeded only, it is said, in restricting the naval programs
of the great democracies Britain and the United States. Yet, looking
back, one sees that the three presidents were no more naive than
everyone else who put his faith in nonaggression pacts and arms control. That was the "fashion" of the day, wrote Lippmann. Few defied
the conventional wisdom. But for the pathetic condition of the U.S.
military in 1939, Harding is blameless, and Coolidge is less culpable
than Hoover, who is less culpable than FDR. From 1921 until 1933,
observed Williams Appleman Williams, the "Republicans in both
houses of Congress were 'more favorable to both army and navy
measures than... Democrats.'"[30]

Not until long after Harding's death did it become clear that
Japan was trampling on the spirit of the Washington treaty by churn-
ing out cruisers, destroyers, and submarines. Yet as late as 1934 FDR
wanted to extend the Washington-London ratios for all categories of
warships. How, without condemning FDR, can we condemn
Harding, Coolidge, and Hoover?

For the deplorable condition of America's military when war broke out, primary responsibility must rest with the men in power from 1933 on. FDR had nine years before Pearl Harbor to turn U.S. industrial capacity, almost ten times that of Japan, to building air and naval forces that would have made America invulnerable. Nor was FDR unwarned. Early in his first term, the president received a visit from an alarmed army chief of staff. Faced with a halving of his army appropriations to balance the budget, General Douglas MacArthur demanded to see FDR. The Old Soldier recounts the confrontation:

> I felt it my duty to take up the cudgels. The country's safety was
> at stake, and I said so bluntly. The President turned the full vials
> of his sarcasm upon me.... The tension began to boil over.... I
> spoke recklessly and said something to the general effect that
> when we lost the next war, and an American boy, lying in the
> mud with an enemy bayonet through his belly and an enemy
> foot on his dying throat, spat out his last curse, I wanted the
> name not to be MacArthur, but Roosevelt. The President grew
> livid. "You must not talk that way to the President!" he roared....
> I felt my Army career was at an end. I told him he had my resig-
> nation as Chief of Staff. As I reached the door his voice came
> with that cool detachment which so reflected his extraordinary
> self-control, "Don't be foolish, Douglas; you and the budget must
> get together on this."[31]

But the army's budget continued to fall.

It needs to be said again: From 1921 to 1933 there was no for-eign menace to cause America to rearm. Germany was defeated, dis-armed, dismembered, demoralized, and democratic. The concern was not whether Germany would arise to wage a war of revenge, but whether Germany would collapse in chaos. Japanese militarists did not take the first step toward Asian empire until ten years after the

Washington conference. In 1931–1932, they occupied Manchuria. How did the public react? Said the *Philadelphia Record*, "[T]he American people don't give a hoot in a rain barrel who controls North China."[32]

American indifference is understandable. John Hay, the architect of the Open Door, had put Manchuria outside China's domain, as had Theodore Roosevelt, who had spoken positively of a Japanese Monroe Doctrine. Indeed, TR wrote his successor, William Howard Taft, to criticize his policy of challenging Japan in Manchuria:

> Our vital interest is to keep the Japanese out of our country, and at the same time to preserve the good will of Japan. The vital interest of the Japanese, on the other hand, is in Manchuria and Korea…. [A]s regards Manchuria, if the Japanese choose to follow a course of conduct to which we are averse, we cannot stop it unless we are prepared to go to war, and a successful war about Manchuria would require a fleet as good as that of England, plus an army as good as that of Germany.[33]

Nor was Japan's creation of the puppet state of "Manchukuo," an act of imperial conquest, beyond the capacity to understand of the British in India, the French in Indochina, or the Americans in the Philippines, Puerto Rico, and Panama.

Hoover denounced the occupation as a violation of Kellogg-Briand and the Open Door, but felt Japan had a case for seizing the buffer state, then ruled by a warlord and in a condition of near anarchy. Japan might justly argue, said Hoover, that its independence was threatened by Stalin's Russia, nursing bitter memories of Port Arthur and Tsushima, and by a nationalist, or worse, a future Communist China, united, xenophobic, and hostile. Seizure of Manchuria, said Hoover, did not threaten any vital U.S. interest: "These acts do not imperil the freedom of the American people, the economic or moral future of our people. I do not propose ever to sacrifice American life for anything short of this."[34]

But Tokyo's conquest should have alerted Herbert Hoover that the marauding Japan of 1931 was not the same nation that had surrendered Shantung. By invading Manchuria, Japan had not only violated Kellogg-Briand and slammed shut the open door there, it had also destroyed the political foundations of the treaties of Washington and London. At this point, both parties should have come out for naval rearmament. Neither did.

CHAPTER 15

The Zeal of the Convert

We have torn up 150 years of traditional American foreign policy. We have tossed Washington's Farewell Address into the discard. We have thrown ourselves squarely into the power politics and the power wars of Europe, Asia and Africa. We have taken the first step upon a course from which we can never hereafter retreat.[1]
—SENATOR ARTHUR H. VANDENBERG, MARCH 11, 1941

The greatest political struggle in American history over foreign policy took place under FDR, but it did not reach virulence until the end of his second term. As publisher Henry Luce asserted, in his first seven years FDR was as "isolationist" as a charter member of America First. The turning point came in May–June 1940, when Hitler's armies overran France in six weeks. The realization that France was now in the Nazi orbit, that Britain might be starved into submission, and that the United States might face a Hitler-dominated Europe convinced some American leaders that England's fight was our fight and that America should intervene, no matter the cost, to save England and stop Hitler.

The "isolationists" were patriotic men and women who, with the appalling legacy of World War I constantly in mind, violently disagreed. With the Battle of Britain won by the fall of 1940, and any German invasion plan dead, they saw no threat from a Nazi empire that had no surface navy and no heavy bombers that could fly the

Atlantic. If Germany lacked the power to subdue England or invade the British Isles, they argued, it presented no peril to a self-sufficient United States, which had many times the industrial capacity of the Third Reich.

Pearl Harbor ended the argument, the interventionists wrote the history, and the "isolationists" faded away, demonized at best as fools, and probably fascist sympathizers. Senator Joseph McCarthy, in his career fighting communists, did nothing to their collaborators, sympathizers, and defenders to compare with what was done to the patriots of America First. But the acolytes of FDR won the great debate as decisively as America won the war. To this day, any who oppose U.S. commitments to fight wars in Europe or Asia, or new global entanglements, must first answer to the intimidating charge that they are nothing but "isolationists."

To understand the politics of the present, we must understand that great political struggle over whether to go to war against Germany.

We forget: From 1918 to 1933, it was not Germany, but the Soviet regime of Lenin and Stalin, with its appalling record of massacre and mayhem, that bristled with hostility toward the West. Defeated and disarmed, afflicted by economic crises, unable to pay the reparations imposed at Versailles, Germany seemed a threat to no one. Indeed, many were having second thoughts about the peace of vengeance the Allies had imposed. Lloyd George had presided over Germany's dismemberment, but did not believe Britain should, or would, fight to enforce the terms of Versailles. A French diplomat quoted the former prime minister thus:

> The British people were not very much interested in what hap-
> pened on the eastern frontier of Germany; they would not be
> ready to be involved in quarrels which might arise regarding

Poland or Danzig or upper Silesia....The British people felt that
the populations in that quarter of Europe were unstable and
excitable; they might start fighting at any time, and the rights
and wrongs of the dispute might be very hard to disentangle. He
[Lloyd George] did not think, therefore, that this country would
be disposed to give any guarantees which might involve them in
military operations in any eventuality in that part of the world.[2]

"For the Polish Corridor, no British Government ever will or
ever can risk the bones of a British grenadier," said Foreign Secretary
Austen Chamberlain in 1925, in conscious echo of Bismarck's dis-
missal of the Balkans.[3] Long after the war, historian A. J. P. Taylor
wrote: "In 1932 men feared, and rightly feared, the collapse of
Germany, not German strength. How could any competent observer
suppose that a country with seven million unemployed, no gold
reserves, and an ever-shrinking foreign trade, would suddenly
become a great military power?"[4] In July 1934, a year and a half after
Hitler took power, the *Times* of London wrote, "In the years that are
coming, there is more reason to fear for Germany than to fear
Germany."[5]

FDR DECLARES NEUTRALITY

The indictment against the Republicans who defeated the Versailles
Treaty and failed to bring America into the League of Nations runs
thus: Had we joined the league and forged an alliance with Britain
and France, we could have expelled Hitler from the Rhineland in
1936, or crushed him at the time of Munich in 1938. There would
have been no World War II.

This scenario has a major flaw: While the Republican Senate had
opposed entry into the League of Nations in 1919, FDR opposed
entry in 1932. Roosevelt did not run against Hoover as an internationalist. When publisher William Randolph Hearst confronted the

Democratic candidate about his views on the League of Nations, Roosevelt flatly declared himself against U.S. membership. Nor was FDR's election seen as a triumph for internationalism. Again, historian Taylor:

> American policy under F. D. Roosevelt became in 1933
> markedly more isolationist than it had been under his Republican
> predecessor....
>
> [T]hough Roosevelt was to embed the United States in
> world policy later, the vote of November 1932 was a victory for
> isolationism. The Democrats were now disillusioned Wilsonians.
> Some believed that Wilson had deceived the American people;
> others that the European statesmen had deceived Wilson. Nearly
> all of them believed that the European Powers, especially the
> former Allies, were incorrigibly wicked and that the less America
> had to do with Europe the better.... The Democratic majority
> in Congress carried a series of measures which made it impos-
> sible for the United States to play any part in world affairs; and
> President Roosevelt accepted these measures without any sign of
> disagreement.[6]

What were "these measures" that tied America's hands? They were the neutrality acts, passed by heavily Democratic Congresses between 1935 and 1937, in alarmed reaction to Mussolini's invasion of Ethiopia in 1935, Hitler's remilitarization of the Rhineland in 1936, and the Spanish Civil War. The neutrality acts were signed without dissent by FDR.

The 1935 act compelled the president, after a state of war had been recognized, to prohibit arms shipments to either side, and gave him the authority to forbid U.S. citizens from traveling on belligerent ships, except at their own risk. The 1936 act forbade loans to belligerents. There were two neutrality acts in 1937. The first embargoed shipments to either side in the Spanish conflict; the second made all the neutrality laws permanent. The three acts were designed to keep America from being drawn into another war because our economy had been mortgaged, by arms sales or loans, to one side. FDR would later say of the last of these laws, "I regret… that I signed that Act."[7]

What brought on this legislation? After the guns fell silent on the Western Front in WWI, historians began burrowing into the archives. Books on how British propaganda had cleverly suckered America into a war that had left 116,000 Americans dead, and gained us nothing, were best-sellers. The court historians had been routed by the revisionists. Americans were convinced that the "war to end all wars" had been fought not for noble ideals or vital interests, but because gullible America had been duped into "pulling England's chestnuts out of the fire."

"The world must be made safe for democracy," Wilson had said. Yet the British, French, and Japanese empires had been enlarged by the war, and we had made the world safe for the greatest enemies democracy had ever seen: Lenin, Stalin, Mussolini, and Hitler. Of the Allies we had saved by spilling all that blood and spending all that treasure, only Finland was paying its war debts to the United States; the rest ignored America's requests for payment. With 25 percent of the American labor force looking for work in 1933, our ex-Allies were seen as ingrates and deadbeats. The real winners in World War I, it was now believed, had been the financiers and arms manufacturers, "the merchants of death."

From 1934 to 1936, North Dakota's populist Republican senator, Gerald P. Nye, held hearings exposing the role of the "great American and European bankers and internationalist arms merchants" in dragging us into war. It was partly in response to Nye's hearings that Congress passed the neutrality acts. All were signed by a president who was then echoing the views of most Americans. In 1935 FDR told Australian Prime Minister Joseph Lyons that the United States would never be drawn into another European war.[8] On August 14, 1936, in a Chautauqua address, Roosevelt thundered out his anti-interventionist and antiwar sentiments:

> We shun political commitments which might entangle us in for-
> eign wars; we avoid connection with the political activities of the
> League of Nations....We are not isolationists except insofar as
> we seek to isolate ourselves completely from war....I have seen
> war....I have seen blood running from the wounded. I have
> seen men coughing out their gassed lungs. I have seen the dead
> in the mud. I have seen cities destroyed....I hate war.[9]

This was a bit of a stretch. Unlike Theodore Roosevelt's four sons, all of whom were combat veterans, one of whom died in World War I, cousin Franklin had manned a desk in Washington. The clos-est he had come to the fighting was a July 1918 trip to France, where he observed a U.S. artillery battery in action, seven kilometers from the front.[10] But his declaration about not intervening in any future European war reflected the opinion of his countrymen, 70 percent of whom believed by 1937 that United States involvement in World War I had been a mistake.[11]

GERMANY'S "BORN LEADER"

Hitler had taken power five weeks before Roosevelt. From its first days, the authoritarian character of the Nazi regime was manifest. Dachau began receiving prisoners as early as March 1933. Jews were soon being subjected to ugly actions and discriminatory laws. In 1934 Ernst Roehm, head of Hitler's army of street-brawling brown-shirts and his only rival for absolute power, was liquidated. Roehm had been caught in a homosexual tryst, and Hitler had his beer-hall comrade shot without trial. About this time Stalin had his rival, Sergei Kirov, assassinated in Leningrad in the gangland style of Al Capone. Comparisons between the two models of "socialism" were inescapable.

On November 12, 1933, fifteen years and a day after the armistice of 1918, Hitler held a plebiscite on German withdrawal from the League of Nations. It carried with 95 percent of the vote in an election even passionate anti-Nazi William Shirer agreed was not faked.[12] Two years later, Hitler took his first step toward overturning the Versailles Treaty. On March 6, 1935, he restored universal military service and announced the formation of a conscript army of half a million men. Under Versailles, Germany was allowed only 100,000 men under arms. Hitler also declared that treaty restrictions against Germany's possession of tanks, heavy artillery, and an air force were a dead letter. His argument: Under the terms of Versailles, all parties had agreed to disarm. Germany had done so; the Allies had not. Thus Germany was no longer bound.

The Allies did nothing. A year later, Hitler brazenly ordered a battalion of lightly armed troops, led by mounted cavalry, to cross the bridges into the demilitarized Rhineland. He nervously waited for the Allied reaction, his generals paralyzed with apprehension. France had 500,000 men under arms, and the German battalion was under orders to withdraw at the first sign of French intervention. It never came. Hitler had gambled and won. The last chance to stop him without risking another European war had slipped by.

Why did the Allies not react? France feared standing up to Germany without Britain, and Britain had an irresolute policy. Many Britons had come to believe the Versailles Treaty had been a dreadful injustice, imposed on a disarmed Germany in violation of the terms of the armistice and of the principle of self-determination. As political scientist Hans Morgenthau would write, "The liberal statesmen of

Western Europe were intellectually and morally unable to resist German expansion as long as it appeared to be justified... by the holy principles of national unification."[13] Men of troubled conscience often feel morally disarmed before their victims. But, in this case, the "victim" had more in mind than rectifying old injustices.

Other Britons were convinced that communism, with its appeal to subject peoples, was a far greater threat to the British Empire. Some even saw Hitler as a potential ally against Stalin. Had he not written in *Mein Kampf* that "the best practicable tie remains with England"?[14]

"Better Hitler than Stalin!" was a slogan of the day. Lloyd George, deeply alarmed at the appeal of communist ideology, visited the German dictator and came away captivated, declaring Hitler "a really great man." Britain's senior statesman returned to write in the *Daily Express* that the führer was "a born leader of men, a dynamic personality with resolute will and dauntless heart who was trusted by the old and idolized by the young."[15]

Nor would public opinion have allowed the British government to use force against Hitler's move into the Rhineland. As historian Taylor wrote:

> There was almost unanimous approval in Great Britain that the
> Germans had liberated their own territory. What [Prime
> Minister Stanley] Baldwin did not add was that he agreed with
> this public opinion. The German reoccupation of the Rhineland
> was, from the British point of view, an improvement and a suc-
> cess for British policy.[16]

By the summer of 1936 Hitler was hosting the Olympic games, to which the United States sent athletes. By 1937 Gertrude Stein was suggesting that Hitler be awarded the Nobel Prize for Peace.[17] That same year Winston Churchill published *Great Contemporaries*, containing his 1935 profile, "Hitler and His Choice," in which Churchill expressed his "admiration for the courage, the perseverance, and the vital force which enabled [Hitler] to challenge, defy, conciliate, or overcome, all the authorities or resistances which barred his path."[18] Hitler and his cohorts, said Churchill, had "showed... their patriotic ardor and love of country...."[19] "[W]e may yet live to see Hitler a gentler figure in a happier age," said Churchill, adding optimistically:

> [H]istory is replete with examples of men who have risen to power by employing stern, grim, and even frightful methods, but who, nevertheless, when their life is revealed as a whole, have been regarded as great figures whose lives have enriched the story of mankind. So may it be with Hitler.[20]

Thus did even Churchill believe and hope as late as 1937.

Then, one by one, the disasters came. In March 1938 Hitler annexed Austria; in September came Munich and the Sudeten crisis. Where were the Americans? During the infamous conferences, writes Henry Kissinger, "Roosevelt felt obliged to emphasize repeatedly that America would not join a united front against Hitler. And he disavowed subordinates and even close friends who so much as hinted at that possibility."[21]

When Prime Minister Neville Chamberlain returned from his Munich conference in 1938—where he had signed away the Sudetenland to Hitler—FDR telegraphed him: "Good man."[22] Undersecretary of State Sumner Welles delivered a radio address giving FDR credit for Munich, referring to "steps taken by the president to halt Europe's headlong plunge into the Valley of the Shadow of Death." Said Welles, "Europe escaped war by a few hours, the scales being tipped toward peace by the president's appeal."[23]

The same attitude prevailed in England. Anthony Eden told his constituents: "Nobody will quarrel with the Government's wish to bring about appeasement in Europe. Any other intention would be as foolish as it would be wrong."[24] The rationale for appeasement was this: Threatened by three potential enemies—Germany, Japan, and Italy—Britain believed that yielding to Berlin's demands for reunification with German minorities separated by Versailles might remove Germany from that list.

APPEASEMENT FAILS

In mid-March 1939 Hitler took a fateful step. He ordered his army into Prague and declared Czechoslovakia a Nazi protectorate. Poland and Hungary each bit off a chunk, and the Slovaks declared their independence.

Back in 1920, H. N. Brailsford, the leading socialist authority on foreign affairs in Britain, had declared that Versailles's "worst offence... was the subjection of over three million Germans to Czech rule."[25] The injustice and folly of Versailles had now produced disaster. Not only had Hitler torn up the Munich accord and humiliated a British prime minister who had sought to appease Germany, he had imposed Nazi rule on non-German peoples. Hitler was no longer taking back what had been taken away; he was on a road of conquest. Now came his inevitable demand for road and rail transit across the "Polish Corridor," formerly German territory, to Danzig, the Hanseatic League port city also severed from the Reich at Versailles. Hitler demanded the return of Danzig as well.

England was in a hellish dilemma. Had Germany been democratic, Parliament might have looked on indifferently. Germany was, after all, demanding only the return of its historic lands, and Germany's claim to Danzig was its strongest. The city was 90 percent German, and its 350,000 people were clamoring to return to their Fatherland. To restore these lands to Berlin might create a bulwark against Stalin's Soviet Union, then convulsed in a horrific purge of the Communist

Party and Red Army, reaching down into all levels of society. But Germany was not ruled by democrats. And by seizing Czechoslovakia, Hitler had shown he could not be trusted and had an agenda not confined to restoring what was lost at Versailles.

This was the British-French dilemma: Was Hitler pursuing a German imperial policy, driving east to capture raw materials, new markets, new *Lebensraum*? Or did Hitler's ambitions extend westward as well? Was he hell-bent on conquering all of Europe? A. J. P. Taylor believes Hitler's ambitions were always—and perhaps only—directed to the east. Hitler's "outlook was 'continental,'" writes Taylor:

> [Hitler] did not attempt to revive the "World Policy" which Germany had pursued before 1914; he made no plans for a great battle-fleet; he did not parade a grievance over the lost colonies, except as a device for embarrassing the British; he was not even interested in the Middle East—hence his blindness to the great opportunity in 1940 after the defeat of France.... He did not wish to destroy the British Empire, nor even to deprive the French of Alsace and Lorraine.... Maybe his ambitions were genuinely limited to the East; maybe conquest there would have been only the preliminary to conquest in Western Europe or on a World scale. No one can tell. Only events could have given the answer; and by a strange twist of circumstances they never did. Against all expectations, Hitler found himself at war with the Western Powers before he had conquered the East. Nevertheless, Eastern expansion was the primary purpose of his policy, if not the only one.[26]

AMERICA'S FAILURE TO PREPARE

Between 1934 and 1938 expenditures for German armaments grew by 470 percent in real terms, a rate equaled only by Japan, though Germany had begun from a tiny base.[27] How did Roosevelt's defense effort compare, considering he had had the backing of Democratic Congresses since 1933? Historian Frederick Marks III writes:

> [FDR] repeatedly blocked the road to American rearmament. While Japan added rapidly to her naval establishment and neared the limits set by the Treaty of Washington, he told reporters, "There isn't any cloud on the horizon at the present time"....
> The year Roosevelt first sought a hemispheric defense program, 1938, was also the year that Germany's chargé in Washington reported incredulously, "Still no military preparations whatever in the United States." In 1939, the U.S. Army ranked nineteenth in the world—behind Portugal and ahead of Bulgaria. In percentage of population under arms it ranked forty-fifth. It stood at less than 70 percent of the peacetime strength authorized by Congress and less than 25 percent in terms of combat readiness. General John J. Pershing considered America in a "lamentable" state.[28]

The claim that FDR battled heroically through the 1930s to build up America's armed forces against the mulish resistance of isolationists is propaganda. As FDR's party controlled the White House and Congress from 1933 to 1941, Republicans cannot be held responsible for the pathetic state of America's armed forces as of September 1, 1939. It is the man who was commander in chief during those seven years who must be held accountable. When France collapsed in June 1940, and Germany and England put hundreds of planes into the air in the Battle of Britain, the United States had a bare minimum of 53 bombers and 187 modern pursuit fighters.[29]

Roosevelt is hailed today for legendary courage in pushing through a draft bill in election year 1940. But polls show the bill had 59 percent support in June, 69 percent in July, and was sponsored

by an anti–New Deal Democrat, Senator Edward R. Burke of
Nebraska, and a Republican, Congressman James W. Wadsworth of
New York—and FDR waited until August 2 to support it. As noted
by historian Marks, "Americans… wanted to spend more on guns
than FDR was willing to request, while Congress appropriated more
for defense than he was ready to spend."[30]

BRITAIN'S DILEMMA

In March 1939 Britain had to decide. By marching into Prague,
Hitler had humiliated Chamberlain, exposing his appeasement policy as fatuous folly and subjugating a people who had never been
part of the Second Reich. He was on the road to conquest, but he
was also headed east. And if Germany intended no attack on France
or the Channel ports, and Hitler's imperial ambitions were in the
east, why was it Britain's duty to fight him to the death? Indeed, if
Britain had had no vital interest in the Rhineland, Austria, or
Czechoslovakia worth fighting for, what was the vital interest in
Danzig? After all, Chamberlain's government always felt the German
claim to Danzig was among its strongest, and Danzig's return
inevitable.

Had Britain made an alliance with France to confront Nazi
Germany with a Western defense wall, without making a commitment to Poland, the Allies might have stayed out of the titanic clash
between the Nazis and the Bolsheviks. The first great blows of
Hitler's war machine would have fallen on Stalin's empire, not the
Western democracies. Such a policy would have left Poland in the
lurch, but no more so than Britain and France did anyway. But Hitler
had blundered. In exposing Chamberlain as a dupe for having trusted
him, he had forced the proud prime minister to make a stand to
redeem himself and British honor. In the words of historian William
Henry Chamberlin:

Hitherto the British Government had been extremely cautious about making firm commitments to defend any part of Europe east of the Rhine. Now it began to toss guarantees about with reckless abandon, and with little regard for its ability to implement these guarantees if they were put to the test.[31]

Thus, when Hitler demanded that Poland negotiate the return of Danzig and grant road and rail transit through the corridor to the city, Great Britain, on March 31, issued a guarantee of Polish territory. If war came, England would be at Poland's side. Many Britons have come to believe this was the greatest blunder of the century, an act of precipitate and ruinous folly. Sir Roy Denman, Labour Party statesman, wrote in 1996 that the British Empire, with its guarantee to Poland, was

> thus placing the decision for peace or war in the hands of a
> swashbuckling, yet inefficient military dictatorship, to which
> Britain could give no effective aid. The fear that after Poland
> Hitler would have attacked Britain was an illusion. As he had
> made clear in *Mein Kampf*, Hitler would have marched against
> Russia. As it was, Britain was dragged into an unnecessary war,
> which cost her nearly 400,000 dead, bankruptcy and the dissolu-
> tion of the British empire.[32]

Even today, there remains an unanswered question: How did Britain propose to save Poland? The only way for Poland to remain independent in the event of a German attack was by military collaboration with Russia. But Stalin had amassed a record of murder and enslavement that dwarfed Hitler's. Estimates of the dead at the hands of the Great Terrorist before September 1939 run to twenty-two million, one thousand times the number that could then be charged to Hitler. Before 1937 Stalin's concentration camps also held one thousand times as many souls as did Hitler's. As late as September 1,

1939, the Gulag held three hundred inmates for every one held by the Third Reich.[33]

The Poles, moreover, were horrified at the idea of inviting into their country the "friendly" troops of a Red Army that Marshal Jozef Pilsudski, on August 15, 1920, had driven back from the gates of Warsaw. Said Polish Marshal Smigly-Rydz, "With the Germans we risk the loss of our liberty, but with the Russians we lose our soul."[34]

Even Foreign Secretary Lord Halifax appreciated Polish reluctance to enter a security arrangement with Stalin's Soviet Union:"An intelligent rabbit would hardly be expected to welcome the protection of an animal ten times its size, whom it credited with the habits of a boa constrictor."[35]

Yet how was Germany to be prevented from overrunning Poland, without Soviet assistance? "Without Russia," Lloyd George warned, "our guarantees are the most reckless commitment any country has ever entered into. I say more—they are demented."[36] George Kennan describes the British-French dilemma:

> [A]s the shades of war closed down over Europe in the summer
> of 1939, the dilemma of Western statesmen, as we now see it in
> retrospect, was clear and inescapable. There was no prospect for
> victory over Germany, unless it were with the help of Russia.
> But for such help, even if it were forthcoming, the Western
> democracies would have to pay heavily in the military conse-
> quences of the war and in the demands that would be raised at
> the peace table. Their military purposes, in other words, were
> mortgaged in advance.[37]

In 1939 the Poles faced a dreadful choice: Hitler or Stalin. They refused to choose, and were attacked by both. "With all the wisdom of hindsight," wrote a scholar of Polish history, "it is impossible to suggest a foreign policy that might have saved Poland."[38]

Not unreasonably, Hitler concluded the Allied war guarantee to
Poland was a bluff. Even if Britain and France declared war, they
could do nothing to interfere with the Wehrmacht's overrunning
of Poland in a few days. And if Britain and France would not fight
to keep him out of the Rhineland, Austria, the Sudetenland, or
Prague, would they die for Danzig? From 1795 to 1919 Poles had
been ruled by German princes, Austrian emperors, Russian tsars.
This had never caused great anguish in London or Paris. Why then
should the end of Polish independence cause the Allies to go to war
in 1939? So Hitler must have thought. On August 11, 1939, he
described to Jacob Burghardt, the Danzig League of Nations com-
missioner, the situation in which British-French guarantees to
Poland had left him:

> Everything I undertake is directed against Russia. If the West is
> too stupid and blind to grasp this I shall be compelled to come
> to an agreement with the Russians, beat the West and then after
> their defeat turn against the Soviet Union with all my forces. I
> need the Ukraine so that they can't starve me out as happened
> in the last war.[39]

On September 1, 1939, Hitler attacked Poland from the west; his
new partner, Stalin, needing two extra weeks to prepare his forces
and assess the Allied reaction, attacked from the east. Britain and
France declared war—on Germany alone. The Poles discovered that
Allied guarantees of their territorial integrity did not cover a Soviet
invasion from the east.

A year earlier, Chamberlain had written to his sister, telling her
he had been reading a life of George Canning, and agreed with
Canning that "Britain should not let the vital decision as to peace
or war pass out of her hands into those of another country."[40] Yet he
had done exactly that; he had given the decision over peace or war

to a Polish regime that had a romantic view of its capacity to fight a modern war.

When British behavior is observed before, during, and after the war, it is hard not to conclude that Britain went to war less for Polish independence than to redeem British honor for Munich and to uphold a tenet of British policy since Louis XIV: prevent any single hostile power from dominating Europe. "The commonest error in politics," Lord Salisbury had warned, "is sticking to the carcasses of dead policies."

If Britain had wanted to punish aggression, Parliament should have declared war on the USSR, too. If Britain wanted to save Poland, it would have taken the offensive in France. But Britain and France sat behind the Maginot Line while Poland was being crucified. And, after half a decade of Nazi occupation, the Polish people learned that Churchill, who had condemned Chamberlain for selling out the Czechs at Munich, had sold them out at Teheran and Yalta by allowing Stalin to keep that half of Poland ceded to him in the Hitler-Stalin Pact. Poland could be compensated with German land. As for Poland's political future, that was Stalin's call.

After Churchill accepted the carving up and communization of Poland without even a burst of his famous eloquent outrages, it is hard to credit the claim that it was for Poland's liberty that Britain went to war.

What would have happened had Chamberlain and Halifax not, in their humiliation, given the war guarantee to Poland? Again, Sir Roy Denman:

> If Chamberlain had not committed the two monumental blunders of his personal involvement and then humiliation in the Czechoslovak affair and then the guarantee to Poland—if he had backed isolation on these issues but accompanied it with a firm

emphasis on rearmament and drawn a realistic line in the sand,
Britain, the sea routes, the Empire, France and the Channel
ports, then he would have faced a rising tide of doubt and dis-
content in the press and more eloquent speeches by Churchill,
but would have had no serious difficulty in carrying with him a
massive House of Commons' majority in favour of staying out of
a German-Polish war. Churchill would never have become
Prime Minister. Germany, after Poland, would have turned on
Russia.[41]

The British-French declarations of war impelled Hitler to attack
in the West to secure his rear before invading Russia. The democracies of the West—Denmark, Norway, Holland, Belgium, France—
were thus overrun and occupied, the British army was thrown off the
continent, and the empire was ensnared in a war that led to its dissolution, as 400,000 British went to their deaths. By redirecting
Hitler's first blow upon themselves, Britain and France bought Stalin
two extra years to prepare for Hitler's attack—and thus saved the
Soviet Union for communism.

Had Britain and France not given the guarantee to Poland,
Hitler would almost surely have delivered his first great blow to
Stalin's Russia. Britain and France would have had additional years to
build up their air forces and armies and to purchase, as neutrals, whatever munitions they needed from the United States. If the revealed
horrors of Nazism in the East mandated a war, the Allies could have
chosen the time and place to strike. Even had Hitler conquered the
USSR at enormous cost, would he then have launched a new war
against a Western Europe where his ambitions never lay? Had Britain
and France not given the war guarantees to Poland, there might have
been no Dunkirk, no blitz, no Vichy, no destruction of the Jewish
populations of Norway, Denmark, Holland, Belgium, Luxembourg,
France, or even Italy.

Even had Hitler, victorious in the East, launched a war in the West, the British and French would have been far better armed and prepared to receive him. Ultimately, it was not Poland that benefited from Britain's war guarantee to Warsaw—Poland lost millions of its people and fifty years of freedom—but Stalin.

HITLER'S IMPERIAL AMBITIONS

September 3, 1939, the day Britain and France declared war on Germany, FDR delivered a fireside chat:

> I have said not once, but many times, that I have seen war and that I hate war. I say that again and again.
>
> I hope the United States will keep out of this war. I believe that it will. And I give you assurance and reassurance that every effort of your Government will be directed toward that end.
>
> As long as it remains within my power to prevent, there will be no black-out of peace in the United States.[42]

FDR was reflecting the will of the nation. In September 1939 a poll showed that only 2.3 percent of Americans wanted to go to war. Only 13.5 percent favored war if Britain and France were on the verge of defeat. By October, after Poland had been overrun, the 13.5 percent fell to 10.1 percent.[43]

After Poland was annihilated in three weeks, the guns fell silent. The Germans sat behind the Siegfried Line, and the French and British behind the Maginot Line. "There is something phony about this war," said Senator Borah, giving the interlude its name, the "Phony War."[44]

But in the East, Stalin was on a rampage. Ten weeks after attacking Poland, he began the "dreadful rape of Finland," as FDR called it, after the Finns refused to hand over the Karelian peninsula at gunpoint. The Soviet Union was expelled from the League of Nations.

In mid-1940 Stalin invaded Estonia, Latvia, and Lithuania, murdering or deporting to Siberia the political and cultural elites of the small Baltic states ceded to him by Hitler in a secret protocol of their partnership agreement.

In April 1940 Hitler suddenly occupied Denmark and Norway, and struck into France on May 10; by mid-June the blitzkrieg had overrun France and hurled the British army off the continent at Dunkirk. Hitler had achieved in six weeks what the kaiser had failed to achieve in four years. The war in the West appeared over.

Following his victory, Hitler made no overt move to threaten U.S. vital interests. He occupied the Atlantic and Channel ports of France; halted his tanks at the Pyrenees; turned the rest of the nation over to the French Vichy government; declined to occupy France's colonies in North Africa; offered England, in exchange for peace, guarantees of the British Empire; visited Paris; and went home, never to return. No one can know the mind of Hitler. But as of mid-1940, his actions argue that beneath the overlay of Nazi ideology, he was driven by a traditional German policy of *Drang nach Osten*, the drive to the East. Having been stripped of its overseas colonies at Versailles, Germany seemed determined to carve a new empire out of Eastern Europe and Bolshevik Russia. William Henry Chamberlin, the historian, held this view of Hitler's ambitions and believed the British-French decision to go to war over Eastern Europe was a monumental blunder of Western history:

> After 1936 there was little prospect of stopping Hitler without a war which was likely to be disastrous to victors as well as vanquished. There was still, however, an excellent chance to keep…
> [Western] Europe out of this war. One can never speak with certainty of historical "might have beens," but, on the basis of the available evidence, the failure of Britain and France to canalize

Hitler's expansion in an eastward direction may reasonably be considered one of the greatest diplomatic failures in history.

Hitler had written in *Mein Kampf*:

"We terminate the endless German drive to the south and west of Europe, and direct our gaze toward the lands in the east. We finally terminate the colonial and trade policy of the pre-war period, and proceed to the territorial policy of the future.

"But if we talk about new soil and territory in Europe today, we can think primarily only of *Russia* and its vassal border states."

That Hitler was treacherous, mercurial, and unpredictable is true. But there are many other indications that his program of conquest was eastward, not westward in orientation. His overtures to Poland for joint action against the Soviet Union have been noted.[45]

In this analysis Hitler had not wanted war with the West. But when the West declared war, he overran France to secure his rear before setting out to conquer the East. In this analysis Hitler saw the world divided into four spheres: Great Britain holding its empire; Japan, dominant in East Asia; Germany, master of Europe; and America, mistress of the Western Hemisphere.

THE DISHONEST ELECTION OF 1940

In late June of 1940, where did the American people stand? With France overrun and the British army driven into the Channel at Dunkirk, 86 percent of Americans said they did not want to go to war against Germany and Italy; only 5 percent wanted to fight.[46] What makes these figures astonishing is that this was the nadir of the Allied cause; still, Americans did not believe that Hitler was a threat to the United States. If FDR believed this to be shortsighted and wrong, he had a moral duty to stand up and say so. An election was impending; he was running for a third term. What better time, what better venue to educate Americans to the mortal threat to their way of life as represented by the partnership of Hitler, Mussolini, and Stalin? But Roosevelt did not; he merely echoed popular sentiment. As Henry Luce wrote, "[F]or seven years Franklin Roosevelt was, for all practical purposes, a complete isolationist. He was more of an isolationist than Herbert Hoover or Calvin Coolidge."[47]

But not only Roosevelt; no national Republican, after the fall of France and during the Battle of Britain, urged America to enter the war. The platform the Democratic Party adopted in the summer of 1940 for the Roosevelt–Wallace ticket read:

> We will not participate in foreign wars, and we will not send our army, naval or air forces to fight in foreign lands outside of the Americas, except in case of attack.... The direction and aim of our foreign policy has been, and will continue to be, the security and defense of our own land and the maintenance of its peace.[48]

Throughout the fall Wendell Willkie and FDR competed in the vehemence of their pledges to stay out of war. "If you elect me president, I will never send an American boy to fight in any European war," said Willkie.[49] He challenged FDR's commitment to peace: "If [Roosevelt's] promise to keep our boys out of foreign wars is no better than his promise to balance the budget, they're already almost on the transports."[50] FDR, said Willkie, was a warmonger who had made secret deals with the British. Stung, the president declared in Boston on October 30, "[M]others and fathers... I have said this before, but I shall say it again and again and again: Your boys are not going to be sent into any foreign wars."[51]

The 1940 campaign was among the most dishonest ever held. Both FDR and Willkie were, by that time, interventionists at heart. After the election, they would work together to steer America into war. Yet neither told the American people the truth as they believed it to be. Both spent the fall election echoing the views of America First.

LINDBERGH AND AMERICA FIRST

The America First Committee (AFC) was born in September 1940, three months after France fell. By then the Royal Air Force had gained the upper hand in the Battle of Britain. There would be no "Sea Lion," code name for Hitler's cross-channel invasion, if ever one had been planned. In its first announcement, the committee issued a statement of its principles:

1. The United States must build an impregnable defense for America.
2. No foreign power, nor group of powers, can successfully attack a prepared America.
3. American democracy can be preserved only by keeping out of the European war.
4. "Aid short of war" weakens national defense at home and threatens to involve America in war abroad.[52]

The AFC also released a statement of objectives that disclosed the proposed activities of the organization:

1. To bring together all Americans, regardless of possible differences on other matters, who see eye-to-eye on these principles. (This does not include Nazists [sic], Fascists, Communists, or members of other groups that place the interest of any other nation above those of our own country.)
2. To urge Americans to keep their heads amid rising hysteria in times of crisis.
3. To provide sane national leadership for the majority of the

American people who want to keep out of the European
war.

4. To register this opinion with the President and with
Congress.[53]

As their principles and policies demonstrate, the leaders of
America First were neither utopians nor pacifists; they believed in
peace through strength. The acting chairman was Brigadier General
Robert E. Wood, chairman of Sears, Roebuck, and quartermaster
general of the army under President Wilson. On the national com-
mittee were: ad executive Chester Bowles; actress Lillian Gish; meat
packer Jay C. Hormel; Brigadier General Hugh S. Johnson, who had
headed FDR's New Deal National Recovery Act; Hanford
MacNider, a decorated war hero and former chairman of the
American Legion; the manufacturer William H. Regnery; Alice
Roosevelt Longworth, daughter of Theodore; novelist Kathleen
Norris; Amos Pinchot, gadfly brother of famed conservationist
Gifford Pinchot; Mrs. Burton K. Wheeler, wife of the Montana senator; and best known of all, Charles A. Lindbergh, the aviator who
had flown the Atlantic into immortality in his single-engine *Spirit of
St. Louis*. Lindbergh did not join the national committee until April
1941, halfway through its life, but he was its biggest draw. Every chapter wanted him as speaker. Wrote H. R. Knickerbocker in late 1941:

> Because Lindbergh had something that appealed so profoundly
> to America that he has not lost it all yet… he towers in influ-
> ence above our other isolationists…. Lindbergh… is… mainly
> responsible for the long hesitation of this country to go to war
> to defend its life.[54]

Presidential speechwriter Robert Sherwood agreed. Lindbergh
"was undoubtedly FDR's most formidable competitor on the radio."[55]
At its peak, AFC claimed 850,000 members, and millions of

supporters across the country. As Bill Kauffman wrote in his history of the AFC:

> Its rallies and newsletters amplified antiwar cries of all strains and accents, from Socialist Norman Thomas to progressive stalwarts Senator Gerald P. Nye and journalist John T. Flynn.... It was populist and patrician, Main Street and windswept prairie, Exeter and Sauk Centre.[56]

Former President Hoover was a supporter. Into the coffers of America First came a $100 check from John F. Kennedy, son of the ambassador to England, with a note: "What you are doing is vital." Kennedy's college roommate Torbert Macdonald recalls Jack's being in strong sympathy with America First: "I can recall distinctly at one stage that Jack thought that the people whose motto was 'America First' were correct and that we were just going to get, needlessly, entangled in what was basically a European war."[57] Future JFK brother-in-law Sargent Shriver was a supporter. At Yale Law School, the AFC was headed by one of its national youth founders and most energetic members:

> Gerald R. Ford, former All-American center in football at the University of Michigan, resigned from the original student executive committee. Ford had been an enthusiastic recruiter for America First. Yet, because he was an assistant football coach at Yale, he feared that the athletic association might frown on his activities and that his job could be in jeopardy.[58]

With Potter Stewart, Ford had been a driving force at Yale. Also a member was the young socialist Murray Kempton, as were the poet e. e. cummings, novelist Sinclair Lewis, and Gore Vidal. The chairman of the *Yale Daily News*, Kingman Brewster, Jr., was an ardent anti-interventionist who helped recruit historian Charles A. Beard. Eddie

Rickenbacker, America's greatest air ace, a rival to the Red Baron and first president of Eastern Airlines, was a member, as was Oswald Garrison Villard. The former editor of the ultra-liberal *Nation*, Villard quit the magazine in disgust when *The Nation* renounced pacifism and whooped it up for war. Villard predicted:

> I believe... that the present editors will some day awake to a
> realization that the course they are now proposing will inevitably
> end all social and political progress, lower still further the stan-
> dard of living, enslave labor, and if persisted in, impose a dictator-
> ship and turn us into a totalitarian state.[59]

The old liberal marveled "that a Hitler beyond seas could so have swept the greatest republic from its moorings."[60] *The Nation's* editor, the Stalinist Freda Kirchway, countered that Villard's was "exactly the policy for America that Nazi propaganda in this country supports."[61] To brand those Americans who wanted to stay out of Europe's war as fascists or Nazi sympathizers was a common tactic. In *The Warhawks*, about the pro-war activists of 1940–1941, Mark Lincoln Chadwin writes:

> Knowing that most Americans—even those opposed to war—
> despised Hitler and Mussolini, the Warhawks worked assiduously
> to pin upon each of the major isolationist figures the image of a
> Nazi, a Fascist sympathizer, or a dupe of the Axis. And, owing
> largely to the indiscretions of their targets, they frequently
> succeeded.[62]

American industrialist Henry Ford was denounced by journalist Herbert Agar as a "fascist... in that he represents one of the main rea-sons for fascism."[63] University of Chicago President Robert Maynard Hutchins was accused by Barry Bingham, the president of the

Louisville Courier Journal, of advocating the "coward's course."[64] In
1940, forty pro-war militants, including journalists Samuel Grafton,
Ralph Ingersoll, and Dorothy Thompson, signed a letter to
Roosevelt demanding that he fire Ambassador to Great Britain
Joseph P. Kennedy as an "enemy of the democratic way of life."[65]
Montana Senator Burton Wheeler was called a "Twentieth Century
Benedict Arnold."[66] Essayist-columnist Alexander Woollcott told his
national radio audience on May 27, 1941, "Whether they [the isola-
tionists] admit it or not, whether they like it or not… they are work-
ing for Hitler."[67]

Most America Firsters were actually small-government Republicans. According to Republican Senator Robert A. Taft, those who
were big on war were Wall Street bankers, society groups, commen-
tators, plutocratic newspapers, magazine writers, the intelligentsia,
communists, Hollywood, and the party's big contributors. Small-
town America and the local chamber of commerce wanted no part
of a new war.[68] The historian with the deepest knowledge of the
America First Committee, Wayne Cole, declared, after long study of
the documents of the AFC and the government files on it:

> The committee's leaders rejected rioting and violence. They
> barred Nazis, Fascists, and anti-Semites from membership, and
> tried to enforce those bans. The committee used orderly demo-
> cratic methods in desperate efforts to keep the United States out
> of the wars raging abroad. The committee's positions on foreign
> affairs were consistent with traditions extending back to the
> beginnings of America's independent history and before…. The
> America First Committee was a patriotic and honorable exercise
> of democracy in action at a critical time in American history.[69]

Upon reflection, George Bush would surely never have said of
the patriots of America First, many of whom he came to know as

friends, that their determination to keep America out of war "flew escort for the very bombers that attacked our men" at Pearl Harbor.[70] Indeed, President Bush's devoted personal friend, Richard A. Moore, whom he named ambassador to Ireland, had been a key organizer of America First.

HITLER REFUSES TO BITE

From June 1940 to June 1941, a conquerors' peace prevailed across Europe. In the East it was the peace of Auschwitz and Katyn, where SS and NKVD killers roamed free and labored long into the night. But not until June 22, 1941, a full year after the fall of France, did Hitler invade the Soviet Union, opening Act III of the great European war and America's historic debate. This was less than six months before Pearl Harbor.

For the two years during which Stalin was Hitler's ally, the USSR had provided the grain and fuel the Germans used to win the Battle of France and fight the Battle of Britain—and the U.S. Communist Party had been insistent that we stay out of the "imperialists' war." But now that Stalin's Russia was Hitler's prey, the Communists howled for intervention. Their position is understandable; the party's allegiance was to Moscow and Stalin. But to most Americans, Hitler's invasion of the USSR changed nothing. They saw no vital interest in Stalin's survival and no moral distinction between Nazis and communists. Both regimes were totalitarian, both were aggressors, both were hostile to Western values, both had innocent blood on their hands. As of June 1941 the body count of those murdered by Stalin still exceeded Hitler's by the millions. To many Americans, Stalin's Russia—spread across a dozen time zones, with an inexhaustible supply of raw materials and oil, possessing an ideology with adherents among elites all over the world, including the United States—was a far greater long-term threat than Hitler's Germany. Most Americans agreed with General Wood when he stated the America First position with clarity and simplicity:

> With the ruthless forces of dictatorship and aggression now
> clearly aligned on both sides [of the European war] the proper
> course for the United States becomes even clearer. We must con-
> tinue to build our defenses and take no part in this incongruous
> European conflict.[71]

Wood believed America must rapidly rearm, but saw no great
moral difference between Hitler and Stalin. He was echoed by
Senator Harry Truman, who, in the words of Henry Kissinger, "rated
the two dictatorships as being morally equivalent, and recommended
that America encourage them to fight to the death."[72] Truman stated:

> If we see that Germany is winning, we ought to help Russia,
> and if Russia is winning we ought to help Germany and that
> way let them kill as many as possible, although I don't want to
> see Hitler victorious under any circumstances. Neither of them
> think [sic] anything of their pledged word.[73]

New York Times military expert Hanson Baldwin came to share
Truman's view that we should have let the two monsters tear each
other to pieces:

> There is no doubt whatsoever that it would have been to the
> interest of Britain, the United States, and the world to have
> allowed—and indeed, to have encouraged—the world's two
> great dictatorships to fight each other to a frazzle. Such a strug-
> gle, with its resultant weakening of both Communism and
> Nazism, could not but have aided in the establishment of a more
> stable peace....[74]

If there had been a point of maximum peril for America in the
war in Europe, it was the summer of 1940, after France had been
overrun and England seemed about to be invaded, with the possible

scuttling or loss of the British fleet. But after the Royal Air Force won the Battle of Britain, the German invasion threat was history. If Goering's Luftwaffe could not achieve air supremacy over the Channel, how was it going to achieve it over the Atlantic? If Hitler could not put a soldier into England in the fall of 1940, the notion that he could invade the Western Hemisphere—with no surface ships to engage the United States and British fleets and U.S. air power dominant in the west Atlantic—was preposterous. Lindbergh made this exact point to the House Foreign Affairs Committee on January 23, 1941:

> If England is able to live at all with bases of the German air
> force less than an hour's flight away, the United States is not in
> greater danger across the Atlantic ocean.... [N]ot a single
> squadron of trans-oceanic bombing planes exists anywhere in
> the world today.... I do not believe there is any danger of an
> invasion of this continent, either by sea or by air, as long as we
> maintain an army, navy, and air force of reasonable size and in
> modern condition, and provided we establish the bases essential
> for defense.[75]

Lindbergh urged Congress to build ten thousand fighter planes. Should the United States discover "any attempt to establish a foreign base in North or South America," the Lone Eagle added, we "should go to war with all our resources."[76] Lindbergh was no pacifist, and the strengthened defense he was calling for was long overdue. In a world at war, even neutrality required American military power, a lesson the United States should have known from its history as far back as 1812.

Six months after Lindbergh testified, Hitler attacked the Soviet Union, a giant of a nation with thousands of tanks and planes and millions of soldiers. The United States was now even more secure. England had stopped Hitler at the Channel and was building planes faster than Germany, and Hitler's legions now faced the Red Army and a Russian winter that had stopped Napoleon. A policy of aid to Britain and the USSR, with a rapid buildup of U.S. military powers, while keeping American boys off foreign battlefields, had mass public support.

But Roosevelt, immediately after he was safely elected to a third term, began to maneuver the United States into the war, even as he assured his countrymen he was taking every step to keep America out. Before the election, Roosevelt had been cautious; now, he was bold, even provocative. He extended the navy's neutrality zone from three hundred miles offshore to mid-Atlantic and put U.S. troops on Greenland and Iceland. In the spring of 1941 the United States aided the British in the search for the *Bismarck*. By July, U.S. naval "patrols" were being extended to Iceland to protect American ships; British ships were allowed in the convoys. None of this was done with the authorization of Congress.

Since Hitler's armies were now deep inside the USSR, and a new front had been opened in North Africa after the British defeated Mussolini there, Hitler did not want to add America to his roster of enemies. He knew U-boat incidents had brought America into the war in 1917, and did not want to repeat the kaiser's fatal blunder. He ordered his submarines to avoid incidents with U.S. ships. But on September 4, 1941, a U.S. destroyer, *Greer*, exchanged fire with a German U-boat.

This is "piracy legally and morally," FDR declared in a fireside chat on September 11: "In spite of what Hitler's propaganda bureau has invented... I tell you the blunt fact that the German submarine fired first upon this American destroyer without warning, and with deliberate design to sink her."[77] The *Greer*, he said, had been on a mail run to Iceland.

Calling German submarines the "rattlesnakes of the Atlantic," FDR ordered U.S. warships to shoot them on sight: "[W]hen you see a rattlesnake poised to strike, you do not wait until he has struck before you crush him."[78] Without authorization from Congress, the president had launched a naval war in the Atlantic.[79]

The truth: The *Greer* affair was a true "Tonkin Gulf" incident. A Senate investigation found the *Greer* was not a mail ship at all. She had been trailing a German submarine for three-and-a-half hours, radioing its position to a British plane that attacked with depth charges, an attack the *Greer* joined. The submarine fired at the American destroyer in self-defense. FDR had deceived the American people.

But if Americans were not being told the truth by the president, the British government was. After communicating with FDR, Churchill told his war cabinet: "[H]e was obviously determined that they should come in.... The president had said that he would become more and more provocative. If the Germans did not like it, they could attack American forces. Everything was to be done to force an incident."[80]

Churchill confidently telegraphed South African statesman Jan Smuts on September 14: "American public have accepted the 'shoot on sight' declaration without knowing the vast area to which it is to be applied, and in my opinion they will support president in fuller and further application of this principle, out of which at any moment war may come."[81]

Yet still, America did not want to go to war. On October 7, 1941, a national poll found that two-thirds of those questioned said it was more important to keep out of war than to defeat Germany at the risk of war.

On October 17, 1941, the USS *Kearny* was hit by torpedoes near Greenland; eleven American lives were lost. President Roosevelt declared an unlimited national emergency, stating, "America has been attacked by Germany." The president neglected to mention that *Kearny* had been dropping depth charges on the submarine before being attacked.[82]

On October 27 the president tried another approach. Speaking at the Mayflower Hotel on Navy and Total Defense Day, FDR riveted the nation by claiming he had come into possession of "a secret map," made in Nazi Germany, that proved Hitler was lying when he said he had no designs on the Western Hemisphere. Hitler's plans for a "new world order," said FDR, included a reorganization of Central and South America into "five vassal states" under Nazi rule. The president claimed he also had come into possession of a Nazi document detailing a plan "to abolish all existing religions," liquidate all clergy, and create an "International Nazi Church":

> [I]n the place of the Bible, the words of *Mein Kampf* will be imposed and enforced as Holy Writ. And in the place of the cross of Christ will be put two symbols—the swastika and the naked sword.
>
> The god of Blood and Iron will take the place of the God of Love and Mercy.[83]

These "grim truths," FDR predicted, will be "hotly denied in the controlled press and radio of the Axis powers."

The map to which FDR alluded was a forgery, done up in the office of Ivar Bryce, who worked for William Stephenson, the top British secret agent in the United States. Writes Nicholas John Cull, author of *Selling War: The British Propaganda Campaign Against American 'Neutrality' in World War II*, "the most striking feature of the episode was the complicity of the president of the United States in perpetrating the fraud."[84]

But Roosevelt's deceit failed to move the nation.

Before Pearl Harbor, FDR never tried to persuade his country that war with Nazi Germany was necessary and America must fight to destroy Hitler. Instead, while accusing the German government of lying about naval clashes in the Atlantic and about Nazi maps and documents, FDR was himself lying to incite national hysteria. There was truth in the cutting remark of Clare Luce in 1944 that FDR "lied us into a war because he did not have the political courage to lead us into it."[85]

On October 22, 1941, the America First Committee sent FDR an open letter calling for a debate in Congress, and an up-or-down vote on a declaration of war on Hitler's Reich. The president refused the challenge and ignored the letter. Seven weeks later, when he went before Congress to ask for a declaration of war on Japan, Franklin Roosevelt did not even mention Hitler or Nazi Germany.

Thus it needs to be said again and again: The America Firsters did not want to "isolate" America from the world; they wanted only to isolate America from the war. The struggle with FDR was over one issue: Should we follow the counsel of Washington and stay out of European wars, or the example of Wilson and go in? By the fall of 1941, the two great combatants were Nazi Germany and Stalinist Russia. Most Americans did not believe their husbands, fathers, or sons should die for either one.

CHAPTER 16

Back Door to War

For a long time I have believed that our best entrance into the war would be by way of Japan.... And, of course, if we go to war against Japan, it will inevitably lead us to war against Germany.[1]

—SECRETARY OF INTERIOR HAROLD L. ICKES,
OCTOBER 18, 1941

America's war with Japan had its roots in two decisions taken four decades before Pearl Harbor: McKinley's decision to annex the Philippines, and the McKinley-Hay declaration of the Open Door policy in China.

Soon after Secretary of State John Hay announced the policy, Japan inquired if the United States would support the Open Door with action, by helping block Russia from taking Manchuria. The United States demurred. Japan settled the issue at Port Arthur and Tsushima.

Japan had demonstrated it would fight to keep Manchuria and Korea from Russia; the Americans had shown they would not. Either Manchuria was not covered by the Open Door, Japan concluded, or the Open Door was bluster and bluff. So from 1931 to 1932, Japan occupied all Manchuria. The United States responded with the Stimson Doctrine—we refused to recognize the occupation or the puppet state Japan created there, "Manchukuo."

By the early 1930s Japan's policy in Asia was a mirror image of Germany's in Europe. As Berlin dreamed of a German empire carved out of the old Russian empire, Tokyo dreamed of a Japanese empire carved out of the Western empires in Asia.

In 1934, with the Amau Doctrine, named for the Foreign Office's Eliji Amau, Japan declared its sole right to supervise China's economic development, a direct challenge to the Open Door. Again, the United States did nothing. Why not? Stated simply, the United States had no vital interest in China. U.S. trade with China was negligible, while China was a primary source of raw materials and a crucial market for Japan. Even more important, Japan had a vital security interest in China. Stalin was establishing a communist power base in Sinkiang and Mongolia, and colluding with Mao Tse-tung. Korea, Manchuria, and Inner Mongolia—pillars of Japan's defense structure—were vulnerable to infiltration.

In the 1930s faraway America did not feel menaced by Stalin's Russia, but to Japan, a vast, brooding Soviet Union that bore bitter memories of Port Arthur and Tsushima represented a mortal threat.

THE UNITED STATES DECLARES "ECONOMIC WAR"

In July 1937, after an incident at Marco Polo Bridge near Peking, Japan invaded China. In December, Japanese planes strafed and sank the *Panay*, a U.S. gunboat on the Yangtze that had been convoying tankers for Standard Oil. Rage swept America. But Japan apologized immediately and offered compensation to the families of the dead and wounded.

Two days after the *Panay* was sunk, Congress took up the Ludlow Amendment, which said there could be no U.S. declaration of war without a national referendum, except in the case of attack or a threat of attack on American soil. Indiana Congressman Louis L. Ludlow, a Democrat and retired newsman, said his constitutional amendment would do more to

keep American boys out of slaughter pens in foreign countries
than any other measure that could be passed. It is based on the
philosophy that those who have to suffer and, if need be, to
die and to bear the awful burdens and griefs of war shall have
something to say as to whether war shall be declared.[2]

Seventy-three percent of the nation favored the Ludlow
Amendment, but the House of Representatives on January 10,
1938, refused, 209–188, to let it be debated. The vote reflected
Roosevelt's control of Congress and the concerns of Republicans
like Arthur Vandenberg of Michigan, who believed the amendment
was a prescription for U.S. paralysis. "[I]t would be as sensible," said
Vandenberg, "to require a town meeting before permitting the fire
department to face a blaze."[3]

By late 1938 the Sino-Japanese War had reached stalemate.
Japan's army held the coastal cities, but Chinese nationalists and
communists held the interior. When France fell in June 1940,
Japan decided to seize its Asian colonies. In September, Tokyo
signed the Tripartite Agreement with Germany and Italy, and its
army occupied the northern half of French Indochina (Vietnam).
Hitler, Stalin, Mussolini, and Hirohito were now all aligned. FDR's
response was an embargo on the sale of scrap iron and steel to
Japan.

After Hitler invaded the USSR in late June 1940, Japan occupied the rest of Indochina. FDR froze all Japanese assets, thus cutting off trade, including oil. He pressed the British and Dutch to
follow. Since Japan's industry and empire were almost totally
dependent on oil from the United States and Dutch East Indies,
America had just grabbed Japan by the throat. Without oil, Japan
could not long continue the war against China; without oil, the
Japanese empire must wither and die.

Six days before he cut the oil lifeline, FDR was warned in a

memo from the navy chief of war plans, Rear Admiral Richmond K.
Turner, of the probable consequences:

> It is generally believed that shutting off the American supply of
> petroleum will lead promptly to an invasion of the Netherlands
> East Indies [by the Japanese].... Furthermore, it seems certain
> that, if Japan should then take military measures against the
> British and Dutch, she would also include military action against
> the Philippines, which would immediately involve us in a Pacific
> War.[4]

Given the risks, the recommendation of Turner's report was "that
trade with Japan not be embargoed at this time."[5] America's senior
naval officer, Admiral Harold Stark, wrote on the report, "I concur in
general."[6] Roosevelt himself was fully aware of what an oil embargo
meant. Pressed by his interventionists—Ickes of Interior, Morgenthau
of Treasury, and Stimson of War—the president gave his cabinet "quite
a lecture" on July 18, warning that if the United States "stopped all
oil, it would simply drive the Japanese down to the Dutch East Indies,
and it would mean war in the Pacific."[7] Yet FDR went ahead. Why?
Some historians contend that it was Assistant Secretary of State Dean
Acheson who ordered no release of Japanese funds, no more export
licenses, thus no sale of oil; and that FDR did not realize the draco-
nian nature of the U.S. sanctions until September.[8] Yet, as Walter
Lippmann wrote, "This was a declaration of economic war" on Japan.[9]
Tokyo now faced a mortal crisis.

Given Japan's aggression in China, its cruelties, the appalling
Rape of Nanking, Tokyo's alliance with Berlin, and its contempt for
the Open Door, America had no obligation to continue providing
Japan with the oil that was fueling its navy and army as they ram-
paged through Asia. But the oil embargo was "economic war" against
an oil-starved nation, and FDR had a moral duty to inform the

nation he had forced Japan into a corner where Tokyo must yield to America's demands—or attack. This Roosevelt did not do. Why not?

Historians give several explanations. One is that FDR did not realize he had just issued a death sentence on the Japanese empire and it must fight or die. Another is that FDR knew the consequences of an oil embargo and approved, because he wanted Japan to attack. A war with Japan, a member of the Tripartite Pact, was the only way he could take us to war in Europe.

When, exactly, FDR decided to shift U.S. policy from all-out aid short of war to taking America into war is difficult to place. But once reelected in November 1940, his rhetoric and actions became openly belligerent. FDR seemed to court a conflict. But while he seemed anxious, even desperate, to get into the war, the nation he had been elected to lead, on a promise to stay out, wanted to stay out. Surveyed in August 1941 on the question, "If you were asked to vote today on the question of the United States going to war against Japan, how would you vote?" Americans, by 76 percent to 24 percent said, "Stay out." As late as October 22, seven weeks before Pearl Harbor, Americans by 74 percent to 13 percent were against going to war with Japan.[10] The American people in the fall of 1941 did not believe that who controlled China or French Indochina was worth fighting about.

On November 25, 1941, Secretary of War Henry L. Stimson confided to his diary that the question of the hour was "how we should maneuver them into the position of firing the first shot."[11] Stimson and FDR knew their history. Only after the Mexican army had killed U.S. soldiers north of the Rio Grande did Polk ask for a declaration of war. Only after the South had fired on Fort Sumter did Lincoln put out a call for volunteers. Only after Germany had sunk four U.S. merchant ships in 1917 did Wilson deliver his war message. FDR needed to maneuver Japan into firing the first shot.

LAST CHANCE FOR PEACE

Japan's rulers estimated that the oil they had hoarded would last two years. But Japan also depended on the Dutch East Indies and British Malaya for tin, rice, bauxite, nickel, and rubber. Cut off from these raw materials as well as oil, Japan's situation would quickly become desperate.

At Roosevelt's urging, the British and Dutch supported America's demand that Japan pull out of China and Indochina and relinquish all conquests since 1937—as the price for lifting the embargo. FDR was demanding that Japan surrender an empire for which it had paid an immense price in blood and treasure, or die for lack of oil, lifeblood of its economy. To Tokyo this was an American ultimatum: Submit or die.

Tokyo had three options: (1) accept the ultimatum, pack, and leave Indochina and China, a humiliating retreat that would mean defeat in the China war and an end to its days as a great power; (2) drive south to seize the sources of rice, rubber, tin, and oil in Malaya and the East Indies; (3) negotiate with the Americans. Japan's concern about the second option was that its leaders believed any attack on British and Dutch possessions meant war with the United States. As America was then engaged in secret war planning with the British and Dutch, Tokyo's concern was justified.

In early December, Lord Halifax received FDR's personal assurance of armed support if Japan went to war against Britain.[12] The president was handing out war guarantees Congress had never authorized and of which the American people were utterly unaware.

Through the summer and into the fall of 1941, Japan sought a way out. Tokyo offered to withdraw from southern Indochina and not to join Germany in an offensive war if the United States would lift the embargo and tell China to negotiate. The United States rejected the offer. Prince Fumimaro Konoye, Japan's prime minister and leader of the peace party, offered to meet FDR anywhere in the Pacific. In a three-hour secret meeting with Ambassador Joseph Grew, Konoye confided that ranking officers in the army and navy were behind him and would accompany him to Juneau, Alaska, and his ship would be equipped with special telephone lines to the emperor, who, said Grew, "would immediately issue a rescript ordering the suspension forthwith of all hostile operations" in China and Indochina.[13] Ambassador Grew wrote in his memoirs:

> We in the Embassy had no doubt that the Prime Minister would
> have agreed, at his meeting with the President, to the eventual
> withdrawal of all Japanese forces from all of Indochina and from
> all of China with the face-saving expedient of being permitted
> to retain a limited number of troops in North China and Inner
> Mongolia temporarily.[14]

Grew believed the United States was on the verge of a diplomatic triumph, without war. But Secretary of State Cordell Hull, fearing a "second Munich," rebuffed the offer.[15] Though the president initially showed interest, he deferred to Hull, and began setting preconditions for any meeting. Konoye was soon replaced by Tojo, and the opportunity was gone.

Hull did later approve a proposal known as the *modus vivendi*. Both nations would give mutual assurances of no further moves into Southeast Asia or the Pacific; Japan would pull out of southern Indochina and cut its forces in north Indochina to 25,000; and the United States would partially lift the embargo, allowing Japan to export and import limited amounts of cotton, oil, food, and medical supplies. FDR was interested, but the plan created a panic among the war hawks. Eden, Churchill, Chiang Kai-shek, his brother-in-law T. V. Soong, and Chiang's American adviser, Owen Lattimore, interceded to kill the *modus vivendi*. Chiang's cables to Washington, according to Hull, were "hysterical."[16] China wanted the United States at war against Japan as desperately as Churchill wanted the United States at war against Germany. But Churchill's note, which reached FDR on November 26, suggested the prime minister was thinking only of Chiang and China:

> Of course it is for you to handle this business and we certainly
> do not want an additional war. There is only one point that dis-
> quiets us. What about Chiang? Is he not having a very thin diet?
> Our anxiety is about China. If they collapse our joint danger
> would enormously increase. We are sure that the regard of the
> United States for the Chinese cause will govern your action. We
> feel that the Japanese are most unsure of themselves.[17]

Hull decided not to give the *modus vivendi* to the Japanese. The last chance for peace in the Pacific slipped away, and it is hard not to conclude that, in their hearts, FDR and his men had already accepted, and welcomed, the prospect of war. On November 26, 1941, Washington told Tokyo America's nonnegotiable demands for lifting the embargo stood: total withdrawal from Indochina and China, acceptance of Chinese sovereignty, and cancellation of Tokyo's tripartite pact with Germany and Italy.[18] Japan's dependence on trade for the necessities of national life had left the empire at the mercy of the United States.

"PUTTING PINS IN RATTLESNAKES"

Thus came the day of reckoning for the Empire of the Sun. Tokyo's options were now reduced to two: diplomatic surrender and humili-ating retreat from Indochina and China, meaning an end to Japan's day as a Great Power—or a desperate lunge south to seize the vital resources for which Japan was starving. Tokyo chose the second course. But to succeed, Japan had to neutralize the one force in the Pacific that could block a drive south: the U.S. battle fleet riding at anchor at Pearl Harbor.

Its only chance of victory, Japan believed, was to strike first, as at Port Arthur, cripple U.S. naval power, capture the Philippines, seize the oil and minerals to make Japan self-sufficient, expand the empire to its limit, and then, behind a ring of navy steel, negotiate a truce with the United States. Not until the American rebuff of November 26 did Japan abandon hope in negotiations, but two months before, it had begun to prepare for the possibility that talks would fail. On September 6, 1941, at an imperial conference, Japan's leaders had ordered preparations for war. Premier Konoye wrote in his memoirs what had been agreed upon:

> The Empire shall perfect war preparations generally by the latter part of October with a determination to be prepared for war with America, England, and The Netherlands in order to assure its independent national existence and self-defense....
>
> In case there is no expectation of achievement of our demands by... diplomatic measures within the first ten days of October, decision shall be made to go to war.[19]

The army needed an October decision to have troops and shipping assembled to strike by the end of November. Japan's hope of victory now rested on an imperial navy made superior in the western Pacific by U.S. failure to match Japanese naval construction after Tokyo broke out of the Washington treaty limits in 1934. In December 1941 Japan had eleven aircraft carriers to six for the United States, and three of the U.S. carriers were assigned to the Atlantic. America had ceded to Japan something it could never have achieved on its own: a fighting chance to defeat the United States in a naval war. The United States had 29 percent of world manufacturing to Japan's 3.8 percent, but had failed to translate its industrial might into military power.[20] Here was the Pacific balance in December of 1941[21]:

	Japan	U.S.	England	Netherlands
Aircraft Carriers	11	3	0	0
Battleships	10	9	2	0
Heavy Cruisers	18	13	1	0
Light Cruisers	23	11	7	3
Destroyers	129	80	13	7
Submarines	67	56	0	13

Reviewing this power equation, weighing the ignominy of retreat against the possibility of glorious victory, Emperor Hirohito authorized his new premier, Hideki ("Razor Brain") Tojo, to launch the attack. On December 8 FDR went before Congress to decry "a date which will live in infamy." The same day, former President Hoover wrote to friends, "You and I know that this continuous putting pins in rattlesnakes finally got this country bitten."[22]

In his address, FDR did not even mention Germany. But Hitler, who had torn up his Munich pact with Britain when it no longer suited him, and had torn up his pact with Russia when it no longer suited him, now honored a pact with a Japan that had just launched a sneak attack on the mightiest nation on earth. Since Japan struck first, Germany was not obligated to join Japan. But whom the gods would destroy they first make mad. On December 11 Hitler declared war on the United States, citing, as one American provocation, the forged map FDR used in his Navy Day address.

LAST DAYS OF AMERICA FIRST

Within hours of Pearl Harbor, America First closed its doors; its leaders pledged themselves to America's victory; its young members went off to enlist; and it passed into history with the statement: "Our principles were right. Had they been followed, war could have been avoided. No good purpose can now be served by considering what might have been, had our objectives been attained.... The time for military action is here."[23]

But a vengeful FDR was not finished with America First. He had unleashed the FBI and IRS on its members, tapped their phones, had them hauled before grand juries, charged them with near-treason, and smeared them as "appeaser fifth columnists" and Nazi sympathizers. William Donovan, future head of the Office of Strategic Services (OSS), had said that "as matters now stand the United States possesses the finest Nazi-schooled fifth column in the world." And FDR had warned in explicit terms:

> Let us no longer blind ourselves to the undeniable fact that the
> evil forces which have crushed and undermined and corrupted
> so many others are already within our own gates. Your
> Government knows much about them and every day is ferreting
> them out.[24]

In his Annual Message to Congress, January 6, 1941, FDR went further:

> The first phase of the invasion of this Hemisphere would not be
> the landing of regular troops. The necessary strategic points
> would be occupied by secret agents and their dupes—and great
> numbers of them are already here, and in Latin America.[25]

Roosevelt's suggestion that there were Nazis, quislings, collaborators, and their "dupes" within echoes Wilson before World War I. Ironically there were "evil forces" and "secret agents and their dupes" within our gates—but they were Stalin's agents and dupes: FDR confidant Alger Hiss, Lauchlin Currie, Harry Dexter White, Judith

Coplin, the Rosenbergs, and all the rest. Honeycombed through the government, ensconced even in FDR's inner circle, these traitors would be exposed. But when FDR's acolytes, who had smeared the leaders of America First as Nazis and Nazi-sympathizers, were themselves accused of being "soft on communism," all hell would break loose at such "smear" tactics. Writes historian Wayne Cole, "Senator Joseph McCarthy did not invent 'guilt-by-association' methods; President Roosevelt and many of his supporters used those methods with great effectiveness against opponents of his foreign policies."[26]

The Nazi "secret agents," against whom FDR and Donovan had railed, were never found. But about the lying and smearing of patriotic Americans, H. Stuart Hughes would write, "[T]he cause justified the dubious means employed."[27] For a half century, Cole has studied the archives of the America First Committee. His conclusion:

> If one were to balance negatives (that is, the morality of the
> "dirty tricks" used by opponents of America First versus the
> magnitude of unsavory or disloyal elements within the commit-
> tee) the America First Committee comes off vastly better than its
> critics. The fact that one disagreed profoundly with the views of
> Lindbergh and believed him totally wrong did not justify accus-
> ing him of disloyalty and Nazi sympathies. Those charges were
> simply not true.[28]

For the sneak attack on Pearl Harbor and the massacre of American sailors that Sunday morning, Japan bears absolute moral responsibility. For partisans of FDR to blame that slaughter on American patriots whose every effort was bent toward keeping us out of war is a classic Big Lie.

Whether or not it had been America's war before December 7, it was our war now. In Yeats's line, "All changed, changed utterly." Americans were united as never before or since by Japan's treachery in attacking our ships and murdering our sailors in their sleep, united in the conviction that the Japanese empire should be destroyed.

Yet there is something deeply wrong about how the United States got into that war. The American people were not children. They knew the history of the First World War; they did not want to fight another. To repeat: They did not want to isolate America from the world, but to isolate America from the war. They did not want to have hundreds of thousands, perhaps millions, of American boys killed in Europe or Asia, because they did not believe America was threatened by Japan's occupation of France's colonies in Asia or Germany's occupation of France itself.

Perhaps they were wrong. But FDR and those who felt they knew better made only feeble attempts to lead Americans to embrace their view and accept the sacrifices of war. Instead, they smeared, persecuted, and blacklisted antiwar leaders and maneuvered us into one collision after another with Germany and Japan so that war would be "thrust upon us." The people of the world's greatest republic, on an issue of life and death, were treated like children who could not understand their true interests, and had to be manipulated and deceived into doing the right thing. Wrote Thomas A. Bailey, a historian sympathetic to Roosevelt:

> Franklin Roosevelt repeatedly deceived the American people during the period before Pearl Harbor.... He was like the physician who must tell the patient lies for the patient's own good....
>
> A president who cannot entrust the people with the truth betrays a certain lack of faith in the basic tenets of democracy. But because the masses are notoriously shortsighted, and generally cannot see danger until it is at their throats, our statesmen are forced to deceive them into an awareness of their own long-run interests. This is clearly what Roosevelt had to do, and who shall say that posterity will not thank him for it?[29]

Posterity has, by and large, thanked him for it. But if the decisions on war or peace are not to be entrusted to the American people and their elected representatives, what has become of our
constitutional republic? If the people are so "notoriously shortsighted" that they cannot "see danger until it is at their throats," what
is the argument for democracy?

The men and women of America First are today reviled as naive
fools at best, fascists and Nazi sympathizers at worst, while FDR is
seen as a leader of vision who saw the Nazi menace for what it was
and moved with dispatch to meet it—against the disloyal opposition
of "isolationists." This is not true history; it is the propaganda of court
historians.

BITTER FRUITS OF AMERICA'S VICTORY

Looking back, one sees that neither FDR nor most of his critics
appreciated fully the character of the totalitarian regimes that had
arisen out of the ashes of the Great War and the vengeful peace
Wilson brought home from Paris. And FDR proved utterly naive
about the character and intentions of Stalin, giving the Great
Terrorist everything he demanded and asking nothing in return, putting his faith in postwar cooperation and a new United Nations to
keep world peace, as Wilson had put his faith in the League of
Nations. At Yalta in 1945, FDR ceded to Stalin rights to the ports of
Darien and Port Arthur and control of the railways in Manchuria.
Said one critical historian:

> The Soviet Union had no more right to hold these ports and
> railways in Manchuria than did Japan.... Roosevelt gave to Stalin
> at Yalta effective control of the same territory over which the
> United States had gone to war with Japan, and by doing so set
> the stage for the Communist conquest of China, and... the war
> in Korea.[30]

In 1949 a young Democratic congressman observed the disaster in Asia and, quoting former U.S. Ambassador to Russia William Bullitt, laid the blame squarely at the feet of FDR and his disciples:

Whatever share of the responsibility was Roosevelt's and whatever share was [General George C.] Marshall's the vital interest of the United States in the independent integrity of China was sacrificed, and the foundation was laid for the present tragic situation in the Far East.[31]

The congressman was John F. Kennedy.

By 1950 Americans were asking what it had all been for. Britain had gone to war to save Poland, only to have Churchill virtually cede Poland to Stalin. FDR had pushed Japan to the brink over China, only to hand over to Stalin Chinese territory we had risked war to liberate. By 1945 Poland was part of Stalin's empire. By 1950 China was one vast killing field where Chinese were no longer dying in the tens of thousands at the hands of the Japanese army, but in the millions at the hands of Mao Tse-tung.

The truth: Whether Chiang's nationalists or Japanese imperialists controlled China in 1941 was not of vital interest to the United States. Yet Roosevelt courted a war with Japan over China that led to the loss of China to Stalin's empire and left us alone in the Far East to contain communism. Result: wars in Korea and Vietnam, 100,000 American dead, 350,000 American wounded, the Stalinization of French Indochina, and genocide in Cambodia.

In 1917 Wilson had gone to war to make the world safe for democracy, and had made the world safe for Lenin, Mussolini, and Hitler. In 1941 Roosevelt had gone to war to make Europe and Asia safe for democracy, and had made Europe safe for Stalinism and Asia safe for Maoism. The crusading globalists, Wilson and FDR, had gone abroad in search of monsters to destroy, and had destroyed them. But in their place came new monsters with nuclear teeth who threatened Western civilization in ways the kaiser never dreamed of. By 1950 communists ruled from the Elbe to the East China Sea, and Stalin, whom Roosevelt had rescued, was building nuclear weapons to target on the United States. Such are the fruits when nations go crusading, instead of putting national interests first.

Churchill, who penned perhaps the most eloquent epitaph of the First World War, wrote in the first volume of his memoirs in March 1948 of the disillusionment of the second great crusade:

> The human tragedy reaches its climax in the fact that after all
> the exertions and sacrifices of hundreds of millions of people and
> of the victories of the Righteous Cause, we have still not found
> Peace or Security, and that we lie in the grip of even worse per-
> ils than those we have surmounted.[32]

Between 1910 and 1950 the West suffered the greatest calamities in the history of civilization. All the great houses of Europe collapsed; all the great Western nations were horribly bloodied in two world wars; all the great empires were destroyed, or in the process of dissolution. Only America was left with the capacity to resist the barbarization of mankind in the name of communism. America did so for four decades to emerge triumphant in the Cold War, the great cause of the lives of many of us. Yet, today, one sees in America the same hubris, the same missionary zeal, the same mindless braying about "hegemony," the same foolish treaty commitments to fight in regions of the world with no relation to U.S. vital interests that one saw in the late European empires. If America is not to end the coming century the way British, French, Germans, and Russians ended this one, we must learn the lessons history has taught us.

PART SIX

1945–1989:
TWILIGHT STRUGGLE

CHAPTER 17

America's Longest War

From Stettin in the Baltic to Trieste in the Adriatic an
iron curtain has descended across the Continent.[1]
—WINSTON CHURCHILL, 1946

We will bury you.[2]
—NIKITA KHRUSHCHEV, 1956

By 1945 Germany had been destroyed and Churchill could
poke about its ruins, but Britain had been reduced to a second-rate
power and Europe's fate would now be decided in Washington and
Moscow. The British Empire was unraveling, and Churchill himself
was about to be pitched out of office as the socialism he despised was
imposed by his opponents. Having fought two wars to slay the
German beast, the British Empire fell on the corpse.

With Germany devastated and divided into occupation zones,
and Stalin's Red Army dominating Europe, George F. Kennan looked
back and ruefully observed:

> Today if one were offered the chance of having back again the
> Germany of 1913—a Germany run by conservative but rela-
> tively moderate people, no Nazis and no Communists—a vigor-
> ous Germany, full of energy and confidence, able to play a part
> again in the balancing-off of Russian power in Europe, in many
> ways it would not sound so bad.[3]

Today the British Empire is history, the United Kingdom is

cracking up, and England's old rival dominates Europe, because Britain abandoned "splendid isolation" to contain a Germany that had grown to its size and power, but did not threaten its vital interests. That the British stand was heroic is undeniable; that British policy was wise is debatable. For in just thirty years after 1914, the greatest empire of the modern world had been reduced to an American dependency. The principal cause of this historic decline was identified by historian A. J. P. Taylor:

> Though the object of being a Great Power is to be able to fight a great war, the only way of remaining a Great Power is not to fight one, or to fight it on a limited scale. This was the secret of Great Britain's greatness so long as she stuck to naval warfare and did not try to become a military power on the continental pattern.[4]

America would do well to study the British experience, to avoid the British fate.

FDR AND THE "CHRISTIAN GENTLEMAN"

Admirers of Churchill and FDR have been hard-pressed to defend their conduct at the wartime conferences. In January 1944 Churchill spoke to British Foreign Minister Anthony Eden of the "deep-seated changes which have taken place in the character of the Russian state and government, the new confidence which has grown in our hearts toward Stalin."[5] After an October 1944 meeting in Moscow, he wrote his wife: "I have had very nice talks with the old Bear. I like him the more I see him. Now they respect us & I am sure they wish to work with us."[6] At Yalta in February 1945, Churchill raised a glass to the monster whose hands dripped with the blood of millions and said, "I walk through this world with greater courage and hope when I find myself in relation of friendship and intimacy with this great man, whose fame has gone out not only over all Russia but the world."[7]

General Sir Alan Brooke, who was there, was most generous in describing the quality of the Yalta speeches as "remarkably low" and consisting "mostly... of insincere, slimy sort of slush!"[8] In reporting to the House of Commons after the conference, Churchill assured the nation that Poland's independence, for which Britain had lost hundreds of thousands of its best and bravest young, was now affirmed:

> The impression I brought back from the Crimea, and from all
> my other contacts, is that Marshal Stalin and the Soviet Leaders
> wish to live in honorable friendship and equality with the
> Western democracies. I feel also that their word is their bond. I
> know of no government which stands to its obligations even to
> its own despite, more solidly than the Russian Soviet
> Government.[9]

At Stalin's behest, Churchill even declared war on democratic Finland in late 1941, when the Finns fought to retake Viborg and the 16,000 square miles that the Red Army had robbed them of in 1940.

FDR was equally smitten with Stalin, and equally accommodating. "Of one thing I am certain," he confided to an aide at Yalta, "Stalin is not an imperialist."[10] Earlier, Roosevelt told William Bullitt, "I think if I give him [Stalin] everything I possibly can, and ask nothing from him in return, *noblesse oblige*, he won't try to annex anything and will work with me for a world of peace and democracy."[11] Writes Henry Kissinger:

> On January 20, 1945, in his fourth inaugural address, Roosevelt
> described his approach [to Stalin] by quoting from Emerson:
> "...the only way to have a friend is to be one." Soon after Yalta,
> Roosevelt characterized Stalin to the Cabinet as "having some-
> thing else in him besides this revolutionist Bolshevist thing." He

ascribed that special quality to Stalin's early education for the priesthood: "I think that something entered into his nature of the way in which a Christian gentleman should behave."[12]

By the summer of 1945 Roosevelt was dead, Churchill was out, and the "Christian gentleman" was still in power. By 1946 Poland, the nation for which Britain had gone to war, had receded into Stalinist darkness and Churchill was warning that an Iron Curtain had descended over Europe. In 1948 Berlin was blockaded, and Czechoslovakia fell to a Soviet-backed coup. In 1949 China fell to Mao's armies, which had been equipped with the Japanese weapons Stalin's armies had captured.

Thus the nations whose independence Churchill and FDR believed had been worth a world war—Czechoslovakia, Poland, China—were lost to a communist empire as brutal and hostile as Hitler's. And no power was left to halt the advance of Stalinism in Europe or Maoism in Asia, except the United States. So, half a decade after America's second crusade to make the world safe for democracy, U.S. troops were again heading to Europe—and to war in Korea.

WILSON'S TRUE HEIR

Although Franklin was a cousin of Theodore, he was the true heir of Wilson, whom he had served as assistant secretary of the navy. From the war's early days, FDR saw himself completing the work of the martyr of peace, by creating a new world order and establishing a United Nations that would succeed where Wilson's League of Nations had failed.

Six months after Pearl Harbor, Roosevelt laid out his postwar plans to a Soviet foreign minister who, two years before, had been in a Berlin bunker laying out postwar plans with Hitler. FDR told Molotov that the United States, Britain, the Soviet Union, and China should, in the new era, act jointly to punish disturbers of the peace.

Japan and Germany would be disarmed and the colonial possessions of "weaker states" would be turned over to a world organization run by the Big Four. Molotov confided that FDR's ideas were likely to win a warm endorsement from Stalin.

In March 1943 Roosevelt presented his plan for a United Nations to Eden. His UN included a General Assembly, where all nations would have a voice and vote, and a Security Council, where real power would reside. "The real decisions," said FDR, "should be made by the United States, Great Britain, Russia, and China, who would be the powers for many years to come and that would have to police the world."[13] In a conversation with aide William Hassett in April of 1943, Roosevelt elaborated on his ideas. Hassett wrote:

> The President said the policy of policing the world [was] not
> insurmountable. He suggested that the United States and China
> would police Asia. Africa would be policed by Great Britain and
> Brazil, the latter because of her proximity to Africa, with other
> interested nations co-operating. The United States will see to the
> protection of the Americas, leaving the peace of Europe to Great
> Britain and Russia.[14]

At Teheran in November 1943, FDR explained to Stalin his plans for the "Four Policemen" responsible for world peace. The USSR, China, the United States, and Britain would have authority to close borders and impose embargoes on nations they determined to be aggressors or disturbers of the peace. If the offending nation did not rectify its behavior, it would be given an ultimatum, defiance of which would lead to bombing and possible invasion.

FDR's plan envisioned endless interventions for permanent peace, but contained no provision for the possibility that one or two of the world's Four Policemen might turn out to be an international criminal.

After Teheran, the United States, Britain, and the USSR sent delegations to Dumbarton Oaks estate in Washington to work out the structure of the new UN. Disagreements arose. England wanted to keep out of UN jurisdiction issues involving the British Empire. France was knocking at the door to be admitted to the Big Four. Fearful of the General Assembly, the USSR wanted sixteen votes—one for each constituent republic. These issues were resolved at Yalta, where Stalin was hailed for statesmanship in settling for three votes in the General Assembly (Russia, Byelorussia, and Ukraine), and where it was decided that Britain, France, China, the USSR, and the United States would each have a Security Council veto.

While Roosevelt's naiveté in putting his trust in Stalin continues to astonish, equally remarkable is how he replicated, step by step, the folly of Wilson. Wilson had compromised again and again on his Fourteen Points to win Allied approval for his League of Nations, and FDR again and again betrayed the principles of the Atlantic Charter to win Stalin's support for his United Nations. At Placentia Bay, Roosevelt and Churchill declared that:

> First, their countries seek no aggrandizement, territorial or other.
>
> Second, they desire to see no territorial changes that do not accord with the freely expressed wishes of the peoples concerned.
>
> Third, they respect the right of all peoples to choose the form of government under which they will live....[15]

Yet, at Teheran, President Roosevelt assented to Soviet annexation of the Baltic republics and eastern Poland and gave Stalin concessions in Manchuria at the expense of China and in violation of his word to Chiang Kai-shek. Both FDR and Churchill accepted Stalin's annexation of East Prussia, Poland's annexation of eastern

Germany, and the "ethnic cleansing" of twelve million to fifteen million German civilians from East Prussia, Pomerania, Silesia, Danzig, the Sudetenland, and the Baltic region—in one of the most hideous crimes of the century. Two million German men, women, and children perished in the "merciless revenge that poured over the entire German civilian population of Eastern Europe... from 1945 to 1948...."[16]

Stalin's rape of East-Central Europe was done without Allied protest. Indeed, in 1944 Churchill had undertaken a cynical mission to Moscow to divide up the Balkan states with Stalin in direct violation of solemn pledges he had made at Placentia Bay.

At Versailles, Lloyd George and Clemenceau had treated Wilson's Fourteen Points as irrelevant. At Teheran and Yalta, Churchill and FDR treated their own Atlantic Charter as irrelevant. Though Roosevelt was a master politician and inspirational leader, his strategic blunders during World War II cost millions their freedom and led to half a century of Cold War.

AMERICA DISARMS

Historians who charge America and Harry Truman with causing the Cold War by abandoning FDR's policy of cooperation with Stalin do both the nation and the man an injustice.

In the months following V-E and V-J Day, Truman did little to resist the national clamor to "bring the boys home." One million soldiers were being discharged each month, but still demonstrations and riots were breaking out among U.S. troops in Tokyo, Guam, China, Calcutta, Hawaii, London, Vienna, Le Havre, Paris, and Frankfurt. "By spring," writes historian William Manchester, "the disturbances had weakened U.S. military morale, damaged American prestige abroad, and dealt the army a heavy blow.... Morale was already at its lowest since Pearl Harbor."[17]

Wives, girlfriends, children, and parents formed "Bring Daddy

Back Home" clubs, as generals, editorial writers, diplomats, and politicians talking up U.S. international responsibilities were brushed aside. Navy Secretary James Forrestal was aghast at the "frenzied demobilization." "The tide of public opinion was impossible to stem," Truman would recall. "Every momma and papa... had to have her [sic] boy home right immediately, and every Congressman, of course, wanted to be reelected."[18] Historian Manchester supports Truman:

> Like Roosevelt before him, Truman had strongly endorsed uni-
> versal military training. Now hope for it evaporated overnight.
> Instead there was grave doubt that the military establishment
> could maintain a skeletal force abroad. Armed strength was
> already down 80 percent. What had been the mightiest air force
> in the world had dwindled from 2,385,000 men to 165,000. The
> navy was discharging 245,000 sailors each month; Nimitz
> warned that not a single squadron was fit for combat....With
> reenlistments declining, General Eisenhower told congressional
> leaders, there was very real danger that the United States would
> "run out of Army."[19]

By the summer of 1946, U.S. ground forces had been cut to two and one-half divisions of largely replacement troops with none of the combat experience of the men mustered out.

The charge that America exploited its power and sole possession of the atom bomb to bully the Soviet Union is propaganda. Truman was not the father of the Cold War, Stalin was. His betrayal of war-time pledges and outrages across Soviet-occupied Europe opened America's eyes to the character of our ex-ally and turned the nation toward confrontation.

One by one, in the euphoria of victory, the shocks came— Stalin's refusal to honor his Yalta commitments to Poland and withdraw troops from Iran; revelations of Soviet wartime espionage; a communist coup in Czechoslovakia and the blockade of Berlin in 1948; the trial of Cardinal Mindszenty in Hungary; explosion of a Soviet atomic bomb and the fall of China to Mao Tse-tung's armies in 1949. And on June 25, 1950, North Korea invaded the South, killing and capturing thousands of ill-prepared U.S. troops. These events, writes one historian, "loosed within American life a vast impatience, a turbulent bitterness, a rancor akin to revolt."[20]

Catholics who before Pearl Harbor had been against intervening in Europe now became zealous supporters of containing and rolling back the Soviet empire. For decades, the Church had been instructing its young in parochial schools, high schools, colleges, on the inherent evil and danger of communism, and the relentless persecution of Catholics under Stalin. In these precincts there was no sympathy for "fellow travelers" proven to have been "soft on communism," and there was great bitterness that their party, the Democratic Party, had abandoned Eastern Europe with so little protest.

Revelations of how Roosevelt had truckled to Stalin at Teheran and Yalta, and the discovery that his administration had been penetrated by Stalin's agents, led to the savage campaigns of the late 1940s and early 1950s in which the cry "soft on communism" reverberated through the land.

The brutality of its politics aside, America by 1950 was as unified as it had been after Pearl Harbor—around the proposition that Stalin and communism were evil and a menace to America's security. This unity, this conviction, were the indispensable pillars of an emerging Cold War consensus that enabled America to rush aid to Greece and Turkey, finance the Marshall Plan, create NATO, fight in Korea, reinstitute the draft, send troops to Europe, face down Moscow in the Cuban missile crisis, and send half a million men to Vietnam.

CONTAINMENT

Did America's Cold War alliances—NATO, CENTO, SEATO, the ANZUS and Rio pact, and security treaties with Korea, Japan, Taiwan—violate Washington's "great rule" against permanent alliances?

No. When created, these were to be temporary alliances to endure only as long as the crisis endured. General Eisenhower and Secretary of State Dean Acheson both assured Congress that U.S. troops would remain in Europe only until Europe could rise to its feet to man its own defenses. Eisenhower estimated that would take ten years.

And a close reading of the Monroe Doctrine would justify NATO as conceived, a temporary alliance to keep the Red Army from overrunning Germany and France. In restating Washington's pledge that America would stay out of Europe's wars, Monroe had added this caveat:

> In the wars of the European powers *in matters relating to themselves* we have never taken any part, nor does it comport with our pol- icy so to do. It is only *when our rights are invaded or seriously men- aced that we... make preparations for our defense* [emphasis added].[21]

By the late 1940s Americans had concluded that a Soviet inva- sion of Western Europe, which a prostrate Germany was powerless to resist, could tilt the balance of power against us; and the communists had declared that their ultimate enemy in this struggle was the United States.

Truman's claim to greatness lies in his early awakening to FDR's folly in trusting Stalin, his leadership in rebuilding Europe, his criti- cal aid to beleaguered Greece and Turkey, and his vision in creating the institutions of Western defense like NATO. His second term, however, was marked by the fall of China in 1949, his failed leader- ship in the "no-win" war in Korea, and almost universal public disapproval. First term, near-great; second term, failure—this is the grade given to Truman by one historian, which seems about right.

For his foreign policy achievements as president, Eisenhower deserves the grade of near-great. He used U.S. nuclear leverage to convince China to end the Korean War and the crisis in the Formosa Straits in 1958, gave the United States eight years of peace and strategic superiority over Moscow, and kept the Western alliance unified through its most dangerous decade. Had Eisenhower had a third term, Cuba would likely have been liberated and quickly subtracted from the Soviet bloc.

VIETNAM

In 1960 Kennedy succeeded Eisenhower after a close election from which he emerged as an aggressive anticommunist. In his inaugural address, JFK declared, "Let every nation know, whether it wishes us well or ill, that we shall pay any price, bear any burden, meet any hardship, support any friend, oppose any foe to assure the survival and the success of liberty."

As Kennedy spoke, he had already been warned by Eisenhower that his test would come in Southeast Asia, and that Laos was the "cork in the bottle." Should Laos fall, Ike had told him, Indochina would be lost. "We may have to fight," said the old general. "You are going to have to put troops in Laos. With other nations if possible—but alone if necessary."[22]

Kennedy's first year was marked by failure and humiliation. The president gave the go-ahead to an invasion of Cuba that had been planned under his predecessor, an invasion that would make "Bay of Pigs" a synonym for debacle. The operation floundered because Kennedy refused to permit U.S. naval and air units to support the Cuban exiles, who were left to be captured or killed on the beach. Containment and the Monroe Doctrine had been defeated ninety miles off the American coast.

In June, Kennedy was verbally assaulted by Khrushchev in Vienna. In August, he sat impotent as the Berlin Wall went up. JFK decided to take his stand in Vietnam, but failed to follow Eisenhower's advice. Laos was not occupied. In a treaty negotiated by Averell Harriman, the United States agreed to neutralize Laos and remove all troops. There was no force left to block Hanoi from sending cadres, weapons, munitions, and, ultimately, combat divisions down the Ho Chi Minh Trail—a network of ten thousand miles of roads, trails, and footpaths, impossible to interdict by air attack alone—into Cambodia and South Vietnam.

Strategists in Moscow, Beijing, and Hanoi knew that North Vietnam was the military machine that would ultimately conquer Indochina. The Pathet Lao in Laos and the Viet Cong in South Vietnam were auxiliaries to pave the way for Hanoi's main force. As Hanoi's General Giap had said in 1950, "Indochina is a strategic unit, a single theater of operations."

When Kennedy embraced Harriman's treaty, putting Laos off-limits to U.S. troops, he forfeited his opportunity to defeat Giap's strategy. To this day I recall, as a young editorial writer in St. Louis, asking an administration defender of LBJ's policy, Cyrus Vance, in a backgrounder at the Jefferson Hotel, how we could permanently defeat the Viet Cong in South Vietnam if we had ceded their Ho Chi Minh supply lines to Hanoi.

The day Kennedy took office, there were 600 U.S. advisers in South Vietnam. By November 22, 1963, there were 16,000. When Lyndon Johnson departed in 1969, there were 535,000 American troops in Vietnam or on the way. Yet none were in Laos astride the communist supply lines, or deployed to threaten the survival of the Hanoi regime. Half a decade into a major war, we were still fighting on the enemy's terms.

Meanwhile, America had been torn asunder over what seemed an endless, "unwinnable" war. Thus when President Nixon sent U.S.

ground troops into Cambodia to root out enemy sanctuaries, this was seen as an *American* widening of the war; and when South Vietnamese troops were sent into Laos in 1971, U.S. troops were forbidden to cross the border. Saigon's army had the strength only to raid the area, not to take and hold it.

While U.S. forces were expanding from a handful of advisers to half a million men, the nature of the war changed. Three weeks before the assassination of President Kennedy, the United States had become an accomplice to a Saigon coup that ended in the murder of South Vietnam's President Diem. Our complicity made Saigon America's client, and Vietnam America's war.

Kennedy's successor, President Lyndon Johnson, soon began to talk boldly about not only defeating communism but also creating a Great Society in the Mekong Delta; by 1965 America was into "nation building," ten thousand miles away, in a country most Americans in 1960 could not have found on a map.

There was something more at work here than a liberal propensity for conducting what one scholar calls "foreign policy as social work." This was an attempt to defeat the enemy *on the enemy's terms*, a concept that ran counter to every strategic principle of warfare, but appealed to the academic-minded "best and the brightest" of the New Frontier. The New Frontiersmen were pursuing Wilsonism—with guns.

A critical turning point in the Vietnam War came with General William Westmoreland's 1967 request for an additional 200,000 troops. He argued to Johnson that the new troops were needed because he was engaged in a "meat-grinder" and barely holding his own. As Norman B. Hannah has argued in *The Key to Failure: Laos and the Vietnam War*:

They could have proposed an alternative—deployment of additional forces (fewer than the requested 200,000) to block the

invasion in southern Laos. They could have explained that this
would change the terms of the war from a test of endurance in
an inconclusive bloodletting to a test of a great nation's military
capability to define the space it intended to defend.[23]

America, which had crushed Japan, a nation many times as powerful, in four years, was unable to defeat tiny North Vietnam, despite
an immense effort, for a fundamental reason: Although the United
States had more than adequate power to defeat Hanoi, it never had
a strategic plan for final victory or the will to pursue such a strategy.

"LONG LIVE THE VICTORY OF PEOPLE'S WAR"

In 1961 Khrushchev coined the phrase "wars of national liberation,"
and Castro's victory seemed a textbook example. But it was Mao
Tse-tung who was the true genius of guerrilla warfare. For Mao, the
guerrilla phase was but an early stage of warfare, designed to gain
fighting experience and recruit a cadre. But guerrillas, and their even
weaker cousins, terrorists, lacked the strength to overthrow a government.[24] To win, revolutionaries must eventually field a conventional army to defeat the regime's army.

Mao's strategy had triumphed in China because, between 1937
and 1945, he had a Japanese buffer between himself and the
Nationalists. Thus he had time to gain control of 100 million
Chinese, from whom to recruit a million-man army, supported by
two million militia, that was able to take on Chiang's Nationalists in
pitched battle.[25] It was the Red Army's defeat of the Japanese in
Manchuria, in the final days of World War II, that gave Mao access to
the captured Japanese weapons and material he would need to esca-
late from guerrilla operations to conventional war.

After Mao's triumph, China proclaimed itself the leader of all
anti-imperialist forces worldwide, and Mao's strategy of "people's
war" was held up as the model to nullify the West's superiority in
technology and weapons. In 1965 China's defense minister, Lin Biao,

published the bible of this strategy, *Long Live the Victory of People's War.* Lin described the Third World as the global countryside. Here, revolutionaries were to recruit their guerrilla armies to drive the West back into its urbanized enclave, there to besiege and destroy it. Lin held that Western nations, like cities cut off from rural markets and resources, must eventually collapse into revolutions of their own.

Lin's strategic vision was breathtaking, but far more destructive to the U.S. war effort in Vietnam was America's response. For in the 1960s there were enough policy-makers who felt a sense of guilt over the history of Western imperialism to engender a spirit of defeatism when confronted by a strategy that was portrayed as nationalist and anticolonial.

America's answer was "counterinsurgency," a policy of doing good works and promoting democracy and economic growth to woo the peoples of the Third World away from the communist way and over to the capitalist, democratic way. The consequent push for reform led the United States to endorse the overthrow of Diem, South Vietnam's most effective leader, on the grounds that he was insufficiently progressive. Lack of reforms or democracy in the North, however, did not seem at all to hinder Hanoi's war effort.

Counterinsurgency as a military strategy meant attrition warfare, based on "search and destroy" missions against elusive guerrillas. These caused high casualties and imposed immense suffering on the people we were trying to protect. The appeal of counterinsurgency was that it was thought to be less costly than conventional war, which was attractive to LBJ who—in his first meeting with the Joint Chiefs as president—talked of cuts in military spending to finance his Great Society.[26]

Yet the rule of thumb had always been that for a regular army to defeat guerrillas, a 10–1 superiority was needed. Johnson thus picked the most expensive war option, and then pursued it incrementally to avoid the higher costs—a formula for failure that produced failure.

THE BREAKING OF JOHNSON

In attempting to beat the enemy at his own game, the United States had both neglected the enemy's weaknesses and forfeited America's strength, its overwhelming military superiority. Johnson also bought into the trendy view that bombing was as much for "signaling" and "bargaining" with an enemy as destroying him.[27] As U.S. diplomat Harlan Cleveland described it, military violence was actually a form of communication:

> The use of force in a dangerous world demands adherence to a doctrine of restraint—the cool, calm, and collected manipulation of power for collective security—and the sophisticated mixture of diplomacy with that power.... [F]orce is just another manner of speaking—with a rather expensive vocabulary. But if force is to be a persuasive form of discourse, its modulations must carry not only the latent threat of more force but equally the assurance that it is under the personal control of responsible men.[28]

LBJ thus used his "Rolling Thunder" bombing campaign as much to impel Hanoi to negotiate as to destroy the enemy base camp. Starting in 1965 there were repeated halts to the bombing for diplomatic overtures. After formal peace talks began in 1968, air strikes were limited to below the 20th parallel, far from Hanoi's heartland and government. The result of using air power as a form of communication: two thousand U.S. aircraft lost and thousands of American KIAs, POWs, and MIAs.

During Johnson's tenure, the North was Hanoi's strategic bastion and Laos and Cambodia its privileged sanctuaries. This allowed Hanoi both to dictate the level of violence and to wage mobile warfare against U.S. and Saigon forces corralled in the South.

Hanoi's strategic advantage became apparent after the 1968 Tet offensive had decimated the Viet Cong, who had tried, too early, to shift to conventional warfare. Though a calamity for the VC, Tet was not a strategic disaster for the North, as Hanoi still retained countless regiments of regular troops. As long as the Hanoi bastion remained secure, North Vietnam could choose the time and place of battle and level of violence.

The Tet offensive, however, proved a disaster for the United States. The morale of America's elites cracked, and many declared the war unwinnable. Antiwar demonstrations grew in size, Johnson's presidency was broken, and a primary challenge mounted against him. After LBJ's withdrawal and Robert Kennedy's assassination, the Democratic Party came apart in the streets of Chicago.

Leadership in the Cold War passed to Richard Nixon's Republicans, and members of America's elite crossed the barricades to join protesters denouncing a cause they had once championed. Suddenly it became "Nixon's War!"

For two decades, the liberal wing of the Democratic Party would bedevil Nixon, Ford, and Reagan on Cold War initiatives from building an anti-ballistic missile (ABM) system, to supporting Saigon, to deploying missiles in Europe, to aiding the Contras in Nicaragua, to building the Strategic Defense Initiative (SDI).

NIXON'S WAR

Even before his 1968 election, Nixon decided the war had to end. His first troop withdrawal of 100,000 was announced in April of 1969. Sensing triumph, the antiwar movement stepped up the pressure. In the fall of 1969 hundreds of thousands descended on Washington to march against the war, some to riot. The president called on the "Great Silent Majority" of Americans to stand by him and support "peace with honor."

They did for four years as the United States transferred the burden of battle to the South Vietnamese. U.S. casualties fell. By 1972

Saigon controlled every provincial capital. Decimated at Tet, the Viet Cong had long since been supplanted by North Vietnamese troops sent down the Ho Chi Minh Trail. When Hanoi launched a spring offensive in 1972, Nixon mined Haiphong and unleashed U.S. air power. Retaliation reached its peak with the "Christmas bombing." Hanoi and Haiphong were hit by B-52s, as the restrictions were lifted on high-value targets. This broke the negotiating deadlock, leading to the Paris Accords of January 27, 1973.

Within weeks of Nixon's second inauguration, most of the POWs were on the way home. For Americans the war was over and—in the winter of 1973—appeared to have been won. The Cold War coalition had been fractured and the left wing of the Democratic Party had defected, but the line had held. Nixon seemed to have defeated both North Vietnam and his domestic enemies. In February 1973 Nixon's approval rating stood at 68 percent. Then came Watergate.

Hanoi had signed a piece of paper but had not altered in the slightest its iron resolve to rule all of Vietnam.

With the breaking of Nixon's presidency, a Democratic Congress began slashing military rations to Saigon to $300 million a year for a war that at its peak in 1968 had cost America one hundred times that sum. With Nixon, then Ford, blocked by Congress from using air power, North Vietnam, rearmed by Moscow, invaded the South early in 1975. Hanoi had now advanced beyond Marshal Lin's "people's war" to conventional war, using Soviet artillery and armor. Saigon resisted heroically but could not stop the onslaught. South Vietnam was overrun and Cambodia taken over by the Khmer Rouge of Pol Pot. The massacres commenced, and the Nobel Prizes awarded the Paris negotiators were washed into history with the blood of our allies.

Nixon achieved greatly in his first term by winning what

appeared to be an honorable peace in Vietnam against the hostility of
the American elite, negotiating arms agreements with Moscow,
opening up China, and creating a new Republican Majority to displace the New Deal coalition of FDR. The political collapse of his
second term, the loss of Southeast Asia, the failure of détente, and
unanswered Soviet cheating on arms agreements denied him, Ford,
and Carter any claim to greatness in foreign policy, though Carter
surely deserves a Nobel Prize for the Israeli-Egyptian peace of Camp
David, which yet endures.

LESSONS OF VIETNAM

While U.S. air power proved effective in destroying enemy targets in
North Vietnam, there were limits to what it could accomplish, so
long as the Americans ruled out any use of ground troops there.
Wrote Lieutenant Colonel Douglas A. Macgregor:

> Again and again, fighter-bombers would clear away surface-to-
> air missiles and fortifications and lose planes and pilots doing so.
> But no American ground forces would move through the
> breach. As a result, in a few weeks, the enemy would rebuild the
> defenses and more American aircraft would be lost in the process
> of attacking them all over again.[29]

Harry G. Summers, Jr., blames America's failure in Vietnam on
our refusal to destroy the enemy's "center of gravity." Clausewitz had
defined a center of gravity as "the hub of all power and movement
on which everything depends.... The point against which all energies should be directed." The leading candidates for this designation
are the enemy's army and capital. As Summers argues, the United
States could not effectively focus on either: "The center of gravity
could not be the North Vietnamese army because we made the conscious decision not to invade North Vietnam to seek out and destroy

its armed forces. For the same reason it could not be Hanoi, the North Vietnamese capital."[30]

Unable to strike with decisive force to end the war at its source, the United States resorted to a campaign of attrition, where success was measured by statistics—bomb tonnage and body counts. U.S. public opinion, another of Clausewitz's centers of gravity, steadily dissipated as the costs and casualties of a prolonged war mounted.

The decisive argument against a "march on Hanoi" was that it would provoke Chinese intervention as in Korea. Fear of a wider war paralyzed the Johnson administration. Yet even with China's massive intervention, Korea was a success compared to Vietnam. The Korean War was shorter by years; U.S. and allied casualties were fewer; South Korea was saved. Had Eisenhower been in power, it is impossible to believe the old general would have accepted the five years of fight-talk-fight with Hanoi that Johnson did. Eisenhower would have won the war with massive force, or cut his losses and come home.

While the communist conquest of Indochina did not diminish U.S. material strength, it did demonstrate America's alarming inability to put its power behind its policy and to prevail in a war that a vast commitment had tacitly declared to be a vital interest. And it was on the wheel of Vietnam that the U.S. establishment was broken, the Cold War consensus first cracked, and the quality and character of America's leadership began to be questioned. Around the Pacific Rim, the fall of South Vietnam was seen as a failure of American power. As foreign policy scholar Peter Rodman has written:

> According to an internal State Department summary of international reaction, the Thai press reflected disillusionment and even alarm at the American willingness to abandon Indochina. The media in the Philippines and South Korea saw the outcome as the United States reneging on a commitment. In Japan, some members of the ruling Liberal Democratic party raised questions

about the reliability of the U.S.-Japan Security Treaty.... Beyond
Asia, the debacle in Vietnam had its effect on American allies
and... on America's adversaries. Reports came in through diplomatic and other channels of other governments reassessing their
ties with us.[31]

Vietnam was a legitimate war of containment that could have
been won in half the time it was fought if the United States had used
its full conventional power at the outset, and refused to set geographic limits on the use of that power. Given how it was fought, it
would have better for Vietnam and the United States had we never
intervened in the mid-1950s to establish a Western ally in the south.
There was, and is, an argument for Vietnam; there was never an argument for fighting it as we did. It is the mark of a Great Power that
when it commits itself to war, it commits itself to victory, and all the
force necessary to prevail. We did not. U.S. soldiers did not lose a
major battle, but America lost—because of a collapse of will of its
political elite.

Ironically, by 1975 the gulf between the two great communist rivals
that had opened up around 1960 had become a canyon. China and the
USSR were deploying armies, air power, and nuclear weapons on the
Siberian-Manchurian border and had fought pitched battles.[32] After
Saigon fell, Soviet warships and bombers moved into former American
bases at Danang and Cam Ranh Bay. But it was Chinese power that
ultimately filled the Asian vacuum left by America's withdrawal.

Washington welcomed this as a balance to the Soviet global
threat. In 1979 China and Vietnam even fought a bloody border
campaign, when Hanoi intervened in Cambodia against Beijing's
ally, the genocidal Pol Pot. Nothing better illustrates the dominance
of national interests over the abstractions of ideology, and the fluidity
of international politics.

The fall of Saigon unleashed a worldwide rampage by Moscow. A Soviet empire that had added only Cuba since World War II began to roll up imperial gains. After the fall of Laos, Cambodia, and South Vietnam, Ethiopia, Angola, Mozambique, Grenada, and Nicaragua soon followed. "Eurocommunism" became the rage on the continent. Then, with the United States paralyzed by a hostage crisis in Iran, Leonid Brezhnev sent the Red Army into Afghanistan, the first use ever of Soviet ground troops outside the bloc.

But now Moscow had overreached. The Afghans put up ferocious resistance, and the Soviet invasion reawakened America, ended détente, and convinced the American people to exchange a president who had sought to accommodate Brezhnev with one who would stand up to him.

THE REAGAN COUNTEROFFENSIVE

With the election of Ronald Reagan came an almost-perfect blend of realism and idealism. The Cold War coalition was revived, the Soviet empire was engaged, and the tide turned. To containment, Reagan added a new dimension: rollback. A conservative, he avoided deliberate provocations and direct challenges to Soviet vital interests, but he skirted arms control agreements with a historic buildup of conventional weapons: a six hundred–ship navy, "Stealth" aircraft, "smart" bombs and missiles, plus SDI, which threatened to cancel out a trillion-dollar Soviet investment in ICBMs, the deadly intercontinental ballistic missiles. When Moscow deployed mobile SS-20 missiles in western Russia, Reagan countered with Pershings in Western Europe. In 1983 he seized on a Marxist coup in Grenada to invade and liberate the island; sent arms to the anti-Soviet guerrillas in Angola, Nicaragua, and Afghanistan; and conducted a sustained ideological offensive against communist doctrine.

The Reagan policy of containment and rollback, of minimum risk and moderate pressure at the peripheries of empire, triumphed.

Mikhail Gorbachev, who came to power in 1985 determined to win in Afghanistan, tried to bully Reagan into giving up SDI at a crucial summit meeting in Reykjavik in 1986. After an all-day final session of the extended summit, Reagan got up from the table and walked away from the greatest arms deal in history.

By the end of Reagan's term, Gorbachev knew the Cold War was lost. When he ordered his army out of Afghanistan, the first significant withdrawal of Soviet troops since the pullout from Austria in the mid-1950s, the curtain began to fall on the Soviet empire. In 1989, as East Germans fled west through Hungary, suddenly the Berlin Wall was down, East Europe was free, the Red Army packed and went home, and the Soviet Union flew apart into fifteen nations. George Bush presided masterfully over the endgame, but Reagan had won the Cold War.

The legacy of Reagan is claimed by many. Some insist that he was a Wilsonian at heart, anxious to spread democracy around the world. They cite his support for the overthrow of Ferdinand Marcos in Manila. But Reagan simply got out of the way of history and accepted the inevitable; he did nothing to bring Marcos down. And the Reagan in whose White House I served for two years was no Wilsonian. He was an anticommunist and a patriot who saw his duty as defending U.S. interests and advancing the defeat of an "evil empire" that threatened his country.

Among the reasons Reagan supported "constructive engagement" with South Africa was his conviction that Pretoria was on the West's side in the Cold War. When one considers the beneficiaries of covert U.S. military aid under Reagan—the Contras, the UNITA rebels of Jonas Savimbi in Angola, the Afghan resistance—all had one thing in common, and it was not a commitment to one man, one vote. All were fighting to oust allies of Moscow. If Reagan enlisted the rhetoric of global democracy, it was to advance the higher cause, the altar piece of his presidency: bringing down the Soviet empire. A truly great president, Ronald Reagan conducted the most successful foreign policy of the twentieth century.

COLLAPSE OF A COLD WAR CONSENSUS

At the Cold War's end, the Cold War coalition collapsed as rapidly as the Soviet empire. For half a century, America had had an enemy that united us. Containment of communism was the cause that gave clarity and coherence to our foreign policy. Almost all the great events of our lives had to do with the Cold War: the Berlin airlift, the Marshall Plan, Korea, the space race, the Wall, the missile crisis, Vietnam, East-West summits, the opening to China, SALT agreements, détente, the "Euromissiles," the Contras, the Reagan Doctrine, SDI. In each presidential campaign, the question of which candidate could better deal with Moscow was almost always paramount. For most of America's foreign policy elite, the Cold War was their vocation; for the American Right, it was the unifying cause.

Now for the first time since Pearl Harbor, the United States had no great enemy and no satisfactory answer to the question in the war movies of our childhood—"What are you going to do, Joe, when this is all over?"

What does the last superpower do when no other power challenges it? What is the moral equivalent of resisting a world-girdling, totalitarian empire? What is America's cause now? Hitler, Tojo, Stalin, Mao, Khrushchev, and Brezhnev united us; their passing brought a fractionalization of foreign policy. We now argue over every policy decision and presidential action because we no longer have an overarching cause to explain or justify them.

From 1945 to 1989 our communist enemy made the job of foreign policy architect simple: Friends stood on America's side; foes sided with Moscow. The difference between crafting foreign policy then and now is the difference between arithmetic and calculus.

AN ABORTED DEBATE

Even before the Wall came down, *The National Interest* magazine invited contributors to a forum on a new foreign policy for an era in which no great enemy threatened. Neoconservatives responded with alacrity and giddy calls for imposing a "Pax Americana" or "global hegemony" on a planet unable to resist the "world's last superpower."

Ex-LBJ aide Ben Wattenberg called for a worldwide crusade for democracy. Columnist Charles Krauthammer wrote that it should be our "wish and work" to "integrate" America, Europe, and Japan in a "supersovereign" entity that would be "economically, culturally, and politically hegemonic in the world."[33] This "new universalism," said Krauthammer, "would require the conscious depreciation not only of American sovereignty but of the notion of sovereignty in general. This is not as outrageous as it sounds."[34]

Not to Krauthammer, but surely to the Patriot Fathers. The Krauthammer superstate would be a betrayal of everything for which the Republic stood. Did we really break free of the British Empire so that we might imitate and surpass it by colluding with Japan and Europe to dictate to mankind? In a rebuttal piece titled "America First—and Second, and Third," I wrote that Krauthammer's vision was un-American, and failed "the fundamental test of any foreign policy: Americans will not fight for it."[35] A nation's purpose, I added, is to be "discovered not by consulting ideologies, but by reviewing its history, by searching the hearts of its people." What is it for which we Americans have always been willing to fight? Lord Macaulay gave us the answer:

> And how can man die better
> Than facing fearful odds
> For the ashes of his fathers,
> And the temples of his gods?[36]

Nowhere in the Constitution is Congress or the president authorized to conscript the wealth of the nation or the blood of its sons for crusades. This is not the Holy Roman Empire. Conservatives who believe our Cold War triumph empowers us to go abroad in search of monsters to destroy should cease calling themselves conservatives. Urging adoption of a policy of "enlightened nationalism," I wrote:

> If the Cold War is ending, what are the terms of honorable peace that will permit us to go home? Are they not: withdrawal of the Red Army back within its own frontiers; liberation of Central Europe and the Baltic republics; reunification of Germany; and de-Leninization of Moscow, i.e., overthrow of the imperialist party that has prosecuted the Seventy Years War against the West?
>
> Once Russia is rescued from Leninism, its distant colonies, Cuba and Nicaragua, must eventually fall, just as the outposts of Japan's Empire, cut off from the home islands, fell like ripe apples into the lap of General MacArthur. Withdrawal of the Red Army from Europe would remove from the hand of Gorbachev's successor the military instrument of Marxist restoration.
>
> The compensating concession we should offer: total withdrawal of U.S. troops from Europe. If Moscow will get out, we will get out. Once the Red Army goes home, the reason for keeping a U.S. army in Europe vanishes. Forty years after the Marshall Plan, it is time Europe conscripted the soldiers for its own defense.[37]

Miraculously, within two years, the great cause we had worked for, prayed for, fought for, all our lives, had triumphed. The Red Army had gone home; the Soviet empire had collapsed; the Baltic states were free; the USSR had broken up into fifteen nations. *Mirabile dictu*—Ukraine was free! Never in history had so odious an empire vanished so swiftly. In two years, the Soviet empire disappeared from the earth, and the Russia over which Boris Yeltsin was presiding extended no further west—save for the tiny enclave of Kaliningrad—than it had at the time of Peter the Great.

All that America had ever sought had come to pass. Yet rather than seize the opportunity to pull up our "trip wires" around the world and shed unwanted commitments—to recapture our freedom of action and restore a traditional foreign policy—Republican internationalists were now joining with Wilsonian globalists to tie America down like Gulliver in some "New World Order" where U.S. wealth and power would be put at the service of causes having nothing to do with the vital interests of the United States.

That **National Interest** *debate was interrupted* by Iraq's invasion of Kuwait. The foreign policy elite rallied to Bush's resolve ("This will not stand!") to go to war. I did not. I did not believe Kuwait was vital to the United States or the emir's regime was worth the life of a single marine.

Saddam, after all, had stolen Kuwait's oil to sell it, and Saudi Arabia could be defended without a war on Baghdad. The nation most likely to achieve hegemony in the Gulf, I argued, was Iran. Iraq, a third as large and populous, was the Arab counter. If we destroyed it, the certain result of war, Iran would be the beneficiary and the United States would be left with the obligation to contain both nations, an open-ended commitment America would be unwilling to sustain.

Finally, I argued, monarchy did not appear to be the wave of the future in the Near East. Soon, all the kings, sheiks, and emirs must go the way of King Farouk of Egypt, King Faisal of Iraq, King Idris of Libya, Emperor Haile Selassie of Ethiopia, and the shah of Iran. Bush won the argument, and the war in the most one-sided military victory in history.

Eight years later, Bush was gone, Saddam was still in power, the coalition had disintegrated, the Arabs had distanced themselves from America, and the United States was virtually alone in trying to force Iraq to disgorge its weapons of mass destruction. "Dual containment" had reached a cul de sac. In 1991 Bush had gone before the UN to declare a New World Order to boisterous applause. Today, the term has been shelved.

As these lines are written, the Senate has approved U.S.-NATO war guarantees to Eastern Europe; we have launched a war on Serbia; and not one Cold War commitment—from defending Japan and Korea to our duty to come to the defense of all of Latin America—has been allowed to lapse. American boys yet unborn are being committed to fight where no American soldiers have ever fought before.

This is a betrayal of the Founding Fathers, a grave injustice to future generations who may have to make great sacrifices in blood to validate our foolish commitments. In that 1990 article, I wrote with conviction: "The day of the realpoliticians, with their Metternichian 'new architectures,' and balance-of-power stratagems, and hidden fear of a world where their op-ed articles and televised advice are about as relevant as white papers from Her Majesty's Colonial Office, is over."[38]

I was wrong. I underestimated the grip that the globalist elites have on power, and the will of these elites never to yield the bureaucratic-military empire—the existence of which gives meaning to their lives. But that hold is weakening.

Lincoln once said they have a right to criticize who have a heart to help. It is not enough to say the interventionists and globalists are wrong. Where are they wrong? Why are they wrong? What is the right foreign policy for America? What ought we to defend at the risk of our country and our own lives? What are the principles of a foreign policy that can ensure America's peace, freedom, and security far into the new century?

PART SEVEN

A Foreign Policy
for America

CHAPTER 18

"Passionate Attachments" and Press Power

*The power of the press in America is a primordial one.
It sets the agenda of public discussion; and this
sweeping political power is unrestrained by any law.
It determines what people will talk about and think
about—an authority that in other nations is reserved
for tyrants, priests, parties and mandarins.*[1]

—THEODORE H. WHITE, 1972

In crafting a foreign policy today, presidents face the same pressures as their predecessors, but magnified by modernity, especially the pressure of media power. As historian Paul Johnson has written, "[T]he first event of its kind in which the media played a salient role—almost a determining one"—was the American Revolution.[2] By 1775, "Americans were already a media-conscious people," and Tom Paine's *Common Sense* was perhaps the most effective pamphlet ever published.[3]

Before the war of 1898, the "yellow press" had become so raucous in its clamor that President Cleveland had to warn Congress that, should it succumb and declare war, he would not send the army to fight. After the *Maine* blew up, the press convicted Spain on no evidence and shrieked for revenge. McKinley was virtually powerless to resist the war fever.

British propaganda in World War I incited such outrage at the "Hun" that when German U-boats were cut loose and U.S. ships sunk, America plunged in with enthusiasm. During World War II, Edward R. Murrow's nightly newscasts from England ("This is London!") moved toward belligerency a nation that had wanted to stay out of another European war.

A photo of a Buddhist monk immolating himself in Saigon during the early days of Vietnam helped convince Kennedy to support a coup that led to the murder of President Diem and Americanization of the war. The photo of a young Vietnamese girl running naked, screaming in pain after a napalm attack, disgusted Americans, as did the photograph of a South Vietnamese police official executing a Viet Cong terrorist. These last two photos became recruiting posters for the antiwar movement.

Adversarial coverage of the Vietnam War helped convince us we were not winning the war, and perhaps ought not. The Tet offensive, in which the Viet Cong lost tens of thousands and saw their infrastructure uprooted, was depicted as a communist triumph. Press coverage helped break Johnson's presidency, as the country imbibed nightly photographic cocktails of war dead and wounded, juiced with journalistic skepticism as to the justice and wisdom of the cause. All added to the impatience of a nation already sickened by the lengthening casualty lists of its sons.

Conversely, a year of nightly television film of Iranian "students" mocking America and burning the Stars and Stripes, as they held fifty-two diplomats and marines hostage in our gutted Teheran embassy, further undercut support for Carter in the hard economic times of 1979 and 1980, and convinced the country it needed a tougher president.

In 1992 TV pictures of starving children persuaded Bush to put U.S. troops into Somalia; TV footage of the body of an army ranger being dragged through the dirty streets of Mogadishu caused Clinton to pull them out. Somalia may be a portent of something worse—an atrocity film that so enrages Americans we become embroiled in a war which, after early casualties, we decide we do not want to fight after all.

Indeed, pictures from the Sarajevo market minutes after it was hit by a mortar shell, coupled with reports of the Srebenica massacre, brought U.S. intervention in a Balkan quarrel most Americans had wanted to stay out of. In Kosovo in 1999 it happened again, after the nation's front pages featured photographs of Albanian victims of Serb atrocities.

Network news shows, and the proliferation of round-the-clock cable channels such as CNN, CNBC, MSNBC, and Fox News, with instant access to every home, have given a few TV producers the power to alter public opinion, almost instantly, and propel presidents to action. This power to inflame underscores the need for presidential patience and courage to resist media-induced clamors for "Action This Day!"

"PASSIONATE ATTACHMENTS"

The one absolutely certain way of bringing this nation to ruin, of preventing all possibility of its continuing as a nation at all would be to permit it to become a tangle of squabbling nationalities.[4]

—Theodore Roosevelt

During the Cold War, Congress would defer to presidents: "Politics stops at the water's edge." But the vanished Soviet threat brought an end to that deference. Today, Congress panders to interest groups that champion foreign countries and causes as routinely as it does to advocates of domestic programs. The result is a foreign policy as incomprehensible as a Jackson Pollock canvas.

With the Cold War no longer America's cause, and containment no longer national policy, U.S. foreign policy is like a great estate gone to probate. Control is up for grabs, and the number of claimants is growing. Most powerful and persistent are ethnic minorities who are passionately attached to foreign lands and who are willing to use their influence, money, and votes to reward politicians who will make their kinsmen's cause America's cause.

Washington warned against "inveterate antipathies" toward some nations and "passionate attachments" to others. An "excessive partiality for one foreign nation and excessive dislike of another" must lead to situations, he cautioned, in which "[r]eal patriots who may resist the intrigues of the favorite are liable to become suspected and odious."[5] Washington had been alarmed to see his country dividing bitterly between those who favored England and those who favored France in the war begun in 1793.

Through the nineteenth century, Washington's warning proved prophetic. Hatred of Britain was fanned by Irish immigrants, preventing any closing of the breach with the Mother Country. In the 1860s the Fenian Society attempted repeated invasions of Canada to provoke a United States–British war it hoped would lead to Irish freedom. Politicians pandered to anti-British sentiment. In 1900 an exasperated Secretary of State John Hay wrote of the Prairie Populist and his Democratic Party:

> Whatever we do, Bryan will attack us as a slave of Great Britain.
> All their state conventions put on an anti-English plank in their
> platforms to curry favor with the Irish (whom they want to
> keep) and the Germans whom they want to seduce. It is too dis-
> gusting to have to deal with such sordid lies.[6]

Outraged by those he believed harbored a higher loyalty to another country, Teddy Roosevelt savaged "hyphenated-Americans." Irish- and German-born immigrants were his special targets:

> The professional German-Americans and Pro-Germans are anti-
> American to the core. They play the part of traitors, pure and

simple. Once it was true that this country could not endure half
free and half slave. To-day it is true that it cannot endure half
American and half foreign. The hyphen is incompatible with
patriotism.[7]

Imitation is the sincerest form of flattery, and Wilson flattered his
nemesis with his 1916 denunciations of the "hyphenates." Colonel
House thought German-Americans were prepared for sabotage and
guerrilla war against the United States in the event of war with
Germany. A touch of paranoia is evident here, for the National
German-American Alliance, even with two million members, would
prove far less influential than an Anglophile elite that tilted toward
Britain and enthusiastically took us in after the kaiser unleashed his
submarines.

In 1917–1918, Jewish influence first came into serious play in
U.S. foreign policy councils when the American Zionist Federation
persuaded Wilson to back Britain's Balfour Declaration calling for a
Jewish homeland in Palestine, then part of the Turkish empire.[8]

While Irish- and German-Americans were the most vocal about
staying out of World War II, Jewish-Americans clamored to have the
United States smash Hitler's regime. The sensitivity and explosiveness
of the ethnic issue was attested to when Charles Lindbergh, the
aviator-hero who had been first to fly the Atlantic alone, in
September 1941 in Des Moines, charged that Jewish influence in
Hollywood and the press was being used to agitate for war.
Lindbergh began his three short paragraphs by saying that he understood why the Jewish community felt as it did:

It is not difficult to understand why Jewish people desire the
overthrow of Nazi Germany. The persecution they suffered in
Germany would be sufficient to make bitter enemies of any
race. No person with a sense of the dignity of mankind can con-
done the persecution of the Jewish race in Germany.[9]

Lindbergh's speech ignited a national firestorm that scorched the America First Committee, and attacks on the Lone Eagle for those three short paragraphs continued for the rest of his life—and beyond.

After World War II, Jewish influence over foreign policy became almost an obsession with American leaders. President Harry Truman described the lobbying for early recognition of Israel in 1948 as the most intense he had ever experienced. Statesman George Kennan said that Jews "pretty well dominated the formation of American opinion with respect to Russian matters."[10] Secretary of State John Foster Dulles complained of "how almost impossible it is in this country to carry out a foreign policy not approved by the Jews. Marshall and Forrestal learned that. I am going to try and have one."[11] In a 1973 interview, J. W. Fulbright, chairman of the Senate Foreign Relations Committee, blurted, "Israel controls the Senate."[12]

While the Israeli lobby is the most powerful of ethnic lobbies, it is not alone. The China lobby helped keep the United States from recognizing Mao's regime for thirty years. Americans of Polish, Lithuanian, Latvian, Estonian, and Hungarian descent moved behind an anticommunist Republican Party that seemed more willing to manifest, in Captive Nations resolutions, its insistence on liberation of their former homelands. With Castro's triumph in 1959, a million Cubans fled to the United States to become passionate supporters of a GOP that opposed any rapprochement. Since the breakup of Yugoslavia, Croatian-Americans have agitated for U.S. support of an independent Croatia, while Serbian-Americans have demanded U.S. support for the same right of secession for their kinsmen in Bosnia. Albanian-Americans have clamored for U.S. air power to punish Belgrade and bring independence to Kosovo. Tiny Armenia, thanks to the powerful Armenian Assembly, now ranks fourth in per capita U.S. foreign aid. The president of Mexico urged Mexican-Americans, right on U.S. soil, to vote Mexico's interests in U.S. elections.

"PANDERING... AN ACCEPTED NORM"

Former Secretary of Defense James Schlesinger and Harvard's Samuel Huntington both warn of the rising power of ethnic lobbies in shaping foreign policy. By the fall of 1997 Armenian-Americans were blocking aid to Azerbaijan though the United States had oil interests there, and Turkey was being deprived of U.S. helicopters and frigates it had purchased because of pressure from Greek-Americans. "There are no Turkish restaurants in my district!" one congressman put it. Easing of the embargo of Havana was blocked by Cuban-Americans who provide the swing votes in New Jersey and Florida. Israel's supporters had veto power over U.S. Middle East policy, and U.S. policy toward Haiti was being driven by pressures from the Congressional Black Caucus. Writes Schlesinger:

> During President Clinton's first term our relations with our clos-
> est ally, Britain, were repeatedly roiled by our interventions in
> Northern Ireland, ultimately driven with an eye on the Irish-
> American vote....Whatever its merits, NATO expansion too has
> been driven by concern over the politics of appealing to voters
> of East European origin.[13]

Schlesinger adds: "Pandering to ethnic constituencies has become an accepted norm. Little embarrassment is expressed—or probably felt."[14] Writes Huntington:

> Economic and ethnic particularism define the current American
> role in the world. The institutions and capabilities... created to
> serve a grand national purpose in the Cold War are now being
> suborned and redirected to serve narrow subnational, trans-
> national, and even nonnational purposes.[15]

Huntington adds this sweeping assertion:

For understanding of American foreign policy it is necessary to
study not the interests of the American state in a world of com-
peting states but rather the play of economic and ethnic interests
in American domestic politics. At least in recent years, the latter
has been a superb predictor of foreign policy stands.[16]

On Capitol Hill the number of caucuses devoted to ethnic
interests has risen in a decade from six to fifteen. As Congress dishes
out foreign aid to some nations and imposes sanctions on others to
appease ethnic groups—with no apparent national interest rationale—U.S. policy appears to allies as chaotic, incoherent, unworthy of
sustained support.[17] The world's last superpower is thus ignored and
defied in a fashion none dared attempt during the Cold War, when
even if one disagreed with American policy, at least one could understand it. U.S. sanctions on Iran are ignored by our NATO allies;
Russia, despite our aid, bedevils U.S. policy in the Balkans; Israel sells
sophisticated weapons to China; Canada and Latin America openly
defy U.S. sanctions on Cuba.

Critics counter that Schlesinger and Huntington today, like
Kennan, Dulles, and Fulbright yesterday, speak only for a WASP elite
that has been dispossessed of its monopoly on foreign policy. All
Americans, these critics argue, whether as individuals, or members of
ethnic groups, or adherents of religious faiths, have a right to try to
shape foreign policy to reflect their values and interests. This "democ-
ratization" of U.S. foreign policy, they contend, is healthy and quin-
tessentially American.

Schlesinger and Huntington, writes *The New Republic*'s Jacob
Heilbrunn, "glide over the fact that policies espoused by a particular
ethnic group may coincide with U.S. interests."[18] And, surely, that has
been true. Greek-Americans supported Truman's aid to Greece that
impeded the communist drive through the Balkans in the 1940s.
Cuban-Americans gave crucial support to Reagan's policy to expel
communism from Nicaragua. Captive Nations resolutions expressed

solidarity with the peoples of East–Central Europe, telling them that we viewed them as allies in a Cold War with an empire that was our enemy as well as theirs.

Yet it is also true that policies espoused by ethnic groups can clash with national interests. Liberation of Eastern Europe was always a distant goal of U.S. foreign policy, but until the late 1990s it was not considered a vital interest. America restricted the weapons used to oppose Moscow's hegemony to the political, economic, and diplomatic. Now Americans of East European descent insist on U.S. guarantees of every frontier of the nations whence their ancestors came. Are such unprecedented security guarantees in the national interest of the United States? When did they become so?

Huntington concedes that ethnic groups "have played active roles in politics throughout American history" but sees both a quantitative and qualitative difference. Today's "ethnic diaspora groups proliferate, are more active, and have greater self-consciousness, legitimacy, and political clout," he writes, adding, "they have begun to drag us into controversies and conflicts unrelated to any U.S. national interest."[19] Schlesinger sees U.S. foreign policy today as little more than a "stapling together of a series of goals" put forth by organized ethnic groups.[20]

Ex-diplomat Chas. W. Freeman, Jr., contends that special interests, including ethnic lobbies, have captured U.S. foreign policy to the point that the idea of a "national interest" is no longer determinant. He writes:

> Foreign policy has been franchised out to special interests. Whichever interest group cares most about an issue gets to shape the policy and to have a big say in the appointment of the officials who will carry it out. Some nations reap disproportionate amounts of taxpayer-funded foreign aid from this system. Others get sanctions imposed on their foes. More than 100 foreign nations are now subject to or threatened with U.S. sanctions.[21]

Though a disability of democracy, this is a condition with which American statesmen will have to live. But it remains a powerful argument against interventionism. To the Lion of Idaho, Senator William Borah, who defied Wilson, it was conclusive. America, he said, "has within her boundary people from almost every land under the sun, still conscious under certain conditions of the 'mystic chords of memory,'" which could, he said, "transfer the racial antipathies... and controversies of the Old World into our very midst."[22] So they have.

This situation argues as well for a new immigration policy to give this country time to assimilate and Americanize the thirty million who have come to these shores in three decades, so that future generations will think of America—not the ancestral homeland—first.

A MORAL IMPERATIVE TO STOP GENOCIDES?

Since the Nazi destruction of the European Jews, a new question has arisen: Do acts of genocide require nations to go to war against regimes that perpetrate them, if those regimes have not attacked one's own country? Have nations a moral duty to go abroad, and go to war, to stop "crimes against humanity"?

The issue first came to a boil long ago—in the Balkans. On June 23, 1876, reports appeared in the *London Daily News* of appalling Turk atrocities against the Bulgarians. "It was alleged that some 25,000 men, women and children had been slaughtered. Grisly details were given of accompanying outrages, arson, sodomy, rape, torture and other atrocious acts."[23] England was in an uproar, though the Ottoman Empire had been its traditional ally against tsarist expansionism.

Prime Minister Benjamin Disraeli initially cast doubt on the reports. Oriental people, he said, "seldom resort to torture but generally terminate their connexion with culprits in a more expeditious manner."[24] Disraeli would be savaged from platform and pulpit for a cruel jibe about the massacres. When the government's investigator returned to confirm that twelve thousand Bulgarians had indeed been slaughtered, Disraeli declared: "We did not uphold Turkey from 'blind superstition, and from a want of sympathy with the highest aspirations of humanity.... *What our duty is at this critical moment is to maintain the empire of England* [emphasis added]."[25]

To Disraeli, the empire came before any sentimentality about dead Bulgarian Christians. In September, however, he was stung by a pamphlet, "The Bulgarian Horrors and the Question of the East," written in white heat by his old rival William Gladstone, who was demanding eviction of the entire Turkish population from Europe. "There is not a criminal in an European gaol, there is not a cannibal in the South Sea Islands," wrote Gladstone, "whose indignation would not arise and overboil at the recital of that which has been done...."[26] An enraged Disraeli rebuffed even the queen's suggestion that he condemn the atrocities, dismissing Gladstone's pamphlet as "vindictive and ill-written—that of course. Indeed in that respect of all the Bulgarian horrors perhaps the greatest."[27]

The British divided as bitterly as over any issue since the battle to repeal the Corn Laws. "Reason vanished and passion prevailed," observed Disraeli biographer Robert Blake. "Liberals carrying the standard of conscience and Tories raising the banner of patriotism met in a head-on clash," wrote historian Virginia Cowles.[28] Queen Victoria was outraged by a speech at a rally where Gladstone had sat on a platform while Edward Freeman, a popular English historian of the Victorian era, brought down the house, declaring, "Perish the interests of England, perish our dominion in India, sooner than we should strike one blow or speak one word on behalf of wrong against the right."[29]

From the publication of the pamphlet to his death, Gladstone would be detested by the queen for putting a moral crusade ahead of his country. To Disraeli, Gladstone was an "unprincipled maniac."[30]

Disraeli was not only driven by rage that his old enemy was trying to ride the Bulgarian massacres back to power; he believed the empire was at stake, and feared that, with the massacres turning the British against the Turks, Russia was being provided with an excuse to go to war and seize Constantinople and the Dardanelles. Disraeli was beside himself. We do not make British foreign policy, he raged, on the basis of "coffee house babble."[31] Writes Blake: "Disraeli had no sympathy with the notion that political questions are ones of morality…. [T]he conflict has coloured the struggle between Left and Right from that day to this."[32]

When the tsar went to war, the British cabinet sent the Royal Navy to defend the Straits. At Plevna, the Russians defeated the Turks, and Bulgarians butchered the Turkish wounded in their hospital beds. Forty-three thousand Turkish prisoners were led on a death march to Russia. Only 15,000 arrived; only 12,000 came home. The 50,000 Turks who died in Russian captivity in that war are long forgotten, but the Bulgarian massacres are yet remembered.[33]

Bismarck shared Disraeli's *realpolitik*. In a famous epigram, he declared, "The Balkans are not worth the bones of a single Pomeranian grenadier." Thus was the pattern set: When vital interests collide with human rights, statesmen put national interests first.

HOW STATESMEN RESPOND TO GENOCIDES

In 1894 the Armenians rose up against the Turks in a rebellion that ended in a fearful massacre of the Armenians. Europe was ablaze with moral indignation, but only Lord Salisbury raised the issue of foreign intervention, an idea rejected when there was no agreement over how the Ottoman estate might be divided up by the European powers.

Armenians were also victims of the first great massacre of the twentieth century. Charged with collaborating with Russia in World War I, some 1,750,000, by one estimate, died as the Turks drove them out of their ancestral homelands. Wrote historian R. J. Rummel:

By foot or rail, the Young Turks initially deported possibly
1,400,000 Armenians overall. Weeks or months of exposure,
thirst, hunger, murder, and abduction reduced their number to
only the very strong.... On average, possibly only 10 percent
survived.[34]

Britain, France, and Russia were already at war with the Turks
and could do no more to save the Armenians. Germany and Austria
at first ignored the reports; then, "in a friendly manner," they sought
to convince the Turks that reports of the massacres were playing into
the hands of Allied propagandists.[35]

After the dissolution of the Ottoman Empire at the end of World
War I, a rebellion led by Kemal Atatürk drove the Allies and Greeks
off Turkish land, whereupon the Turks turned in vengeance on the
Armenians again, killing an estimated 700,000. None of the Western
Allies had any stomach for intervention, including the Americans.

So it has gone. In *Death by Government*, Rummel lists the century's genocides against ethnic minorities and civilian populations.
Adding up four—concentration camp killings by the Bolsheviks, the
forced collectivization of the kulaks, the planned famine in Ukraine,
and the Great Terror purge of the Communist Party and Red
Army—Rummel puts the total dead at the hands of Lenin and Stalin
at close to fifty million. Excepting a feeble Allied intervention at the
end of World War I, no nation considered stepping in to stop the
slaughters.

Mass deportation of the European Jews to the east did not begin
until 1942, when the United States was already at war. At Casablanca
FDR declared that Berlin's unconditional surrender was our war
aim, even before the extent of the killings was known. As V-E Day
did not come until more than three years after Pearl Harbor, it is difficult to see what more could have been done by the United States
to destroy Hitler's regime much sooner. Once the United States

became a belligerent, it lost any leverage or ability to intervene diplomatically on behalf of the victims of Hitler.

Mao's eradication of the "rich landlords" in the Great Leap Forward, and the purges in the Cultural Revolution, took the lives of millions. But the British, with Hong Kong at risk, recognized Mao's regime and traded with it during a Korean War in which British soldiers also died. America never considered intervention; when Nixon went to Beijing to toast Mao, the U.S. establishment applauded his realism.

In 1975 came the Khmer Rouge's destruction of between 15 percent and 25 percent of Cambodia's population of eight million. From the first hours of Pol Pot's triumph, as the cities and hospitals of Phnom Penh were emptied at gunpoint, the world knew what was afoot. But no one begged the United States to go back to stop the killing.

Among Rummel's other episodes of "democide" this century are the Bengal/Hindu genocide in the India-Pakistan war of 1971, the slaughter of half a million ethnic Chinese in Indonesia in 1965, the Japanese army's "Rape of Nanking," Idi Amin's butcheries in Uganda, the Indonesian bloodbath in East Timor, and the Tutsi-Hutu massacres in Burundi twenty-five years ago, and in Rwanda this decade. Not one of these horrors provoked foreign intervention, with the exception of the belated effort to stop the killing in Rwanda.

Generally, then, statesmen do not take their countries to war to stop genocide unless their own kinsmen are the victims. Cultural genocide in Tibet and the persecution of Christians are not allowed to interfere with America's China trade. Would we have gone to war to liberate Kuwait had the emir not sat atop vast oil reserves? Fair question, since, when Nasser's army was using poison gas on Yemenis, no one intervened. "It is unworthy of a great state to dispute over something which does not concern its own interests," said Bismarck.[36]

While statesmen may echo Gladstone, they more often emulate Disraeli and Bismarck. But Gladstone is making a comeback. Writes British commentator Frank Johnson: "Gladstone with his agitation against 'Turkish ethnic cleansing' in Bulgaria invented the 'ethical foreign policy'.... Gladstone's Balkan policy is also, for good or ill, President Clinton's."[37]

THE NEW RELIGIOUS CRUSADERS

Another complication in shaping a new foreign policy is the zeal of religious activists to use America's leverage to force changes in the policies of countries that deny their people full religious freedom. And Congress has shown itself responsive.

Economic sanctions, it is said, compelled Ian Smith's Rhodesia to give up the ghost and South Africa to transfer power to the black majority. If sanctions worked to end apartheid, it is argued, why can they not work to end religious persecution and discrimination? So human rights activists, friends of Tibet, Evangelical Christians, Catholic and Jewish champions of religious liberty, and the right-to-life movement have united to try to strip China of its most-favored-nation trade status. These annual battles have spawned a religious rights movement that has begun targeting all restrictions on religious freedom imposed in the name of social order.

With Islamic fundamentalism on the rise, minorities, Christians especially, face repression from Algeria to Indonesia. Catholics and animists have been massacred in Sudan and seen their wives raped and children sold into slavery. In Egypt, Copts are the victims of pogroms. In Saudi Arabia, religious freedom does not exist; Christian converts who try to spread the faith can face a death sentence. In Iran, life for the Bahais has been hell.

Religious discrimination is practiced in many countries. In Russia, Evangelical Christians and Catholics have been forbidden to proselytize. Austria recognizes three tiers of religions with differing rights; Seventh Day Adventists, Jehovah's Witnesses, and the Church of Scientology are excluded. In Latin America, opposition is growing to Evangelical preachers. In Israel, the Orthodox have effected the first passage of a law prohibiting non-Jewish religions from working for conversions among Israelis, with a three-year prison sentence for violators.[39]

Any crusade for religious tolerance is going to attract Americans. This one has brought together Left and Right. Invariably, the demand is for the United States to use its diplomatic leverage and economic clout—including sanctions—on regimes that persecute people of faith or deny them full religious freedom. As scores of nations do not share the American belief in an absolute free market for religious faiths, this crusade invites constant collisions between the United States and regimes from China to Russia to Saudi Arabia and Sudan, and raises anew a question as old as the Republic:

In an imperfect world, to what extent should the internal policies and practices of foreign countries determine the U.S. relationship? Can the United States be friendly to a country that is unfriendly to our ideal of religious freedom?

AGENTS OF INFLUENCE—AND TRANSNATIONALS

Against the insidious wiles of foreign influence (I conjure you to
believe me, fellow-citizens) the jealousy of a free people ought
to be *constantly* awake, since history and experience prove that
foreign influence is one of the most baneful foes of republican
government.[39]

—George Washington, Farewell Address, 1796

Washington would be astonished at what goes on in the city that bears his name. Former secretaries of state, senators, congressmen, cabinet officers, trade reps, diplomats, and bureaucrats have signed on as "registered agents" for foreign companies, countries, and causes.[40]

Foreign regimes are as bold in buying influence in Washington as our former public servants have become in selling it. In 1997 the Justice Department began an investigation into charges that Asian nations, including China, funneled millions of dollars into the presidential and Senate campaigns of 1996, in the belief U.S. foreign and trade policy were on the auction block.

Another new force in shaping foreign policy is the transnational corporation, a mutant of the multinational. These giant global companies no longer claim allegiance to the nations of their birth, and their political power in Washington has grown commensurate with their financial power.

In February 1997 Boeing, the U.S. aircraft company begun in 1916 in Seattle, got a new chairman. In his baptismal interview, Philip Condit said he would be happy if, twenty years hence, no one thought of Boeing as an American company. Boeing's new goal was reportedly "to forge links with non-U.S. companies in a drive to rid itself of its image as an American group."[41] Added Condit: "I believe we are moving toward an era of global markets and global companies. I think it is advantageous that your workforce, your executive corps, reflect that. I would expect the nationalities of our executives to be considerably broader."[42]

Asked about the danger of defense technology thefts in joint projects with foreign companies, Condit brushed off the concern: "I'm a believer that technology transfers very readily. I think trying to say 'I've got a technological edge and I'm going to hold on to it' is impossible."[43]

Would not this stance compromise Boeing's role as a pivotal U.S. defense contractor? Condit went on: "As we move in an international direction... the U.S. government will have to find ways—of dealing with that."[44] A part of Boeing's assembly line is in China, and when asked if he had concerns about human rights violations there, Condit retorted:

Oh, yeah, absolutely. And I'm going to put it in context: they are
the same ones that I have about human rights violations in the
United States.... Some of the struggles we've had with civil
rights don't look all that shiny. People have been shot. People
have been beaten. I happened to be in China during the
Rodney King beating.[45]

Needless to say, Boeing's influence has been deployed against any
sanctions on the nation that may emerge as America's great twenty-
first–century antagonist.

Seeing themselves as first citizens of a new world, these Masters
of the Universe dream of a day when the nation-state is as obsolete
as the feudal castle. "The expansion of our consciousness to the
global level offers mankind perhaps the last real chance to build a
world order that is less coercive than that offered by the nation-state,"
wrote A. W. Clausen, ex-president of BankAmerica Corporation.[46] In
echo, William I. Spencer, former president of First National City
Corporation, declared, "The political boundaries of nation-states are
too narrow and constricted to define the scope and sweep of modern business." We must "defang the nationalist monster," says Peter
Drucker.[47] Carl A. Gerstacker of Dow Chemical Company once
mused aloud about a brave new world:

I have long dreamed of buying an island owned by no nation
and of establishing the World Headquarters of the Dow
Company on the truly neutral ground of such an island,
beholden to no nation or society.[48]

A spokesman for Dow rival Union Carbide seconded
Gerstacker: "It is not proper for an international corporation to put
the welfare of any country in which it does business above that of
any other."[49] Putting America first shows a lack of loyalty to the

corporation. No man can serve two masters, and the company comes before the country.

In *Between Two Ages*, three decades ago, future National Security Adviser Zbigniew Brzezinski saw the new power center emerging. "A global human consciousness is for the first time beginning to manifest itself," exulted Brzezinski.[50]

> Today we are again witnessing the emergence of transnational elites… composed of international businessmen, scholars, professional men, and public officials. The ties of these new elites cut across national boundaries, their perspectives are not confined by national traditions, and their interests are more functional than national.[51]

Global capitalists have become acolytes of global governance. They wish to see national sovereignty diminished and sanctions abolished. Where yesterday American businesses suffered damage to their good name for selling scrap iron to Japan before Pearl Harbor, today it is not uncommon to read of satellite and missile technology, even supercomputers, sent abroad and ending up in the hands of the military of potentially hostile nations. Once it was true that what was good for the Fortune 500 was good for America. That is no longer true, and what is good for America must take precedence.

"NO MORE VIETNAMS!"

With the memory still raw of 58,000 Americans coming home in caskets from Vietnam, U.S. statesmen must take account of a new restraint on intervention—a deep antipathy among Americans for spilling the blood of our soldiers, if our country is not attacked. Because of Vietnam, the Silent Majority wants to stay out of wars unrelated to U.S. vital interests. At their peril do political leaders underestimate this determination.

People forget: Even Ronald Reagan at the peak of his popularity and persuasive power was almost unequal to the task of convincing the country to support a pro-American Nicaraguan resistance fighting to oust a pro-Soviet junta openly hostile to the United States. And Reagan was forced to evacuate all U.S. forces from Lebanon after a terrorist bomb blew up the barracks there, killing 269 U.S. Marines. The public was uninterested in the mission for which they had been sent, and wanted them home.

Bush was able to rally the nation to fight the Gulf War only because he had in Saddam Hussein a villain out of central casting who had used poison gas, committed naked aggression, threatened the oil supply of the industrial democracies, and was said to be building atomic and chemical weapons. Still, Bush's war resolution won Senate approval only by a vote of 52–48.

Clinton was forced to pull U.S. forces out of Somalia after just one fire fight, and has carefully kept U.S. troops in Bosnia out of harm's way to minimize the possibility of casualties that might create an instant clamor to "bring the boys home." In the war against Serbia, the United States restricted itself to air strikes and missile attacks, avoiding any casualties in the first ten weeks of combat. America's refusal to accept casualties, says former Defense Secretary James Schlesinger, argues for brief and relatively bloodless U.S. interventions, or none at all.

> The public is not prepared to tolerate significant casualties unless
> there is a direct threat to the United States or its principal allies,
> or what will be seen as an obvious threat to our interests. Thus,
> public expectations dramatically narrow the room for maneuver
> for U.S. leaders. Such are the "lessons" not only from Vietnam,
> but from Lebanon, Somalia, and Bosnia.[52]

NUCLEAR PROLIFERATION

A related and powerful argument against any interventionist foreign policy is the proliferation of nuclear weapons and ballistic missiles. Eight nations are known today to have atomic weapons: the United States, Russia, Britain, France, China, Israel, India, and Pakistan. South Africa was a nuclear power, but dismantled its weapons. North Korea may have a small arsenal. Three former Soviet republics, Belarus, Ukraine, and Kazakhstan—now independent nations—had control of nuclear weapons but returned them to Moscow. Iran is said to be building them. South Korea, Taiwan, and Japan have the capability, but have forsworn building the weapons, as have Brazil and Argentina. Iraq had a nuclear program before Desert Storm. And the terrorist organization of Osama Bin Laden reportedly sought to buy nuclear weapons from rogue military elements after the USSR broke up.

Chemical and biological weapons have been called "the poor man's atom bomb." Many nations have developed them. Russia was accused of using them in Afghanistan, Egypt of using them in Yemen, and Iraq of using them on its own people. Libya is said to be building them in the desert.

The United States, Russia, and China have ICBMs; the British and French have submarine-launched ballistic missiles; the Israelis and North Koreans have medium-range missiles. Iran's missile program is said to depend on the North Koreans. Iraq used Scuds on U.S. bases and Israel during Desert Storm. These rockets, which can carry nuclear, biological, and chemical weapons, are in the arsenals of many countries. With the technology of nuclear weapons almost fifty-five years old, and that of cruise and ballistic missiles (the German V-1 and V-2 rockets) even older, the eventual spread of such weapons to any advanced nation that wishes to possess them would seem but a matter of time and choice.

If there is a silver lining to this darkening cloud, it is that nuclear weapons have not been used since August 1945, and they have served as both a deterrent to attack and a force for restraint on those who possess them. Had America not had a monopoly on nuclear weapons, the Soviet Union might have taken Berlin and driven to the Channel in the late 1940s, and the Chinese might not have agreed to an armistice in Korea.

No nation with nuclear weapons has ever had its homeland invaded or its cities subjected to attack, with the exception of Israel in Desert Storm. Yet, even here, Saddam Hussein's refusal to use chemical warheads on his Scuds, when he had used them on his own people, was probably due to his fear that American or Israeli retaliation might be nuclear.

While possession of these weapons may deter any future invasion of Israel, or of China by Russia, or the reverse, the weapons are also an insurance policy—should Iraq or Iran acquire them—against another Desert Storm. North Korea's possession of a nuclear capability has probably bought that regime security against being overrun by U.S. or South Korean forces in any new Korean war.

For U.S. strategists, the spread of nuclear weapons is an immensely inhibiting factor. Large concentrations of U.S. troops are virtual hostages to atomic weapons. Had Hitler possessed them, Normandy would have been suicidal. Had China had them in 1950, Truman would never have let MacArthur approach the Yalu River. Because Russia had them, America observed as the Hungarian Revolution was drowned in blood. Had Saddam Hussein had nuclear weapons, the army of Desert Storm would never have crossed the Iraqi border. Indeed, there might have been second thoughts among our Arab and NATO allies about even joining the coalition.

Nuclear weapons are the great inhibitors and the great equalizers. They raise the potential cost of future conflicts, and they are the most powerful of arguments against fighting any war to the death, as we did World War II—for a Hitler would surely have used them. And when one considers that today, nuclear, chemical, and biological weapons can be delivered by such conventional means as merchant ships and truck bombs, the case against going abroad in search of monsters to destroy becomes conclusive.

IS THERE "COMMON GROUND"?

The growing domination of U.S. foreign policy by ethnic groups and media elites able to focus public attention and incite public hysteria raises these questions: Are there vital national interests apart from, and even in conflict with, the special interests that have a preemptive claim upon us as Americans, which we will defend with all we have, including the lives of our young? Are there causes that justify risking nuclear retaliation on the United States? If so, what are they?

Americans are as divided as they have ever been over foreign policy. Disagreements cross philosophical and party lines. Liberals and conservatives can be found on both sides of questions from NATO expansion to Bosnia to Haiti to Kosovo, from imposing sanctions on China to lifting sanctions on Iraq, Iran, and Cuba. It is time we found that common ground upon which we can all stand as Americans.

CHAPTER 19

Claimants to Kennan's Legacy

If there's no Cold War, what's the
point of being an American?

—Rabbit Angstrom

Containment was the seventh American foreign policy tradition, given its name by George Kennan in 1947 in his famous Mr. X article in *Foreign Affairs*. With the end of the Cold War, however, foreign policy went to probate, and by 1999 three rival schools were claimants. Before we can consider a new foreign policy behind which all Americans can unite, we must briefly review the case for each.

GLOBAL DEMOCRACY AS PANACEA

First are the multilateralists who have held power under Clinton. These true heirs of Wilson see in the global spread of free trade, one-man, one-vote democracy, and disarmament agreements from SALT treaties to chemical weapons bans, the means whereby mankind attains the age-old dream of world peace. America can be truly itself and truly secure, they argue, only inside a world system where democracy has spread over the planet and a global government has emerged capable of securing justice for all nations and keeping the peace. To that end, nations must yield some of their sovereignty. Adherents of this view may be found fighting to

further empower supranational institutions like the UN, the World
Bank, the International Monetary Fund (IMF), and the World
Trade Organization (WTO), and to create new global institutions
such as a permanent Nuremberg tribunal with power to prosecute
"war criminals" from any nation.

The roots of this foreign policy vision may be found in
Western history. As historian William Hawkins writes, Wilson's
three themes—free trade, disarmament, and world government—
are of an ancient lineage.

> This triplet runs through the works of the great classical liber-
> als from David Hume to Thomas Paine and Immanuel Kant
> on to Jean-Baptiste Say and Richard Cobden. It was repeated
> as items three, four, and fourteen in President Woodrow
> Wilson's Fourteen Points, issued in January 1918, a plan
> Wilson said "rejects the standards of national selfishness that
> once governed the counsels of nations and demands that they
> shall give way to a new order of things." Three-quarters of a
> century later, they form the core of President Bill Clinton's
> vision of a post–Cold War "new order."[1]

A representative figure of the Wilsonian school would be the
late George W. Ball, once described as "part of a new transnational
élite that felt frustrated and unduly restricted by the traditional
nation-state system."[2] Ball once vented his exasperation at the
antiquated notion of borders:

> The urgent need of modern man [is] to use the world's
> resources in the most efficient manner. That can be achieved
> only when all the factors necessary for the production and use
> of goods—capital, labor, raw materials and plant facilities—are
> freely mobilized and deployed according to the most efficient

pattern—and that in turn will be possible only when national boundaries no longer play a critical role in defining economic horizons.[3]

Where does one's loyalty lie? That issue has been raised by the Wilsonian globalists. To whom, and to what, do we owe allegiance, and love? Is it still the country, or does the "international community" take precedence? Is the age of the nations over? Strobe Talbott, Clinton's roommate at Oxford and architect of his Russian policy, believes so:

> All countries are basically social arrangements.... No matter how permanent and even sacred they may seem at any one time, in fact they are all artificial and temporary.... Within the next hundred years... nationhood as we know it will be obsolete; all states will recognize a single, global authority. A phrase briefly fashionable in the mid-20th century—"citizen of the world"—will have assumed real meaning by the end of the 21st.[4]

To Talbott, the WTO, IMF, and World Bank are "protoministries of trade, finance and development for a united world."[5] Richard N. Gardner, Clinton's ambassador to Spain, twenty-five years ago declared allegiance to this vision, and counseled a policy of pursuing it through stealth to avoid awakening the slumbering giant of American patriotism:

> [T]he "house of world order" will have to be built from the bottom up.... An end run around national sovereignty, eroding it piece by piece, will accomplish much more than the old-fashioned frontal assault.[6]

David Callahan, research fellow at the Twentieth Century
Fund, is of this school. He had called for "preventive engagement"
in ethnic conflicts from Burundi to Bosnia, Chechnya, and the
Transniester Republic—to douse nationalist blazes before they
spread. "[M]ost ethnic conflicts are unwinnable wars that only
guarantee future cycles of violence," insists Callahan. America
should intervene to "make them less common, and, when they do
occur, to reduce both their intensity and their duration."[7]

Callahan endorsed Presidential Decision Directive 25. This was
the basis for Clinton's "Policy on Reforming Multilateral Peace
Operations," issued in May 1994, which urged a standing UN "rapidly deployable mission headquarters" and a UN airlift capability:
"On a case by case basis, the president will consider placing appropriate forces under the operational command of a competent UN
commander for specific UN operations authorized by the Security
Council."[8] Putting U.S. troops under UN command became a blaz-
ing issue in the Republican primaries of 1996.

As this globalist view is quasireligious in character, adherents tend
to look on opponents as worse than obstructionists. Historian Charles
Beard wrote on the eve of America's entry into World War II:

> According to the internationalist hypothesis, Americans who
> advocate peace for the United States in the presence of
> European and Asiatic wars are not peace advocates in the true
> sense.... [T]hey are isolationists pursuing a policy which leads
> to armaments and wars. In internationalist literature, these
> peace advocates are frequently represented as selfish, cowardly,
> and immoral persons, who merely wish "to save their own
> skins," who refuse to recognize the obligations of the United
> States to other nations suffering not from their own follies but
> from the neglect of the American people.[9]

THE HEGEMONIST TEMPTATION

The second school is the Republican-neoconservative establishment that held power under President Bush and believes America
should exploit its hour of power to impose a Pax Americana. This
elite believes that the great lesson of history was Munich in 1938,
that the way to deal with dictators and disturbers of the peace is
ruthlessly and early, that while it is best to act in concert with
other nations, it is often necessary to act alone.

In early 1998 this elite was calling for air strikes on Iraq, followed by a marines' march to Baghdad to hang Saddam Hussein.
It supported Clinton on NATO expansion and U.S. intervention
in Bosnia and war in Kosovo. Its criticism was that he did too little and acted too late.

George Bush spoke for this school in his October 1, 1991,
address to the UN on the "New World Order." Declared Bush, "I
see a world of open borders, open trade, and... open minds, a
world that celebrates the common heritage that belongs to all the
world's people, taking pride not just in hometown or homeland
but in humanity itself."[10] Our vision must encompass more than
America; it must embrace the world.

Republican internationalists and neoconservatives, with
nationalists and traditionalists, hold that the world is a dangerous
place, full of enemies anxious to exploit American weakness. They
are dismissive of efforts to reform tyrants who crawl to power over
the corpses of their predecessors and believe United States security rests on U.S. power and the will to use it. They, too, believe in
superiority in all spheres critical to the nation's defense: air, sea,
space, and technology.

Nationalists and traditionalists part company with neoconservatives on their contention that peace is indivisible and requires
U.S. dominance of every region. Many of the latter argue that
unless democracy is secure everywhere, it is secure nowhere, that

the only certain way to prevent monsters from molesting us is to strangle them in their crib. This sense of "none-is-safe-unless-all-are-safe" can be found in American statesmen from Elihu Root, who said, "To be safe, democracy must kill its enemy when it can and where it can. The world cannot be half democratic and half autocratic," to Dean Rusk, who said the "United States cannot be secure until the total international environment is ideologically safe."[11]

These thinkers see foreign policy as a sword against the enemies of American values and against threats not only to our own interests but to those of our friends and allies, whom they now number in the scores. Where the nationalist sees the United States as the "balancer of last resort," not an "intervener of first resort," neoconservatives and internationalists see the United States as a frontline fighting state in Europe, the Middle East, the Gulf, and Korea, and on the Pacific Rim.

In this vision, the United States should impose a "benevolent global hegemony" on mankind and stand at the epicenter of a worldwide alliance of democracies, united by trade and investment, whose combined power would dwarf any combination that might rise to challenge it. Theirs is the vision of America as Rome, with imperial allies, not imperial provinces.

A colorful rendering of this vision appeared in a *Foreign Affairs* article—"Toward a Neo-Reaganite Foreign Policy"—by William Kristol and Robert Kagan, which chastised conservatives for lack of manliness in not supporting a new imperium by which the United States would go out into the world to slay dragons as our national vocation. Here is a sampling:

> Conservatives these days succumb easily to the charming old metaphor of the United States as a "city on a hill." They hark back... to the admonition of John Quincy Adams that

America ought not go "abroad in search of monsters to
destroy." But why not? The alternative is to leave monsters on
the loose, ravaging and pillaging to their hearts' content, as
Americans stand by and watch. What may have been wise
counsel in 1823, when America was a small, isolated power in
a world of European giants, is no longer so, when America is
the giant. Because America has the capacity to contain or
destroy many of the world's monsters, most of which can be
found without much searching, and because the responsibility
for the peace and security of the international order rests so
heavily on America's shoulders, a policy of sitting atop a hill
and leading by example becomes in practice a policy of cowardice and dishonor.[12]

Set aside that Adams made that speech in 1821; a policy of
America as global bounty hunter was far removed from Reagan's
vision. His foreign policy was crafted to prevail in a long struggle
by putting ideological, not military, pressure on Moscow, by deter-
ring a direct Soviet challenge with the modernization of the U.S.
military, and by aiding proxies—Contras in Nicaragua, Jonas
Savimbi's UNITA in Angola, the Afghan mujahedin—to bleed the
"Evil Empire" at its periphery.

Kristol and Kagan watched perhaps too many episodes of
Have Gun, Will Travel in childhood. Reagan did not send
Americans out to destroy monsters, whether in Beijing, Teheran,
Baghdad, Hanoi, Phnom Penh, Damascus, or Havana. He was not
some global gunslinger. Only three times under Reagan would
members of the U.S. military lose their lives in action—in the
unwise intervention in Lebanon, in the capturing of a Soviet pawn
in Grenada, and in the raid on Libya in retaliation for the terrorist bombing of a Berlin nightclub frequented by American troops.

Upon what authority would a president use the armed forces of the United States to attack nations that did not attack us? The men and women of the U.S. military volunteer to defend America—its honor, citizens, and vital interests—not to serve as Hessians of a New World Order. What criteria would our global bounty hunters use to decide which tyrants were to be destroyed? This thinking is sophomoric. The declaration of such a policy would instantly isolate America by convincing any remaining allies that America had taken terminal leave of its senses and that further association with us was dangerous folly. Not every beast needs to be hunted down and killed; some are best left alone to live and die in their part of the forest.

FATAL FLAWS IN THE GLOBALIST VISION

In the media, bureaucracy, Congress, and the think tanks, the strength of these schools remains prodigious, but out of proportion to their strength in the nation. Indeed, with the post–Cold War era a decade old, it may be said that both schools are being repudiated by massive indifference.

The neo-Wilsonians, like Wilson and FDR, have discovered that the "international community" is a fiction, a figment of their imaginations. Our NATO allies, save Britain, refused to back us in the recent Gulf crisis and have yet to contribute to a NATO expansion supposedly done for their benefit. Russia routinely sells weapons to anti-American regimes and is the greatest thorn in the side of U.S. policy-makers in the Balkans and the Gulf. Israel, beneficiary of perhaps $100 billion in American aid, takes for itself the West Bank land it wishes to keep, ignores U.S. complaints, and sells advanced weapons, dependent on U.S. technology, to China. The Gulf nations, wary of the "Arab street," refuse to support the United States against Iraq and move closer to their Islamic brothers in Iran. The Japanese reject our economic advice, and Japan and China ignore our demands for open markets for U.S. goods.

The fatal flaw in the globalist vision is that it is utopian. It envisions a world that has never existed and can never exist, because it is contrary to fallen human nature. History has shown again and again that men do not give loyalty, love, and allegiance to entities greater than the nation. No "world community" can ever replace the *patria*. Ultimately, men fight and die for the "ashes of their fathers and the temples of their gods," not some New World Order. Who would give his life—for the United Nations?

In crises, men invariably take care of their own wives and children first; so, patriots will always put their country first. "Our country... may she always be in the right; but our country, right or wrong." Despite the trendy disparagement of the idea, Stephen Decatur's toast yet resonates.

Republican internationalists and neoconservatives understand this. Their dream of America as a "benevolent global hegemon" fails for a different reason: It is not rooted in America's history or its heart—and if it cannot be found there, it will not move a people. Unlike Romans and British, Americans make poor imperialists. A brief, bloody Philippine insurrection cured America of the lust for empire, which is why we never annexed Cuba. After World Wars I and II, the United States could have dictated to the world. Instead, the universal clamor was to "bring the boys home." This is not the hardy stuff of empire. Americans will fight when they feel their honor has been impugned—as with the *Maine* and at Pearl Harbor—and they will sustain an interventionist policy if some great hostile power clearly intends our destruction, as we believed the empire of Lenin and Stalin did. But no malevolent empire threatens us today, and despite the efforts to create a new Hitler in Saddam Hussein and Slobodan Milosevic, they both fall short of the mark. Thus, all that heroic chatter about global hegemony, a crusade for democracy, and "On to Baghdad!" has faded away.

Americans don't want to build a New World Order; they want to build a better America. Perhaps that is unheroic, but that is who we are.

ENLIGHTENED NATIONALISM

The third school, denounced as neoisolationist, is more accurately described as traditionalist-nationalist, or in Lippmann's phrase, "enlightened nationalism," and it is carrying the day by default, for it is only marginally represented in the foreign policy debate. Yet this idea alone can unite America—because every American will agree there are bottom-line vital interests that must be defended to the death; and the more narrow the definition, the greater the willingness to stand together and fight.

This school holds America to be a completed nation. As its frontiers have been forever established, its Manifest Destiny has been attained; its foreign policy should be first a shield, only then a sword, of the nation. These Americans believe in the Old Republic and in putting America first. They see our role not as a knight-errant that sets out to right the wrongs of a sinful world, but as the coiled rattlesnake that threatens none so long as it is not threatened and its domain is not intruded upon. They hold it to be folly to think we can convert all nations to U.S.-style democracy or should squander the public treasury in so witless an enterprise.

With MacArthur, these Americans believe that only the dead know the end of war, and that the wisest policy remains that of the Founding Fathers: Maintain the power to defend ourselves from all enemies, but stay out of wars that are not ours and husband our might to confront enemies that threaten us. No great nation can be truly isolationist, and America never was. But we can reclaim our independence and restore our freedom of action by letting lapse Cold War commitments that must involve us in virtually every great conflict of the new century. Primary responsibility for the defense of Eastern and Central Europe, of the Balkan countries, of the Middle East, of the Persian Gulf, of Korea, Japan, Australia, Thailand, Pakistan, and the Philippines, of Latin America, must be first and foremost the people of these countries themselves—not Americans. We are but 4 percent of the world's population and cannot be held eternally responsible for the peace and security of half the planet.

Catholics are raised to believe the Church is with us to the end of the world. As such, Holy Mother Church had to come to terms with Roman emperors, barbarian rulers, kings, and despots until each in turn passed away, as she continued her stately progress down through the ages. This confidence, this serenity, this detachment from the transient conflicts of modernity would serve the Republic well. In times of crisis, let us recall Lincoln's words: "And this, too, shall pass away."

No nation has the luxury America does, of time, space, and power, to observe at a distance and assess whether some emergent menace is a true peril—to us. As Coolidge once said, when you see ten troubles coming up the road, often the best thing to do is nothing, because nine will fall into the ditch before they reach you. In the age we have entered, Washington's wisdom is worth revisiting. Remarking on America's great distance from the blood-soaked continent, he implored:

> Why forego the advantages of so peculiar a situation? Why quit our own to stand upon foreign ground? Why, by inter-weaving our destiny with that of any part of Europe, entangle our peace and prosperity in the toils of European Ambition, Rivalship, Interest, Humour or Caprice?
>
> 'Tis our true policy to steer clear of permanent Alliances, with any portion of the foreign world. So far... as we are now at liberty to do it.[13]

Now, let us write a foreign policy that will protect and preserve this Republic and enable future generations to look back on the twenty-first century and say that it, too, was an American Century.

CHAPTER 20

A Republic, Not an Empire

America is not to be Rome or Britain.
It is to be America.[1]

—CHARLES A. BEARD, 1939

[W]e must consider first and last the American national
interest. If we do not, if we construct our foreign policy
on some kind of abstract theory of our rights and duties,
we shall build castles in the air. We shall formulate
policies which in fact the nation will not support with
its blood, its sweat, and its tears.[2]

—WALTER LIPPMANN, 1943

The year 1989 was the American moment. With the fall of
the Berlin Wall, and then the dissolution of the Soviet empire and the
Soviet Union, the United States was left as the world's sole superpower. No nation could challenge us. The Gulf War showed our military supremacy, the 1990s our economic supremacy.

But such moments never last. In 1763, Britain, with France
humiliated, bestrode the world like a colossus. Not since Rome had
the world seen such an empire. Yet, within a dozen years, the colonists
in America were refusing to pay taxes or quarter British troops,
embargoing British goods, and talking rebellion and secession.
Eighteen years after the French had been driven out of North
America, French troops and ships at Yorktown would help drive the
British out of their thirteen North American colonies, the crown
jewels of the empire.

If today we are incensed by the ingratitude of allies thwarting our leadership, after we succored and defended them through half a century of Cold War, imagine how the Mother Country must have felt about the Americans for whom she had won so much in the Seven Years War. Asked his thoughts on the American colonists, Samuel Johnson replied, "Sir, they are a race of convicts, and ought to be thankful for anything we allow them short of hanging."[3] Dr. Johnson's sentiments about the rebellious Americans mirror ours today about our own thankless allies.

But such is the way of the world. And if America has had one great failing in the 1990s, it has been not to grasp that our hegemony was surely transient, that, unlike a good father preparing his children to stand on their own, we failed to insist that our allies begin to provide for their own defense and take control of their own destinies. Rather than yield gracefully as Europe and Asia asserted their new independence, we have behaved like a possessive parent.

The world has changed. Nations that welcomed our guidance after World War II, and nestled under America's wing in the Cold War, now seek to go their own way. As Americans came to resent British hegemony, they have begun to resent and resist ours. They no longer want our tutelage and direction. It is time to let go of empire.

Any true foreign policy must grow out of a nation's history and its heart. It cannot be grafted on; it must be organic, and rooted in the nation's vital interests. But what are vital interests? Lippmann said they were "those interests which the people of the nation are agreed they must defend at the risk of their lives."[4] What, then, are we willing to send America's young to fight and die for? Our foreign policy will take shape when we have the answer to that question.

REAFFIRMING AND REFINING
MONROE'S DOCTRINE

Americans have always been prepared to fight to prevent any hostile power from establishing a strategic beachhead in the Western Hemisphere. Jefferson would have gone to war rather than let Napoleon take Louisiana from a weakened Spain. Polk would have gone to war rather than let the British take California. Johnson and Seward would have invaded Mexico, if necessary, to expel the puppet regime of Napoleon III.

In his first days, the next president should restate the U.S. position that the Monroe Doctrine is the cornerstone of American foreign policy, and that the United States will consider it unacceptable for any hostile regime to create a bastion in this hemisphere. The United States should, moreover, declare it will not tolerate any regime bordering the Caribbean, in Central America, or in Mexico, controlled by, or allied to, a hostile foreign power, as Cuba and, for a time, Nicaragua were during the Cold War. Already, China's agents have begun to displace Americans at entry ports to the Panama Canal. It should be U.S. policy to effect their peaceful removal.

But the United States should disavow any right or intention to intervene in any Latin American country that does not threaten us or its neighbors. On many occasions, the now-democratic countries of Latin America have reverted to authoritarian regimes, military and civilian, of the Left and Right. So long as these regimes do not align themselves with hostile powers and do not threaten us or their neighbors, they should be left to deal with their own internal problems. Only if America is directly affected, as with Fidel Castro's Mariel exodus, or some mass emigration from Mexico caused by revolutionary chaos, should the United States intervene. As for the Rio pact, the United States should give notice of withdrawal. We do not need military allies in this hemisphere to defend ourselves, and we ought not to be giving out pledges that we will defend every nation here. There is no vital American interest in what kind of regimes rule in the southern cone of South America. In the Falklands War, the United States sided with its European ally, Britain, against a hemispheric ally, Argentina, for the elemental reason that Britain is closer to America in every way.

TO REMAIN ONE NATION, ONE PEOPLE

Sheltered behind thousands of miles of ocean, America has been the most fortunate of nations in its geography. Neither Canada nor Mexico has been a security concern in this century. That is changing. In the new century, Quebec may declare independence, and the Maritime and Western provinces could separate from Ottawa. Americans may profoundly regret a breakup of Canada, but we are not a disinterested party; Canada is the most important country on earth for us. Should it come apart, the United States should offer trade agreements and security alliances to each successor state, and statehood itself, should any breakaway Canadian province wish it. As for Greenland, the last great empty space in the Western Hemisphere, the huge island should remain permanently inside the U.S. defense perimeter, and eventually be formally annexed by the United States. Unlike Puerto Rico, Greenland lacks the requisites of nationhood.

Across our two thousand–mile border with Mexico, a mighty political storm is brewing. Cross-border crime is rising; narcotics are pouring into this country. Mexico's ruling party, afflicted with sclerosis, corruption, and repeated financial crises, has failed to raise the living standard of most of Mexico's ninety-three million people. Our southern border is certain to require far greater policing and possibly a permanent presence of American troops. In ex-Defense Secretary Caspar Weinberger's book *The Next War*, an anti-American regime in Mexico forces U.S. military intervention.

The most immediate and serious problem facing the United

States in this hemisphere lies in mass immigration. Since 1965 America has added thirty million people. Each year, as many immigrants enter, not all legally, as there are people in New Hampshire and Vermont. One-tenth of the population of Mexico, the Caribbean islands, and Central America is already here—and more are coming. If immigration continues at present levels, America will cease to be a First World nation by 2040. A majority of Americans will no longer claim Europe as their ancestral home.

No nation has ever undergone so radical a demographic alteration and survived. With ethnic and racial militancy rising, and nations cracking up—from the Soviet Union, Czechoslovakia, and Yugoslavia, to Great Britain, Canada, and Italy—we need to take stock of where we are headed.

The Melting Pot is not working as it once did; assimilation is not taking place as before. Many newcomers have shown no desire to become Americans; some exhibit hostility to learning English; others manifest open contempt for the country. At the U.S.-Mexico soccer game at Los Angeles Coliseum in 1998, the National Anthem was booed by 90,000; the U.S. flag was torn down; the U.S. team was showered with insults and debris as it left the field.[5] Immigrants now make up a growing share of the inmate population in federal and state prisons; a third of the early arrestees in the Los Angeles riot were illegal aliens.

Mexican interference in America's internal affairs is increasing. Mexican consuls have worked against state ballot initiatives. In Texas, President Ernesto Zedillo urged Mexican-Americans to vote his country's interests in U.S. elections, and offered dual citizenship to recapture the allegiance of these Americans. Officials in Mexico City have said they will do nothing to impede illegal immigration into the United States. Hispanic militants talk of America as "the occupying power" and of creating an "Aztlan" nation in the Southwest separate from the United States.

Americans have always known instinctively that the great dangers come from within. Abraham Lincoln spoke this truth in an 1838 address to the Young Men's Lyceum of Springfield, Illinois:

> At what point shall we expect the approach of danger?... Shall
> we expect some transatlantic military giant, to step the Ocean,
> and crush us at a blow? Never! All the armies of Europe, Asia and
> Africa combined... with a Buonaparte for a commander, could
> not by force, take a drink from the Ohio, or make a track on the
> Blue Ridge, in a trial of a thousand years.... If destruction be our
> lot, we must ourselves be its author and finisher. As a nation of
> freemen, we must live through all time, or die by suicide.[6]

The greatest threat today to the survival of the Republic may well lie in the loss of our American identity as one nation, and one people, if we become what Theodore Roosevelt called a "polyglot boarding-house" for the world. America can absorb individuals who come here to become Americans; we cannot import the diasporas of foreign nations that are determined to remain citizens-in-exile of foreign lands.

Wilson said, "Some Americans need hyphens in their names because only part of them has come over."[7] This trend back toward hyphenated-Americanism is not a sign of national vitality, but of a dying patriotism and approaching disunion. Lest we forget: Mass immigration led to Spain's loss of West Florida in 1810 and detachment of Texas from Mexico in 1836. The Americans who had emigrated there remained loyal to America. Continued mass immigration, legal and illegal, threatens America's national unity and may yet bring the eventual breakup of this country. Indeed, for the first time since 1861, voices of secession can be heard in the land.

It should become U.S. policy in the year 2000 to declare that the era of mass immigration has ended, that henceforth 250,000 new

immigrants will be permitted in each year, and that illegal immigration will be halted—and illegal aliens returned home. As Ronald
Reagan said, a country that cannot control its borders isn't really a
country anymore.

The campaign to make Puerto Rico, annexed in 1898, the fifty-first
state must be defeated. Puerto Rico is a *nation,* with its own language,
history, culture, flag, and even its own Olympic team and Miss
Universe contestant. Its intellectual and cultural elite is deeply
nationalistic. Not in any election has a majority of the island's
3.8 million people voted for U.S. statehood. Three-fourths of the
Puerto Rican people do not speak English. To make this island a state
means making America a bilingual nation and denying to Puerto
Rican patriots and nationalists, forever, their right to join the family
of nations. We cannot do that and remain true to our anticolonial
heritage. And if we end all hope of these people for independence,
we will create our own Quebec and invite a Northern Ireland–type
insurgency in the Caribbean.

    Annexed without its assent in the Spanish-American War,
Puerto Rico should forever retain the right of self-determination.

As for Cuba, the U.S. Cold War policy of isolation and containment
succeeded. Keeping Castro afloat cost the Soviet Union $5 billion a
year, advancing the bankruptcy of the regime. But Cuba is no longer
a strategic colony of a hostile empire or a threat to Central America
or the Caribbean. The threat from Cuba today lies in the potential
for political upheaval with the passing of Castro and Castroism. A
million refugees could be sent fleeing toward Florida. America's
interests dictate a peaceful transfer of power. Castro may be the
enemy of America; the Cuban people are not.

CONTAINMENT OF CHINA?

With 22 percent of the world's population, China is the power that some predict will surpass America as the world's largest economy and most powerful nation by 2020. Perhaps. But as China has grown powerful, it has grown truculent. Though China's economy depends on $70 billion in annual exports to the United States, Beijing has insulted an American secretary of state, disrupted Taiwan's elections with missile tests, invaded offshore islands, sold missiles to Iran, sent nuclear technology to Pakistan, and persecuted Christians, Tibetans, and dissidents in defiance of timid United States expressions of concern about human rights and religious freedom. In April 1996 Russia and China proclaimed a "strategic partnership." In November of that year, Beijing agreed to pay for future purchases of Russian planes and warships from a $140 billion hoard of hard currency amassed from its huge annual trade surpluses with the United States.[8]

Yet, despite its bellicosity, China does not today threaten any vital U.S. interest, and its emergence as a world power need not mean inevitable conflict. For China is already contained—by geography. To the north is a suspicious Russia with a huge nuclear arsenal, fearful China will one day try to reclaim the "lost territories" taken by the tsars. To China's west are Moslem peoples that harbor a deep religious and ethnic antipathy to China. To the south are Vietnam and India, neither a candidate for satellization. To the east are Korea, Japan, Taiwan, and the American navy.

The most likely causes of a clash with China are the offshore islands of Asia. The Senkakus, claimed by China, are occupied by Japan, and the United States has a security treaty requiring us to protect all Japanese-administered territory. The Paracels in the South China Sea are claimed by Vietnam as well as China. The Spratlys, further south, which dominate the sea lanes to the Persian Gulf and may have huge oil and gas deposits, are claimed by six nations—China, Vietnam, Taiwan, Malaysia, Brunei, and the Philippines. "Whoever controls the Spratlys will gain regional hegemony in the next century," contends one Japanese strategist.[9]

The father of China's navy has spoken of building a blue-water fleet to dominate the western Pacific from the Asian coast out to the second chain of islands. While perhaps boastful talk, that would encompass the entire Pacific Rim all the way to Guam. But before that, a crisis is almost certain to erupt over the island claimed by China as its long-lost province—Taiwan.

Separated by one hundred miles of sea, with twenty-one million industrious people and a weapons pipeline to America, Taiwan would not be easy prey. And should Beijing blockade the island, it would rupture its trade ties with the United States, bankrupting China, and risk a clash with the U.S. Navy. Since Jimmy Carter abrogated our security treaty, America is not obliged to go to war to defend Taiwan, but the question of how we would deal with a blockade or missile attack on Taiwan is among the most crucial facing the next president.

In considering that question, we should realize that in any clash with Beijing, America would be without allies. In the 1996 crisis in the Taiwan Strait, not a single Asian nation publicly endorsed the deployment of U.S. aircraft carriers off the China coast. Only where their own security is the issue do our Asian allies become true allies. As these nations are far more threatened than we by a militarist expansionist China, the present situation should be unacceptable to the United States.

If we look ahead a decade, we see that the great threat China might pose to the United States would be if it managed to neutralize the Pacific Rim and Japan as it pursued a program of imperialist expansion. If all the dynamic potential of East Asia were placed into the balance against us, we would be forced back across the Pacific to Hawaii. While such a development would be a strategic defeat for the

United States, it would be an unvarnished disaster for Free Asia, ending its hopes of freedom, liberty, and prosperity.

So long, however, as the United States guarantees the security of the nations of Free Asia, they, like Europeans, will never undertake to provide for, or to pay for, their own defense. The United States should thus unilaterally declare in force the Nixon Doctrine laid down by the president in Guam in 1969: In future Asian wars, America will provide the weapons of defense for free nations, but Asian soldiers, sailors, and airmen must do the fighting. As the century closes, we should end our role, taken up at Manila Bay, as a frontline fighting state in Asia, and become Free Asia's arsenal of democracy and strategic reserve of freedom.

While the United States should maintain military relations with the friendly states of Asia, we should dissolve all security treaties that require us to go to war, instantly, in the event of some attack on Thailand, Australia, or the Philippines. No vital interest of ours is at risk in these nations. Only by taking away the security blanket will we shock Free Asia into doing what it should have done long ago: organize militarily, as it has economically, to provide for the common defense. Only when the assumption of automatic U.S. rescue is removed will a new balance of power emerge.

In 1964 Lyndon Johnson declared to a nation concerned we would get involved in war in Vietnam, "[W]e are not about to send American boys nine- or ten thousand miles away from home to do what Asian boys ought to be doing for themselves."[10] This time we ought to mean it.

A NEW CHINA POLICY

United States policy toward China should be neither to aggravate nor to appease Beijing. But allowing China to run near $60 billion annual trade surpluses at our expense, while we guarantee low-interest loans to Beijing from the Asian Development Bank and

World Bank, is appeasement. American imports from China and investments there are financing military forces that may one day threaten Asia and the U.S. fleet. As trade and aid have not made China more reasonable, the United States should reward Chinese truculence by treating China as the Great Power rival it claims to be.

Specifically, Beijing does not deserve the same preferential trade treatment as Britain. The United States should negotiate a reciprocal treaty with China that imposes on its goods at least the same tariffs and taxes Beijing imposes on ours, and we should veto any additional World Bank and Asian Development Bank loans to China. These are nothing but foreign aid.

Should China move against any of its neighbors, including Taiwan, a firebell would ring across Asia. With bitter memories of colonization by Europeans and Japanese, these nations would surely arm to defend their liberty. But the first defense perimeter of Free Asia should be manned by Asians themselves, united in regional alliances, with the United States relegated to the supporting role Nixon envisioned. Like Shakespeare's Fortinbras, it has been the role of America to come in at the end, not at the beginning of the family wars of Asia and Europe. Let other nations play Hamlet.

KOREA AND JAPAN

Currently, the United States has mutual security treaties requiring us to act to repulse any attack on South Korea or Japan. Yet neither nation is obligated to go to war if America is attacked. Both of these treaties should be rewritten.

Half a century after the Korean War, four decades after the Chinese troops left Korea, 37,000 U.S. troops remain in the South, most along the DMZ. Why should Americans be first to die in any second Korean war? Our last two Far East wars cost 100,000 lives, sundered our country, poisoned our politics, and crippled two

presidents. We are not going to send another army to fight a third.
The nation would not tolerate it, and no vital interest justifies it.

With twice the population of the North and twenty times its
economic power, South Korea, with access to U.S. weapons and U.S.
strategic support, is capable of manning its own defense. American
troops on the DMZ should be replaced by South Koreans; the
United States should remove it forces from the peninsula; and any
United States participation in a future Korean war should be
restricted to air and naval support.

But if America leaves, we are told, North Korea will attack. That
begs the question: When will South Korea's army be able to defend it
from a hermit nation half its size on the edge of starvation? Under
Reagan, the United States "broke" Moscow by outinvesting it in
weaponry and outproducing it. Why cannot South Korea do the same?

Since Vietnam, we have bought Asia twenty-five additional years
of security. Our assignment is complete, our mission done. In his
farewell address in 1951, Douglas MacArthur urged us to establish a
Pacific defense perimeter on "a chain of islands extending in an arc
from the Aleutians to the Marianas held by us and our free allies.
From this island chain we can dominate with sea and air power every
Asiatic port from Vladivostok to Singapore and prevent any hostile
movement into the Pacific."[11] MacArthur's strategy did not envision
any retreat to California. He was no more an "isolationist" than
Eisenhower, who advocated a similar policy for Europe. Had
Kennedy followed General MacArthur's advice there would have
been no Vietnam.

Whether or not MacArthur's counsel was right then, it is right
now. The French did not leave Asia until driven out. When the
British departed, wars exploded even as the Union Jack was coming
down. In this period of relative tranquility, America should devise a
new policy to reflect the new situation in this dynamic region. There
is no perfect time to let go; there is no guarantee that once we are
gone all will be well. But no better time will come to divest ourselves

of extravagant commitments to go to war to defend nations that are fully capable of manning their own defenses.

America does have a vital interest in ensuring that Japan's industrial might and military potential are not placed in any global balance against us. But our interest in an independent Japan is no greater than its own. Yet in this partnership, Tokyo has done most of the taking. Japan runs up huge trade surpluses at our expense, while denying Americans fair access to its markets. While we spent 6 percent to 9 percent of GDP on defense in the Cold War, Japan's defense spending never exceeded 1 percent. America is obligated to fight for Japan; Japan has no corresponding obligation. We need a new partnership agreement by which the burdens and benefits, risks and responsibilities, are more equitably shared. Japanese leaders, like former Prime Minister Morihiro Hosokawa, also believe the century's end should see a drastically reduced U.S. military presence in their country.[12]

As it is essential that Germany reassume its historic role as Europe's bulwark against any threat from the East, it is essential that Japan cease to be a U.S. dependency and assume its rightful role in the power balance in Asia. With an economy four times that of China, there is no reason Japan cannot invest in adequate air and naval forces to defend itself.

THE GULF

America's interest in the Persian Gulf is, as former Secretary of State James Baker put it in a word, oil. The Gulf has 25 percent of the world's supply and an equal share of known reserves, and U.S. dependency on imported oil is growing. Every day, America imports ten million barrels, more than half its daily consumption. Even at the relatively low price of $14 a barrel, this adds $50 billion annually to the current account deficit and is, autos and textiles–apparel aside, the largest item in our mammoth merchandise trade deficit. Of our $250 billion defense budget, the Gulf accounts for an estimated

$50 billion.[13] If the emir of Kuwait did not sit atop an ocean of oil, the United States would not have restored him to his throne.

Yet our present Gulf policy of dual containment of Iran and Iraq is unsustainable. American air power and naval power remain adequate to prevent Iran from closing the Gulf and to deter Iraq from reconquering Kuwait, but the balance is shifting. Saddam Hussein proved as much when he marched into the U.S.-guaranteed "safe haven" in Kurdistan. Secretary of State Madeleine Albright admitted as much when she secretly instructed UN weapons inspectors to make no challenge inspections that were likely to result in military confrontation.

Since 1991, moreover, America, France, and Britain have cut their defenses by as many soldiers, sailors, and airmen as fought in the Gulf War. As Western power contracts, Iran's grows. Saudi Arabia is also less stable than in 1991. The presence of five thousand American troops and fifty thousand civilians there calls to mind the huge U.S. presence in Iran prior to the revolution, and is resented deeply enough by some Saudi radicals to justify in their eyes acts of terrorism. Saudis see us as making a protectorate of a nation that is supposed to protect the holy places of Islam. Even Saudi friends are wary of their country becoming a U.S. dependency. Thus, permission for the permanent positioning of U.S. weapons has been denied.

A revolution in Saudi Arabia would sweep away the West's position in the Gulf. But in preparing for any such catastrophe, the United States has some impressive resources. We still produce 40 percent of the oil we consume. We have secure access to the oil fields of Canada, Mexico, Venezuela, and West Africa to our own Strategic Petroleum Reserve, and to limitless deposits of natural gas and coal which would come on stream in any run-up of oil prices to $40 a barrel. Should an Islamic republic of Saudi Arabia join an embargo of the West, it might cause global recession; but it would trigger an oil boom in Canada, Mexico, the North Sea, Venezuela, Kazakhstan, Russia, the Caspian region, and the Far East, as well as in Texas, Louisiana, and Alaska. Other OPEC nations would rush to fill

Western orders. The longer an embargo continued, the more independent the industrial democracies would become, and the more desperate would be the situation of the embargoing states. When it ended, its creators would find their market had largely vanished; and when they began pumping at former levels to recoup lost income, they would produce a global glut and a collapse in worldwide oil prices, as happened in the early 1980s. The oil weapon is a classic two-edged sword.

Yet America needs an insurance policy. Steps that might be taken to ensure U.S. energy independence include: (1) an end to draw-downs of the Strategic Petroleum Reserve, and topping it off; (2) opening up the Alaska Natural Wildlife Refuge to exploratory drilling; (3) reconsideration of the use of nuclear power to generate electricity; (4) rapid development of the oil resources of Russia, the Caspian, and Central Asia; (5) multiplication of pipelines from the Caspian and the Gulf; and (6) study of the potential of an oil import fee to stimulate conservation and new drilling, and to make clean coal and natural gas more competitive. Tax revenue from any fee could be rebated to states, citizens, and companies that had to bear its cost.

Like the British Empire, the United States cannot police the Gulf forever. With the United States building only six warships each year, within three decades our navy will be one-third the size of Reagan's navy, which Bush used to triumph in Desert Storm. But as oil is worthless, even to hostile nations, unless they can sell it for cash, the United States does not need to guard the oil fields of the Near East to have access to their production.

It is time to abandon a sterile policy of dual containment for a more active diplomacy, especially with Iran. While the memory of the holding of American hostages twenty years ago remains fresh, and Iran has undoubtedly had a hand in terrorism, we ought not forget that, twenty years after the Chinese were killing Americans in Korea, Richard Nixon was in Beijing toasting Chairman Mao. Nothing

Iran's regime has done, despicable as it may be, compares with what Mao's men did. As for Saddam, murderous though he may be, he is not a threat to America; should he use a weapon of mass destruction against U.S. forces, or smuggle one into our country, his destruction would be total—and he knows it.

ISRAEL AND THE MIDDLE EAST

In the Middle East, the United States has a NATO ally in Turkey, Arab friends in Jordan and Egypt, and a commitment that America will not let Israel go down and will assure its access to the weapons needed for its self-defense. No U.S. government will renege on that commitment.

But Israel will not know peace as long as it occupies Arab land. Withdrawal from the Golan Heights, south Lebanon, and the West Bank, and the creation of a Palestinian homeland are, as almost all Israelis now concede, necessary conditions of peace. But they are not sufficient conditions. The Israelis must have guarantees that any territory given up is not used as a base for terrorist or military attacks.

In the Arab world there is the perception that America is not an honest broker, that we apply a double standard to the Arabs, that in any collision the United States will invariably side with Israel. Much of the prestige America had at the time of the Gulf War has been lost. When Arab nations boycotted a U.S.-promoted conference in Qatar, and attended an Islamic conference in Teheran in 1997, it was a reflection of the shifting sentiment in the region.

The way to restore that prestige is for the United States to preside over a just peace between the Palestinians and the Israelis. But there is another American interest here—that is not to let this country become ensnared in this bitter and interminable quarrel by either imposing peace or policing it. We have already allowed ourselves to be drawn into the Balkan quagmire; to repeat this in the Middle East is to invite another Lebanon.

As the peace process moves forward, the United States should begin to disengage militarily from the Middle East. While we have friends and allies there, no vital U.S. interest is at risk in this volatile region—as there are no more Soviet client states there. As for the specter of Islamic fundamentalism, the huge U.S. military presence and the perception of American dictation and domination only exacerbates that problem.

Specifically, the United States should end foreign aid to Israel and Egypt, which runs to $5 billion yearly, and lay out what we believe to be the elements of an honorable peace: (1) return of the Golan Heights to Syria, and their demilitarization; (2) Israeli withdrawal from Lebanon, with a right of return if Hezbollah uses the territory for attacks; (3) a flag and a land of their own for the Palestinians, with a Vatican enclave-capital in Arab East Jerusalem; any Palestinian state on the West Bank and Gaza should be demilitarized—i.e., no fighter aircraft, no artillery, no missiles, no mortars, no tanks; and (4) a permanent commitment to Israel of access to U.S. weapons to enable it to maintain a security edge, with Israeli guarantees of no further transfers of U.S. weapons technology to China.

Would this make Israel invulnerable to terrorist attack? No, but there are no such guarantees, even for America. But the absence of a negotiated peace is a guarantee of future war. Ultimately, the choice is for Israelis and Arabs to make.

NEITHER ISOLATIONIST
NOR INTERVENTIONIST

And so we now come squarely and closely face to face with
the issue which Americans hate most to face. It is that old, old
issue with those old, old battered labels—the issue of
Isolationism versus Internationalism.

We detest both words. We spit them at each other with the
fury of hissing geese.[14]

—Henry Luce,
"The American Century," 1941

From mid–1940 to December 1941 America's great debate was over one question: Should America go to war to prevent Hitler from dominating Europe? On December 11, 1941, Hitler ended the debate by declaring war on the United States. With NATO in 1949 the United States declared that we would go to war, and nuclear war if necessary, to prevent Stalin from overrunning Europe.

This extraordinary commitment was justified under Washington's dictum that we may rely upon "temporary alliances for extraordinary emergencies." But, even in 1949, America's red line was at the Elbe. We did not go to war when Moscow crushed the Hungarian Revolution of 1956, erected the Berlin Wall in 1961, invaded Czechoslovakia in 1968, or ordered Solidarity crushed in 1981. In each crisis a Cold War president said in effect to Moscow: Revolting though your actions are, they do not imperil us, for who rules Eastern Europe has never been a vital interest of the United States. "Our power is on the sea and in the air, not on the land, and our interest in the interior of the European continent is indirect," Lippmann wrote in 1943. "To encourage the nations of Central and Eastern Europe to organize themselves as a barrier against Russia would be to make a commitment that the United States could not carry out."[15]

That remains true. With the Cold War won, it is time that Europe, a continent as populous and prosperous as North America, reassumes full responsibility for its own defense. We are not Romans; we cannot remain in Germany four hundred years. With Russians no longer occupying East Germany, Eastern Europe, the Baltic states, or Ukraine, Western Europe has never been more secure. France and Great Britain, with nuclear weapons, have never been in less danger, and are capable of defending themselves. A united and democratic Germany, the economic powerhouse of Europe, is fully capable of resuming its historic role of defending Central Europe. America cannot forever play the roles history and geography have given to other nations. Nor is there any valid reason Americans should. After all, how long should 260 million Americans have to defend 360 million rich Europeans—from 160 million impoverished Russians?

The United States should withdraw all its ground troops from Europe and amend the NATO treaty so that involvement in future European wars is an option, not a certainty. The trip wires put down by Acheson and Dulles, which would put America at war with a nuclear-armed Russia the instant it has crossed one of half a dozen frontiers, should be pulled up, and the mandate of the Constitution should be restored: Before America goes to war, Congress must declare war.

The Balkan wars that followed the breakup of Yugoslavia have lasted for nearly a decade, but, until we attacked Belgrade in 1999, America remained unaffected. We have no vital interest in that blood-soaked peninsula to justify a permanent military presence that could mire us down in a guerrilla war and invite terrorist retaliation. The Balkans are not our backyard; they are Europe's backyard, and responsibility for policing the peninsula belongs to them, not us.

HANDLING A WOUNDED BEAR

With communism dead, there is no great quarrel between America and Russia, no region on earth where our vital interests clash. Why create such a quarrel? America and Russia are not natural enemies. For us to give war guarantees to nations once part of the tsar's domain must be seen by Moscow as a violation of *its* Monroe Doctrine. For decades, we bristled at Russian troops in Cuba and submarines in Cienfuegos. How do we expect Russians to react to U.S. troops in Poland or Lithuania? Wounded and amputated, bereft of its cubs, the Russian Bear ought not to be provoked.

Lest we forget: The Russian army was not run out of Central Europe by NATO. It went home voluntarily in an unanticipated triumph for the West. Why then provoke Russia by threatening it with

with war if it should ever attempt to return? The United States is not going to treat a Belarussian attack on Bialystok like a Russian attack on Boston. Why declare that we will? Rather than encircling Russia, let us enlarge Russia's stake in peace. Bringing Russia into the European Union would be a far wiser guarantee of Europe's security than a threat to go to war to defend frontiers most Americans could not find on a wall map.

With its population shrinking from birth control, rampant abortion, and early deaths due to crowded living conditions, horrid health conditions, alcoholism, and pollution—and with Islamic fundamentalism rising to the south and a hungry China eyeing Siberia—Russia is a natural ally for the United States. But by moving NATO onto Mother Russia's front porch, we are driving her into the arms of Beijing and creating the hostile alliance it is in our vital interest to prevent.

In 1961 Eisenhower told Kennedy the time was right for Europe to raise the armies for its own defense, that the huge U.S. military presence was creating an unhealthy dependency. He urged JFK to bring the troops home. Nearly four decades later, with the Cold War over and the Red Army history, let us follow Ike's advice: Transfer command of NATO ground forces to a German general, and, after detaching the U.S. Sixth Fleet, transfer NATO's southern command at Naples to a French admiral. The role of America in Europe should not be as a frontline fighting state, but, again, as the arsenal of democracy and strategic reserve of the West.

Blessed by Providence with thousands of miles of ocean between us and a Eurasian land mass out of which have come all the great wars of the twentieth century, America is the most fortunate of nations. Why surrender this providential blessing? Remember the wisdom of our first and greatest president:

> Why forego the advantages of so peculiar a situation? Why quit
> our own to stand upon foreign ground? Why, by interweaving

our destiny with that of any part of Europe, entangle our peace
and prosperity in the toils of European Ambition, Rivalship,
Interest, Humour or Caprice?

    'Tis our true policy to steer clear of permanent Alliances,
with any portion of the foreign world.[16]

The Atlantic and Pacific Oceans are America's security belt, but
entangling alliances, history shows, are transmission belts of war.
Historian Charles Beard put the fundamental issue well: "It is not:
Shall we Love Europe?... It is: How can this country avoid war?"[17]

RECAPTURING AMERICA'S LOST SOVEREIGNTY

America is the most self-sufficient of nations, and our first and greatest tradition is liberty. Yet America has in recent years been yielding
up its sovereignty to the agencies of an embryonic world government, in a betrayal of our history and heritage.

    Among these agencies are the United Nations, where a cam-
paign is under way to strip the veto power from the permanent
members of the Security Council, and to convert the General
Assembly into a Parliament of Nations, where each nation has equal
voting rights. In the World Trade Organization, created in 1994, the
United States has already yielded to the principle of one nation, one
vote, and agreed to fight in federal courts for WTO decisions, even
when they go against the states of the American union.

    In Rome in 1998, an international criminal court for war crim-
inals, a standing Nuremberg tribunal, was established with the right
to prosecute citizens of any nation; the nation whose citizens are
indicted need not give its assent. With its new Law of the Sea Treaty,
moreover, the United Nations is reaching for control of—and a right
to royalties on—the resources on the seabeds of the world's oceans.

    The International Monetary Fund (IMF), designed at Bretton
Woods in 1944 to help maintain fixed exchange rates, has evolved

into an agency for funneling Western capital to failing regimes—to maintain interdependency and prevent a return to the economic nationalism of Washington, Hamilton, Lincoln, and Teddy Roosevelt. The World Bank and its sister banks have become welfare windows for the Third World, where loans are made that everyone knows will never be paid back. As with the IMF, the purpose is a steady siphoning off of America's wealth to the client states of these institutions. Through control of these agencies, international bureaucrats exercise influence and power over the United States. In 1998 one UN bureaucrat traveled across the United States to investigate human rights violations on the death rows of our state prisons.

All this is being done in the name of altruism, interdependence, and global democracy, but it is really about power; it is really about who shall rule us. In every nation, there is a struggle under way between those who put the country first and those who believe the Age of Nations must come to an end, that only world governance can lead to world peace. This is the world struggle that has succeeded the Cold War, that will decide the destiny of mankind. In that war our antagonists are the globalists, and our allies are the patriots of every country.

Like Gulliver on the beach of Lilliput, America sleeps, even as it is tied down with silken threads, so that when it awakens it will be unable to move. The dream of the managerial elites of the New World Order is that, one day, America will pass into history to become simply the wealthy Western hemispheric province of their domain, and they will control its wealth and direct its power—to their own ends. If we let that happen, if we let ourselves be robbed of this legendary estate, history will write of us that we were nothing but foolish and incompetent heirs.

With the 1998 crisis of the global economy, Americans began to awaken to the perils of interdependency. As the Asian contagion spread, they began to see its costs when the IMF was forced to pump more than $180 billion into Thailand, Indonesia, Korea, Russia, and Brazil to prevent the financial crisis from engulfing us all. They began to realize we cannot depend on foreign markets for future prosperity, for these markets can be closed, or collapse overnight. Americans must begin to rely more upon one another, and less upon foreign lands, and take control again of their economic and political destiny.

Specifically, the United States Senate should reject the UN Law of the Sea Treaty, and American diplomats should work for worldwide rejection of the UN international criminal tribunal—and refuse to cooperate in any way. U.S. trade laws should be rewritten to guarantee American businesses and workers privileged access to our own markets. After all, this country belongs to us, not to the world. And we should set it as America's goal to reduce our dependence on imports for the needs of our national life, and reduce our dependence on trade for our national prosperity.

The United States should give notice to the WTO and negotiate reciprocal trade treaties with all nations, including China and Japan, that run $60 billion trade surpluses at our expense while denying us equal access to their markets. As for the UN, we should warn the secretary general that any attempt to weaken the U.S. veto power will result in America's withdrawal. And U.S. troops should never again be placed under UN command.

RECLAIMING THE REPUBLIC

"What are you going to do, Joe, when this is all over?" was the question we heard in the war movies of our childhood. What is America's destiny? The answer depends upon another question: How do we see America? As the "world's last superpower," whose wealth and might must be used to reshape the world in our own image? Or as the land of liberty to be loved and preserved for itself? Is it our duty and destiny to go out into the world to seek monsters to destroy, or do we instead keep before us the Founding Fathers' goal of defending the peace and freedom of our own country and becoming a light unto the nations? Do we follow the vision of Washington or the temptation of Wilson?

America "is strategically immune in being insulated, invulnerable, impermeable, and impervious, and thus has few security reasons to become engaged politically and militarily," wrote historian Eric Nordlinger. In a world of hawks and doves, he suggested a different model:

> …[T]he metaphorical aviary of security studies… should be expanded to include eagles. They are powerful, keen sighted, high-flying, remotely perched, and thus eminently well-protected birds. Symbolizing strength and freedom, the bald-headed eagle also happens to be America's national bird.[18]

Trumpet calls to empire customarily fall on unreceptive ears when they reach these shores. By nature and history we Americans lack the patience and perseverance of imperial peoples. We are not the party of empire; we are the party of liberty. So let us set about creating a new impenetrable shield for the Republic, crafting a new foreign policy rooted in the national interest, so America may pass through the turbulent decades before us, serene and secure, and men will look back, one hundred years hence, and say, that, yes, the twenty-first century, too, was an American Century.

NOTES

Chapter 1: How Empires Perish

1. John V. Denson, "War and American Freedom," *The Costs of War: America's Pyrrhic Victories*, ed. John V. Denson, 2nd expanded edition (New Brunswick, N.J.: Transaction Publishers, 1999), p. 9.

Chapter 2: Courting Conflict with Russia

1. Steven D. Feller, "Foreign Entanglements," *Ripon Forum*, Winter 1998, p. 25.
2. Bill Kauffman, *America First!: Its History, Culture, and Politics* (Amherst, N.Y.: Prometheus Books, 1995), p. 143.
3. Barton Gellman, "Keeping the U.S. First; Pentagon Would Preclude a Rival Superpower," *Washington Post*, March 11, 1992, p. A1.
4. Barton Gellman, "Pentagon War Scenario Spotlights Russia; Study of Potential Threats Presumes U.S. Would Defend Lithuania," *Washington Post*, February 20, 1992, p. A1.
5. Ibid.
6. Ibid.
7. Gellman, "Keeping the U.S. First," p. A1.
8. Ibid.
9. Ibid.
10. Ibid.
11. Ibid.
12. Ibid.
13. Gellman, "Pentagon War Scenario," p. A1.
14. Barbara Conry, "New Problems for NATO—Potential Conflicts Involving the Czech Republic, Hungary, and Poland," *NATO Enlargement: Illusions and Reality*, eds. Ted Galen Carpenter and Barbara Conry (Washington: Cato Institute, 1998), p. 85.
15. "'Munich Danger' Is Rising Over

Europe Again," Czech News
Agency, March 12, 1996.

16. Christopher Layne, "Why Die for
Gdansk? NATO Enlargement and
American Security Interests,"
NATO Enlargement, p. 54.

17. Richard Reeves, *President Kennedy:
Profile of Power* (New York: Simon
& Schuster, 1993), p. 23.

18. Walter Lippmann, *U.S. Foreign
Policy: Shield of the Republic*
(Boston: Little, Brown, 1943),
pp. 148–49.

19. Layne, "Why Die for Gdansk?"
p. 54.

20. Thomas M. Magstadt, "Flawed
Democracies: The Dubious
Political Credentials of NATO's
Proposed New Members," *Policy
Analysis*, March 6, 1998
(Washington: Cato Institute,
1998), p. 1.

21. Susan Eisenhower, "Perils of
Victory," *NATO Enlargement*,
pp. 105–06.

22. Ibid., p. 110.

23. Stanley Kober, "Russia's Search
for Identity," *NATO Enlargement*,
pp. 130–31.

24. Eisenhower, "Perils of Victory,"
p. 111.

25. Ibid.

26. Ibid., p. 114.

27. Gene Smith, *The Dark Summer: An
Intimate History of the Events That
Led to World War II* (New York:
Macmillan, 1987), p. 185.

28. John Bartlett, *Familiar Quotations*,
16th edition (Boston: Little, Brown
and Company, 1992), p. 344.

Chapter 3: America's Future Wars

1. James Chace, "A Strategy to
Unite Rather Than Divide
Europe," *NATO Enlargement:
Illusions and Reality*, eds. Ted Galen
Carpenter and Barbara Conry
(Washington: Cato Institute,
1998), p. 177.

2. Doug Bandow, "The New
American Century: Searching for
Foes in the Post–Cold War Era,"
Chronicles, June 1998, p. 18.

3. Walter Lippmann, *U.S. Foreign
Policy: Shield of the Republic*
(Boston: Little Brown, 1943),
pp. 9–10.

4. John M. Collins, "Military
Preparedness Principles
Compared with U.S. Practices,"
Congressional Research Service,
January 24, 1994, p. 94–48S.

5. *Treaties and Alliances of the World:
An International Survey covering
Treaties in Force and Communities of
States* (New York: Charles
Scribner's Sons, 1968), p. 100.

6. "U.S.-Ukraine Security
Committee Report," News
Release, Office of Assistant
Secretary of Defense/Public
Affairs, November 15, 1996.

7. William Drozdiak, "European
Allies Balk at Expanded Role for
NATO," *Washington Post*, February
22, 1998, p. A27. Quoted by Gary
Dempsey, "Washington's Kosovo
Policy," *Policy Analysis*, October 8,
1998 (Washington: Cato Institute),
p. 20.

8. J. A. S. Grenville and Bernard Wasserstein, *The Major International Treaties Since 1945: A History and Guide with Texts* (London and New York: Methuen, 1987), p. 127.

9. Steven Erlanger, "U.S. Signs Accord to Protect Israel from Mass-Destruction Arms," *New York Times*, November 2, 1998, p. A13.

10. Grenville and Wasserstein, *The Major International Treaties*, p. 119.

11. Bill Gertz, "Cohen Says North Korean Missile is Big Threat; U.S. Defenses Not Ready for Nodong," *Washington Times*, July 10, 1998, p. A1.

12. Grenville and Wasserstein, *The Major International Treaties*, p. 124.

13. *Treaties and Alliances*, p. 190.

14. "Manila Cites U.S. Pact in spat over Spratlys," *Washington Times*, November 13, 1998, p. A15.

15. *Treaties and Alliances*, p. 188.

16. "Southeast Asia Treaty Organization," *West's Encyclopedia of American Law* (St. Paul: West Group, 1998), p. 311; *Background Notes*, Thailand, November 1994 (Washington: U.S. Department of State/Bureau of Public Affairs, 1994), p. 8.

17. Grenville and Wasserstein, *The Major International Treaties*, p. 112.

18. *Treaties and Alliances*, p. 144.

19. Ibid.

20. H. W. Brands, *What America Owes the World: The Struggle for the Soul of Foreign Policy* (New York:

Cambridge University Press, 1998), p. 303.

Chapter 4: The Myth of American Isolationism

1. Walter A. McDougall, *Promised Land, Crusader State: The American Encounter with the World Since 1776* (New York: Houghton Mifflin, 1997), p. 68.

2. *Public Papers of the Presidents of the United States: George Bush, 1991*, Bk. II, *July 1 to December 31, 1991* (Washington: Government Printing Office, 1992), p. 1574.

3. "Former President Bush Delivers Remarks at the Republican National Convention," Federal Document Clearing House Incorporated, August 12, 1996, p. 2.

4. Christopher Layne, "Bush's 'Isolationist' Straw Man," *Washington Post*, December 22, 1991, p. C7.

5. Wayne S. Cole, *Determinism and American Foreign Relations During the Franklin D. Roosevelt Era* (Lanham, Md.: University Press of America, 1995), p. 92.

6. Ibid.

7. McDougall, *Promised Land, Crusader State*, p. 57.

8. Alexander DeConde, *A History of American Foreign Policy* (New York: Charles Scribner's Sons, 1963), p. 124.

9. Joseph Stromberg, "The Spanish-American War as Trial Run, or Empire as Its Own Justification,"

The Costs of War: America's Pyrrhic Victories, ed. John V. Denson (New Brunswick, N.J.: Transaction Publishers, 1997), pp. 171–72.

10. Ibid., p. 173.
11. Joseph Burkholder Smith, *James Madison's Phony War: The Plot to Steal Florida* (New York: Arbor House, 1983), p. 42.
12. McDougall, *Promised Land, Crusader State*, p. 40.
13. Ibid.
14. Walter Lippmann, *Isolation and Alliances: An American Speaks to the British* (Boston: Little, Brown, 1952), pp. 8, 10–11.
15. Ibid., p. 11.
16. Ibid, pp. 14–15.
17. Cole, *Determinism and American Foreign Relations*, p. 96.
18. Peter Brimelow, *Alien Nation, With a New Afterword by the Author* (New York: HarperCollins, 1996), p. 293.

Chapter 5: Birth of an American Foreign Policy

1. Richard M. Ketchum, ed., *The American Heritage Book of the Revolution* (New York: American Heritage Publishing, 1971), p. 71.
2. Alexander DeConde, *A History of American Foreign Policy* (New York: Charles Scribner's Sons, 1963), p. 21.
3. Ibid., pp. 33–34.
4. John C. Fitzpatrick, ed., *The Writings of George Washington from the Original Manuscript Sources 1745–1799*, vol. 30, *June 20,*

1788–January 21, 1790 (Washington: Government Printing Office, 1939), p. 187.
5. James Thomas Flexner, *George Washington and the New Nation (1783–1793)* (Boston: Little Brown and Company, 1970), p. 69.
6. Ibid., p. 73.
7. Fitzpatrick, *The Writings of George Washington*, vol. 27, *June 11, 1783–November 28, 1784* (Washington: Government Printing Office, 1938), p. 475.
8. Flexner, *George Washington*, p. 73.
9. Melvin Small, *Democracy & Diplomacy: The Impact of Domestic Politics on U.S. Foreign Policy, 1789–1994* (Baltimore: Johns Hopkins University Press, 1996), pp. 2–3.
10. Patrick J. Garrity, "Warnings of a Parting Friend," *The National Interest*, Fall 1996, p. 16.
11. George Washington, "Farewell Address," *The Annals of America*, vol. III, *1784–1796*, publisher William Benton (Chicago: Encyclopedia Britannica, 1968), p. 611.
12. Michael Lind, *Hamilton's Republic, Readings in the American Democratic Nationalist Tradition* (New York: Free Press, 1997), p. 35.
13. Small, *Democracy & Diplomacy*, p. 4.
14. Fitzpatrick, *The Writings of George Washington*, vol. 35, *March 30, 1796–July 31, 1797*, pp. 231–32.
15. Paul Johnson, *A History of the*

American People (New York: HarperCollins, 1997), p. 231.

16. Fitzpatrick, *The Writings of George Washington*, vol. 35, p. 234.

17. Charles A. Beard, *A Foreign Policy for America* (New York: Alfred A. Knopf, 1940), pp. 17–18.

Chapter 6: "Mr. Madison's War"

1. Hamilton, Jay, et al., *The Federalist: A Commentary on the Constitution of the United States* (New York: Modern Library, 1941), p. 87.

2. Thomas A. Bailey, *A Diplomatic History of the American People,* 7th ed. (New York: Meredith, 1964), pp. 94–95.

3. Ibid., p. 98.

4. Ibid.

5. Alexander DeConde, *A History of American Foreign Policy* (New York: Charles Scribner's Son, 1963), p. 76.

6. Richard Brookhiser, "In Love With Revolution," *New York Times*, November 17, 1996, Section 7, p. 23.

7. DeConde, *American Foreign Policy*, p. 77.

8. Ibid., p. 78.

9. Ibid., p. 81.

10. Henry Kissinger, *Diplomacy* (New York: Simon & Schuster, 1994), p. 31; Bailey, *Diplomatic History*, p. 108.

11. Samuel Eliot Morison and Henry Steele Commager, *The Growth of the American Republic,* vol. 1 (New York: Oxford University Press, 1962), pp. 377–78.

12. DeConde, *American Foreign Policy*, p. 86.

13. *Dictionary of American History*, rev. ed., vol. II (New York: Charles Scribner's Sons, 1976), p. 16.

14. DeConde, *American Foreign Policy*, p. 92; Bailey, *Diplomatic History*, p. 124.

15. Paul Leicester Ford, ed., *The Works of Thomas Jefferson*, vol. IX (New York: G. Putnam's Sons, 1905), p. 220.

16. John Steele Gordon, *Hamilton's Blessing: The Extraordinary Life and Times of our National Debt* (New York: Walker, 1997), pp. 44–45.

17. Ibid., p. 45.

18. Paul Johnson, *A History of the American People* (New York: HarperCollins, 1997), p. 257.

19. Joseph Burkholder Smith, *James Madison's Phony War: The Plot to Steal Florida* (New York: Arbor House, 1983), pp. 40–41.

20. DeConde, *American Foreign Policy*, p. 121.

21. Bailey, *Diplomatic History*, p. 166.

22. Ibid.

23. Walter A. McDougall, *Promised Land, Crusader State: The American Encounter with the World Since 1776* (New York: Houghton Mifflin, 1997), p. 35.

24. Robert H. Ferrell, *American Diplomacy: A History* (New York: W. W. Norton and Company, 1959), p. 64.

25. Michael Kraus, *The United States to 1865* (Ann Arbor: University of Michigan Press, 1959), p. 321.

26. Johnson, *A History of the American People*, p. 261.
27. Bailey, *Diplomatic History*, pp. 144–45.
28. Ibid., pp. 155–56.
29. Ibid., p. 156.
30. Robert A. Rutland, *James Madison and the Search for Nationhood* (Washington: Library of Congress, 1981), p. 121.
31. Morison and Commager, *The Growth of the American Republic*, p. 422.
32. DeConde, *American Foreign Policy*, p. 111.
33. Rutland, *James Madison and the Search for Nationhood*, p. 122.
34. Marquis James, *The Life of Andrew Jackson* (Indianapolis: Bobbs-Merrill Company, 1938), p. 29.
35. Bruce Catton and William B. Catton, *The Bold and Magnificent Dream* (Garden City, N.Y.: Doubleday, 1978), pp. 461–62.
36. Harold Faber, *From Sea to Sea: The Growth of the United States*, 2nd ed. (New York: Charles Scribner's Sons, 1992), p. 57.
37. Catton and Catton, *The Bold and Magnificent Dream*, p. 462.
38. Ibid.
39. Robert H. Ferrell in note to PJB (Buchanan Files).
40. Robert Remini, *Andrew Jackson and the Course of American Empire: 1767–1821* (New York: Harper & Row, 1977), pp. 298–99.
41. DeConde, *American Foreign Policy*, p. 89.
42. Julian P. Boyd, ed., *The Papers of Thomas Jefferson*: vol. 8, *February to 31 October 1785* (Princeton, N.J.: Princeton University Press, 1953), p. 427.
43. Kissinger, *Diplomacy*, p. 33.
44. Bailey, *Diplomatic History*, p. 141; Morison and Commager, *The Growth of the American Republic*, pp. 400–01.
45. Ferrell, *American Diplomacy*, p. 81.
46. DeConde, *American Foreign Policy*, p. 138.

Chapter 7: How We Took Florida

1. Wayne S. Cole, *Determinism and American Foreign Relations During the Franklin D. Roosevelt Era* (Lanham, Md.: University Press of America, 1995), p. 11.
2. Thomas A. Bailey, *A Diplomatic History of the American People,* 7th ed. (New York: Meredith, 1964), p. 165.
3. Robert Remini, *Andrew Jackson and the Course of American Empire: 1767–1821* (New York: Harper & Row, 1977), p. 47.
4. Marquis James, *The Life of Andrew Jackson* (Indianapolis: Bobbs-Merrill, 1938), p. 283.
5. Ibid.
6. Ibid., pp. 283–84.
7. Bailey, *Diplomatic History*, p. 169.
8. Ibid.
9. James, *The Life of Andrew Jackson*, p. 291.
10. David S. Heidler and Jeanne T. Heidler, *Old Hickory's War: Andrew Jackson and the Quest for Empire* (Mechanicsburg, Pa.: Stackpole Books, 1996), p. 231.
11. Ibid., p. 184.

12. Bailey, *Diplomatic History*, pp. 170–71.
13. Heidler and Heidler, *Old Hickory's War*, p. 189.
14. Bailey, *Diplomatic History*, p. 170.
15. Kenneth Neill Cameron, ed., *Percy Bysshe Shelley: Selected Poetry and Prose* (New York: Rinehart & Co., 1958), p. 33.
16. Samuel Eliot Morison and Henry Steele Commager, *The Growth of the American Republic*, vol. 1 (New York: Oxford University Press, 1962), p. 450.
17. Heidler and Heidler, *Old Hickory's War*, p. 218.
18. Ibid., p. 183.
19. Ibid., p. 184.
20. Bailey, *Diplomatic History*, p. 172.
21. Heidler and Heidler, *Old Hickory's War*, p. 191.
22. Ibid., p. 199.
23. Harold Faber, *From Sea to Sea: The Growth of the United States*, 2nd ed. (New York: Charles Scribner's Sons, 1992), p. 70.
24. Bailey, *Diplomatic History*, p. 174.
25. Walter A. McDougall, *Promised Land, Crusader State: The American Encounter with the World Since 1776* (New York: Houghton Mifflin, 1997), p. 78.
26. Ibid., p. 89.
27. Remini, *Andrew Jackson and the Course of American Empire*, p. 50.
28. H. W. Brands, *What America Owes the World: The Struggle for the Soul of Foreign Policy* (New York: Cambridge University Press, 1998), p. 8.
29. Ibid., pp. 8–9.
30. Eric A. Nordlinger, *Isolationism Reconfigured: American Foreign Policy for a New Century* (Princeton, N.J.: Princeton University Press, 1995), p. 186.

Chapter 8: "Jimmy Polk's War"

1. Robert H. Ferrell, *American Diplomacy: A History* (New York: W. W. Norton, 1959), p. 85.
2. Hank Burchard, *Washington Post*, Weekend, April 19, 1996, p. 57.
3. Alexander DeConde, *A History of American Foreign Policy* (New York: Charles Scribner's Sons, 1963), p. 183.
4. Ibid., p. 184.
5. Thomas A. Bailey, *A Diplomatic History of the American People*, 7th ed. (New York: Meredith, 1964), pp. 241–42.
6. Samuel Eliot Morison, *The Oxford History of the American People* (New York: Oxford University Press, 1965), p. 439.
7. John Steele Gordon, *Hamilton's Blessing: The Extraordinary Life and Times of Our National Debt* (New York: Walker, 1997), pp. 60–64.
8. Frederick Merk, *Slavery and the Annexation of Texas* (New York: Alfred A. Knopf, 1972), p. 210.
9. Bailey, *Diplomatic History*, p. 244.
10. Samuel Eliot Morison and Henry Steele Commager, *The Growth of the American Republic*, vol. 1 (New York: Oxford University Press, 1962), pp. 601–02.
11. Ibid., p. 602.
12. Jennifer Roback Morse, "Constitutional Rules, Political

Accidents, and the Course of History: New Light on the Annexation of Texas," *Independent Review*, Fall 1997, p. 188.

13. John Spencer Bassett, ed., *Correspondence of Andrew Jackson*, vol. 6, *1839–1845* (Washington: Carnegie Institution of Washington, 1933), p. 278.

14. Ferrell, *American Diplomacy*, pp. 97–98.

15. Ibid., p. 98.

16. Bassett, *Correspondence of Andrew Jackson*, pp. 313, 302.

17. Bailey, *Diplomatic History*, p. 245.

18. Marquis James, *The Life of Andrew Jackson* (Indianapolis: Bobbs-Merrill, 1938), p. 767.

19. Ibid., p. 768.

20. Ibid., p. 769; Bassett, *Correspondence of Andrew Jackson*, pp. 286–87.

21. Bailey, *Diplomatic History*, p. 247.

22. Ibid., p. 248.

23. Bassett, *Correspondence of Andrew Jackson*, pp. 329–30; James, *The Life of Andrew Jackson*, p. 776.

24. James, *The Life of Andrew Jackson*, p. 786.

25. Bailey, *Diplomatic History*, p. 255.

26. David M. Pletcher, *The Diplomacy of Annexation: Texas, Oregon, and the Mexican War* (Columbia: University of Missouri Press, 1973), pp. 353–54.

27. DeConde, *American Foreign Policy*, p. 199.

28. James D. Richardson, ed., *A Compilation of the Messages and Papers of the Presidents* (New York:

Bureau of National Literature, Inc., 1897), vol. V, p. 2292.

29. Bailey, *Diplomatic History*, p. 257.

30. Harold Faber, *From Sea to Sea: The Growth of the United States* (New York: Charles Scribner's Son, 1992), p. 130.

31. Bailey, *Diplomatic History*, p. 259.

32. Morison and Commager, *The Growth of the American Republic*, p. 615.

33. Ibid., pp. 609, 613.

34. Bailey, *Diplomatic History*, p. 263.

35. Michael Kraus, *The United States to 1865* (Ann Arbor: University of Michigan Press, 1959), p. 433.

36. Morison and Commager, *The Growth of the American Republic*, p. 617.

37. Robert H. Ferrell, *American Diplomacy: A History*, rev. and expanded ed. (New York: W. W. Norton, 1969), p. 231.

38. Kraus, *The United States to 1865*, p. 434.

39. Walter A. McDougall, *Promised Land, Crusader State: The American Encounter with the World Since 1776* (New York: Houghton Mifflin, 1997), p. 52.

40. Peter Brimelow, "A Modest (?) Proposal," *Forbes*, March 27, 1995, p. 58.

41. Timothy Keesee, Ed.D., Mark Sidwell, Ph.D, eds., *United States History for Christian Schools* (Greenville, SC: Bob Jones University Press, 1991), p. 251.

42. Melba Porter Hay, ed., *The Papers of Henry Clay*, Volume 10,

Candidate, Compromiser, Elder Statesman, January 1, 1844, to June 29, 1852 (Lexington: University Press of Kentucky, 1991), pp. 945–46.

43. Eric A. Nordlinger, *Isolationism Reconfigured: American Foreign Policy for a New Century* (Princeton, N.J.: Princeton University Press, 1995), p. 186.

44. DeConde, *American Foreign Policy*, p. 218.

45. McDougall, *Promised Land, Crusader State*, p. 75.

46. H.W. Brands, *What America Owes the World: The Struggle for the Soul of Foreign Policy* (New York: Cambridge University Press, 1998), p. 8.

47. DeConde, *American Foreign Policy*, p. 219.

Chapter 9: "One War at a Time"

1. Thomas A. Bailey, *A Diplomatic History of the American People*, 7th ed. (New York: Meredith, 1964), p. 299.

2. Alexander DeConde, *A History of American Foreign Policy* (New York: Charles Scribner's Sons, 1963), p. 243.

3. Robert H. Ferrell, *American Diplomacy: A History*, rev. and expanded ed. (New York: W. W. Norton, 1969), p. 270.

4. DeConde, *American Foreign Policy*, p. 242.

5. Christopher Layne, "Kant or Cant: The Myth of the Democratic Peace," *Debating the*

Democratic Peace, eds. Michael E. Brown, Sean M. Lynn-Jones and Steven E. Miller (Cambridge, Mass: MIT Press, 1995), p. 171.

6. Ibid., p. 170; DeConde, *American Foreign Policy*, p. 246.

7. Layne, "Kant or Cant," p. 172.

8. Ferrell, *American Diplomacy*, p. 281.

9. DeConde, *American Foreign Policy*, p. 246.

10. Ibid.

11. Charles A. Beard, *A Foreign Policy for America* (New York: Alfred A. Knopf, 1940), p. 96.

12. Patrick J. Garrity, "Warnings of a Parting Friend," *National Interest*, Fall 1996, p. 20.

13. DeConde, *American Foreign Policy*, p. 251.

14. Ibid., p. 258.

15. Ibid.

16. Ferrell, *American Diplomacy*, pp. 302–03.

17. Ibid., p. 305.

18. Ibid., p. 306.

19. Bailey, *Diplomatic History*, p. 360.

20. Ibid., p. 364.

21. Ibid., p. 366.

22. Ferrell, *American Diplomacy*, p. 309.

23. Walter A. McDougall, *Promised Land, Crusader State: The American Encounter with the World Since 1776* (New York: Houghton Mifflin, 1997), p. 10.

Chapter 10: "Splendid Little War"

1. Foster Rhea Dulles, *The United States Since 1865* (Ann Arbor: University of Michigan Press, 1959), p. 161; H.W. Brands, *What*

America Owes the World: The Struggle for the Soul of Foreign Policy (New York: Cambridge University Press, 1998), pp. 33–34.

2. Alexander DeConde, *A History of American Foreign Policy* (New York: Charles Scribner's Sons, 1963), p. 356.

3. Robert H. Ferrell, *American Diplomacy: A History* (New York: W. W. Norton, 1959), pp. 179.

4. Walter A. McDougall, *Let the Sea Make a Noise: Four Hundred Years of Cataclysm, Conquest, War and Folly in the North Pacific* (New York: Avon Books, 1993), p. 373.

5. Ferrell, *American Diplomacy*, pp. 177–81.

6. Ibid., pp. 180–81.

7. Ralph K. Andrist, ed., *The American Heritage History of the Confident Years* (New York: American Heritage Publishing Company, 1969), p. 297.

8. Charles A. Beard, *A Foreign Policy for America* (New York: Alfred A. Knopf, 1940), pp. 54–55.

9. Thomas Marc Parrott, ed., *Shakespeare: Twenty-Three Plays and the Sonnets*, rev. ed. (New York: Charles Scribner's Sons, 1953), p. 424.

10. *Papers Relating to the Foreign Relations of the United States 1895*, Part I (Washington: Government Printing Office, 1896), p. 558; Thomas A. Bailey, *A Diplomatic History of the American People,* 7th ed. (New York: Meredith, 1964), p. 441.

11. Christopher Layne, "Kant or Cant: The Myth of the Democratic Peace," *Debating the Democratic Peace*, eds. Michael E. Brown, Sean M. Lynn-Jones and Steven E. Miller (Cambridge, Mass.: MIT Press, 1995), p. 175; DeConde, *American Foreign Policy*, p. 332.

12. *Foreign Relations of the United States*, Part I, pp. 564–65.

13. Barbara W. Tuchman, *The Proud Tower: A Portrait of the World Before the War, 1890–1914* (New York: Macmillan, 1966), p. 31.

14. Dulles, *The United States Since 1865*, p. 162; Bailey, *Diplomatic History*, p. 444.

15. Tuchman, *The Proud Tower*, p. 31.

16. Ibid., p. 32.

17. Allan Nevins, *Grover Cleveland: A Study in Courage* (New York: Dodd, Mead, 1938), p. 647; Walter Lippmann, *U.S. Foreign Policy: Shield of the Republic* (Boston: Little, Brown, 1943), p. 91.

18. Robert Debs Heinl, *Dictionary of Military and Naval Quotations* (Annapolis: United States Naval Institute, 1966), pp. 8–9.

19. McDougall, *Let the Sea Make a Noise*, p. 391. As for "jingo," the term had its origin in an English drinking song written by G. W. Hunt in 1878, as the popular mood built for a confrontation with Russia, which was then pressing upon Constantinople and the Dardanelles:

We don't want to fight
But, by jingo, if we do
We've got the ships,
We've got the men,
We've got the money, too!

20. *A Compilation of the Messages and Papers of the Presidents* (New York: Bureau of National Literature, 1912), vol. viii, p. 6241.

21. Bailey, *Diplomatic History*, p. 452.

22. Ralph Raico, "American Foreign Policy—The Turning Point, 1898–1919," *The Failure of America's Foreign Wars*, eds. Richard M. Ebeling and Jacob G. Hornberger (Fairfax, Va.: Future of Freedom Foundation, 1996), p. 58.

23. DeConde, *American Foreign Policy*, p. 344.

24. Bailey, *Diplomatic History*, p. 454.

25. Ibid.; Dulles, *The United States Since 1865*, p. 165.

26. Ibid.

27. Andrist, *The American Heritage History of the Confident Years*, p. 304.

28. *Messages and Papers of the Presidents*, vol. VIII, p. 6262.

29. George F. Kennan, *American Diplomacy 1900–1950*, expanded ed. (Chicago: University of Chicago Press, 1951), p. 9.

30. Ferrell, *American Diplomacy*, p. 197.

31. DeConde, *American Foreign Policy*, p. 343; Bailey, *Diplomatic History*, p. 456.

32. Bailey, *Diplomatic History*, p. 457.

33. Ibid., p. 455.

34. Orestes Ferrara, *The Last Spanish War: Revelations in "Diplomacy"* (New York: Paisley Press, 1937), p. 127.

35. Ferrell, *American Diplomacy*, p. 200.

36. Ibid.

37. Bailey, *Diplomatic History*, p. 461.

38. Ibid., 463; *Times* of London, April 14, 1898, p. 3:1.

39. DeConde, *American Foreign Policy*, p. 345.

40. Charles S. Olcott, *William McKinley*, vol. II (Boston: Houghton Mifflin, 1916), pp. 166–67.

41. Kennan, *American Diplomacy*, p. 13.

42. *Washington Post*, June 3, 1898.

43. Eric F. Goldman, *Rendezvous with Destiny: A History of Modern American Reform* (New York: Vintage Books, 1956), p. 54.

44. Ferrell, *American Diplomacy*, p. 205.

45. Ibid.

46. Joseph Stromberg, "The Spanish American War as Trial Run, or Empire as Its Own Justification," *The Costs of War: America's Pyrrhic Victories*, ed. John V. Denson (New Brunswick, N.J.: Transaction Publishers, 1997), p. 182.

47. Thomas Fleming, "From Bryan to Buchanan," *Chronicles*, March 1996, p. 10.

48. Julius W. Pratt, *Expansionists of 1898: The Acquisition of Hawaii and the Spanish Islands* (Baltimore: Johns Hopkins Press, 1936), p. 347.

49. Kennan, *American Diplomacy*, p. 18; Albert K. Weinberg, *Manifest Destiny: A Study of Nationalistic Expansionism in American History*

(Baltimore: Johns Hopkins Press, 1935), p. 306.

50. Bill Kauffman, "His Country's Own Heart's Blood: American Writers Confront War," *Costs of War*, p. 343; Bill Kauffman, *America First!: Its History, Culture, and Politics* (Amherst, N.Y.: Prometheus Books, 1995), p. 36.

51. John V. Denson, "War and American Freedom," *Costs of War*, p. 34.

52. C. Vann Woodward, *Tom Watson: Agrarian Rebel* (New York: Macmillan, 1938), p. 335.

53. Albert Galloway Keller and Maurice R. Davie, eds., *Essays of William Graham Sumner*, vol. 2 (New Haven: Yale University Press, 1934), pp. 266, 274.

54. Ibid., p. 303.

55. DeConde, *American Foreign Policy*, p. 354.

56. Melvin Small, *Democracy & Diplomacy: The Impact of Domestic Politics on U.S. Foreign Policy, 1789–1994* (Baltimore: Johns Hopkins University Press, 1996), p. 31.

57. Walter A. McDougall, *Promised Land, Crusader State: The American Encounter with the World Since 1776* (New York: Houghton Mifflin, 1997), p. 40.

58. Fleming, "From Bryan to Buchanan," p. 10.

59. DeConde, *American Foreign Policy*, p. 352.

60. Henry Cabot Lodge and Charles F. Redmond, eds., *Selections from the Correspondence of Theodore Roosevelt and Henry Cabot Lodge 1884–1918* (New York and London: Charles Scribner's Sons, 1925), vol. I, p. 384; McDougall, *Promised Land, Crusader State*, pp. 113, 239 (fn 35).

61. Bailey, *Diplomatic History*, p. 465.

62. Ibid., p. 478.

63. Kennan, *American Diplomacy*, p. 19.

64. Andrist, *The American Heritage History of the Confident Years*, p. 327.

65. Goldman, *Rendezvous with Destiny*, p. 54.

66. Margaret Leech, *In the Days of McKinley* (New York: Harper & Brothers, 1959), p. 258.

67. Goldman, *Rendezvous with Destiny*, p. 54; Dulles, *The United States Since 1865*, p. 168.

68. Dulles, *The United States Since 1865*, p. 168.

69. Brands, *What America Owes the World*, p. 35; Ferrell, *American Diplomacy*, pp. 172–73.

70. McDougall, *Let the Sea Make a Noise*, p. 437.

71. Denson, "War and American Freedom," *Costs of War*, p. 33.

72. Ferrell, *American Diplomacy*, p. 206; Bailey, *Diplomatic History*, p. 471.

73. Leech, *In the Days of McKinley*, p. 345. McKinley's remarks were not published until two years after the president was assassinated; some historians question whether this is truly a verbatim rendering of what McKinley actually said to the clergymen.

74. Newman C. Eberhardt, *A Summary of Catholic History*, vol. 2 (St. Louis: Herder, 1961), p. 84.

75. Kurt Glaser, "Nineteenth Century Messianism and Twentieth Century Interventionism," *Modern Age*, Winter 1973, p. 22.

76. Ferrell, *American Diplomacy*, p. 202.

77. Brands, *What America Owes the World*, p. 37.

78. Beard, *A Foreign Policy for America*, p. 72.

79. Ibid., p. 63.

80. Brands, *What America Owes the World*, p. 184.

81. Nathan Miller, *Star-Spangled Men: America's Ten Worst Presidents* (New York: Scribners, 1998), p. 56.

82. McDougall, *Let the Sea Make a Noise*, p. 452.

83. Bailey, *Diplomatic History*, p. 517.

Chapter 11: The New Imperialists

1. Holcomb B. Noble, "Henry Steele Commager, History Scholar and Defender of the Constitution, Is Dead at 95," *New York Times*, March 3, 1998, Section D, p. 23.

2. Thomas A. Bailey, *A Diplomatic History of the American People,* 7th ed. (New York: Meredith, 1964), p. 482; Robert H. Ferrell, *American Diplomacy: A History*, rev. and expanded ed. (New York: W. W. Norton, 1969), p. 412.

3. Alexander DeConde, *A History of American Foreign Policy* (New York: Charles Scribner's Sons, 1963), p. 366.

4. Ibid., p. 365.

5. Bailey, *Diplomatic History*, p. 483.

6. DeConde, *American Foreign Policy*, p. 366.

7. Peter Schran, "The Minor Significance of Commercial Relations Between the United States and China, 1850–1931," *America's China Trade in Historical Perspective*, eds. Ernest R. May and John K. Fairbank (Cambridge, Mass.: Harvard University Press, 1986), pp. 239–40, 253.

8. Henry Kissinger, *Diplomacy* (New York: Simon & Schuster, 1994), p. 41.

9. DeConde, *American Foreign Policy*, p. 372.

10. Bailey, *Diplomatic History*, p. 482.

11. H. W. Brands, *What America Owes the World: The Struggle for the Soul of Foreign Policy* (New York: Cambridge University Press, 1998), p. 244.

12. DeConde, *American Foreign Policy*, p. 373.

13. Ibid.

14. Ferrell, *American Diplomacy*, p. 476.

15. Ibid., p. 468.

16. Kissinger, *Diplomacy*, p. 40.

Chapter 12: "He Kept Us Out of War"

1. Walter A. McDougall, *Promised Land, Crusader State: The American Encounter with the World Since 1776* (New York: Houghton Mifflin, 1997), p. 122.

2. John V. Denson, "War and American Freedom," *The Costs of War: America's Pyrrhic Victories*, ed.

John V. Denson (New Brunswick, N.J.: Transaction Publishers, 1997), p. 33.

3. Ibid.

4. Henry Kissinger, *Diplomacy* (New York: Simon & Schuster, 1994), p. 43.

5. Theodore Roosevelt, "America First—a Phrase or a Fact?" *America and the World War: Fear God and Take Your Own Part* (New York: Charles Scribner's Sons, 1926), p. 261.

6. Ibid., p. 268.

7. Eric A. Nordlinger, *Isolationism Reconfigured: An American Foreign Policy for a New Century* (Princeton, N.J.: Princeton University Press, 1995), p. 55.

8. Quote 871, *Respectfully Quoted* (Washington: Library of Congress/Congressional Research Service, 1989), p. 167.

9. McDougall, *Promised Land, Crusader State*, p. 131.

10. Ray Stannard Baker, *Woodrow Wilson: Life and Letters*, vol. 6, *Facing War, 1915–1917* (Garden City, N.Y.: Doubleday, Doran, 1937), p. 249.

11. Ibid., pp. 249–50; Arthur S. Link, ed., *The Papers of Woodrow Wilson*, vol. 37, *May 9–August 7, 1916* (Princeton, N.J.: Princeton University Press, 1981), p. 223.

12. Baker, *Woodrow Wilson*, p. 251.

13. Ibid., p. 252.

14. Ibid., p. 253.

15. Ibid.

16. Ibid., p. 254.

17. Ibid., p. 257; Donald Bruce Johnson and Kirk H. Porter, compilers, *National Party Platforms 1840–1964* (Urbana: University of Illinois Press, 1966), p. 200.

18. Baker, *Woodrow Wilson*, p. 258.

19. Link, *The Papers of Woodrow Wilson*, vol. 38, *August 7–November 19, 1916*, pp. 132–33.

20. Melvin Small, *Democracy & Diplomacy: The Impact of Domestic Politics on U.S. Foreign Policy, 1789–1994* (Baltimore: Johns Hopkins University Press, 1996), pp. 43, 45.

21. Link, *The Papers of Woodrow Wilson*, vol. 5, *Campaigns for Progressivism and Peace, 1916–1917*, p. 104.

22. Ibid., pp. 104–05.

23. Ibid., p. 106.

24. Ibid., pp. 106–07.

25. Ibid., p. 107.

26. Ibid., p. 108.

27. Ibid., pp. 109–10.

28. Thomas A. Bailey, *A Diplomatic History of the American People,* 7th ed. (New York: Meredith, 1964), p. 588.

29. Link, *The Papers of Woodrow Wilson*, vol. 5, p. 111.

30. Ibid.

31. Clarence Manion, *The Conservative American: Yesterday, Today, and Tomorrow* (Shepherdsville, Ky.: Victor Publishing, 1966), p. 25.

Chapter 13: "Wilson's War"

1. Arthur S. Link, ed., *The Papers of Woodrow Wilson*, vol. 41, *January 24–April 6, 1917* (Princeton, N.J.: Princeton University Press, 1983), p. 527.

2. Peter Clarke, *Hope and Glory: Britain 1900–1990* (London: Penguin Books, 1996), p. 83.

3. Ralph Raico, "World War I: The Turning Point," *The Costs of War: America's Pyrrhic Victories*, ed. John V. Denson, 2nd expanded edition (New Brunswick, N.J.: Transaction Publishers, 1999), p. 220.

4. Ralph Raico, "American Foreign Policy—The Turning Point, 1898–1919," *The Failure of America's Foreign Wars*, eds. Richard M. Ebeling and Jacob G. Hornberger (Fairfax, Va.: The Future of Freedom Foundation, 1996), p. 67; Thomas A. Bailey, *A Diplomatic History of the American People*, 7th ed. (New York: Meredith, 1964), p. 567.

5. Walter A. McDougall, *Promised Land, Crusader State: The American Encounter with the World Since 1776* (New York: Houghton Mifflin, 1997), p. 126.

6. Elting E. Morison, ed., *The Letters of Theodore Roosevelt*, vol. II, *The Years of Preparation 1898–1900* (Cambridge, Mass.: Harvard University Press, 1951), p. 1112.

7. Richard W. Leopold and Arthur S. Link, eds., *Problems in American History* (Englewood Cliffs, N.J.: Prentice-Hall, 1957), p. 492.

8. Robert H. Ferrell, *American Diplomacy: A History*, rev. and expanded ed. (New York: W. W. Norton, 1969), p. 492.

9. William Henry Chamberlin, *America's Second Crusade* (Chicago: Henry Regnery Company, 1950), p. 5.

10. Edward Grey, *Viscount Grey of Fallodon, Twenty-Five Years: 1892–1916* (New York: Frederick A. Stokes, 1925), pp. 101–02, 108–11; Raico, "World War I: The Turning Point," p. 226.

11. Chamberlin, *America's Second Crusade*, p. 10.

12. Bailey, *Diplomatic History*, p. 565.

13. Ibid.

14. Raico, "World War I: The Turning Point," p. 222.

15. Wayne S. Cole, *An Interpretative History of American Foreign Relations* (Homewood, Ill.: Dorsey Press, 1968), p. 355.

16. Robert Lansing, *War Memoirs of Robert Lansing* (Indianapolis, New York: Bobbs-Merrill, 1935), p. 128. Quoted in Colin Simpson, *The Lusitania* (Boston: Little Brown, 1972), p. 55.

17. H. W. Brands, *What America Owes the World: The Struggle for the Soul of Foreign Policy* (New York: Cambridge University Press, 1998), p. 58.

18. Ibid.

19. Edwin Borchard and William Potter Lage, *Neutrality for the*

United States, 2nd ed. (New
Haven:Yale University Press,
1940), pp. 221, 229.

20. Cole, *Interpretive History,*
pp. 357–58.

21. Charles Callan Tansill, *America
Goes to War* (Boston: Little,
Brown, 1938), p. 258.

22. Ibid., p. 429.

23. Brands, *What America Owes the
World,* p. 70.

24. Tansill, *America Goes to War,* pp.
258–59; William Jennings Bryan
and Mary Baird Bryan, *The
Memoirs of William Jennings Bryan*
(Philadelphia: John C. Winston,
1925), pp. 395–99.

25. Robert Tucker, "An Inner Circle
of One: Woodrow Wilson and His
Advisers," *National Interest,* Spring
1998, p. 23.

26. Raico, "World War I: The Turning
Point," p. 219.

27. Tucker, "An Inner Circle of
One," p. 13.

28. Ibid., p. 15.

29. Ibid., p. 26.

30. Bailey, *Diplomatic History,* p. 583.

31. Ibid.

32. Tansill, *America Goes to War,*
p. 653.

33. Bailey, *Diplomatic History,* p. 575.

34. Ibid., p. 574.

35. Ibid.

36. John Milton Cooper, *The Vanity of
Power: American Isolationism and the
First World War, 1914–1917*
(Westport, Conn.: Greenwood
Publishing Corp., 1969), p. 197.

37. Ibid.

38. McDougall, *Promised Land,
Crusader State,* p. 130.

39. Arthur S. Link, ed., *The Papers of
Woodrow Wilson,* vol. 40, *November
20, 1916–January 23, 1917*
(Princeton, N.J.: Princeton
University Press, 1982), p. 409.

40. Ibid., pp. 408–09.

41. Foster Rhea Dulles, *The United
States Since 1865* (Ann Arbor:
University of Michigan Press,
1959), p. 249.

42. Barbara Tuchman, *The
Zimmermann Telegram,* new ed.
(New York, Macmillan, 1966),
p. 139.

43. Ibid., p. 141.

44. Link, *The Papers of Woodrow
Wilson,* vol. 41, pp. 526–27.

45. Link, *The Papers of Woodrow
Wilson,* vol. 37, *May 9–August 7,
1916,* p. 113.

46. Robert H. Ferrell, *American
Diplomacy: A History,* rev. and
expanded ed. (New York: W. W.
Norton, 1969), p. 501.

47. Link, *The Papers of Woodrow
Wilson,* vol. 41, p. 525.

48. Brands, *What America Owes the
World,* p. 194.

49. Ferrell, *American Diplomacy,* rev.
and expanded ed., p. 517.

50. Henry A. Kissinger, *Diplomacy*
(New York: Simon & Schuster,
1994), p. 225.

51. C. Paul Vincent, *The Politics of
Hunger: The Allied Blockade of
Germany, 1915–1919* (Athens:
Ohio University Press, 1985),
p. 79; Kissinger, *Diplomacy,* p. 239.

52. Dulles, *The United States Since 1865*, p. 268.

53. Bailey, *Diplomatic History*, p. 611.

54. Robert H. Ferrell in note to PJB (Buchanan Files).

55. Raico, "World War I: The Turning Point," p. 240.

56. Ibid., 203.

57. Erik von Kuehnelt-Leddihn, *Leftism Revisited: From De Sade and Marx to Hitler and Pol Pot* (Washington: Regnery Gateway, 1990), p. 218.

58. Quote based on Roy Denman, *Missed Chances: Britain & Europe in the Twentieth Century* (London: Indigo, 1997), pp. 47–48; Ray Stannard Baker, *Woodrow Wilson & World Settlement*, vol. 2 (Garden City, N.Y.: Doubleday, Page, 1923), p. 501.

59. Otto Friedrich, *Before the Deluge: A Portrait of Berlin in the 1920s* (New York: Harper & Row, 1972), pp. 49–50.

60. Denman, *Missed Chances*, p. 34.

61. Friedrich, *Before the Deluge*, p. 68.

62. W. H. Auden, *The Collected Poetry of W. H. Auden* (New York: Random House, 1945), p. 57.

63. John Maynard Keynes, *The Economic Consequences of the Peace* (London: Macmillan, 1919), p. 34.

64. Marvin Olasky, "Woodrow Wilson's Folly: The Private and Public Life of a President," *Philanthropy, Culture & Society*, Capital Research Center, March 1998, p. 6.

65. Count Harry Kessler, *Walter Rathenau: His Life and Work* (New York: Howard Fertig, 1969), p. 271.

66. Link, *The Papers of Woodrow Wilson*, vol. 40, p. 536.

67. George F. Kennan, *American Diplomacy* (Chicago: University of Chicago Press, 1951), p. 69.

68. Keynes, *Economic Consequences of the Peace*, p. 279.

69. Link, *The Papers of Woodrow Wilson*, vol. 56, *March 17–April 4, 1919*, p. 260; Denman, *Missed Chances*, p. 41.

70. Kissinger, *Diplomacy*, p. 272.

71. John Greenleaf Whittier, as quoted in John Bartlett, *Familiar Quotations*, 16th edition (Boston: Little, Brown and Company, 1992), p. 443.

72. Bailey, *Diplomatic History*, p. 615.

73. John Steele Gordon, *Hamilton's Blessing: The Extraordinary Life and Times of Our National Debt* (New York: Walker, 1997), p. 103.

74. Winston S. Churchill, *The World Crisis*, vol. 2 (New York: Charles Scribner's Sons, 1929), pp. 1–2.

75. Dulles, *The United States Since 1865*, p. 271; Karl Schriftgiesser, *The Gentleman from Massachusetts: Henry Cabot Lodge* (Boston: Little, Brown, 1944), p. 311.

76. Bailey, *Diplomatic History*, p. 606.

77. Link, *The Papers of Woodrow Wilson*, vol. 55, *February 8–March 16, 1919*, p. 418.

78. McDougall, *Promised Land, Crusader State*, p. 142.

79. Bailey, *Diplomatic History*, p. 614.

80. Robert H. Ferrell, *American Diplomacy: A History* (New York: W. W. Norton, 1959), p. 311.

81. "This is Not Peace," *New Republic*, May 24, 1919, cover.

82. "A Punic Peace," *New Republic*, May 24, 1919, p. 71; "Peace At Any Price," *New Republic*, May 24, 1919, p. 101.

83. "Peace At Any Price," p. 100.

84. Eric F. Goldman, *Rendezvous with Destiny: A History of Modern American Reform* (New York: Vintage Books, 1956), pp. 206–09; Ferrell, *American Diplomacy*, p. 299.

85. Goldman, *Rendezvous with Destiny*, p. 206.

86. Paul Johnson, *A History of the American People* (New York: HarperCollins, 1997), p. 652.

87. Link, *The Papers of Woodrow Wilson*, vol. 56., p. 398.

88. Roland N. Stromberg, *Collective Security and American Foreign Policy: From the League of Nations to NATO* (New York: Frederick A. Praeger, 1963), p. 30.

89. Robert Lansing, *The Peace Negotiations: A Personal Narrative* (Boston: Houghton Mifflin, 1921), p. 139.

90. John A. Garraty, *Henry Cabot Lodge: A Biography* (New York: Alfred A. Knopf, 1968), p. 312.

91. Johnson, *A History of the American People*, p. 653.

92. Olasky, "Woodrow Wilson's Folly," p. 7.

93. Ibid.

94. Ibid.

95. Quote based on Arthur Bernon Tourtellot, ed., *Woodrow Wilson: Selections for Today* (New York: Duell, Sloan, and Pierce, 1945), p. 238; Link, *The Papers of Woodrow Wilson*, vol. 63, *September 4–November 5, 1919*, p. 42.

96. McDougall, *Promised Land, Crusader State*, p. 144.

97. Johnson, *A History of the American People*, p. 653.

98. Bailey, *Diplomatic History*, p. 615.

99. William Appleman Williams, "The Legend of Isolationism," *The Shaping of American Diplomacy*, ed. William Appleman Williams (Chicago: Rand McNally, 1956), p. 660.

100. McDougall, *Promised Land, Crusader State*, p. 144.

101. Bailey, *Diplomatic History*, p. 624.

102. McDougall, *Promised Land, Crusader State*, pp. 144–45.

Chapter 14: Disarmament Decade

1. William Appleman Williams, "The Legend of Isolationism," *The Shaping of Foreign Policy*, ed. William Appleman Williams (Chicago: Rand McNally, 1956), p. 657.

2. A. J. P. Taylor, *The Origins of the Second World War* (New York: Atheneum, 1961), p. vi.

3. Melvin Small, *Democracy & Diplomacy: The Impact of Domestic Politics on U.S. Foreign Policy, 1789–1994* (Baltimore: Johns

Hopkins University Press, 1996), p. 53.

4. Thomas A Bailey, *A Diplomatic History of the American People*, 7th ed. (New York: Meredith, 1964), pp. 639–40.

5. Mark Sullivan, *Our Times: The United States 1900–1925*, vol. vi, *The Twenties* (New York: Charles Scribner's Sons, 1935), p. 193.

6. Foster Rhea Dulles, *The United States Since 1865* (Ann Arbor: University of Michigan Press, 1959), p. 280; Bailey, *Diplomatic History*, p. 647.

7. Bailey, *Diplomatic History*, pp. 643–44.

8. Robert H. Ferrell, *American Diplomacy: A History* (New York: W. W. Norton, 1959), p. 339.

9. Walter Lippmann, *U.S. Foreign Policy: Shield of the Republic* (Boston: Little, Brown, 1943), p. x.

10. *Saturday Evening Post*, March 26, 1921.

11. George W. Norris, Governor of the Federal Reserve Bank of Philadelphia, August 6, 1921.

12. *Dallas News*, October 12, 1921.

13. Bailey, *Diplomatic History*, p. 648.

14. Frederick W. Marks III, *Wind Over Sand: The Diplomacy of Franklin Roosevelt* (Athens, Ga.: University of Georgia Press, 1988), p. 8.

15. Ibid.

16. Ferrell, *American Diplomacy*, p. 331.

17. Henry A. Kissinger, *Diplomacy* (New York: Simon & Schuster, 1994), p. 374.

18. Alexander DeConde, *A History of American Foreign Policy* (New York: Charles Scribner's Sons, 1963), p. 496.

19. *Public Papers of the Presidents of the United States: Herbert Hoover, March 4 to December 31, 1929* (Washington: Government Printing Office, 1974), pp. 165–66.

20. Ray Lyman Wilbur and Arthur Mastick Hyde, *The Hoover Policies* (New York: Charles Scribner's Sons, 1937), p. 593.

21. Bailey, *Diplomatic History*, p. 653.

22. Robert Gordon Kaufman, *Arms Control During the Pre-Nuclear Era* (New York: Columbia University Press, 1990), p. 149.

23. Samuel I. Rosenman, compiler, *The Public Papers and Addresses of Franklin D. Roosevelt*, vol. 3, *The Advance of Recovery and Reform, 1934* (New York: Random House, 1938), p. 165.

24. Kissinger, *Diplomacy*, p. 372.

25. Otto Friedrich, *Before the Deluge: A Portrait of Berlin in the 1920s* (New York: Harper & Row, 1972), p. 127.

26. Ferrell, *American Diplomacy*, pp. 324, 327; Dulles, *United States Since 1865*, p. 285; Bailey, *Diplomatic History*, p. 661.

27. DeConde, *American Foreign Policy*, p. 538.

28. Wayne S. Cole, *An Interpretive History of American Foreign Relations* (Homewood, Ill.: Dorsey Press, 1968), p. 423.

29. DeConde, *American Foreign Policy*,
    p. 540.
30. Williams, "The Legend of
    Isolationism," pp. 658–59.
31. Douglas MacArthur, *Reminiscences*
    (New York: McGraw-Hill, 1964),
    p. 101.
32. Dulles, *United States Since 1865*,
    p. 281.
33. Michael Hunt, *Crises in U.S.
    Foreign Policy: An International
    History Reader* (New Haven: Yale
    University Press, 1996), p. 74.
34. Wilbur and Hyde, *The Hoover
    Policies*, p. 601.

**Chapter 15: The Zeal of the
Convert**

1. Arthur M. Vandenberg, Jr., and Joe
   Alex Morris, eds., *The Private
   Papers of Senator Vandenberg*
   (Boston: Houghton Mifflin,
   1952), p. 10.
2. *Papers Respecting Negotiations for an
   Anglo-French Pact* (London: His
   Majesty's Stationery Office, 1924),
   pp. 112–13.
3. Henry A. Kissinger, *Diplomacy*
   (New York: Simon & Schuster,
   1993), p. 273; A. J. P. Taylor, *The
   Origins of the Second World War*
   (New York: Atheneum, 1961),
   p. 54.
4. A. J. P. Taylor, *The Origins of the
   Second World War* (New York:
   Atheneum, 1961), p. 67.
5. Ibid., p. 76.
6. Ibid., pp. 61, 66–67.
7. Samuel I. Rosenman, compiler,
   The Public Papers and Addresses of

    Franklin D. Roosevelt, vol. 8,
    War—and Neutrality (New York:
    Macmillan, 1941), p. 516.
8. Robert H. Ferrell, *American
   Diplomacy: A History*, rev. and
   expanded ed. (New York: W. W.
   Norton, 1969), p. 601.
9. Rosenman, *The Public Papers and
   Addresses of Franklin D. Roosevelt,*
   vol. 5, *The People Approve* (New
   York: Random House, 1938),
   pp. 288–89.
10. Joseph Alsop, *FDR: A Centennial
    Remembrance* (New York: Viking
    Press, 1982), p. 53.
11. Gallup Poll, January 20–25, 1937,
    Public Perspective, August/
    September 1997, p. 21.
12. Roy Denman, *Missed Chances:
    Britain & Europe in the Twentieth
    Century* (London: Indigo, 1996),
    pp. 71–72.
13. H. W. Brands, *What America Owes
    the World: The Struggle for the Soul
    of Foreign Policy* (New York:
    Cambridge University Press,
    1998), p. 158.
14. Denman, *Missed Chances*, p. 64.
15. John Toland, *Hitler* (Garden City,
    N.Y.: Doubleday, 1976),
    pp. 398–89.
16. Taylor, *Origins of the Second World
    War*, pp. 99–100.
17. Toland, *Hitler*, p. 409.
18. Winston S. Churchill, *Great
    Contemporaries* (Chicago:
    University of Chicago Press,
    1973), p. 265.
19. Ibid.
20. Ibid., pp. 268, 261.

21. Kissinger, *Diplomacy*, p. 381.

22. Nicholas John Cull, *Selling War: The British Propaganda Campaign against American 'Neutrality' in World War II* (New York: Oxford University Press, 1995), p. 21; Denman, *Missed Chances*, p.118.

23. William Henry Chamberlin, *America's Second Crusade* (Chicago: Henry Regnery Company, 1950), p. 99.

24 Alan Campbell Johnson, *Sir Anthony Eden* (London: Robert Hale, Ltd., 1955), pp. 159–60.

25. Taylor, *Origins of the Second World War*, p. 189.

26. Ibid., pp. 69–70.

27. Alan S. Milward, *War, Economy, and Society 1939–1945* (Chicago: University of Chicago Press, 1979), p. 47.

28. Frederick W. Marks III, *Wind over Sand: The Diplomacy of Franklin Roosevelt* (Athens, Ga.: University of Georgia Press, 1988), p. 112.

29. Ibid.

30. Ibid.

31. Chamberlin, *America's Second Crusade*, p. 57.

32. Denman, *Missed Chances*, p. 3.

33. John Lewis Gaddis, *We Now Know: Rethinking Cold War History* (Oxford: Clarendon Press, 1997), pp. 9–12, fn.'s pp. 298–99; Alan Bullock, *Hitler and Stalin: Parallel Lives* (New York: Alfred Knopf, 1992), pp. 392, 507; *Encyclopaedia Judaica*, vol. 5 C-Dh (Jerusalem: Macmillan/Keter, 1971), p. 78; Colon Cross, *Adolf Hitler*

(London: Hodder and Stoughton, 1973), pp. 218–21; Bernd Wegner, "The 'Aristocracy of National Socialism': The Role of the *SS* in National Socialist Germany," *Aspects of the Third Reich*, ed. H. W. Koch (London: Macmillan, 1985), p. 443.

34. Alexander DeConde, *A History of American Foreign Policy* (New York: Charles Scribner's Sons, 1963), p. 576; Gene Smith, *The Dark Summer: An Intimate History of the Events That Led to World War II* (New York: Macmillan, 1987), p. 185.

35. Smith, *The Dark Summer*, p. 164.

36. Ibid., p. 163.

37. George F. Kennan, *American Diplomacy, 1900–1950* (Chicago: University of Chicago Press, 1951), pp. 76–77.

38. Adam Zamoyski, *The Polish Way: A Thousand-Year History of the Poles and Their Culture* (London: John Murray Ltd., 1987), p. 353.

39. Denman, *Missed Chances*, p. 65.

40. Ibid., p. 121.

41. Ibid., p. 151.

42. Rosenman, *Public Papers and Addresses of Roosevelt*, vol. 8, pp. 463–64.

43. "The *Fortune* Survey: Supplement II on War," *Fortune*, November 1939, n.p.

44. Cull, *Selling War*, p. 34.

45. Chamberlin, *America's Second Crusade*, pp. 49–50.

46. Hadley Cantril, ed., *Public Opinion 1935–1946* (Princeton, N.J.:

Princeton University Press, 1951), p. 971.

47. Henry R. Luce, "The American Century," *Life*, February 17, 1941, p. 63.

48. Donald Bruce Johnson and Kirk R. Porter, compilers, *National Party Platforms 1840–1964* (Urbana: University of Illinois Press, 1966), p. 382.

49. Robert H. Ferrell, *American Diplomacy: A History* (New York: W. W. Norton, 1959), p. 376.

50. Robert Smith Thompson, *A Time for War: Franklin Delano Roosevelt and the Path to Pearl Harbor* (New York: Prentice Hall Press, 1991), p. 276.

51. Rosenman, *Public Papers and Addresses of Roosevelt,* vol. 9, *War—and Aid to Democracies* (New York: Macmillan, 1941), p. 517.

52. Wayne S. Cole, *America First: The Battle Against Intervention 1940–1941* (Madison: University of Wisconsin Press, 1953), pp. 15–16.

53. Ibid., p. 16.

54. Kenneth S. Davis, *The Hero: Charles A. Lindbergh and the American Dream* (Garden City, N.Y.: Doubleday, 1959), p. 400.

55. Ibid.

56. Bill Kauffman, *America First!: Its History, Culture and Politics* (Amherst, N.Y.: Prometheus Books, 1995), p. 18.

57. Nigel Hamilton, *JFK: Reckless Youth* (New York: Random House, 1992), p. 287.

58. Justin D. Doenecke, ed., *In Danger Undaunted: The Anti-Interventionist Movement of 1940–1941 as Revealed in the Papers of the America First Committee* (Stanford, Cal.: Hoover Institution Press, 1990), p. 8; Justin D. Doenecke, "The America First Committee," *Chronicles,* December 1991, pp. 18–19.

59. Oswald Garrison Villard, "Issues and Men," *Nation,* June 29, 1940, p. 782.

60. Ibid.

61. Kauffman, *America First!* p. 19.

62. Mark Lincoln Chadwin, *The Warhawks: American Interventionists Before Pearl Harbor* (New York: W. W. Norton, 1968), p. 208.

63. Ibid., p. 125.

64. Ibid., p. 128.

65. Ibid., pp. 127, 129.

66. Ibid., p. 213.

67. Ibid., p. 210.

68. Ibid., pp. 19–20; Kauffman quotes Murray Rothbard, "The Foreign Policy of the Old Right," *Journal of Libertarian Studies,* Winter 1978, p. 88.

69. Wayne S. Cole, *Determinism and American Foreign Relations During the Franklin D. Roosevelt Era* (Lanham, Md.: University Press of America, 1995), p. 40.

70. *Public Papers of the Presidents of the United States: George Bush, 1991 Book II, July 1 to December 31, 1991* (Washington: Government Printing Office, 1992), p. 1574.

71. Cole, *Determinism,* p. 45.

72. Kissinger, *Diplomacy*, pp. 425–26.

73. Ibid., pp. 425–26; James P. Warburg, *Turning Points Toward Peace* (New York: Current Affairs Press, 1955), p. 40.

74. Hanson W. Baldwin, *Great Mistakes of the War* (New York: Harper, 1949), p. 10.

75. Wayne S. Cole, *Roosevelt and the Isolationists, 1932–1945* (Lincoln: University of Nebraska Press, 1983), pp. 417, 416.

76. Ibid., p. 417.

77. Rosenman, *Public Papers and Addresses of Roosevelt,* vol. 10, *The Call to Battle Stations* (New York: Harper Brothers, 1950), pp. 384–85.

78. Ibid., p. 390.

79. Cole, *Roosevelt and the Isolationists,* pp. 443–44; Kissinger, *Diplomacy,* p. 392; Ferrell, *American Diplomacy* (1959), pp. 382–83.

80. Ralph Raico, "The Case for an America First Foreign Policy," *The Failure of America's Foreign Wars* (Fairfax, Va.: Future of Freedom Foundation, 1997), p. 27.

81. Martin Gilbert, *Winston S. Churchill,* vol. vi, *Finest Hour, 1939–1941* (Boston: Houghton Mifflin, 1983), p. 1188, fn. 2.

82. Rosenman, *Public Papers and Addresses of Roosevelt,* vol. 10, p. 418; Ferrell, *American Diplomacy,* (1959), p. 383.

83. Rosenman, *Public Papers and Addresses of Roosevelt,* vol. 10, p. 440.

84. Cull, *Selling War,* p. 172.

85. Thomas A. Bailey, *The Man in the Street: The Impact of American Public Opinion on Foreign Policy* (New York: Macmillan, 1948), p. 12.

Chapter 16: Back Door to War

1. Harold L. Ickes, *The Secret Diary of Harold L. Ickes,* vol. 3, *The Lowering Clouds, 1939–1941* (New York: Simon & Schuster, 1955), p. 630.

2. Wayne S. Cole, *Roosevelt and the Isolationists 1932–1945* (Lincoln: University of Nebraska Press, 1983), p. 254.

3. Ibid., p. 258.

4. Bruce R. Bartlett, *Cover-Up: The Politics of Pearl Harbor— 1941–1946* (New Rochelle, N.Y.: Arlington House, 1978), p. 38.

5. Ibid.

6. Ibid.

7. Cole, *Roosevelt and the Isolationists,* p. 489.

8. Walter McDougall, *Let the Sea Make a Noise: Four Hundred Years of Cataclysm, Conquest, War and Folly in the North Pacific* (New York: Avon Books, 1993), pp. 606–07.

9. Walter Lippmann, *U.S. War Aims* (Boston: Little, Brown, 1944), p. 23.

10. Hadley Cantril, ed., *Public Opinion 1935–1946* (Princeton, N.J.: Princeton University Press, 1951), p. 975.

11. Richard Current, *Secretary Stimson: A Study in Statecraft* (New Brunswick, N.J.: Rutgers University Press, 1954), pp. 4, 155.

12. Raymond A. Esthus, "President

Roosevelt's Commitment to Intervene in a Pacific War," *Mississippi Valley Historical Review*, June 1963, p. 34; Bartlett, *Cover-Up*, pp. 59–60.

13. Joseph C. Grew, *Turbulent Era: A Diplomatic Record of Forty Years, 1904–1945*, ed. Walter Johnson (Freeport, N.Y.: Books for Libraries Press, 1952), p. 1329.

14. Ibid., p. 1355.

15. Ibid., p. 1334.

16. William Henry Chamberlin, *America's Second Crusade* (Chicago: Henry Regnery Company, 1950), p. 166.

17. Ibid., p. 167.

18. Foster Rhea Dulles, *The United States Since 1865* (Ann Arbor: University of Michigan Press, 1959), p. 441.

19. Cordell Hull, *The Memoirs of Cordell Hull* (New York: Macmillan, 1948), vol. 2, p. 1102.

20. Paul Kennedy, *The Rise and Fall of the Great Powers: Economic Change and Military Conflict from 1500 to 2000* (New York: Random House, 1987), p. 330.

21. Cesare Salmaggi and Alfredo Pallavisini, *2194 Days of War* (New York: Gallery, 1979), p. 174.

22. Sheldon Richman, "New Deal Nemesis: The Old Right Jeffersonians," *Independent Review*, Fall 1996, pp. 216–217.

23. Sheldon Richman, "The America First Committee," *Freedom Daily*, April 1995, p. 26.

24. Samuel I. Rosenman, compiler,

The Public Papers and Addresses of Franklin D. Roosevelt, vol. 9, *War—and Aid to Democracies* (New York: Macmillan, 1941), p. 638.

25. Ibid., p. 666.

26. Wayne S. Cole, *Determinism and American Foreign Relations During the Franklin D. Roosevelt Era* (Lanham, Md.: University Press of America, 1995), p. 41.

27. H. Stuart Hughes, "A Question of Confidence," *New York Review of Books*, February 17, 1977, p. 20.

28. Cole, *Determinism*, p. 42.

29. Thomas A. Bailey, *The Man in the Street: The Impact of American Public Opinion on Foreign Policy* (New York: Macmillan, 1948), pp. 11–13.

30. Anthony Kubek, *How the Far East Was Lost: American Policy and the Creation of Communist China, 1941–1949* (Chicago: Henry Regnery Company, 1963), pp. 108, 111.

31. Ibid., p. 112; *Congressional Record*, February 21, 1949, p. A993.

32. Chamberlin, *America's Second Crusade*, p. 183.

Chapter 17: America's Longest War

1. John Bartlett, *Familiar Quotations*, 16th edition (Boston: Little, Brown and Company, 1992), p. 622.

2. Ibid., p. 690.

3. Ralph Raico, "American Foreign Policy—The Turning Point, 1898–1919," *The Failure of*

America's Foreign Wars, eds. Richard M. Ebeling and Jacob G. Hornberger (Fairfax, Va.: Future of Freedom Foundation, 1996), p. 75.

4. A. J. P. Taylor, *The Origins of the Second World War* (New York: Atheneum, 1961), p. xviii.

5. Ralph Raico, "Rethinking Churchill," *The Costs of War: America's Pyrrhic Victories*, ed. John V. Denson, 2nd expanded edition (New Brunswick, N.J.: Transaction Publishers, 1999), p. 279.

6. Ibid.

7. Henry Regnery, "War and Leadership," *Modern Age*, Summer 1989, pp. 205–06.

8. Ibid., p. 205.

9. Ibid., p. 206.

10. Robert Nisbet, *Roosevelt and Stalin: The Failed Courtship* (Washington: Regnery Gateway, 1988), p. 73.

11. Ibid., p. 6.

12. Henry A. Kissinger, *Diplomacy* (New York: Simon & Schuster, 1994), p. 417.

13. Richard M. Ebeling, "Covering the Map of the World—The Half Century Legacy of the Yalta Conference," *The Failure of America's Foreign Wars*, p. 184.

14. Ibid., pp. 184–85.

15. William Henry Chamberlin, *America's Second Crusade* (Chicago: Henry Regnery Company, 1950), pp. 140–41.

16. Alfred-Maurice De Zayas, *The German Expellees: Victims in War and Peace* (New York: St. Martin's Press, 1986), p. xvii.

17. William Manchester, *The Glory and the Dream: A Narrative History of America 1932–1972* (New York: Bantam Books, 1974), p. 405.

18. Melvin Small, *Democracy & Diplomacy: The Impact of Domestic Politics on U.S. Foreign Policy, 1789–1994* (Baltimore: Johns Hopkins University Press, 1996), p. 83.

19. Manchester, *The Glory and the Dream*, p. 409.

20. Eric F. Goldman, *The Crucial Decade—And After: America, 1945–1960* (New York: Random House, 1960), p. 113.

21. Walter A. McDougall, *Promised Land, Crusader State: The American Encounter with the World Since 1776* (New York: Houghton Mifflin, 1997), p. 70.

22. Richard Reeves, *President Kennedy: Profile of Power* (New York: Simon & Schuster, 1993), p. 31.

23. Norman B. Hannah, *The Key to Failure: Laos and the Vietnam War* (New York: Madison Books, 1987), p. 233.

24. J. Bowyer Bell, *The Myth of the Guerrilla: Revolutionary Theory and Malpractice* (New York: Alfred A. Knopf, 1971), pp. 3–60.

25. Trevor Newitt Dupuy, *The Military History of the Chinese Civil War* (New York: Franklin Watts, 1969), p. 62.

26. H. R. McMaster, *Dereliction of*

Duty: Lyndon Johnson, Robert McNamara, The Joint Chiefs of Staff and the Lies That Led to Vietnam (New York: HarperCollins, 1997), p. 49.

27. Peter W. Rodman, *More Precious Than Peace: The Cold War and the Struggle for the Third World* (New York: Scribner, 1994), p. 120.

28. Ibid., p. 121.

29. Douglas A. Macgregor, *Breaking the Phalanx: A New Design for Landpower in the 21st Century* (Westport, Conn.: Praeger, 1997), p. 17.

30. Harry G. Summers, Jr., *On Strategy: A Critical Analysis of the Vietnam War* (Novato, Cal.: Presidio Press, 1982), p. 129.

31. Rodman, *More Precious Than Peace*, pp. 130–31.

32. Robert A. Scalapino, "Asia in a Global Context: Strategic Issues for the Soviet Union," *The Soviet Far East Military Buildup: Nuclear Dilemmas and Asian Security*, eds. Richard H. Solomon and Masataka Kosaka (Dover, Mass: Auburn House, 1986), p. 26.

33. Patrick J. Buchanan, "America First—and Second, and Third," *National Interest*, Spring 1990, p. 77.

34. Ibid.

35. Ibid.

36. John Bartlett, *Familiar Quotations*, 16th edition (Boston: Little, Brown and Company, 1992), p. 425.

37. Buchanan, "America First," pp. 78–79.

38. Ibid., p. 79.

Chapter 18: "Passionate Attachments" and Press Power

1. Theodore H. White, *The Making of the President 1972* (New York, Atheneum, 1973), p. 245.

2. Paul Johnson, *A History of the American People* (New York: HarperCollins, 1997), p. 140.

3. Ibid., pp. 140, 154.

4. Arthur M. Schlesinger, Jr., *The Disuniting of America: Reflections on a Multicultural Society* (New York: W. W. Norton, 1991), p. 118.

5. Daniel Boorstin, ed., *An American Primer* (New York: New American Library, 1968), p. 224.

6. Melvin Small, *Democracy & Diplomacy: The Impact of Domestic Politics on U.S. Foreign Policy, 1789–1994* (Baltimore: Johns Hopkins University Press, 1996), p. 32.

7. Theodore Roosevelt, *America and the World War: Fear God and Take Your Own Part* (New York: Charles Scribner's Sons, 1926), p. 201.

8. Small, *Democracy & Diplomacy*, p. 46.

9. Bill Kauffman, *America First!: Its History, Culture, and Politics* (Amherst, N.Y.: Prometheus Books, 1995), pp. 20–21; Kenneth S. Davis, *The Hero: Charles A. Lindbergh and the American Dream* (New York: Doubleday, 1959), p. 411.

10. Jacob Heilbrunn, "Huntington's Disease," *New Republic*, December 8, 1997, p. 4.

11. Small, *Democracy & Diplomacy*, p. 100.

12. Kauffman, *America First!*, p. 152.

13. James Schlesinger, "Fragmentation and Hubris," *National Interest*, Fall 1997, p. 5.

14. Ibid.

15. Samuel P. Huntington, "The Erosion of American National Interests," *Foreign Affairs*, September/October 1997, p. 9.

16. Ibid., p. 11.

17. Ibid., p. 8.

18. Heilbrunn, "Huntington's Disease," p. 5.

19. Huntington, "Erosion of American National Interests," p. 10.

20. Ibid., p. 11.

21. Chas. W. Freeman, Jr., "Foreign Policy for Sale...," *Wall Street Journal*, June 16, 1998, p. A18.

22. Small, *Democracy & Diplomacy*, p. xvi.

23. Robert Blake, *Disraeli* (New York: St. Martin's Press, 1967), p. 592.

24. Ibid., p. 593.

25. Ibid., p. 594.

26. Ibid., p. 598.

27. Ibid., p. 602.

28. Virginia Cowles, *The Russian Dagger: Cold War in the Days of the Czars* (New York: Harper & Row, 1969), pp. 97–98.

29. William Hawkins, "South Africa: Another Balkan Crisis," *Continuity: A Journal of History*, Fall 1987, p. 43.

30. Blake, *Disraeli*, p. 606.

31. Richard T. Shannon, *Gladstone and the Bulgarian Agitation 1876* (Hamden, Conn.: Archon Book, 1975), p. 45; William Hawkins, "National Interests Do Not Beckon U.S. to Bosnia," *Human Events*, October 30, 1993.

32. Hawkins, "South Africa: Another Balkan Crisis," p. 41.

33. Cowles, *The Russian Dagger*, p. 113.

34. R. J. Rummel, *Death by Government* (New Brunswick, N.J.: Transaction Books, 1994), p. 221.

35. David Fromkin, *A Peace to End All Peace: Creating the Modern Middle East 1914–1922* (New York: Henry Holt, 1989), p. 212.

36. Hawkins, "National Interests Do Not Beckon U.S. to Bosnia."

37. Frank Johnson, "Blood, Iron and Bibles," *National Interest,* Fall 1998, p. 12.

38. Larry Witham, "Activists Fight Battle for Religious Liberty All Over the World," *Washington Times*, June 14, 1998, p. A6.

39. Boorstin, *An American Primer*, p. 224.

40. Ibid.

41. Michael Skapinker, "Boeing Keen for New Joint Ventures with BAe," *Financial Times*, March 12, 1997, p. 18.

42. Michael Skapinker, "Flight Plan From Seattle," *Financial Times*, March 12, 1997, p. 13.

43. Ibid.

44. Ibid.

45. "The Appease China Sweepstakes (Cont.)," *Weekly Standard,* September 8, 1997, p. 4.

46. A.W. Clausen, "The International Corporation: An Executive View," *The Annals of the American Academy of Political and Social Science,* September 1972, p. 21.

47. Richard J. Barnet and Ronald E. Müller, *Global Reach: The Power of the Multinational Corporations* (New York: Simon & Schuster, 1974), pp. 18–19.

48. Ibid., p. 16.

49. Ibid.

50. Zbigniew Brzezinski, *Between Two Ages: America's Role in the Technetronic Age* (New York: Viking Press, 1970), p. 58.

51. Ibid., p. 59.

52. James Schlesinger, "Raise the Anchor or Lower the Ship: Defense Budgeting and Planning," *National Interest,* Fall 1998, p. 7.

Chapter 19: Claimants to Kennan's Legacy

1. William Hawkins, "The Surrender of Political and Military Sovereignty," *Chronicles,* October 1995, p. 18.

2. Wesley T. Wooley, *Alternatives to Anarchy: American Supranationalism Since World War II* (Bloomington: Indiana University Press, 1988), p. 169.

3. Ibid., p. 168.

4. Strobe Talbott, "The Birth of the Global Nation," *Time,* July 20, 1992, p. 70.

5. Ibid., p. 71.

6. Richard N. Gardner, "The Hard Road to World Order," *Foreign Affairs,* April 1974, p. 558.

7. David Callahan, *Unwinnable Wars: American Power and Ethnic Conflict* (New York: Farrar, Strauss and Giroux, 1997), pp. 20–21.

8. William Hawkins, "Clinton's UN Peacekeeping Plan Still Flawed," A Background Paper Prepared by the Republican Research Committee, House of Representatives, June 1994, p. 6.

9. Charles A. Beard, *A Foreign Policy for America* (New York: Alfred A. Knopf, 1940), p. 88.

10. Sam Francis, "American Conservatives and the Globalist Challenge," *America Asleep: The Free Trade Syndrome and the Global Economic Challenge* (Washington: U.S. Business and Industrial Council Education Foundation, 1991), p. 140.

11. Christopher Layne, "Kant or Cant: The Myth of the Democratic Peace," *Debating the Democratic Peace,* eds. Michael E. Brown, Sean M. Lynn-Jones, and Steven E. Miller (Cambridge, Mass: MIT Press, 1995), p. 198.

12. William Kristol and Robert Kagan, "Toward a Neo-Reaganite Foreign Policy," *Foreign Affairs,* July 17, 1996, p. 31.

13. John C. Fitzpatrick, ed., *The Writings of George Washington from*

the Original Manuscript Sources, vol. 35, *March 30, 1796–July 31, 1797* (Washington: Government Printing Office, 1940), p. 234.

Chapter 20: A Republic, Not an Empire

1. H. W. Brands, *What America Owes the World: The Struggle for the Soul of Foreign Policy* (New York: Cambridge University Press, 1998), p. 132.

2. Walter Lippmann, *U.S. Foreign Policy: Shield of the Republic* (Boston: Little, Brown, 1943), p. 137.

3. Robert H. Ferrell, *American Diplomacy: A History*, rev. and expanded ed. (New York: W. W. Norton, 1969), p. 31.

4. Lippmann, *U.S. Foreign Policy*, p. 86.

5. Patrick J. Buchanan, "Anti-Americanism in L.A.," *Creators Syndicate,* March 6, 1998.

6. Roy P. Basler, ed., *The Collected Works of Abraham Lincoln*, vol. 1 (New Brunswick, N.J.: Rutgers University Press, 1953), p. 109.

7. Woodrow Wilson (Address, May 14, 1914), *The Pocket Book of Quotations* (New York: Simon & Schuster, 1952), p. 6.

8. "China Expands Reach with Russian Destroyers," *Jane's Defence Weekly*, January 15, 1997, p. 5.

9. Joe De Courcy, "China and the Threat of War in East Asia," *Intelligence Backgrounder*, May 1996;

reprinted in *St. Croix Review*, November 1996.

10. *Public Papers of the Presidents of the United States: Lyndon B. Johnson, 1963–64*, Bk. II—*July 1 to December 31, 1964* (Washington: Government Printing Office, 1965), p. 1391.

11. Douglas MacArthur, *Reminiscences* (New York: McGraw-Hill, 1964), p. 401.

12. "U.S. to Continue Troop Deployment in Asia, Cohen Says," Japan Economic Newswire, *Kyodo News Service,* July 10, 1998.

13. "The Persian Gulf War: Five Years Later. The Storm Isn't Over," *Independent Petroleum Association of America*, February 1996, p. 71.

14. Henry R. Luce, "The American Century," *Life*, February 17, 1941, p. 63.

15. Lippmann, *U.S. Foreign Policy*, pp. 9–10.

16. John C. Fitzpatrick, ed., *The Writings of George Washington from the Original Manuscript Sources*, vol. 35, *March 30, 1796–July 31, 1797* (Washington: Government Printing Office, 1940), p. 234.

17. Brands, *What America Owes the World*, p. 122.

18. Eric A. Nordlinger, *Isolationism Reconfigured: An American Foreign Policy for a New Century* (Princeton, N.J.: Princeton University Press, 1995), p.6.

ACKNOWLEDGMENTS

While I alone bear responsibility for interpreting the historic events described in *A Republic, Not an Empire*, and for all the foreign policy recommendations, I have benefited immensely from the counsel and assistance of many friends in writing it. They all have my gratitude for their generosity in reading my manuscript before it went to press, to try to ensure that, at least in its facts, it was as free of error as it might be.

Among these are Robert Ferrell, one of America's great historians, and professor emeritus at Indiana; Ted Galen Carpenter of Cato Institute; historian Ralph Raico of Buffalo State; foreign policy scholar Christopher Layne; Lyndon K. "Mort" Allin, a special assistant to three presidents; and history scholar and writer William Hawkins.

For the twelve weeks he spent trying to trace the near one thousand footnotes back to their original sources, Frank Mintz deserves special thanks.

Others who helped with individual chapters include Wayne Cole, the nation's foremost authority on the America First Committee; Alexander DeConde, who is among the most respected of our historians of American diplomacy; Bernard Way, a teacher at Christendom College; Sam Francis, the columnist-author; Peter Brimelow of *Forbes*; researcher-writer Steve Sniegoski; Terry Jeffrey of *Human Events*; John Meroney of American Enterprise Institute; and Doug Bandow of Cato Institute. And, again, my gratitude goes to Fredi Friedman, editor of this book as well as *The Great Betrayal* and *Right from the Beginning*, and, I can only hope, of all my future books.

INDEX

ABOUT THE AUTHOR

Patrick J. Buchanan is a political commentator and nationally syndicated columnist. He has been a founding panelist on three national television shows on CNN and NBC, authored four books, and served as a senior White House adviser to Presidents Nixon, Ford, and Reagan. Buchanan is making his third run for the Republican presidential nomination. He lives with his wife, Shelley, in McLean, Virginia.

ALSO BY PATRICK J. BUCHANAN

The Great Betrayal

Right from the Beginning

Conservative Votes, Liberal Victories

The New Majority